Arthur Dumas

201 West 103rd Street
Indianapolis, Indiana 46290

To Cindy, Mom, Dad,
and Leslie.

FIRST EDITION

International Standard Book Number: 0-672-30594-1

Library of Congress Catalog Card Number: 94-66276

98 97 96 95 4 3 2 1

Interpretation of the printing code: the rightmost double-digit number is the year of the book's printing; the rightmost single-digit, the number of the book's printing. For example, a printing code of 95-1 shows that the first printing of the book occurred in 1995.

Composed in AGaramond and MCPdigital by Macmillan Computer Publishing

Printed in the United States of America

Trademarks

Publisher
Richard K. Swadley

Aquisitions Manager
Greg Wiegand

Managing Editor
Cindy Morrow

Development Editor
Scott Allen Parker

Software Development Specialist
Keith Davenport

Copy Editor
Susan Christophersen

Production Editor
Katherine Stuart Ewing

Editorial Coordinator
Bill Whitmer

Editorial Assistants
Carol Ackerman
Sharon Cox
Lynette Quinn

Technical Reviewer
Jeff Beckley

Marketing Manager
Gregg Bushyeager

Cover Designer
Tim Amrhein

Book Designer
Alyssa Yesh

Director of Production and Manufacturing
Jeff Valler

Imprint Manager
Juli Cook

Manufacturing Coordinator
Paul Gilchrist

Production Analysts
Angela D. Bannan
Dennis Clay Hager
Mary Beth Wakefield

Graphics Image Specialists
Jason Hand
Clint Lahnen
Dennis Sheehan
Jeff Yesh

Page Layout
Mary Ann Cosby
Judt Everly
Casey Price
Jill Tompkins
Scott Tullis
Dennis Tor Wesner

Proofreading
Don Brown
Mona Brown
Michael Brumitt
Cheryl Cameron
Kimberly K. Hannel
Donna Harbin
Marcella Logan
Erika Millen
SA Springer
Tim Taylor

Indexer
Greg Eldred

Overview

Contents

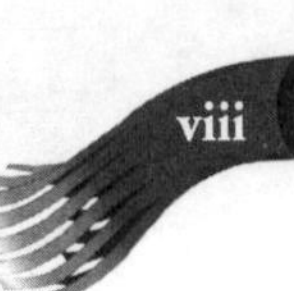

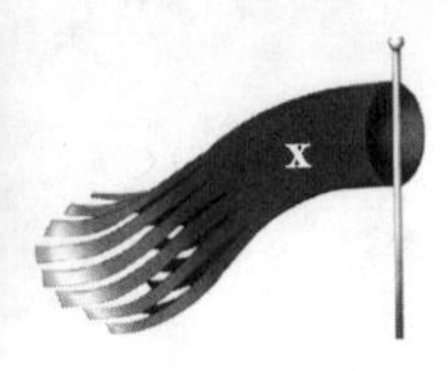
x

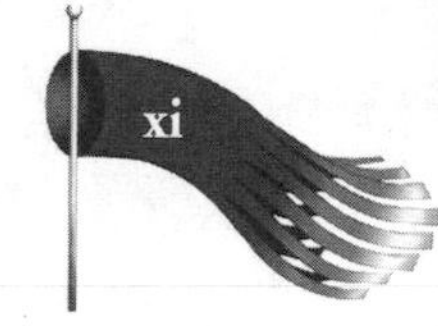

Acknowledgments

I would like to thank everyone at Sams Publishing for their help in bringing this book to fruition. In particular, thanks go to Susan Christophersen, Keith Davenport, Kathy Ewing, Stacy Hiquet, and Scott Parker.

Thanks go to Jeff Beckley for his technical input. I would also like to express my appreciation for the help Robert Mowery provided with the overall concept of this book.

Gratitude is also expressed to the many software developers who have produced the WinSock specification, and to the many more who are diligently working on its successor.

Lastly, I would like to thank my wife, Cindy, for her encouragement and support during the development of this book.

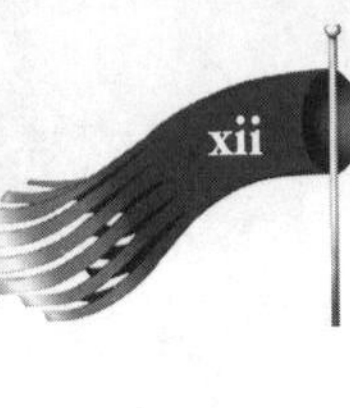

About the Author

Arthur Dumas is a software engineer in Rochester, New York. He can be reached on CompuServe by sending e-mail to `74004,3231`. Through the Internet, send e-mail to `74004,3231@compuserve.com`.

Introduction

The Windows Sockets specification describes a common interface to which networked Windows programs can be written. WinSock provides for binary and source code compatibility with several vendors' network protocol stacks. This allows a single version of a networked application to run on any number of computers with the Windows operating system.

The focus of the WinSock 1.1 specification, and the focus of this book, is the TCP/IP protocol suite (Transmission Control Protocol/Internet Protocol), although the WinSock specification isn't limited to just TCP/IP. TCP/IP programming is traditionally done using the Berkeley sockets programming model. WinSock expands on the Berkeley model to allow sockets to better work in the event-driven world of Windows.

This book examines several practical examples using traditional WinSock programming techniques. In addition, a class library is developed that encapsulates the basic functionality of WinSock. Several more programs are developed using this class library.

Audience

This book can be used by Windows programmers familiar with Microsoft Visual C++ and the Microsoft Foundation Classes. If you are just learning the Windows programming paradigm, there are several good books available to help you. Sams Publishing offers the following titles:

Teach Yourself TCP/IP in 14 Days (ISBN: 0-672-30549-6)
Teach Yourself Windows Programming in 21 Days (ISBN: 0-672-30344-2)
Teach Yourself Visual C++ 2 in 21 Days (ISBN: 0-672-30534-8)

Requirements

The programs in this book are designed to produce either 16-bit or 32-bit executables. The included 16-bit executables were compiled with Visual C++ 1.5. The 32-bit programs were compiled with Visual C++ 1.1 for Windows NT. As this book goes to press, Visual C++ 2.0 is being introduced. Several of the included programs were tested with a beta edition of Visual C++ 2.0, and no problems were encountered, but no guarantee is provided.

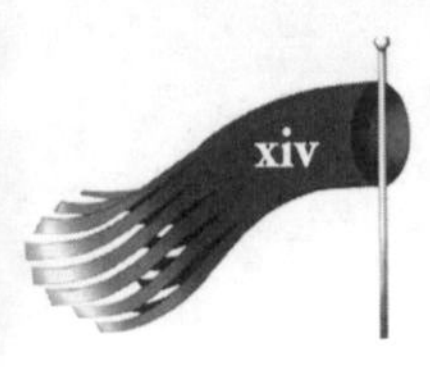

The system requirements for running this book's programs are either Windows 3.1 or later with a WinSock compatible TCP/IP protocol stack, or Windows NT 3.1 or later with its built-in stack.

Book Overview

Part I: Introduction to Networking

Chapter 1 describes the basic of computer networking. If you're familiar with the goals and topologies of computer networks, and are well-versed with network programming models, feel free to skip this chapter.

Chapter 2 covers the TCP/IP protocol suite. The ISO OSI Reference Model is compared with TCP/IP. Computer addressing and message routing are also discussed in this chapter.

Chapter 3 covers Berkeley sockets that provides the foundation for WinSock. WinSock is compared to Berkeley and the specific enhancements that allow sockets to work in the Windows environment are discussed.

Chapter 4 provides a brief overview of the Visual C++ development environment. If you are a seasoned user of Visual C++, this chapter can be skipped.

Part II: Basics of WinSock Programming

Chapters 5 through 7 cover the basics of WinSock programming, including the function calls needed to produce networked applications.

Chapter 8 presents several sample applications that make use of the functions described in Chapters 5 through 7. The first part of this chapter describes how the 16-bit and 32-bit projects are maintained. The first program is used to discover information about your WinSock-compatible TCP/IP stack. With the second program you can perform database lookups. The next set of programs echoes a datagram packet between themselves. The last set of programs echoes stream data between themselves.

Part III: WinSock Class Library

Chapter 9 describes the goals of the WinSock class library developed in Chapters 10 through 13.

Chapters 10 though 13 describe several classes (`CWinSock`, `CDatagramSocket`, and `CStreamSocket`) designed to simplify WinSock programming.

Part IV: Programming with the WinSock Class Library

Chapter 14 uses the classes discussed in Part III to implement the datagram and stream echo programs first seen in Chapter 8.

Chapter 15 covers a practical client-server database application. The server is implemented as a Multiple-Document Interface application that uses a distinct window to monitor the accesses of the clients being served.

Chapter 16 presents a Finger application that can be used to query a UNIX computer about its users.

Part V: Appendixes

Appendix A is a listing of the WINSOCK.H header file, which you will refer to often for structure and variable definitions.

Appendix B is a description of WinSock error codes listed in numeric order.

Source Code Listings

The full source code for each program is listed on the enclosed disk. Few of the programs are displayed in their entirety in the text of this book.

Conventions Used in This Book

Structures, variables, and anything else that may appear in the source code of a program appear in a `monospace` typeface. *Italics* highlight technical terms when they first appear in the text and are sometimes used to emphasize important points.

I

Introduction to Networking

1

Networking and Network Programming

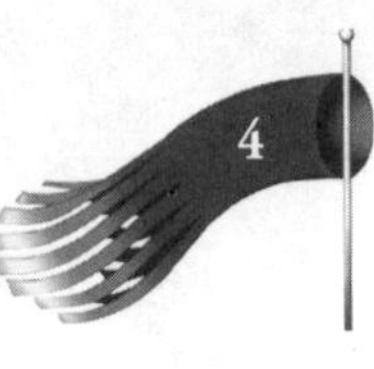

The purpose of this book is to show you how to make network-aware applications that run on the Microsoft Windows and Windows NT operating systems using the Windows Sockets (WinSock) Application Programming Interface (API). To that end, several practical examples are examined that utilize the basic functionality of WinSock.

Network operating systems, such as Windows for Workgroups and Windows NT, provide basic file and printer sharing services. This most basic level of functionality is provided "out of the box." Network-aware applications are programs that use the capabilities of a collection of connected computers. Network-aware programs range from custom applications that transfer data among computers on a network to mainstream applications that enable electronic mail and remote database access. The WinSock API is a library of functions that a programmer can use to build these network-aware applications. WinSock has its roots in Berkeley sockets as introduced in the Berkeley Software Distribution of UNIX. WinSock uses the TCP/IP (Transmission Control Protocol/Internet Protocol) suite, which provides the formal rules of behavior that govern network communications between all computers running this particular computer networking protocol.

Before I begin the examination of network programming, look at the basics of computer networking in general. A network can be loosely defined as a collection of two or more computers that have some sort of communication path between them. A network can be loosely classified as either a local area network (LAN) or wide-area network (WAN). The use of the terms *LAN* and *WAN* is somewhat misleading because which term you use is relative to the particular network installation you're describing. Generally speaking, a LAN covers a much more geographically restricted area than does a WAN. Whereas a LAN may connect computers within an office building, a WAN may connect computers spread across the country. With the advances in networking hardware and software, many widely dispersed LANs can now be connected to form a much larger homogeneous WAN. Devices known as *bridges* and *routers* allow for this connection of disparate LANs. Computer networks aren't new, but they weren't accepted in the personal computer realm until perhaps the late 1980s, when computer firms began offering cost-effective and reliable networking for the desktop PC. At that time, the primary goal of the PC network was to provide a central repository for files and to allow printers to be shared among many users. It hasn't been until relatively recently that businesses have realized the true potential of a PC network.

Goals of Networking

The goals of PC networking have been expanding over the last few years—from simple file and printer sharing to access of fax machines, modems, and enterprise-wide electronic mail systems. All the while, the essential goals of networking have always been to share resources and to provide a medium for communications.

Resource Sharing

For the sake of this discussion, a network resource is either a device or a capability on the network that's available for use by network users. The computer that the network resources are attached to is called the *server.* The other computers that access those resources over the network are called clients. The typical PC network user today takes shared file and printer access for granted. But there are now other resources that also can be made available to the user. Among them are fax machines, modems, compute servers, and database servers.

Files

The traditional use of PC networks has been and probably always will be to act as a repository for files. By storing files in a common location accessible to coworkers, for example, much productivity can be gained. Several products exist from Microsoft and other vendors that provide this capability. Windows for Workgroups is one such product. It's classified as a peer-to-peer network, which means that there's no dedicated, central-file server. Instead, any computer on the network can share files with any other; any computer on the network can act as either a client, server, or both. Windows NT and Windows NT Advanced Server expand on this idea by providing a much more robust file-sharing capability and better file system security.

Figure 1.1 shows two computers labeled Computer A and Computer B. Each has access to files on the File and Print Server and stored on the computer server. To illustrate the difference between the central-file server model and the peer-to-peer model, examine the following scenario, where Computer A has a file on its hard disk that it would like to make available to Computer B. In the central-file server model, Computer A must connect to the File and Print Server, place the file on the server's hard disk, and then inform Computer B that the file is available. Computer B then connects to the File and Print Server and accesses the file deposited there by Computer A. Using a peer-to-peer network, Computer A could simply give Computer B permission to access the file on Computer A's hard disk.

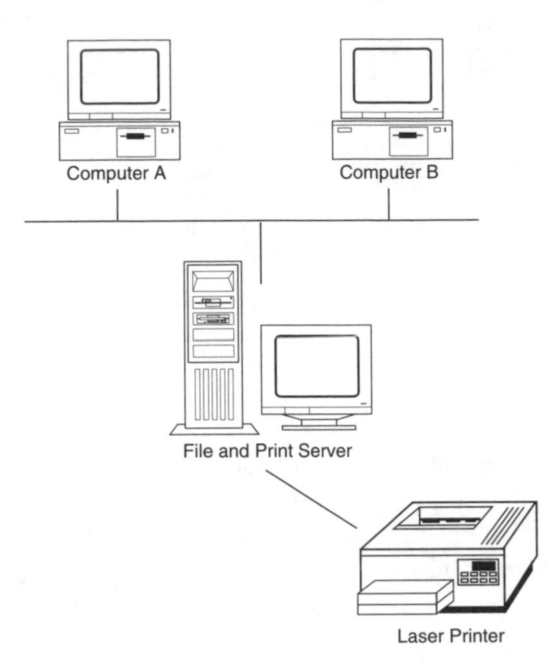

FIGURE 1.1.
File and printer resource sharing.

At a minimum, a computer network with a file server, whether it be centralized or peer-to-peer, prevents the use of the infamous "sneaker net" whereby files are transferred between computer users by first putting the desired files onto a floppy disk and then walking that floppy over to the designated recipient.

Printers

Another popular use of PC networks is to make printers available to all network users. This obviously provides a great cost savings by reducing the number of expensive printers and the cost of the maintenance and management of those devices. Windows for Workgroups and Windows NT provide printer-sharing capabilities. As Figure 1.1 shows, the two computers labeled Computer A and Computer B, as well as the File and Print Server computer, have access to the laser printer attached to the File and Print Server. When the user seated at Computer A prints a document, it's sent to the File and Print Server where it's printed. If a user at Computer B tries to print a document while Computer A's document is still printing, Computer B's document is stored in a temporary location on the File and Print Server. This process is called printer spooling. As soon as the first submitted print job belonging to Computer A's user is complete, the next job, belonging to Computer B's user, is begun.

A Windows NT-based network fully supports the remote management of networked printers. An administrator of a Windows NT network can monitor the status (to see if the paper is out, for example) of a remotely located printer and also manipulate the queue

of jobs waiting to be printed. He could, for instance, pause a print job sent by a user at 1:00 to make a print job submitted at 1:05 print first. The administrator can control other printer options such as which hours of the day the printer is available, who on the network can access the printer, and which users' print jobs have higher priority than others.

Fax Machines

The fax "machines" that are now being attached to computer networks are really just specialized modems that can communicate with other fax "modems" and more traditional stand-alone fax machines. There are several benefits to networked fax modems. Most documents that are eventually faxed are created with a computer's word processing program, printed on a traditional laser or dot-matrix printer, and then fed into a traditional fax machine. The networked fax modem saves these last two time-consuming steps by allowing the word processing program to "print" directly to the fax device. Most fax modems appear as just another printer to the word processing program. When the user selects the fax modem as the "printer" to print to, the user is asked to fill out a fax cover sheet which includes the recipient's name and the telephone number of the recipient's fax machine. A fax modem also allows a fax to be easily distributed to multiple recipients at different telephone numbers.

Microsoft at Work fax software is a component of the Microsoft at Work architecture (to be discussed shortly). This software allows networked computers running Windows to share a fax modem attached to one of the networked computers.

Modems

Standard modems, as opposed to fax modems, are also being used now as shared devices on PC networks. In the past, users who had a regular need for modem communications had to have their own personal modems. More often than not, that modem was very underutilized. By arranging several modems in a modem pool reachable by a network, many more users can have access to modem communications without the expense of personal modems. When users need to access a modem, they request one from the modem pool and then proceed as if that modem were theirs alone. When they're finished with the modem resources, those resources are freed and made available to the next user who requests them. Figure 1.2 shows four computers and a two-modem pool. The Modem Pool Server is the computer that manages the modem pool. Computers A, B, and C have access to these modems. When Computer A requests the use of a modem, the Server removes that modem from its availability list. When Computer B requests a modem, the Server assigns the second modem to Computer B. If Computer C then requests a modem, the request is placed in a queue. As soon as Computer A or B relinquishes its "borrowed" resource, Computer C gets use of that freed modem.

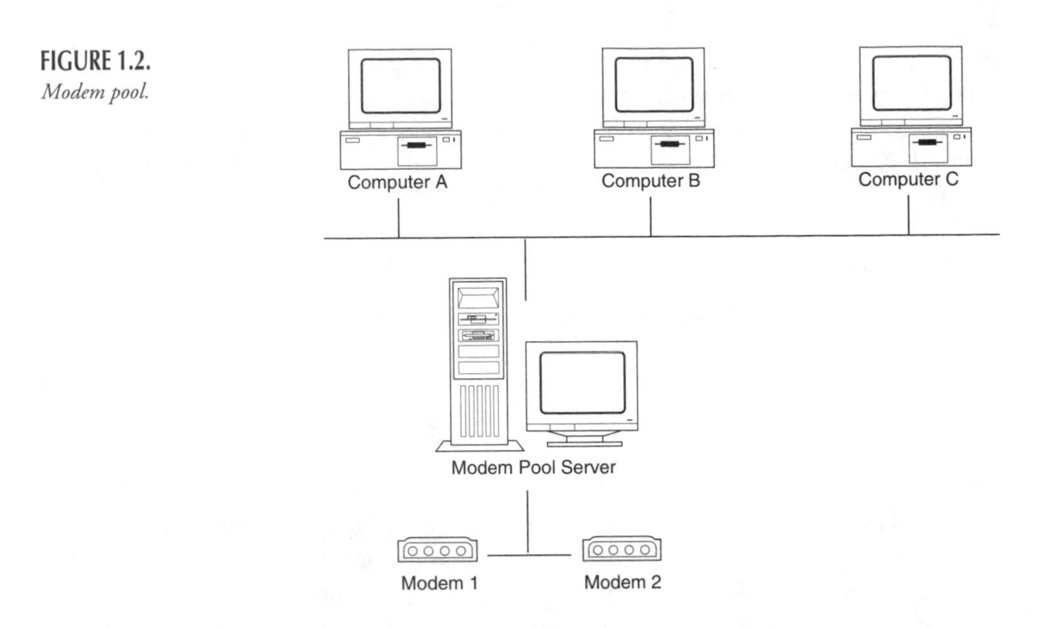

FIGURE 1.2.
Modem pool.

Modem access can also operate in the opposite direction. It's possible to have remote users dial into the computer network. Once they're logged to the network, the remote users have the same access to network resources as users whose computers are physically attached to the network. Microsoft's Remote Access Service (RAS) includes this capability for Windows for Workgroups and Windows NT.

Compute Servers

Another shared resource that can be found attached to some PC networks is the compute server. This device is usually a very powerful computer that's geared toward performing specialized tasks. For example, compute servers can be tuned for exceptional floating-point calculation performance. A compute server isn't necessarily practical for use as a general-purpose computer, so users access this resource from a workstation or desktop PC. The results of the compute server's work can be displayed on the local desktop PC using a remote graphical user interface. This graphical interface is based on the X Windows system developed at the Massachusetts Institute of Technology.

Another way to take advantage of a compute server is to use Remote Procedure Calls (RPC) in your desktop application. Using RPCs, the application on the desktop computer makes calls to functions that happen to execute on the remote compute server. When the function has completed, the results are returned to the desktop computer as if the function call took place locally. Figure 1.3 shows one possible scenario with a powerful mainframe compute server serving the needs of both an X Windows workstation and a PC using RPCs.

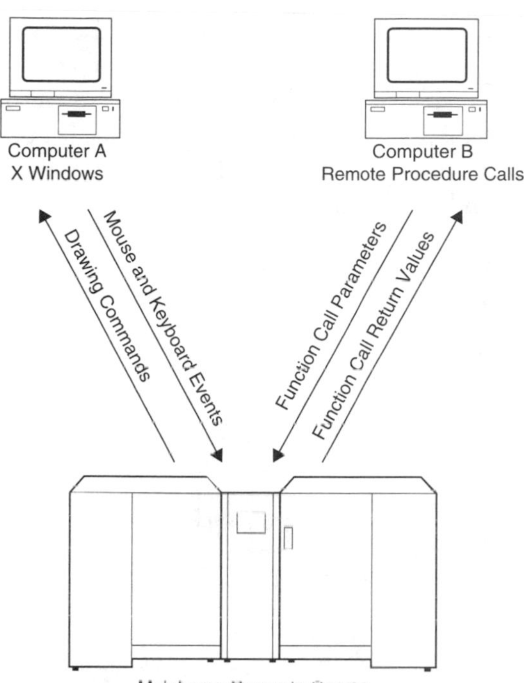

FIGURE 1.3.
Compute server.

Database Servers

The networked database server is similar to the compute server but is more common in today's business environment. With this network resource, desktop PCs can query and modify a database that's made available to the entire enterprise. Figure 1.4A shows one possible configuration. The user seated at the client computer sends a query to the database server. The database server receives the query parameters and processes the request. When the database server has completed the necessary processing, a response is returned to the client computer. This configuration is known as client/server architecture. The client/server programming model is explained later in this chapter.

Several vendors, including Microsoft, Oracle, and Sybase, provide database servers that are geared toward the high-end client/server market. Many companies, such as Borland, Gupta, Microsoft, PowerSoft, and Oracle, provide tools necessary to build the client portion of the client/server solution.

A client/server database is especially useful when several people need access to the same information. This architecture is desirable because it allows people in different locations, possibly even on opposite sides of the globe, to share and modify common information. The client/server database architecture not only makes it easy to locate users at disparate locations but also allows freedom in the location of the databases. With this scenario, as shown in Figure 1.4B, the database can be maintained where it makes the most sense. In an order entry system, for example, it might make sense to have the billing department maintain the customer records in one database while the inventory records are maintained by the parts department in a different database stored on another database server. During order entry time, the order entry clerk can access both databases and get the most up-to-date information.

Database server.

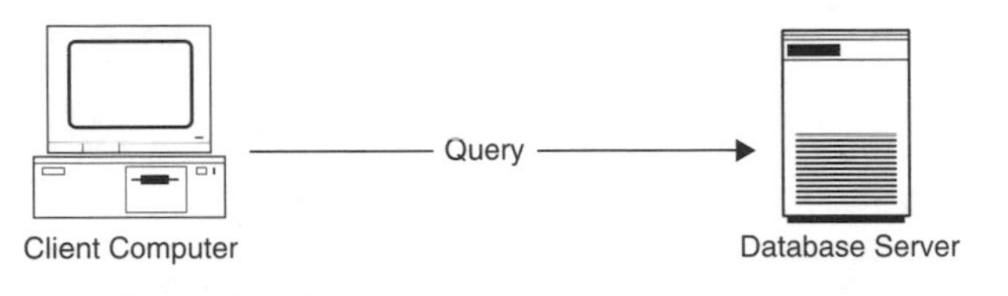

Step 1: The client sends a query to the database server

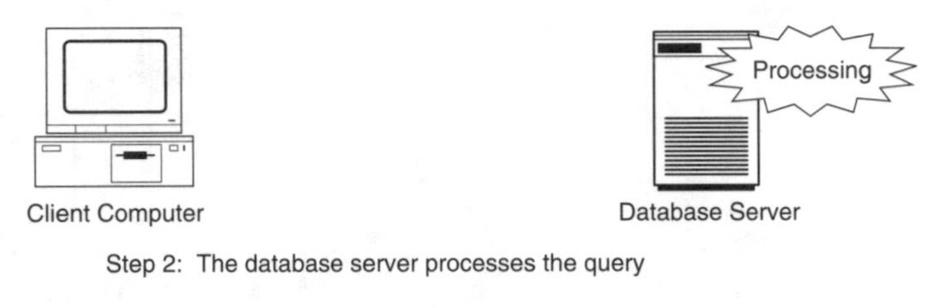

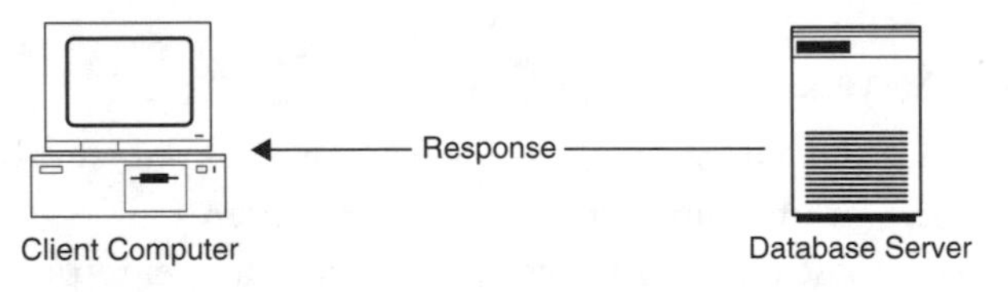

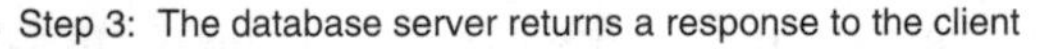

Communications Medium

The complementary, and somewhat overlapping, goal for a computer network is to act as a communications medium. In a basic sense, if this communications medium didn't exist, neither would the ability to share any network resources, as described earlier. In this context, however, the communications medium allows network users to communicate better with each other. To facilitate this human-to-human communication, many networked software tools have been built. Among them are electronic mail systems, workgroup scheduling programs, and electronic forms processing systems.

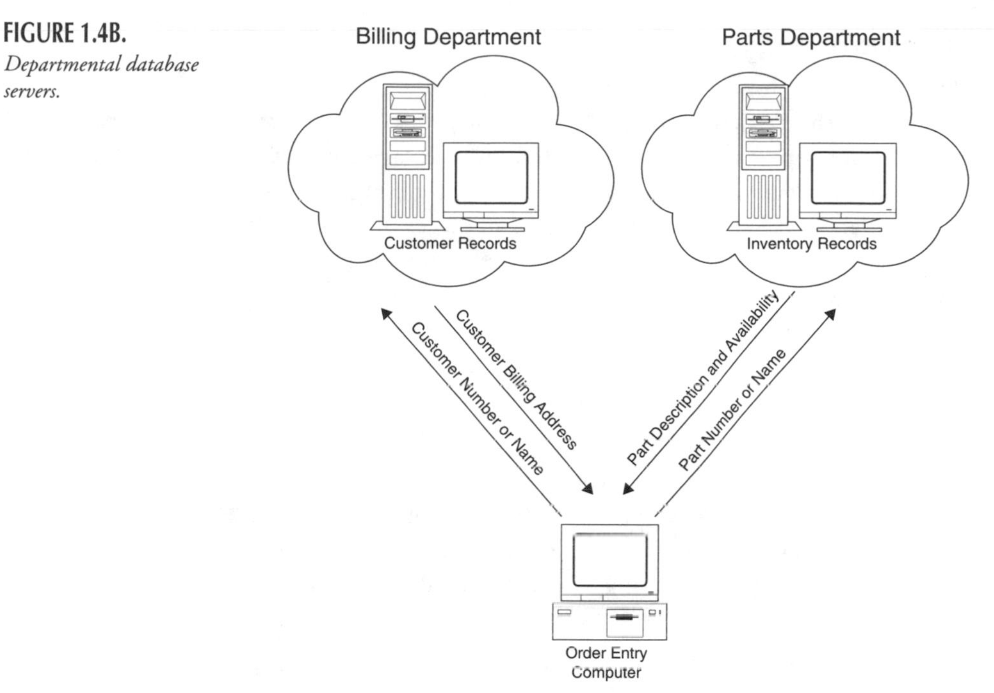

FIGURE 1.4B.
Departmental database servers.

Electronic Mail

Electronic mail, known as *e-mail*, has had wide acceptance in the arena of larger computer systems such as those that run a UNIX operating system derivative. PC networks now have e-mail capability, too. Not only can e-mail be shared between PC network users, but it can be routed to users on other networks that are based on high-end workstations or multiuser computers. This capability means that all computer users in a business setting can use electronic communications among themselves and can still use the best computer and operating system combination to meet their primary job responsibilities.

Modern e-mail systems have been extended further so that embedded or attached objects can be sent. These objects can be as simple as additional textual information or as diverse as a computer-playable video presentation or a financial spreadsheet. When recipients read their e-mail, the attachments are immediately available.

Windows for Workgroups and Windows NT are bundled with e-mail support.

Electronic Forms

With electronic forms an organization can easily exchange structured information. E-forms are the modern-day equivalent of the printed paper form. A simple example of a form is the popular "While You Were Out" message your secretary might fill out. By combining e-forms with an e-mail system, your messages will appear as nicely formatted, standardized e-mail messages instead of pieces of paper scattered about your desk. Another use of an e-form might be by a salesman who enters a customer's order on his laptop computer while on site. The e-form is then either immediately transferred to a host computer using a modem or transferred at the end of the business day in a batch-type mode where all the day's orders are sent.

Workgroup Scheduling

Workgroup scheduling helps coworkers manage their time and communicate with each other more effectively. A network scheduling program provides network computer users with the ability to view and modify each other's day planners. This ability makes it easier to schedule group meetings, make personal appointments, and assign tasks to an available individual. Microsoft's Windows for Workgroups and Windows NT include a scheduling program that has this capability.

Chat

A chat utility can replace a phone call for simple one-to-one or one-to-many communications. Under a UNIX-based operating system, the chat utility is called talk. In the Windows and Windows NT environment, the chat utility is called Chat and is executed by running the WINCHAT.EXE program. With both programs you can connect to at least one other network user and then type messages back and forth.

World Wide Web and Mosaic

On a more global scale, the World Wide Web (WWW) is gaining in popularity. The WWW was started at CERN, the European Laboratory for Particle Physics. Its original purpose was to facilitate the communication between fellow particle physicists. WWW is a distributed system with which users can access documents of varying types, from simple text files to graphical images stored in the GIF or JPEG format. The data may

contain links to other related data. By traversing these links, information on a particular topic can be found. This world-wide connection is made possible by the Internet, a collection of an estimated 2,000,000 interconnected computer systems spread the world over.

To traverse the Web, as it is known, the user needs a sophisticated Web client or browser. The browser's duties involve traversing the links, retrieving data of miscellaneous types, and providing viewers for that data. One of the best Web browsers available is Mosaic, developed at the National Center for Supercomputing Applications. Figure 1.5 shows Mosaic for Windows connected to a computer that Microsoft has made available for support of its products. Pointing the mouse cursor at the folder and clicking the mouse button causes Mosaic to redraw the screen with the newly selected folder's information. When users see data files they would like, another mouse click causes files to be retrieved to the users' machines where they're displayed, if there are appropriate viewers available, or saved to disk for later examination.

Webs are even finding a place for internal use in the corporation. The data stored at a Web site is inherently cross-platform. This means a company can produce a document once, possibly including multimedia-type extensions, and have that document available for viewing by users of Windows, Macintosh, or UNIX computers. All that is needed is a Web browser for each platform.

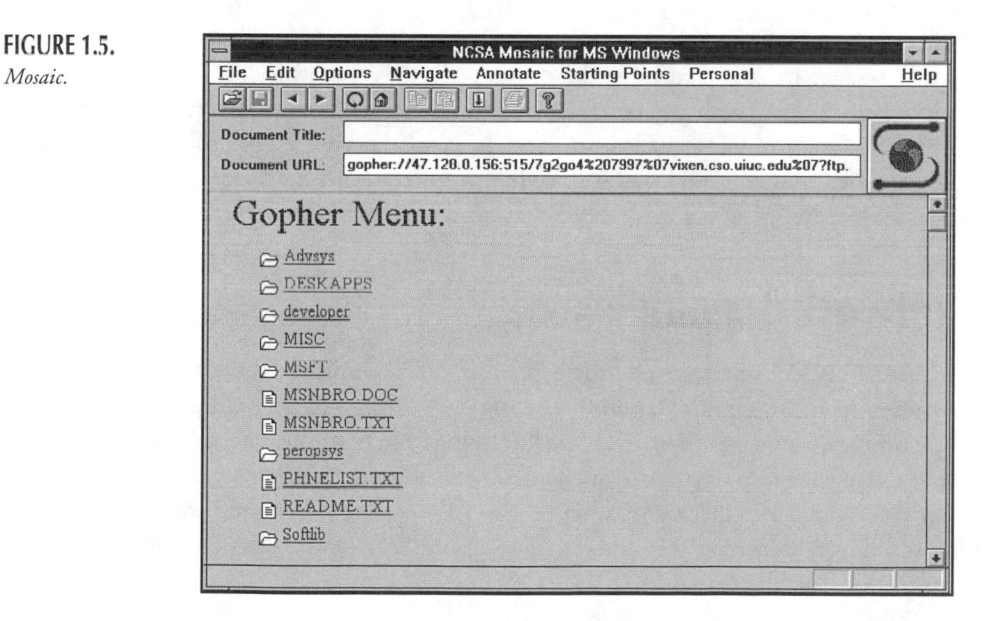

FIGURE 1.5.
Mosaic.

Coming Soon

The future promises more networking options. One exciting area of development involves wireless communications. Usually associated with the notion of a Personal Digital Assistant, wireless communications will allow access to an enterprise's network from anywhere on the planet. Imagine being able to access your e-mail messages from the beach.

Another area of interest, particularly to Microsoft, is to make network resources more easily shared and utilized. To meet this goal, Microsoft initiated the Microsoft at Work program in 1993. One component of Microsoft at Work discussed earlier was Microsoft at Work fax software, with which network users can send faxes and computer files directly from their desktop computers. Soon we will see other Microsoft at Work-enabled devices, such as telephones and photocopiers. These devices will have a touch screen surface with a simplified Windows interface and will also be available as network resources. With an "At Work" enabled photocopier, for example, a network user will be able to send a print job directly from his favorite word processor program and have the desired number of copies printed, collated, and stapled.

As networks get more sophisticated and the amount of network traffic they can handle increases, video conferencing becomes more viable. Video conferencing usually involves the use of a multimedia-enabled computer that includes a video camera and microphone. With such a configuration, two or more users can see and hear each other, as well as type messages back and forth as the outdated Chat type utility allows. By combining video conferencing with a networked "white-board" utility, on which networked users can see and manipulate visual computer data, coworkers are able to collaborate on work even though they may be located in different offices, different states, or even different countries. It might be a while before that kind of network bandwidth exists though.

Network Topologies

The previous sections described the capabilities of a computer network. But how are all of these file, print, fax, and compute resources connected so as to allow the typical desktop computer to access them? Network topology refers to the way networked computers and network resources are connected. The three most widely used topologies are bus, ring, and star. Note that the following network topology diagrams are logical views of the topologies they represent and don't necessarily match the physical (electrical) interconnections on the networks.

Bus Network

The bus network topology, shown in Figure 1.6, connects each computer to a single cable. At each end of the cable is a terminating resistor or a terminator. An electrical signal is passed back and forth along the cable past the computers and between the two terminators. The bus carries a message from one end of the network to the other. As the bus passes each computer, the computer checks the destination address on the message. If the address in the message matches the computer's address, the computer receives the message. If the address doesn't match, the bus carries the message to the next computer, and so on.

Bus topology is passive, meaning that computers only listen for data being sent on the network and aren't responsible for moving data from one computer to the next. If one computer fails, it doesn't affect the entire LAN. On the other hand, if a cable breaks, the entire cable segment (the length between the two terminators) loses its connectivity, so that the entire segment isn't functional until the cable can be repaired.

Each computer attached to a bus network can transmit data whenever it "wants." This capability means that two computers may try to transmit simultaneously. This occurrence is called a collision. A collision is detected by the network hardware of the sending computers. When a collision is detected, the packets of data that generated the collision are retransmitted.

The limitation of bus networks is the speed of data transmission relative to the number of computers on the network. As more computers are added to the network, more collisions are bound to happen. As more collisions occur, more retransmissions take place and the overall network performance degrades.

Ethernet is one example of a common bus network found on many local area networks. Ethernet is also the most popular LAN architecture in use today.

NOTE

Ethernet was developed by the Xerox Corporation in 1972 as the follow-up to some research done at the University of Hawaii. Ethernet first became commercially available in 1975 as a 2.94 Mbps network able to connect up to 100 computers spread over a 1-kilometer cable. Xerox Ethernet soon became popular, and work was done with the Intel Corporation and Digital Equipment Corporation to extend Ethernet's capability to 10 Mbps. Today, 100 Mbps Ethernet is gaining in popularity.

Ethernet networks can be wired with different types of cable, each with its own benefits and drawbacks. Three popular specifications for Ethernet topologies are 10BASE2, which uses thin coaxial cable (Thinnet) that can carry a signal up to approximately 607 feet; 10BASE5, which uses Thicknet cabling that can carry a signal for about 1,640 feet; and 10BASET, which uses unshielded twisted-pair cable that can carry a message for about 328 feet between a computer and the hub to which the computer is connected.

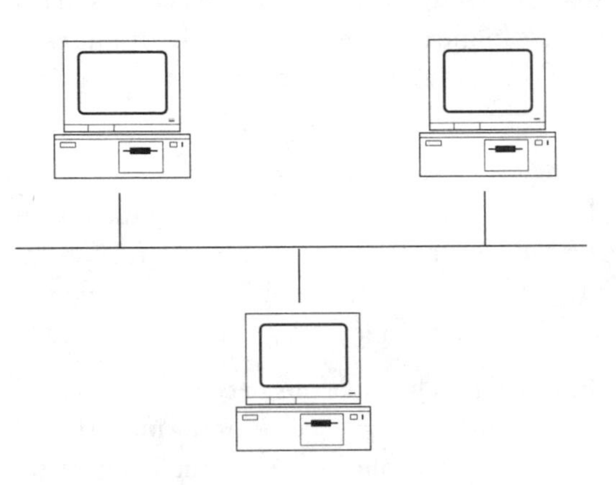

FIGURE 1.6.
Bus network.

Ring Network

Figure 1.7 shows a ring network. In a ring network, a packet of data (often called a token) is continually moving around the ring from one computer to the next. To send data, a computer on the network must wait for the circulating token to pass by. When the token arrives, it's examined to see whether it's empty. If it's empty, the computer that wishes to transmit adds its data to the token packet and addresses the packet to a destination. As the token passes by the destination computer, the computer looks at the address and because the message is addressed to itself, extracts the data, and replaces the token packet's data with a delivery acknowledgment message. The token then continues to circle the ring and eventually returns to the sending computer. The sending computer examines the token packet to see if it contains the data it sent or an acknowledgment message. If it doesn't find an acknowledgment message, the sender knows that the data wasn't received, possibly because the destination computer wasn't operating. The sender then clears the token packet and passes it along the ring to allow subsequent computers their chance to use the network's communication resources. The token passing scheme is in contrast to the bus topology whereby any computer can send at any moment and the protocol must detect collisions. Collisions of this nature can't occur on a ring network.

NOTE

The first design of a network passing a token ring is attributed to E. E. Newhall in 1969. IBM first publicly supported a token-ring topology in March 1982, and announced its first token-ring network product in 1984.

Data on the IBM token-ring network is transmitted at either 4 or 16 Mbps, depending on the actual implementation. For computers to communicate with each other, all network cards must be configured similarly to communicate at either 4 or 16 Mbps on the network. Networked computers are connected by shielded and/or unshielded twisted-pair cable to a wiring concentrator called a Media Access Unit or MAU (rhymes with cow). Each MAU can support as many as 72 computers that use unshielded wire or up to 260 computers using shielded wire. Each ring can have as many as 33 MAUs allowing for a theoretical maximum of 8,580 computers on the network.

FIGURE 1.7.
Ring network.

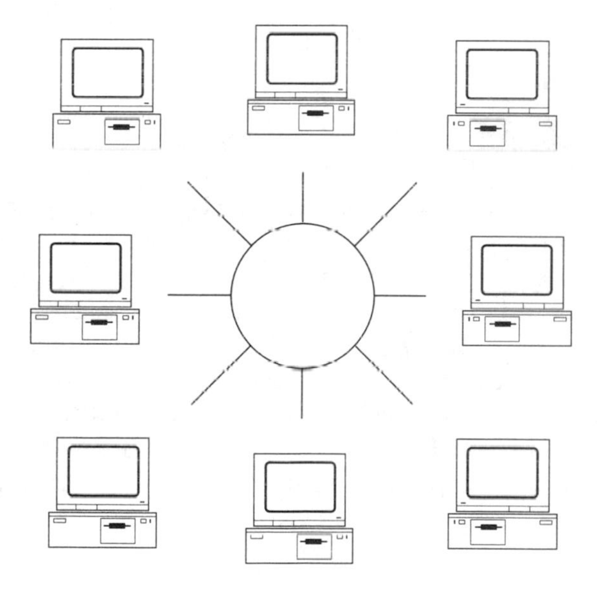

Star Network

To transmit data between any two computers in a star network, shown in Figure 1.8, requires that data be sent via the centrally located computer, called a hub. The hub provides a common connection so that all the computers can communicate with one another. To extend the star network, hubs can be connected to one another. The major problem with star networks is that if the centrally located hub isn't operating, the entire network becomes unusable. A benefit of a star network is that no computer, other than the centrally located hub, can interrupt network traffic.

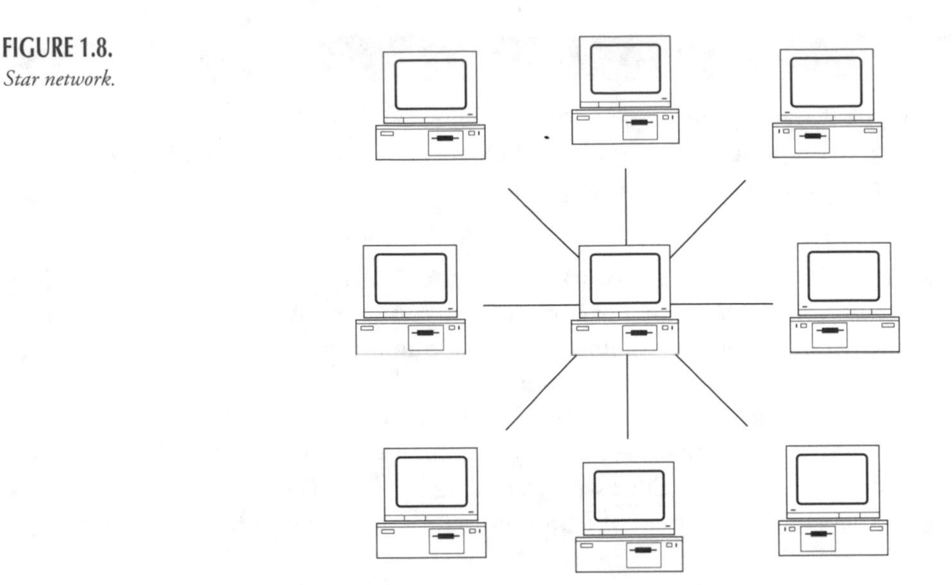

FIGURE 1.8.
Star network.

Internetworking

The previous section detailed different network topologies. This section will show that these disparate networks can be interconnected and may even be separated by thousands of miles. This scenario is called internetworking. Figure 1.9 shows a well connected network composed of a bus network, a ring network, a satellite connection to a remote server, and a dial-up modem connection. Notice the device called the Gateway. This device is used to connect the bus network to the ring network. Its job isn't only to bridge the two networks hardware-wise but also to route data between the two when the destination of a data packet isn't local to either the bus or ring network. Routing and gateways are described more fully in Chapter 2, "TCP/IP Overview." In this network, the laptop computer has the same access to resources connected to the bus network's Workstation computer as does the bus network's Macintosh computer. Of course the access times may not be the same for the laptop computer and the Macintosh.

Does Network Topology Matter?

Fortunately, the average application programmer has little need to know the topology details of the network his software will run on. Most of these details are hidden from

the application program by a networking application programming interface (such as WinSock). The application programmer will need to be concerned with these nitty-gritty details if the application being developed has any special requirements, such as fault tolerance or guaranteed response times. The programmer may also be concerned about the underlying network hardware. Ethernet was listed earlier as an example of a bus network. Some networks may not be as simple as Figure 1.6 appears. As several local area networks are interconnected, and as wide area network links, such as those provided by satellites, are added, network topology becomes an issue with the network application programmer. You can't assume that data will reach its destination in less than 100 milliseconds, for example. The best advice is to make your network programs as configurable and robust as possible, especially with regard to time-out values.

FIGURE 1.9.
Internetworking.

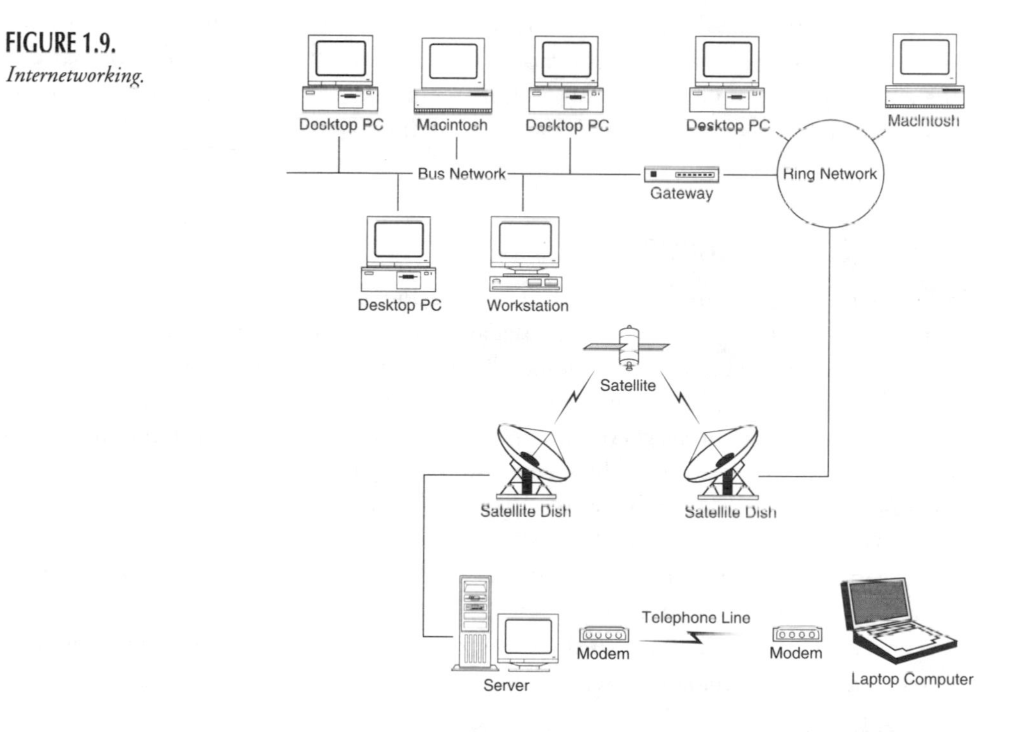

Look at Figure 1.9 as an example of a network configuration that requires flexible network applications. If the server is acting as a database server, it must serve the client computers on the bus network, the ring network, and the telephone line. The network access times are different for the Macintosh on the bus network than they are for the laptop computer dialed with a 9,600-baud modem, for example.

The application programmer should make the server aware of the disparity in performance when it communicates with the many other computers it serves. Those other computers must likewise be knowledgeable about their connectivity to the server. The client software running on the laptop computer may have a five-second time-out for database access while the bus network's Macintosh may need a 10-second time-out to make up for the delays introduced by the satellite link. Attention to details such as this early in a network application's development cycle may save a lot of aggravation later.

Network Programming Models

The previous section discussed ways that computers and other resources can be attached to a network. But what do we do now that we have networked computers that can communicate with one another and share common resources? We need software that can take advantage of the network. This section begins a discussion of network programming. Network programming can be thought of in two primary contexts: client/server and distributed.

Client/Server Computing

In the client/server computing model, an application is split into two parts: a front-end client that presents information to the user and collects information from the user, and a back-end server that stores, retrieves, and manipulates data and generally handles the bulk of the computing tasks for the client. In this model the server is usually a more powerful computer than the client, oftentimes a minicomputer or mainframe, and serves as a central data store for many client computers, making the system easy to administer. Client/server architecture increases workgroup productivity by combining the best features of stand-alone PCs with the best features of minicomputers and mainframes. Client/server architecture makes the best use of high-end server hardware and reduces the load on client PCs. Load reduction, in turn, provides superior performance and minimizes network traffic. Figure 1.4A shows one example of a client/server interaction with a client accessing a database server.

A server is any program that runs on a networked computer and can provide a service. A server receives a request over the network, performs the necessary processing to service that request, and returns the result to the requester. The client is the program that sends a request to a server and waits for a response.

For a client and server to communicate and coordinate their work, an interprocess communication (IPC) facility is needed. The subject of this book, WinSock, can be used to satisfy this requirement. Chapter 15, "Practical Client/Server Database Application," introduces an example that will demonstrate client and server database implementations.

One server program can service several client requests at the same time. For this reason, implementing servers tends to be more difficult than implementing clients. To provide the capability of supporting several client requests simultaneously, servers are usually built in two parts: a single master that accepts requests and one or more slaves that actually process and respond to the individual requests.

Client/server architecture contrasts with the classical centralized architecture popularized by typical mainframe installations. In a centralized environment, the "clients" are little more than dumb terminals that act as simple data entry/display devices. There's a minimum of work done at the terminal. The user typically fills in the fields of a form before sending the field data to the central computer. All processing and screen formatting is done on the central computer, and the dumb terminal simply displays the preformatted data. In a client/server environment, the client has much greater intelligence and more freedom with the final visual presentation of the data to the user. Instead of the data being preformatted to match the way it will be viewed, it's sent back in its "raw" format, and the application running on the client computer "decides" how to display that data. Thus the "front end" that the user sees can be customized while the "back end" remains unchanged.

Distributed Computing

The distributed architecture can be thought of in two different ways: precollection and parallel processing.

Precollection is the act by which background processes on networked computers concurrently collect and propagate information before that information is requested. An example would be a program that requests the status of every other computer on the local network. In the client/server environment, the client program would have to send a request to each computer on the network and wait for a response. This procedure is potentially very time-consuming. In a distributed implementation, each computer on the local network would have a process that runs continually in the background and that reports status information to every other computer on a regular interval. When the program is run to request the status information of every other computer on the local network, the response comes back immediately because the information was precollected in each local computer. Of course this solution wouldn't work well if the information being requested was time sensitive, because the delay in the updates would make the response outdated. Shortening the time between the updates sent by the networked computers wouldn't work well either because of the possibility of saturating the network's data-handling capabilities.

When most people think of parallel processing, they think of a computer that has more than one processing unit. *Parallel computing* in a distributed system environment means taking advantage of more than one computer on the network to perform a specific task. Suppose that you, as a software developer, want to do a large project build late at night when few other programmers are at work. Wouldn't it be nice to take advantage of all that idle processing power lying in each programmer's workstation or desktop PC? With a build utility that was designed for a distributed environment, your build could execute in a parallel fashion with certain modules being compiled on certain computers and other modules being compiled on other computers. The project build could be completed in a greatly reduced time. This assumes that the source code going into the build is located somewhere on the network and is as easily accessible by all other computers as it is to your own. If the source code is located on your local computer, the overhead in shipping it across the network to the other computers might overshadow the benefit of multiple modules being built simultaneously.

Summary

This chapter has discussed the basics of computer networking and network programming. The primary purpose of most computer networks is to allow for the sharing of resources such as files, printers, modems, and fax machines, and to facilitate the communication of the people using the networked computers. Network topology refers to the way networked computers and network resources are connected to each other, with the most popular topologies being bus, ring, and star. To take advantage of the network's connectivity, network-aware application software is used. The client/server and distributed models are two popular methodologies followed when writing networked software. To write this networked software, a network application programming interface (API) is used by the programmer. One such network API, and the focus of this book, is WinSock. The following two chapters will discuss TCP/IP, the underpinnings of WinSock, and WinSock itself.

2

TCP/IP Overview

Computer network protocols are formal rules of behavior that govern network communications. The Transmission Control Protocol (TCP) and Internet Protocol (IP) are just two of the data communication protocols encompassed by the Internet Protocol Suite. This protocol suite is usually referred to as TCP/IP partly because TCP and IP are two of the most important protocols of the collection. TCP/IP includes a set of standards that specify how networked computers communicate and how data is routed through the interconnected computers.

TCP/IP provides the application programmer with two primary services: connectionless packet delivery and reliable stream transport. These will be discussed in detail later in this chapter. TCP/IP has several distinguishing features that have led to its popularity, including

Network Topology Independence. TCP/IP is used on bus, ring, and star networks. It's used in local-area networks as well as wide-area networks.

Physical Network Hardware Independence. TCP/IP can utilize Ethernet, token ring, or any number of physical hardware variations.

Open Protocol Standard. The TCP/IP protocol suite standard is freely available for independent implementation on any computer hardware platform or operating system. TCP/IP's wide acceptance and the fact that TCP/IP is available on platforms ranging from supercomputers to desktop personal computers makes it an ideal set of protocols to unite different hardware and software.

Universal Addressing Scheme. Each computer on a TCP/IP network has an address that uniquely identifies it so that any TCP/IP enabled device can communicate with any other on the network. Each packet of data sent across a TCP/IP network has a header that contains the address of the destination computer as well as the address of the source computer.

Powerful Client-Server Framework. TCP/IP is the framework for powerful and robust client-server applications that operate in local-area networks and wide-area networks.

Application Protocol Standards. TCP/IP doesn't just provide the programmer with a method for moving data around a network among custom applications. It also provides the underpinnings of many application-level protocols that implement such common functionality as e-mail and file-transfer capabilities.

The current incarnation of the Windows Sockets library is built on TCP/IP, although there's nothing inherent in WinSock precluding it from utilizing an alternate protocol

stack. In fact, work is in progress on the next version of WinSock, which will support the use of Novell's IPX/SPX, Apple's Appletalk, and other popular network protocols.

NOTE

The term *protocol stack* has been mentioned a few times now. It refers to the way some network communication protocols, including TCP/IP, are composed of several logical layers of software where each layer communicates with the layer directly above and below itself. At the top of this stack is the application layer that you, as the applications programmer, provide. The bottom of the stack is generally thought to be the layer that communicates with the network hardware (that is, the Ethernet or Token Ring). The upcoming section titled "ISO OSI Protocol Stack" provides a more complete definition of a protocol stack.

TCP/IP History

The history of the TCP/IP protocol suite can be traced back to one of the first wide-area networks consisting of computers from different manufacturers running different operating systems.

ARPANET

This experimental network was called ARPANET, and its development was sponsored by the Defense Advanced Research Projects Agency (DARPA) in 1969 with the goal of creating a network to provide robust data communications among computers from different vendors. Before ARPANET, most computer networks were homogeneous, consisting of computers from the same hardware manufacturer running the same operating system.

The ARPANET's popularity became apparent, and in 1975, it was converted from an experimental network into a fully operational network that was used for daily communications among researchers at the connected sites. But research into network protocols continued and the Internet Protocol Suite resulted. The TCP/IP protocols were adopted as Military Standards in 1983, and all computers connected to the ARPANET were required to adopt the new protocol. The ARPANET was then split into two networks: the MILNET, used for unclassified military communications, and the new, much smaller ARPANET, used for further research. MILNET and ARPANET together became known as the Internet.

Berkeley Software Distribution

DARPA was also interested in expanding the Internet by attaching university computing sites. At that time, most university computer science departments were running a version of the UNIX operating system developed at the University of California at Berkeley. This implementation of UNIX is known as the Berkeley Software Distribution or BSD UNIX. DARPA funded Bolt Beranek and Newman, Inc. to implement TCP/IP for UNIX and funded Berkeley to incorporate the protocols into its software distribution. This funding, combined with the fact that many university computer science departments were adding more computing resources that needed to be interconnected, all but guaranteed a wide audience for TCP/IP.

The programmers for BSD UNIX didn't simply take TCP/IP as it came from Bolt Beranek and Newman. They added an abstracted layer for the use of application developers called sockets. Sockets, which WinSock is based on, make it easy for the application programmer to write networked code. The BSD programmers also added several utilities to their UNIX that were built upon pre-existing commands used in the standalone computing environment. For example, the new remote copy command `rcp` was introduced. This command extended the standard copy command called `cp` to the network. Network-aware utilities such as these, and the power that can be wielded from them, helped BSD UNIX and its TCP/IP gain wide acceptance.

With the popularity of BSD UNIX at universities, the size of the connected Internet grew. The even wider acceptance of TCP/IP soon after BSD's inclusion of the protocols led to an astronomical Internet growth rate that has yet to peak. In 1983, the Internet connected a handful of computing sites. Today, the Internet connects two million computers and forty million people spread all over the world.

NOTE

The use of the term *internet* is sometimes confusing because it's used haphazardly to mean so many different things. TCP/IP is another name for the Internet Protocol Suite. TCP/IP and Internet Protocol are used interchangeably. Originally, if someone said their computing site had an internet, it meant there were two or more networked computers that used the Internet Protocol between them. The term *internet* (notice the lower case *i*) is now used to refer to any collection of physically separate networks that share the same communication protocols (not necessarily TCP/IP) to appear as a single logical network. The term *Internet* (notice the upper case *I*) is used to refer to the worldwide collection of interconnected computer networks that run the TCP/IP protocols.

Request for Comments

No single company or group "owns" TCP/IP. The protocols are freely distributable, and anyone is allowed to incorporate them into his or her operating system or computer network. You may be wondering how TCP/IP is expanded and how the application protocols mentioned earlier are developed. The answer lies in Internet Request for Comments (RFC).

RFCs provide for an informal method of establishing new TCP/IP protocol standards. RFCs usually begin as Internet drafts. After the Internet community has had a chance to critique the draft it becomes an RFC. RFCs are numbered sequentially, so later RFCs have higher numbers than those created earlier. Some RFCs supersede earlier ones, but the new RFC will always make note of that.

The number an RFC receives is distributed by an organization at SRI International called the Network Information Center or the NIC (pronounced nick). The NIC is funded by the Defense Communication Agency (DCA), which manages the military's computer network infrastructure. The NIC isn't only responsible for an RFC's number, it's also responsible for the storage and distribution of TCP/IP protocols, allotment of Internet addresses, and the registration of the names of Internet-connected computers.

One example of an RFC is RFC 742, which defines the finger protocol. The finger protocol is usually accessed by the user using a finger program. Finger allows a user to find out certain information about a specific user on a specific networked computer or all users on a specific networked computer. The finger protocol describes the communications that must take place between the finger client program that a user runs and a finger server that continuously runs on the computer that's being "fingered." You'll build a finger client program for Windows in a later chapter.

ISO OSI Reference Model

A group called the International Standards Organization (ISO) introduced the Open Systems Interconnection (OSI) Reference Mode, a layered network architecture, with the goal of international standardization of computer network protocols. The OSI model is said to be an open systems architecture because it connects computer systems that are open for communications with other systems. The connected computer systems don't have to be from the same manufacturer and don't have to run the same operating system. TCP/IP and the OSI model share a similarity in this regard.

The Seven-Layer OSI Model

The OSI model is composed of seven layers as shown in Figure 2.1. Taken together, these layers define the functions of data communication protocols. Each layer of the OSI model represents a function performed when data is transferred between cooperating applications across a connecting network. A layer doesn't have to define a single protocol; it defines a function that's performed by any number of protocols. For example, the finger protocol and a file transfer protocol both fit into the Application Layer. According to Andrew Tanenbaum's Computer Networks book, the layers were defined with the following ideals in mind:

A layer should be created where a different level of abstraction is needed.

Each layer should perform a well-defined function.

The function of each layer should be chosen with an eye toward defining internationally standardized protocols.

The layer boundaries should be chosen to minimize the information flow across the interfaces.

The number of layers should be large enough that distinct functions don't have to be thrown together in the same layer out of necessity, and small enough that the architecture doesn't become unwieldy.

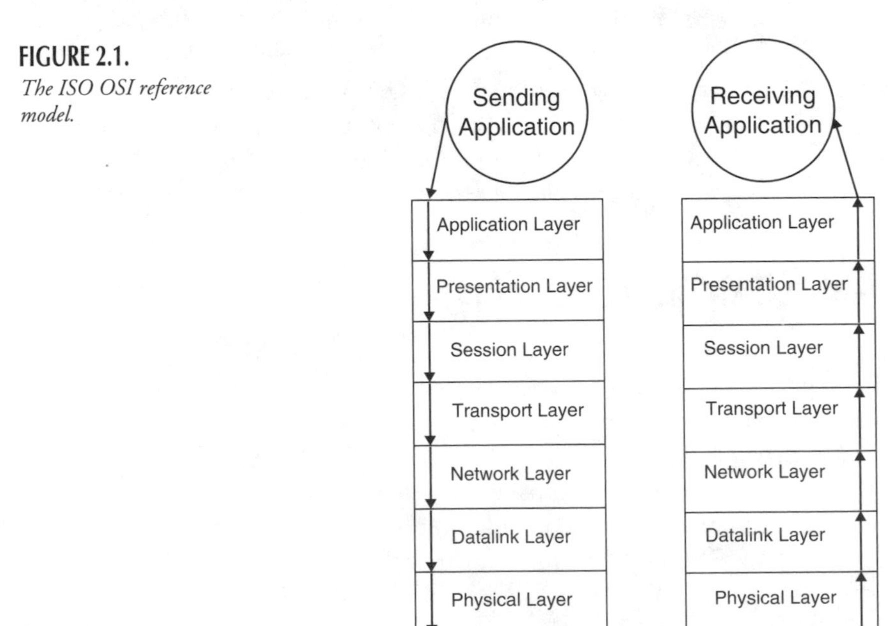

FIGURE 2.1.
The ISO OSI reference model.

Application Layer

The application layer provides end-user services such as file transfer and e-mail. This is the layer closest to what the user of the computer sees and manipulates. The finger protocol described earlier fits into this layer because it's the protocol that defines the client application's interaction with the server application providing the finger service. The finger client communicates with its peer finger server. A peer is a protocol implementation that resides in the equivalent layer on a remote system.

Presentation Layer

The presentation layer controls how data is represented. This is the layer in which data compression might take place, for example. Using data compression as an example, when data passes from the application layer to the presentation layer, the presentation layer compresses the data before passing it on to the session layer. When data arrives, it's passed from the session layer to the presentation layer where it's uncompressed and passed on to the application layer. Hence, the presentation layer really performs a data manipulation function, not a communication function.

Session Layer

The session layer manages the process-to-process communication sessions between hosts. It's responsible for establishing and terminating connections between cooperating applications.

Transport Layer

The transport layer performs end-to-end error detection and correction. This layer guarantees that the receiving application receives the data exactly as it was sent.

Network Layer

The network layer manages network connections. It takes care of data packet routing between source and destination computers as well as network congestion.

Datalink Layer

The datalink layer provides reliable data delivery across the physical network. It doesn't assume that the underlying physical network is necessarily reliable.

Physical Layer

The physical layer is concerned with transmitting and receiving raw bits over a physical communication channel. Ethernet is one example of such a channel. This layer has knowledge of voltage levels and of the pin connections to the physical hardware media.

These seven layers and the way they're represented as building blocks stacked one on top of the other has led to the term protocol stack or simply stack.

TCP/IP and the OSI Model

TCP/IP doesn't directly follow the OSI model. Although each network model has the goal of facilitating communication among different makes and models of computers, even when those computers are running dissimilar operating systems, each network model has resulted in different implementations. Whereas the OSI model is driven by a large standards organization, which takes a long time to formulate and adopt a standard, TCP/IP was driven by the immediate need of the United States government. TCP/IP development isn't burdened with the same stringent requirements as OSI. Most of TCP/IP's advances have been made by individuals and small groups through the issuance of RFCs. The process of creating and adopting an RFC is more expeditious than the equivalent procedure in the ISO. This has led some to say TCP/IP isn't a very "pure" architecture. Pure or not, TCP/IP is the set of protocols used to connect more computers in the world today than any other.

Although OSI and TCP/IP differ, it's still useful to use the seven-layer model as a frame of reference when discussing data communications. Figure 2.2 shows the layered architecture of TCP/IP.

FIGURE 2.2.
TCP/IP layered architecture.

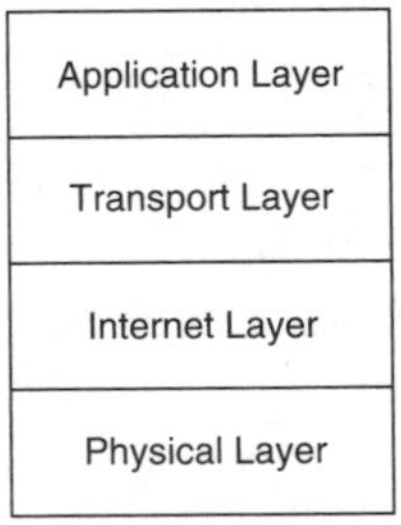

Application Layer
Transport Layer
Internet Layer
Physical Layer

Application Layer

The application layer consists of applications that make use of the network. A file-transfer utility and the finger program discussed earlier are examples of programs that fit into the application layer. The application and presentation layers of the OSI model fit into this layer of the TCP/IP architecture. For example, if data transferred between two peer

programs is going to be compressed, the application "is responsible" for the compression and decompression. In effect, the transport layer is absorbed into the application instead of being a separate entity as it is in the OSI model. For the sake of discussion, however, you can still think of the transport function as a logical layer.

Transport Layer

The transport layer provides end-to-end data delivery. The OSI model's session and transport layers fit into this layer of the TCP/IP architecture. The notion of OSI's session connection is comparable to TCP/IP's socket mechanism. A TCP/IP socket is an end-point of communications composed of a computer's address and a specific port on that computer. OSI's transport layer has an equivalent in TCP/IP's TCP. TCP provides for reliable data delivery and guarantees that packets of data will arrive in the order they were sent, with no duplicates and with no data corruption.

Internet Layer

The internet layer defines the datagram and handles the routing of datagrams. The datagram is the packet of data manipulated by the IP protocol. A datagram contains the source address, destination address, and data, as well as other control fields. This layer's function is equivalent to that of the OSI's network and datalink layers. The IP (as in the right-hand side of TCP/IP) is analogous to the network layer. It's responsible for encapsulating the underlying network from the upper layers. It also handles the addressing and delivery of datagrams. The datalink layer isn't usually represented in the TCP/IP architecture, but IP could be used to support this function.

Physical Layer

TCP/IP makes no effort to define the underlying network physical connectivity. Instead, it makes use of existing standards provided by such organizations as the Institute of Electrical and Electronic Engineers (IEEE), which defines RS232, Ethernet, and other electronic interfaces used in data communications.

The movement of a packet of data through the layers in a TCP/IP network is shown in Figure 2.3. When a packet of data is sent, it travels to the transport layer where the transport header is added. Next the internet layer adds its header. Finally, the physical layer attaches its header. When a packet of data is received, the process is reversed, resulting in the application's reception of the intended data.

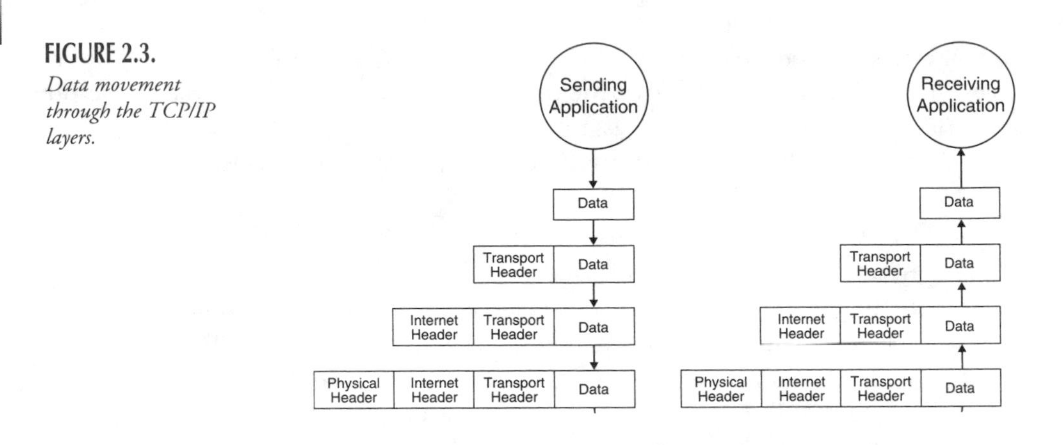

FIGURE 2.3.
Data movement through the TCP/IP layers.

TCP/IP Addressing Scheme

One of TCP/IP's distinguishing features described previously is its universal addressing scheme whereby each computer on a TCP/IP network has an address that uniquely identifies it. This universal addressing scheme extends even to the world-wide Internet, connecting more than two million computers that are connected to thousands of separate networks.

It's IP's responsibility to deliver datagrams among the TCP/IP networked computers. To make such deliveries possible, each computer has a unique IP address composed of a 32-bit number. The IP address contains sufficient information to uniquely identify a network and a specific computer on the network.

Network Classes

Because a computer's IP address must uniquely identify not only the computer but also the network the computer is attached to, the IP address is split between a network identifier (net id) part and a host identifier (host id) part. The split between these two identifiers isn't the same for all IP addresses. The class of the address determines how many bits of the IP address are reserved for network identification and how many are reserved for host identification. There are five classes of IP address with only the first three relevant to the majority of users. Classes A, B, and C are for general-purpose use; classes D and E are reserved for special purposes and future use. Figure 2.4 shows the format of an IP address.

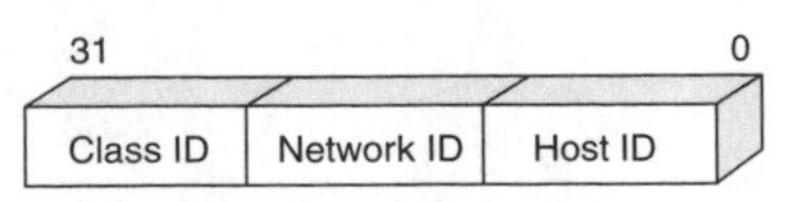

FIGURE 2.4.
IP address format.

As far as the application programmer is concerned, no discernible difference exists among a class A, B, or C address. A computer with a class A address can communicate with a computer with a class C address just as well as a class A computer can communicate with another computer with a class A address. Table 2.1 shows the maximum number of networks and hosts that can exist for the different classes.

Table 2.1. IP address class allocation.

Network Class	*Networks*	*Hosts per Network*
A	126	16,777,214
B	16,382	65,534
C	2,097,150	254

Not all network identifiers or host identifiers are available for use. Some addresses are reserved for special use. If Table 2.1 is compared to the following class descriptions, you'll see that not all bit combinations are included in the counts of Table 2.1.

Class A

Class A IP addresses are identified by a high-order bit of zero. The next highest order seven bits identify the network. The remaining 24 bits identify the host.

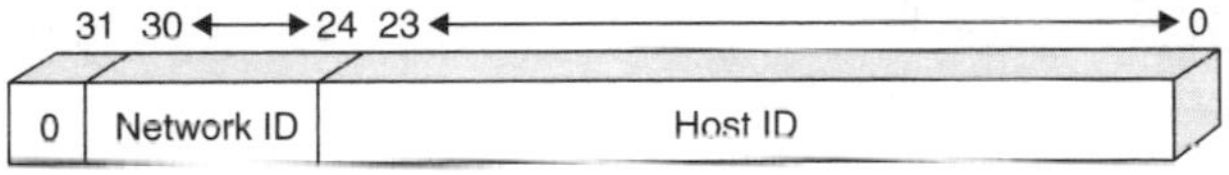

FIGURE 2.5.
Class A IP Address Format.

Class B

Class B IP addresses are identified by a high-order bit of one and the next highest order bit set to zero. The next highest order fourteen bits identify the network. The remaining 16 bits identify the host.

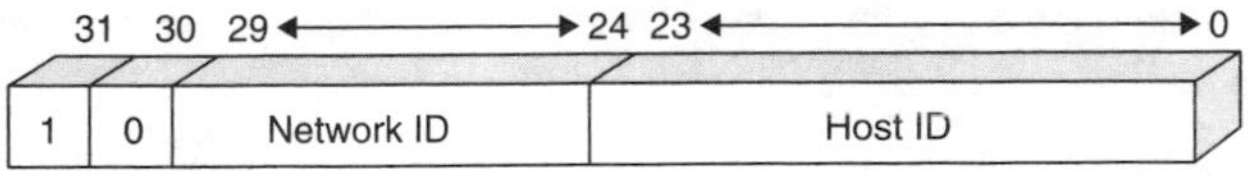

FIGURE 2.6.
Class B IP address format.

Class C

Class C IP addresses are identified by a high-order bit sequence of one one zero. The next highest order twenty-one bits identify the network. The remaining eight bits identify the host.

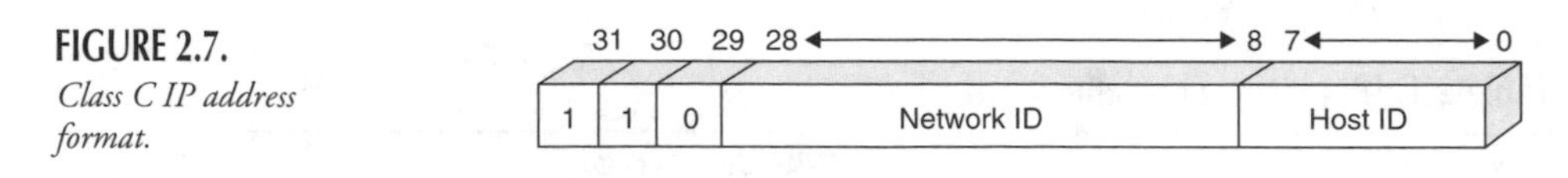

FIGURE 2.7.
Class C IP address format.

Dotted Decimal Notation

If the format of an IP address sounds confusing, don't worry. An IP address is usually represented by the dotted decimal notation. An IP address' dot notation is comprised of 4 decimal values in the range of 0 to 255 separated by a period or dot (.). Each value represents 8 bits of the IP address. The 4 values together are the 32 bits of the IP address.

I'll use the IP address of my computer as an example. Its address in dotted decimal format is 166.78.4.139. Figure 2.8 shows the binary interpretation of this IP address. Bit 31 is a 1, so that indicates this computer is either a class B or C network. Bit 30 is a 0 indicating that the computer does belong to a class B network. The earlier discussion of network classes said that class B addresses allowed 14 bits for the network id part and 16 bits for the host id part. The dividing line separating the network part from the host part is between bits 15 and 16. You can read this to mean the computer resides on network 166.78 and is host 4.139.

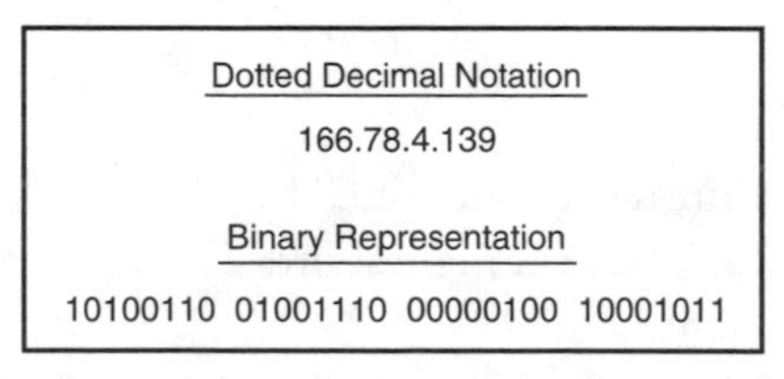

FIGURE 2.8.
IP address decoding.

NOTE

If remembering the dotted decimal notation of a computer still sounds too confusing, read on: The implementors of TCP/IP realized that humans would need an easy method of accessing this information, so they devised a method whereby a simple-to-remember textual name symbolizes an IP address. The name-to-IP-address translation is supported by several methods with the

simplest being a plain ASCII file where each line of the file has the IP address in dotted decimal notation to the left and the textual name to the right. This file is customarily named `hosts` and is referred to as the *host file.*

The host file implementation is fine for a small network with relatively few computers, but the management of such a file becomes unwieldy or impossible as the network grows to thousands of hosts, as in the Internet or any large corporate network. In this environment, a name server is utilized. A *name server* is a computer that provides a name to IP address resolution. When a request to translate a certain name to its IP address arrives at the name server, it does a database lookup to see if it has this information. If not, the request is passed on to an authoritative server. *Authoritative servers* are maintained with official data provided by the group responsible for the assignment of IP addresses.

Subnetting

Subnetting is a method of locally modifying the use of the network and hosts bits. By moving the dividing line that separates the host id part from the network id part, more networks can be created at the same time the maximum number of hosts on each network is reduced. A subnet mask is used to define the new dividing line. It's represented in dotted decimal notation in much the same way as an IP address is. The bits that are set to one represent the network portion; the remaining bits that are set to zero represent the host portion.

Earlier, I determined that the IP address of my computer resided on network 166.78 and had a host id of 4.139. Officially speaking this is correct. But as it turns out, the network administrators at my site have decided to use a network mask of 255.255.255.0 to logically partition the address space into more networks. Looking at the logical view, my network id is 166.78.4 and my host id is 139. Another way of saying this is my computer is host 139 on subnet 166.78.4.0. Notice that the low order byte is 0. Performing a logical AND operation between my complete IP address and the subnet mask results in the subnet 166.78.4.0. The component that remains—139—is the host part.

TIP

The subnet mask doesn't have to be partitioned on even 8-bit boundaries. As an example, suppose that my subnet mask is 255.255.255.128. Performing the logical AND operation between this subnet mask and 166.78.4.139 results in 166.78.4.1 with a remaining portion of 11. Hence my computer would be host 11 on subnet 166.78.4.1.

The NIC and Internet IP Addresses

You should see now that IP address space is a limited resource. You have also learned that any computer attached to the global Internet must have a unique IP address. The Network Information Center is the group responsible for the assignment of IP addresses and domain names. To get an official IP address and have your host name officially recognized, you must register with the NIC. Depending on your needs, the NIC will most likely allocate to you either a class B or C network identifier. Class A network space is very rare—remember that there are only 126 possible class A networks—and is almost exhausted.

When you register, you'll also need to choose a domain name. Domain names are organized into a hierarchical structure with the root-level domain at the top. The top-level domains in the United States are

COM for commercial organizations
EDU for educational organizations
GOV for governmental organizations
MIL for military organizations
NET for network support organizations
ORG for organizations that don't fit into any other category

Other top-level domains are generally reserved for country codes. For example, the United Kingdom belongs to the top-level UK domain, and Australia belongs to the top-level AU domain.

My personal computer, with IP address 166.78.4.139, has a fully qualified name of GOOBER.PING.COM. It's a member of the PING.COM domain which is in turn a member of the top-level COM domain. Figure 2.9 shows a hierarchical representation of the domains mentioned thus far.

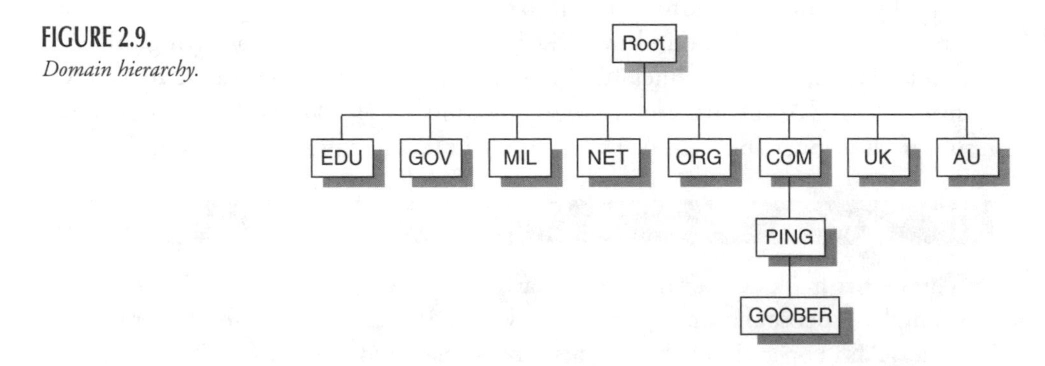

FIGURE 2.9.
Domain hierarchy.

Routing

Routing is the method by which packets of data are sent from one computer to another in the most efficient way possible. The routing process is composed of several components as follows:

Determining what paths are available between the source and destination computers

Selecting the "best" path between the source and destination computers where "best" may mean different things depending on the goals

Using those paths to reach other computers

Adjusting the datagram formats to fit into the underlying physical network technology

In a TCP/IP network, routing is performed by the IP layer. The network id of the destination computer's IP address as well as the subnet mask are used by the IP layer to make routing decisions.

Default Gateway

In an interconnected computer network, or internet, some method is required to deliver data to computers that reside on another connected network. By specifying a default gateway, the IP layer of the sending computer "knows" to what destination it should forward data that has a destination which isn't on the local network. See Figure 2.10 for a simple network arrangement. When 166.78.4.139 sends data to 166.78.4.10, the IP layer takes the subnet mask, in this case 255.255.255.0, and performs a logical AND operation on both the source and destination IP addresses. The result in this case is 166.78.4.0 for both addresses, which tells the IP layer that both computers are on the same subnet. The data is sent directly to 166.78.4.10. When 166.78.4.139 sends data to 166.78.1.5, the IP layer again uses the subnet mask, and the results are 166.78.4.0 for the source and 166.78.1.0 for the destination. These numbers don't match, which signals the IP layer that the computers reside on different subnets. The sending computer can't send directly to 166.78.1.5. The data must be sent to the default gateway, which is a computer that has two IP addresses and resides on two distinct subnets. The data is first sent to 166.78.4.2 and then forwarded on to 166.78.1.5.

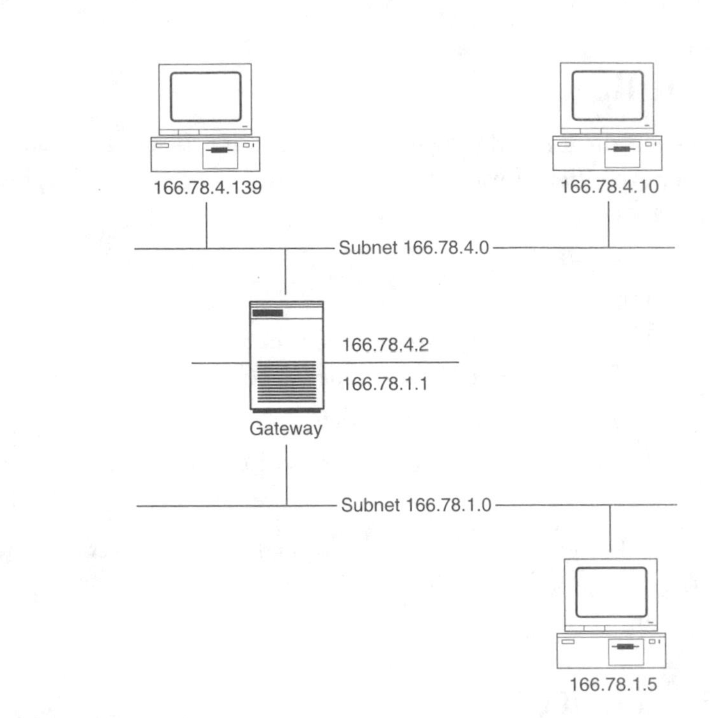

FIGURE 2.10.
Network routing.

Multiple Default Gateways

It's also possible to have multiple default gateways. With this configuration, a subnet doesn't rely on one gateway to the connected networks. Instead the data can use several paths to leave the source subnet. The IP layer uses the subnet mask, the IP addresses of the gateways, and the IP address of the destination computer to decide the most efficient route from sender to receiver.

Internet Layer

The internet layer is shown in Figure 2.2. It defines the datagram and handles the routing of those datagrams. IP is the most important protocol of the TCP/IP protocol suite, because it's used by all other TCP/IP protocols and all data must flow through it. IP is also considered the building block of the Internet.

Although the application programmer doesn't usually see this layer, a brief overview is beneficial.

IP

IP is a connectionless protocol, which means that no end-to-end association is established before data is transmitted. This is in contrast to a connection-oriented protocol that exchanges control information between hosts to establish a connection before data is transmitted. IP doesn't guarantee reliable data delivery either. Packets of data could arrive at their destination out of order, duplicated, or not at all. IP relies on other layers, such as the TCP transport protocol, to provide the reliability feature.

The basic building block of IP is the datagram. Each datagram, or packet of data, has a source and destination address. Routing of data is done at the datagram level. As a datagram is routed from one network to another, it may be necessary to break the packet into smaller pieces. This process is called fragmentation and it's also the responsibility of the IP layer. Fragmentation is required on some internets because the many hardware components that make up the network have different maximum packet sizes. IP must also reassemble the packets on the receiving side so that the destination host receives the packet as it was sent.

Address Resolution Protocol

Unfortunately, network hardware (that is, the Ethernet card you plug into your computer) doesn't understand IP addresses. The Address Resolution Protocol (ARP) is used to map the logical IP addresses and host names—that humans like to use—into the physical addresses that the underlying network hardware mandates. This protocol operates by broadcasting a message onto the local network, saying in effect, "Is the computer with IP address `xxx.xxx.xxx.xxx` out there?" If the computer with the designated IP address is listening, it returns a message with its physical hardware address to the source. Any other computer that receives the broadcast request message ignores it. This protocol only works on the local network because the format of the physical network address is dependent on the hardware used in the network. For example, if an Ethernet was in use, the response to the ARP request would be a 48-bit number that uniquely identifies every Ethernet device in existence.

Internet Control Message Protocol

The Internet Control Message Protocol (ICMP) is another low-level protocol rarely used by the application programmer. It uses IP datagrams to send messages that perform flow control, error reporting, routing manipulation, and other informational functions for TCP/IP.

The application programmer most certainly will make use of the ping utility, one of the most common programs that uses ICMP. Ping uses ICMP's echo function to test the response of a networked host. By getting a response from ping, you're assured that network routing is in place between the two computers and that the remote computer is indeed running.

NOTE

You'll develop a version of ping in a later chapter. That version of ping will use an application-level protocol from the transport layer instead of the internet layer's ICMP.

Transport Layer

IP is responsible for getting datagrams from computer to computer. The transport layer is responsible for delivering that data to the appropriate program or process on the destination computer. The two most important protocols of the transport layer are User Datagram Protocol (UDP) and Transmission Control Protocol (TCP). UDP provides connectionless datagram delivery; TCP provides a reliable stream-oriented delivery service with end-to-end error detection and correction.

To facilitate the delivery of data to the appropriate program on the host computer, the notion of a port is used. A port is a 16-bit number that denotes an end-point of communication within a program. An IP address and port combination taken together uniquely identify a network connection into a process. The socket paradigm developed by the University of California at Berkeley makes more intuitive the use of IP addresses and ports.

NOTE

The application programmer is responsible for ensuring that two or more processes don't utilize the same port.

Application programmers use UDP and TCP in the majority of their networked programs.

User Datagram Protocol

The User Datagram Protocol (UDP) allows data to be transferred over the network with a minimum of overhead. UDP overhead is low because it provides only unreliable data delivery. There's no method in the protocol to verify that the data reached the destination exactly as it was sent. The data may be lost, duplicated, or arrive out of order.

These limitations don't make UDP useless, though. The low overhead in UDP transmission—because there's no need to establish a connection—and the lack of reliability makes UDP very efficient. UDP can be used when the application programmer puts error-case handling into the application. For example, suppose that you had a simple client-server relationship where the client sends a small piece of data to the server and expects within two seconds a response in the form of a small piece of data. If the client doesn't receive a response within two seconds, it can assume the data didn't make it to the server successfully and so it may retransmit the request. If the client does receive a response from the server, that can be used as an acknowledgment that the data did reach its destination.

Figure 2.11 shows the format of a UDP message. The message contains a 16-bit source and destination port.

FIGURE 2.11.
UDP message format.

Source Port	Destination Port
Length	Checksum
Data...	

Transmission Control Protocol

The Transmission Control Protocol (TCP) verifies that data is delivered in order and without corruption. Associated with this feature is extra overhead in the generation and maintenance of a connection.

TCP provides for the transmission of a reliable, connection-oriented stream of bytes. TCP's reliability comes from its inclusion of a checksum into each packet of data transmitted. On reception, a checksum is generated and compared to the checksum included in the header of the data packet. If the checksums don't match, the receiver communicates that fact to the sender, and the data is automatically resent. Application programmers don't have to be concerned with this function because the lower layers mask it. TCP is considered connection-oriented because the two end-points of communications exchange a handshaking dialogue before data transmission can begin. This handshake guarantees to the sender that the receiver is alive and ready to accept data.

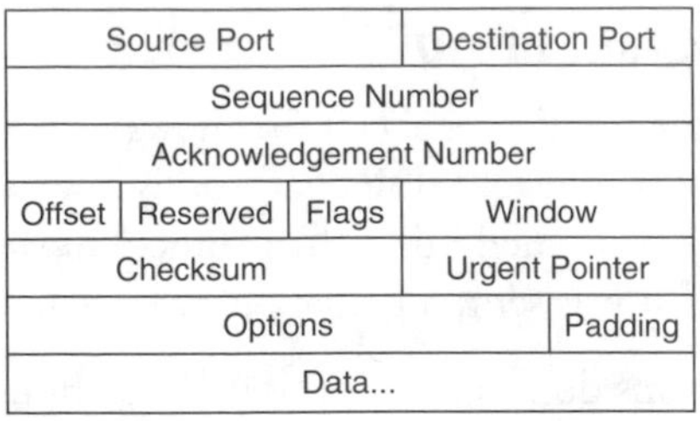

FIGURE 2.12.
TCP message format.

Source Port			Destination Port	
Sequence Number				
Acknowledgement Number				
Offset	Reserved	Flags	Window	
Checksum			Urgent Pointer	
Options				Padding
Data...				

Figure 2.12 shows the format of a TCP message. The message contains a 16-bit source and destination port as does the UDP message. But this message also includes sequencing fields as well as a data checksum field. These additional entries in the message are there to support TCP's reliable data transport.

Well-Known Ports

UDP and TCP use the IP address and the port number to uniquely identify a particular process on a TCP/IP networked computer. But your application program shouldn't use just any port. Some ports are called reserved ports because they have been given a special meaning. Some RFCs describe application-level services that most TCP/IP networked computers run. These network-accessible services "listen" at a well-known port so that client programs need only know the IP address of the remote host. For example, consider the finger program. It takes as its parameter a host name or host IP address. The finger program connects to the host at the well-known port that has been reserved for the finger service. If you were to write a program that waited for connections on a well-known port, you might get client programs trying to attach to your service that were expecting another program on the back-end.

Summary

This chapter discussed the principal components of a TCP/IP network. TCP/IP protocols are independent of the underlying network hardware on which they reside. Each computer on a TCP/IP must have a unique IP address that universally discloses the computers identification. TCP/IP is particularly well suited for use in an internetworking environment where several disparate networks need to be connected. Gateways allow the IP data to travel between two or more interconnected networks. The application programmer will make the most use out of TCP/IP's transport level interfaces of UDP and TCP. The socket paradigm is used to assist the application programmer with network coding. The next chapter discusses WinSock's use of sockets and the extensions necessary to support the Microsoft Windows architecture.

3

WinSock Overview

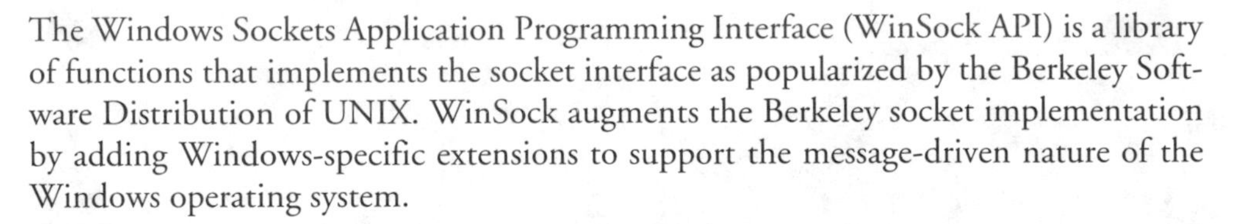

The Windows Sockets Application Programming Interface (WinSock API) is a library of functions that implements the socket interface as popularized by the Berkeley Software Distribution of UNIX. WinSock augments the Berkeley socket implementation by adding Windows-specific extensions to support the message-driven nature of the Windows operating system.

WinSock version 1.1 is bound to the TCP/IP protocol suite. Although future versions of WinSock are expected to support Novell's IPX/SPX, Apple's Appletalk, and other popular network protocols, this book concentrates on the socket interface to the TCP/IP protocol stack.

The WinSock specification allows TCP/IP stack vendors to provide a consistent interface to their stacks so that application developers can write an application to the WinSock specification and have that application run on any vendor's WinSock-compatible TCP/IP protocol stack. This is contrast to the days before the WinSock standard when software developers had to link their applications with libraries specific to each TCP/IP vendor's implementation. This limited the number of stacks that most applications ran on because of the difficulty in maintaining an application that used several different implementations of Berkeley sockets. WinSock has removed that barrier. Application programmers write to the WinSock API and link their applications with the WINSOCK.LIB import library (or WSOCK32.LIB in the case of Win32). The application can then be installed on a computer that has a WinSock TCP/IP stack, from any number of vendors, and dynamically link to the WINSOCK.DLL (or WSOCK32.DLL) provided by the vendor. Figure 3.1 is a block diagram of WSOCK32.DLL interaction in a 32-bit program on Windows NT. Although the actual WINSOCK.DLL is specific to each TCP/IP stack vendor, the interface into that dynamic link library remains consistent, hence any program linked with the WinSock import library should work.

CAUTION

I say *should* work because not all TCP/IP vendors' stacks operate in exactly the same way. Some simply have bugs and others interpret the WinSock or TCP/IP protocol standards differently. In some cases, the WinSock specification itself is ambiguous.

As discussed in Chapter 2, a socket is simply an end-point of communication. A TCP/IP socket is comprised of an IP address and a port. Some ports are reserved for well-known services and others are for use by your applications. Sockets can be set up to provide either a reliable, connection-oriented stream service or an unreliable, connectionless datagram service.

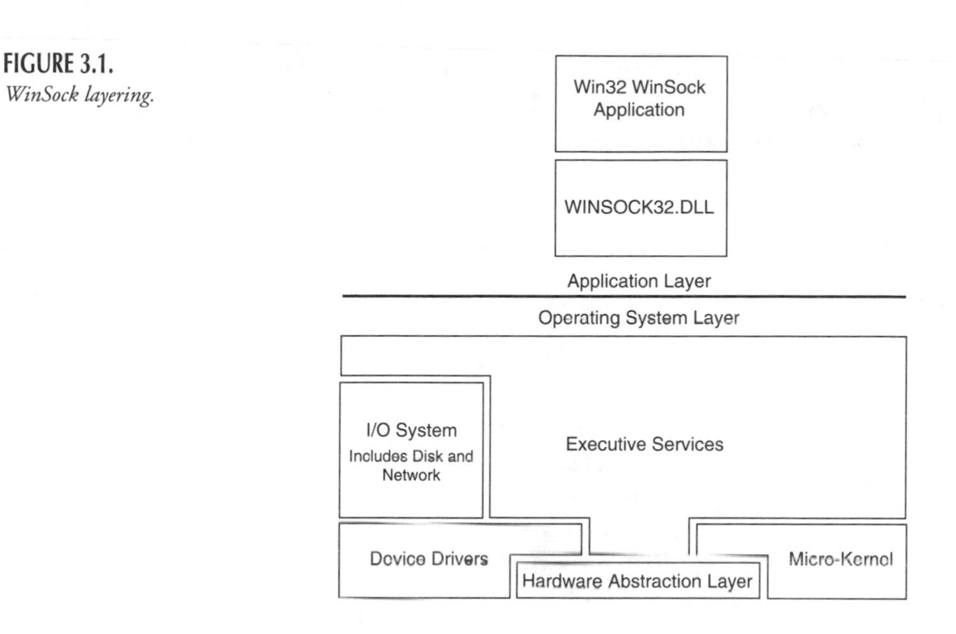

FIGURE 3.1.
WinSock layering.

The reliable stream socket is based on the TCP. It requires that a connection be established before two processes can send or receive data between themselves. The data sent between the connected processes is simply a stream of bytes. There are no record delimiters in the data stream. For example, if the sending process sends 100 bytes, the receiving process may receive that data as a single chunk of 100 bytes or two chunks of 50 bytes each. If your application depends on records being sent, you must provide application-level headers in the data stream; TCP won't preserve the packet size for you on the receiving side.

The connection-oriented stream service is well suited to the client-server architecture. In a typical client-server interaction, the server creates a socket, gives the socket a name, and waits for clients to connect to the socket. The client creates a socket and connects to the named socket on the server. When the server detects the connection to the named socket, it creates a new socket and uses that new socket for communication with the client. The server's named socket continues waiting for connections from other clients. See Figure 3.2 for an illustration of this simple client-server interaction.

The unreliable, connectionless datagram socket is based on the User Datagram Protocol. It doesn't require that a connection be established before two processes can send data to and receive data from each other. The data sent between any two processes is contained in a single packet. The sender sends the packet and the receiver receives the entire packet. Consequently, this type of socket can be easily used to send records; no application-level headers are required. The limitations in this socket service are that data may not be received at the destination, that data may be duplicated, and that data may arrive out of order.

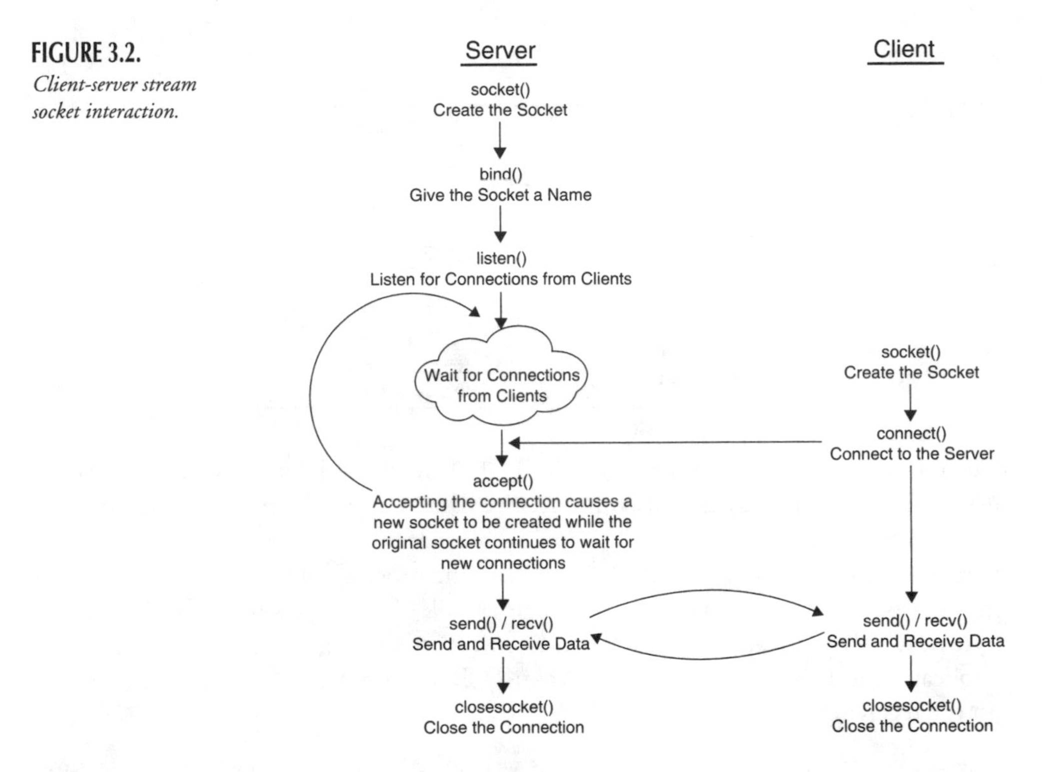

FIGURE 3.2.
Client-server stream socket interaction.

Berkeley Sockets Versus WinSock

Those familiar with Berkeley sockets may want to examine the following list, which describes some differences between the Berkeley socket implementation and WinSock.

WinSock Version 1.1 supports the TCP/IP domain for interprocess communication on the same computer as well as network communication. In addition to the TCP/IP domain, sockets in most UNIX implementations support the UNIX domain for interprocess communication on the same computer and the Xerox XNS domain.

The return values of certain Berkeley functions are different. For example, the `socket()` function returns –1 on failure in the UNIX environment; the WinSock implementation returns INVALID_SOCKET.

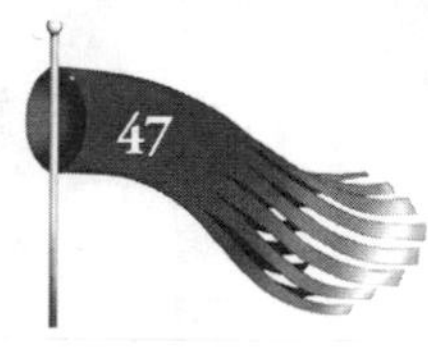

Certain Berkeley functions have different names in WinSock. For example, in UNIX the `close()` system call is used to close the socket connection. In WinSock, the function is called `closesocket()`. See the next item for the reason.

WinSock socket handles may not be UNIX-style file descriptors. In a UNIX environment, a socket handle can be operated on in much the same way as any other file handle (that is, an actual disk file). In most WinSock implementations, with the possible exception of the Win32 environment of Windows NT, socket handles can't be operated on in the same fashion as generic file descriptors.

Several new functions were added to WinSock to support the message-driven architecture of Windows. These are discussed in the following section.

WinSock Extensions to Berkeley Sockets

WinSock has several extensions to Berkeley sockets. Most of these extensions are due to the message-driven architecture of Microsoft Windows. Some extensions are also required to support the nonpreemptive nature of the 16-bit Windows operating environment. Windows NT and the 32-bit follow-up operating system to Windows 3.11 remove the nonpreemptive limitations, but the additional WinSock functions are still useful for reasons discussed later.

Windows Message-Driven Architecture

Although this book is not geared toward the beginning Windows programmer, this section gives a brief overview of the Windows architecture. If you're familiar with Windows message-driven architecture, feel free to jump ahead to the section titled WinSock Asynchronous Functions.

At the heart of every Windows program is a message loop and one or more window procedures. The message loop retrieves messages from the program's message queue and dispatches them to the appropriate window procedure for execution. Windows is considered to be a message-driven or event-driven system because no part of the program runs unless a message or event triggers it. Messages are generated by user actions such as typing on the keyboard or moving the mouse and by internal operating system activity.

The two major components of a Windows program are its message loop and its windows. As described previously, the message loop retrieves messages and calls the window procedure appropriate for the window. The message that is retrieved from the message queue contains a handle to the window to which the message should be routed.

The window procedure to call is dependent on the window class of the destination window. Some window classes are declared by the application programmer, and other predefined window classes are supplied by the Windows operating system. These predefined window classes are called controls. A few of the predefined controls are listed here:

EDIT	Used to view and edit text
LISTBOX	Used to display a list from which the user can select one or more items
STATIC	Used to display static text that is often used as labels for other controls

To better explain the message-driven nature of Windows, you can examine the following contrived sample application with a sizable main window, an edit control, and a static text label to the left of the edit control. The program's display is shown in Figure 3.3.

FIGURE 3.3.
Sample Application with Three Windows.

The sizable main window has a user-defined window class. The most important properties, or styles, of the main window are

`WS_CAPTION`	Gives the window its title bar
`WS_MINIMIZEBOX`	Adds the minimize button to the top right of the title bar allowing the window to be minimized into an icon
`WS_MAXIMIZEBOX`	Adds the maximize button to the top right of the title bar allowing the window to be maximized to fill the entire screen
`WS_SYSMENU`	Adds the system menu to the top left of the title bar
`WS_THICKFRAME`	Gives the window its sizing capabilities

The static text label is another window of the application. To the programmer new to Windows, it may seem strange that a static text label is a window. A lot of what the user thinks of as simple screen elements, such as buttons, list boxes, and edit boxes, are really

just specialized windows. This static-text label is known as a child window because it is anchored to the main window; the main window is the parent to the static-text label. This window has the predefined window class of STATIC and its functionality is limited. The static control can respond to messages that tell it to change its text or return its textual contents to the caller. Notice I said "respond to messages." The static control acts just like any other window in that it lies dormant until it receives a message. When a message comes in destined for the static control, the window procedure for the static control is called with parameters that specify the action that should be taken. One such message might be `WM_SETTEXT`, which tells the control to change the text it's displaying on the screen.

The last window of the application is the edit box. It has the predefined window class of EDIT. The edit control designates a rectangular child window in which the user can type text from the keyboard. The user selects the control and gives it the keyboard focus by clicking in it or moving to it by pressing the Tab key. The user can type text when the control displays a flashing caret. The mouse can be used to move the cursor, select characters to be replaced, or position the cursor for inserting characters. The Backspace key can be used to delete characters. You can tell from this description of the EDIT control, taken from the Windows Software Development Kit documentation, that this type of window knows about a lot more messages than the static control.

Now that you've read about the three windows that make up this sample application, look at the program flow once it is up and running. The heart of the program is its message loop. A message loop commonly used looks like this:

```
while (GetMessage(&msg, NULL, 0, 0))
{
  TranslateMessage(&msg);
  DispatchMessage(&msg);
}
```

This code fragment retrieves messages from the application's message queue and dispatches the messages to the destination window by calling its window procedure. If the user positions the mouse cursor over the edit box and presses the left mouse button, the edit control receives the input focus. The edit control knows it has focus when the `WM_SETFOCUS` message is dispatched to it. When this happens, the edit control displays the blinking caret to show where the next key pressed will be displayed. Figure 3.4 shows the message flow for the following `WM_CHAR` event. When the user types a key on the keyboard, a `WM_CHAR` message is generated. One of the qualifiers to this message is the actual key pressed. The edit control receives this notification and paints the newly typed character in the box. If the user then positions the mouse cursor outside the edit box but still inside the main application window, the edit box will receive a `WM_KILLFOCUS` message telling it to remove the blinking caret, and the main window then receives a `WM_SETFOCUS` message.

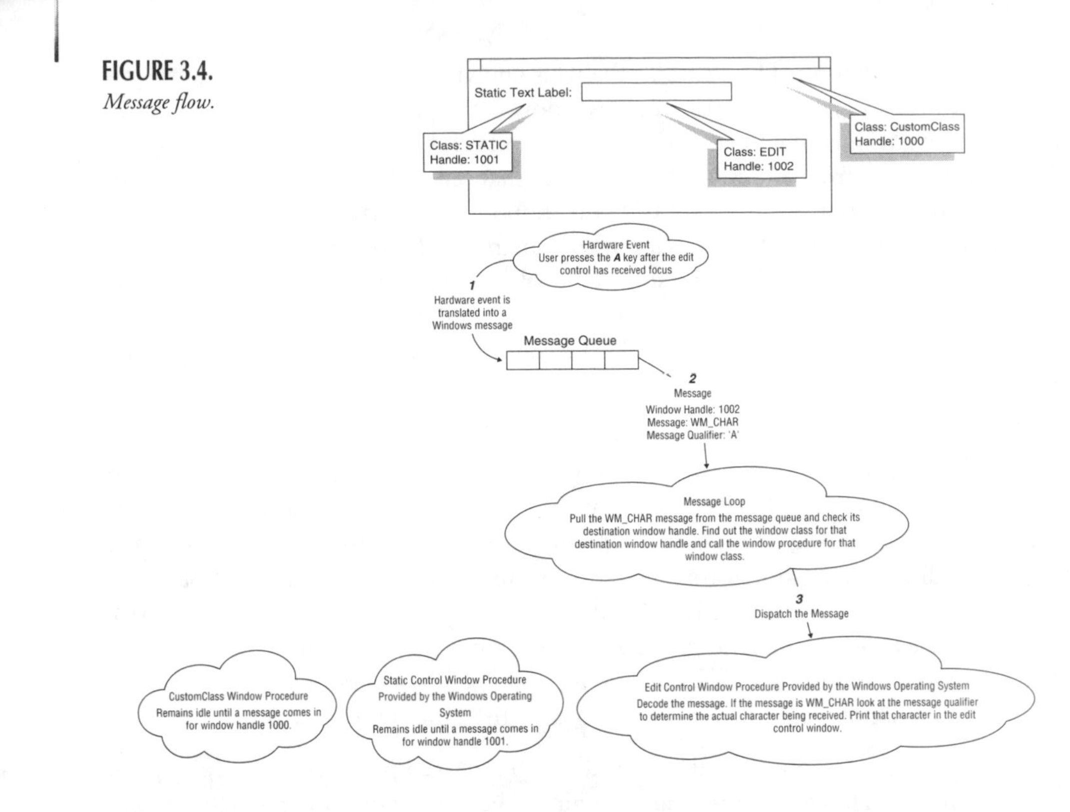

FIGURE 3.4.
Message flow.

The 16-bit Windows environment is cooperatively multitasked. This means that the applications running must cooperate with one another so that multiple tasks or programs can run simultaneously. They do this by continuously running the message loop described previously. If an application calls the `GetMessage()` function and there are no messages waiting for that application, Windows switches tasks and allows another program to run. That newly running program runs through its message loop until it has no more messages to process, and the procedure continues through all the programs running on the computer. In this environment, it's very easy for a single program to prevent all others from running. For example, if the edit box in the previously described example took 10 seconds to process the `WM_CHAR` message, no other tasks on the computer would run for at least 10 seconds. Not only would other tasks not run but if the user rapidly typed several keys in succession, it would take 10 seconds for each keystroke to be reflected on the screen. It is imperative in the nonpreemptive multitasking Windows environment to process a message swiftly and return to the message loop. If a program doesn't follow this rule, the performance of the entire computer system will suffer.

Windows NT is a preemptive multitasking operating system. This means that the operating system itself determines when a new task should run. It doesn't depend on an application checking for messages in order for a task switch to occur. If, as described previously, an application took 10 seconds to process a `WM_CHAR` message, other applications could still run before that 10 seconds elapsed. That particular application would experience poor performance, but it wouldn't degrade the performance of any other program running on the computer at that time. It's generally considered bad practice for a program to have poor response time to a user's commands. Users won't be happy if they have to wait 10 seconds for a character to appear on the screen. If an operation that was executed in response to a message takes a long time to run, the user interface of the program should remain responsive to the user. That is why it's advisable for an application to check its message queue often, even in the preemptive environment of Windows NT.

WinSock Asynchronous Functions

WinSock was originally designed for the nonpreemptive Windows architecture. For this reason, several extensions were added to traditional Berkeley sockets.

Blocking Versus Nonblocking

Many of the Berkeley socket functions take an indeterminate amount of time to execute. When a function exhibits this behavior, it is said to block; calling the function blocks the further execution of the calling program. In the Berkeley UNIX environment, for which sockets were originally developed, this didn't pose a serious problem because the UNIX operating system would simply preempt the blocking program and begin running another program. Windows (unlike Windows NT) can't preempt a task, so all other programs are put on hold until the blocking call returns. The designers of WinSock knew this posed a serious problem, so they added special code in the blocking functions to force the message loop of other applications to be checked. But this was still not the most efficient technique.

Berkeley sockets already have the notion of blocking versus nonblocking for some operations. For example, the `send()` function used to send data to a remote host may not return immediately, so the programmer is given the option of creating the socket with blocking or nonblocking sends. If the socket is created in blocking mode, it won't return until the data has been delivered. If it's created in nonblocking mode, the call to the `send()` function returns immediately and the program must call another function called `select()` to determine the status of the send. Windows and Windows NT can use the `select()` method of nonblocking calls, but the best thing to do in a Windows program is to use the special Windows asynchronous functions.

The special Windows asynchronous functions begin with the prefix `WSAAsync`. These functions were added to WinSock to make Berkeley sockets better fit the message-driven paradigm of Windows. The most common events to use the asynchronous functions for are the sending and receiving of data. Sending data might not happen instantly, and receiving data most certainly will cause a program to wait unless it is receiving a constant stream of bytes. By creating a socket for nonblocking sends and receives and using the `WSAAsyncSelect()` function call, an application will receive event notification messages to inform it when it can send data or when data has arrived and needs to be read. In the mean time, when there is no data communications occurring, the rest of the program remains fully responsive to the user's actions. The `WSAAsyncSelect()` function and its use with sending and receiving data on a nonblocking socket is discussed beginning in Chapter 7, "Socket Functions."

WinSock even extends Berkeley's nonblocking support to functions that could still cause a Berkeley UNIX program to block. The concept of a name server was introduced in Chapter 2, "TCP/IP Overview." The name server's job is to take as input the plain text representation of a computer's name and return that computer's IP address. The name server is usually a networked computer distinct from the one running WinSock programs that you develop. The services of a name server require that a message be sent over the network from the computer using the WinSock program to the computer running the name server. This network communication could take an indeterminate amount of time. WinSock has compensated for that fact by extending the functions that utilize the services of a name server. These functions are among those grouped into a category of functions called the database functions or the `getXbyY` functions. `GetXbyY` is used to refer to these database functions because the function names take the form of get X by Y, or put another way: "Given Y, what is the corresponding X?" In the name server example, the function used is called `gethostbyname()`; given the computer's name, what is its host information? In Berkeley UNIX, the `getXbyY` functions may block. WinSock adds asynchronous versions of the `getXbyY` functions called `WSAAsyncGetXbyY`. The `gethostbyname()` function is complimented by the nonblocking WinSock function called `WSAAsyncGetHostByName()`, for example. A call to a `WSAAsyncGetXbyY` function returns immediately with an identifying handle. When the actual work performed by the function has completed, a message is sent to the application notifying completion of the function with the specified handle. The database functions, in both their blocking and asynchronous forms, are discussed in a Chapter 6, "Conversion and Database Functions."

The WinSock asynchronous functions were added primarily for the benefit of the nonpreemptive Windows environment. You may be questioning their worth in the truly preemptive multitasking Windows NT environment. The `WSAAsync` functions have an important use even in Windows NT. They allow your applications to remain responsive to the user. Users won't enjoy working with your program if it forces them to wait for completion of a long event. Most users expect a way to cancel operations that take a long time. For example, suppose that you have a program that takes as input a computer's plain-text name. The user enters the name and then presses a button labeled Look Up, which causes the `gethostbyname()` function to be called. Using `gethostbyname()` will cause the program to hang for an indeterminate amount of time until the request is carried out. Under Windows NT other programs would still run, but under Windows the performance of all programs would be degraded. This program could be modified to use `WSAAsyncGetHostByName()` instead of `gethostbyname()`. As soon as users press the Look Up button, the `WSAAsyncGetHostByName()` function is called and returns an identifying handle. If users wish to cancel the search, they can press the Cancel button, which terminates the request with that identifying handle. Users would maintain full control instead of being at the mercy of the program.

Summary

This chapter discussed WinSock as compared to the original Berkeley sockets interface popularized by BSD UNIX. WinSock includes most of the Berkeley functionality with many extensions to support the event-driven nature of Windows. The use of some of these extensions is mandatory for proper program execution; the use of others is optional but desirable because they provide a user interface responsive to the user's requests. Later chapters will fully explore the benefits of using the WinSock extended functions. The next chapter discusses the Microsoft Visual C++ development environment.

4
Visual C++

Microsoft's Visual C++ product has greatly simplified the development of Windows programs. The application developer is no longer required to start every project with the same hundred lines of mandatory code just to display the most basic of windows. The Microsoft Foundation Class library (MFC) encapsulates most of that drudgery, allowing the programmer to start working on the real problem instead of the plumbing. The samples presented in this book make use of MFC and Visual C++.

Visual C++ Components

The Visual C++ package includes several tools that are tightly integrated with each other and to the Microsoft Foundation Class library. The combination of these tools makes it easy to create a framework from which the application begins.

Visual Workbench

Visual Workbench is the program you will spend the most time in. It includes a color-coded text editor which highlights keywords in your C and C++ source code. The Visual Workbench also encompasses a build manager which manages makefiles that can be used from within Visual Workbench or from the command line. This build manager is used to add new source files to a project, change compiler and linker options, and automatically generate source code dependencies. The Visual Workbench also includes a source level debugger. Debugging, and coding in general, is made much simpler by the help facility built into Visual Workbench. By placing the caret on a Windows, C, or C++ keyword and pressing the F1 key, help on that topic is displayed. Figure 4.1 shows Visual Workbench operating on the TEST project with two source code windows open for editing.

AppWizard

AppWizard is one component of the Visual Workbench. It automates the task of creating a minimalistic Windows program by prompting you with several options and then creating the skeleton source code necessary for that application. The skeleton program created by AppWizard supports window management, a basic menu structure, and basic menu commands. Some of the options offered determine whether the application will have:

> Multiple Document Interface or Single Document Interface. A MDI application can have one or more child windows within the main application window. The Visual Workbench is an example of a MDI application because it allows you to have several source code windows open at any one time.

Initial Toolbar. The toolbar is a row of bitmap buttons that appears beneath the application's menu.

Printing and Print Preview.

Context Sensitive Help.

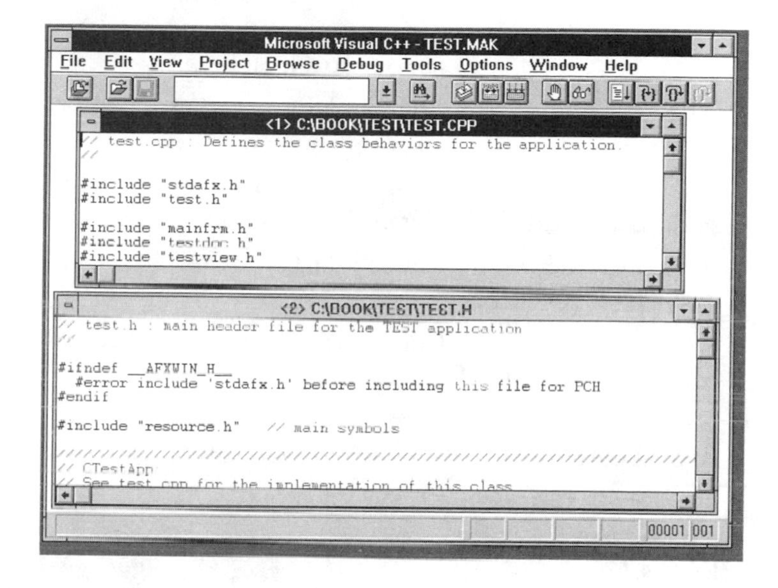

FIGURE 4.1.
Visual Workbench.

Figure 4.2 shows the option dialog of AppWizard. The output of AppWizard is several C++ source and header files, the project makefile, and the resource file. Below is a list of files for an AppWizard-generated project called TEST. The TEST project uses the Single Document Interface.

TEST.MAK	Project file compatible with Visual Workbench and command-line tool NMAKE.
TEST.H.	Main include file for application; includes other project-specific include files and declares the CTestApp application class.
TEST.CPP	Main application source file. Contains the application class CTestApp.
TEST.RC	Listing of all resources the program uses. It includes icons, bitmaps, and cursors stored in the RES subdirectory. File can be edited directly with App Studio.
RES\TEST.ICO	Icon file used as application's icon. Icon is included by the main resource file TEST.RC.

RES\TEST.RC2	Contains resources not edited by App Studio. Initially contains a VERSIONINFO resource that you can customize for your application.
TEST.DEF	Contains information about the application that must be provided so that it runs with Microsoft Windows. Defines parameters such as name and description of application and size of initial local heap.
TEST.CLW	Contains information used by ClassWizard to edit existing classes or add new classes.
MAINFRM.H and MAINFRM.CPP	Contain frame class CMainFrame, which is derived from CFrameWnd and controls all SDI frame and features.
TESTDOC.H and TESTDOC.CPP	Contain the CTestDoc document class.
TESTVIEW.H and TESTVIEW.CPP	Contain the CTestView view class.
STDAFX.H and STDAFX.CPP	Used to build a precompiled header file to make and compiles substantially faster.
RESOURCE.H	Defines resource IDs. App Studio reads and updates this file.

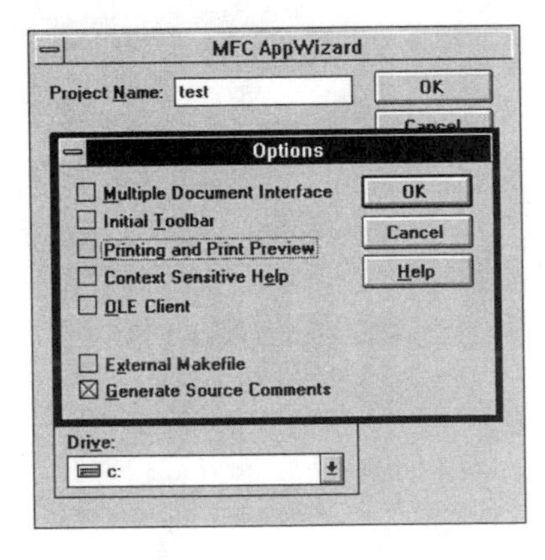

FIGURE 4.2.
AppWizard options.

App Studio

App Studio is used to create and edit Windows resources. With it, you can manipulate the resources for menus, dialog boxes, bitmaps, icons, cursors, strings in a string table, and keyboard accelerators. App Studio automatically generates unique resource IDs for the resources you create. These IDs are stored in the RESOURCE.H file by default. Figure 4.3 shows App Studio editing the resource file from the TEST project listed previously.

FIGURE 4.3.
App Studio.

ClassWizard

ClassWizard is perhaps the most empowering component of the Visual C++ development environment. With it, you can derive classes from several standard MFC base class objects and to add member functions and variables to those classes. ClassWizard is used to map Windows messages, as well as user-defined messages, to specific member functions. With just a few mouse clicks, you can associate a specific message to a particular function name. ClassWizard creates the function prototype for that function in the header file for the class and also creates a stub function for you to add code to in the C++ file.

A common use of ClassWizard is to associate a class derived from CDialog with a dialog resource created with App Studio. First you design a dialog resource with App Studio and then launch ClassWizard. If ClassWizard is launched directly from App Studio and the dialog resource being edited doesn't yet have a class associated with it, ClassWizard will automatically prompt you for a class name for the new dialog box class. Once the basic class is created, you can link member functions to the buttons and controls of the dialog box. You can also associate variables to the controls of the dialog box. For example, if the dialog box contains an edit control used to enter a numeric value, you can link an integer variable to that control. The integer variable becomes a member variable to the dialog's class object. When your application needs the value entered into that edit control, it simply references the integer member variable.

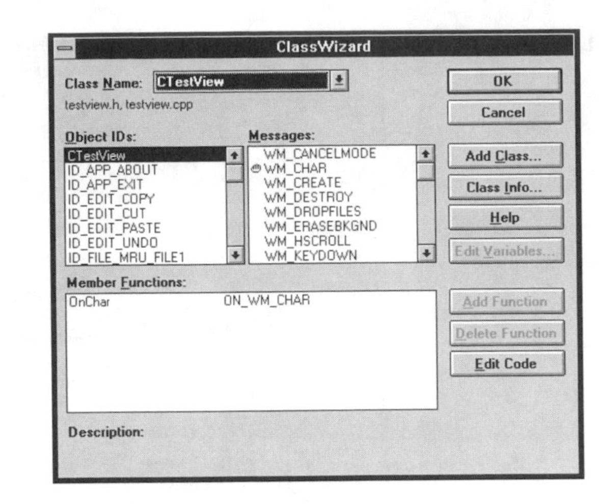

FIGURE 4.4.
ClassWizard.

Class Browser

The Class Browser is integrated into Visual Workbench. You can use it to view class hierarchical relationships. You can select a class and view all classes derived from it or view the class from which it was derived. Figure 4.5 shows the base class graph of the `CTestApp` object from the TEST application. The browser shows us that `CTestApp` is derived from `CWinApp`. Clicking `CTestApp` reveals specific information for that object in the other part of the class browser viewer. The upper-right portion shows the member functions particular to `CTestApp`. Double-clicking one of these names puts you into the Visual Workbench editor at the appropriate spot in the source file for `CTestApp`. The lower-right portion shows the source files where the `CTestApp` object is implemented.

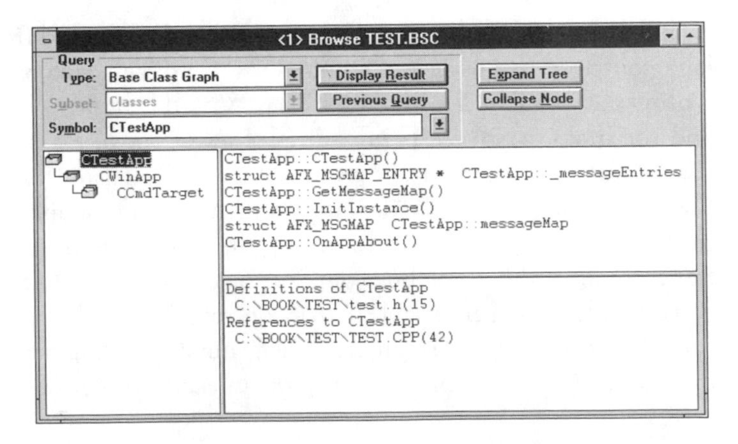

FIGURE 4.5.
Class Browser.

Message Mapping in an MFC Program

You will remember from the discussion in Chapter 3 that Windows is an event-driven operating system that relies on messages being delivered to the appropriate destination window in order for program execution to take place. Visual C++ makes the coding of message-based code almost trivial. With ClassWizard, you can define an object derived from a list of standard MFC objects. These base class objects are windows that expect to receive messages. ClassWizard allows for an easy mapping between messages and functions that perform the desired operations in response to those messages. After creating your derived class from the applicable base class, ClassWizard will create the member functions that you need to run in response to a message stimulus. A member function is created in the class declaration and a stub code for the member function is inserted into the implementation file for the class. The base classes from which your classes can be derived already have many member functions ready to be overridden by your special purpose code. One of these member functions reacts in response to the WM_CHAR message, which tells the window that the user has pressed a key on the keyboard. Figure 4.4 shows ClassWizard with the WM_CHAR message mapped to `OnChar`. The code created by ClassWizard in the class declaration for the TEST application follows:

```
class CTestView : public CView
{

...

//{{AFX_MSG(CTestView)
  afx_msg void OnChar(UINT nChar, UINT nRepCnt, UINT nFlags);
  //}}AFX_MSG
  DECLARE_MESSAGE_MAP()
}
```

Notice that the code ClassWizard adds is placed between the commented lines `//{{AFX MSG(CTestView)` and `//}}AFX MSG`. The appropriate code in the implementation file follows:

```
...

BEGIN_MESSAGE_MAP(CTestView, CView)
  //{{AFX_MSG_MAP(CTestView)
  ON_WM_CHAR()
  //}}AFX_MSG_MAP
END_MESSAGE_MAP()

...

void CTestView::OnChar(UINT nChar, UINT nRepCnt, UINT nFlags)
{
  // TODO: Add your message handler code here and/or call default
```

```
  CView::OnChar(nChar, nRepCnt, nFlags);
}

...
```

When a WM_CHAR message comes in that is destined for the `CTestView` window, the message map is examined to see how the message should be routed. Because ON_WM_CHAR is in the message map, MFC knows that the application has a message handler in place. The WM_CHAR message is one for which there is a default handler already in place in `CTestView`'s base class of `CView`. MFC knows that WM_CHAR maps to the `OnChar` member function. You will see in a later chapter how to add user-defined message handlers that are unique to your application. Because MFC doesn't know of these message handlers, you have to specify in the message map the name of the member function that handles that message.

Support Files for Building WinSock Applications

To compile an application that uses the WinSock API, you need the WinSock header file WINSOCK.H, which contains all the function prototypes and structure definitions. Linking the application requires either WINSOCK.LIB or WSOCK32.LIB depending on whether you're targeting the 16-bit or 32-bit Windows platform. WINSOCK.H and WSOCK32.LIB are included with Visual C++ 1.1 for Windows NT. WINSOCK.H and WINSOCK.LIB are available from your TCP/IP stack provider.

To ensure source code compatibility between the 16-bit and 32-bit programs, the standard 16-bit Windows include file VER.H must be named WINVER.H, as it is named in the 32-bit environment. If you're using a 16-bit compiler, I suggest going into the compiler's include directory and copying VER.H to WINVER.H.

A detailed discussion of how to build WinSock applications is included in Chapter 8, "Sample Applications."

Summary

The Visual C++ integrated development environment has greatly simplified development of Windows programs. The well-integrated tools make it easy to create applications that use the MFC library. The WinSock class library developed later in this book will make extensive use of MFC's functionality. The development of these classes will show the power and flexibility of Visual C++.

II

Basics of WinSock Programming

5

Startup and Shutdown Functions

The WinSock functions your application needs are located in the dynamic link library named WINSOCK.DLL or WSOCK32.DLL depending on whether the 16-bit or 32-bit version of Windows is being targeted. Your application is linked with either WINSOCK.LIB or WSOCK32.LIB as appropriate. The include file where the WinSock functions and structures are defined is named WINSOCK.H for both the 16-bit and 32-bit environments. Before your application uses any WinSock functions, the application must call an initialization routine called `WSAStartup()`. Before your application terminates, it should call the `WSACleanup()` function.

WSAStartup

The `WSAStartup()` function initializes the underlying Windows Sockets Dynamic Link Library (WinSock DLL). You will remember that the WinSock API is independent of the specific TCP/IP stack vendor. This is what gives WinSock-compliant applications the capability of running on any number of TCP/IP stacks. The `WSAStartup()` function gives the TCP/IP stack vendor a chance to do any application-specific initialization that may be necessary. `WSAStartup()` is also used to confirm that the version of the WinSock DLL is compatible with the requirements of the application.

The prototype of the WSAStartup() function follows:

```
int PASCAL FAR WSAStartup(WORD wVersionRequired, LPWSADATA lpWSAData);
```

The *`wVersionRequired`* parameter is the highest version of the WinSock API the calling application can use. The high-order byte specifies the minor version number and the low-order byte specifies the major version number. The *`lpWSAData`* parameter is a pointer to a `WSADATA` data structure that receives details of the WinSock implementation.

Version Checking

One objective of the `WSAStartup()` function is to confirm that the WinSock implementation meets the requirements of the application. As of the summer of 1994, Versions 1.0 and 1.1 of WinSock have been released. Most WinSock compliant TCP/IP stacks in use today, including the stacks supplied by Microsoft, implement Version 1.1 of the WinSock specification.

The *`wVersionRequired`* parameter in the call to `WSAStartup()` has a high-order byte that specifies the minor version number and a low-order byte that specifies the major version number. The following code shows how a *`wVersionRequired`* parameter is constructed that has a requirement of WinSock Version 1.0:

```
wVersionRequired = MAKEWORD(0, 1);
```

The second parameter to the `WSAStartup()` function is a pointer to a `WSADATA` data structure. After the call to the initialization function, this structure contains information detailing the WinSock implementation. The `WSADATA` structure has the following format:

```
typedef struct WSAData {
  WORD            wVersion;
  WORD            wHighVersion;
  char            szDescription[WSADESCRIPTION_LEN+1];
  char            szSystemStatus[WSASYS_STATUS_LEN+1];
  unsigned short  iMaxSockets;
  unsigned short  iMaxUdpDg;
  char FAR *      lpVendorInfo;
} WSADATA;
```

To verify that the WinSock compliant stack meets the version requirements of your application, the application should check the value in *wVersion* after the `WSAStartup()` function returns. For example, if your application requires WinSock Version 2.0, compare the high-order byte of *wVersion* to 0 and the low-order byte to 2. If either of these comparisons fail, the application should display a message to the program's user explaining the failure. The following code fragment shows a typical implementation:

```
WORD wVersionRequested = MAKEWORD(1, 1); // WinSock 1.1 requested
WSADATA wsaData;                         // WinSock details
int nErrorStatus;                        // error status

nErrorStatus = WSAStartup(wVersionRequested, &wsaData);
if (nErrorStatus != 0)
{
  // display an error message explaining that WinSock
  // initialization has failed and return

  return;
}

// check the WinSock version information

if ( (LOBYTE(wsaData.wVersion) != LOBYTE(wVersionRequested)) ||
 (HIBYTE(wsaData.wVersion) != HIBYTE(wVersionRequested)) )
{
  // display an error message explaining that the WinSock
  // implementation doesn't meet the version requirements
  // of the application

  WSACleanup();        // terminate WinSock use
  return;
}
```

This code segment, or something resembling it, is placed early in a program's execution path. Typically it is found in `WinMain()` of a program built with the Windows SDK or `CWinApp::InitInstance()` for an MFC program.

In the preceding code, notice that the `WSADATA` structure has *`wVersion`* and *`wHighVersion`* as member variables. *`wHighVersion`* has the same format as *`wVersion`* and *`wVersionRequested`*. A WinSock DLL may contain support for multiple WinSock versions. For example, it's common for a WinSock DLL to support Versions 1.0 and 1.1. If the application requests Version 1.0 from a WinSock DLL that supports 1.0 and 1.1, *`wVersion`* will contain 1.0 and *`wHighVersion`* will contain 1.1. This says that the WinSock DLL will supply Version 1.0 functionality to the application but it has the capability of supporting Version 1.1 functionality. The following table lists application and WinSock interaction for differing application version requirements and WinSock capabilities:

App Ver	*WinSock Ver*	*`wVersion` Requested*	*`wHigh` `wVersion`*	*End Version*	*Result*
1.1	1.1	1.1	1.1	1.1	App uses 1.1
1.0, 1.1	1.0	1.1	1.0	1.0	App uses 1.0
1.0	1.0, 1.1	1.0	1.0	1.1	App uses 1.0
1.1	1.0, 1.1	1.1	1.1	1.1	App uses 1.1
1.1	1.0	1.1	1.0	1.0	App fails
1.0	1.1	1.0	--	--	`WSAStartup()` fails
1.0, 1.1	1.0, 1.1	1.1	1.1	1.1	App uses 1.1
1.1, 2.0	1.1	2.0	1.1	1.1	App uses 1.1
2.0	1.1	2.0	1.1	1.1	App fails

The general rules that `WSAStartup()` follows are as follows:

If *`wVersionRequested`* matches one of the versions supported by the WinSock DLL, set *`wVersion`* to *`wVersionRequested`* and set *`wHighVersion`* to the highest WinSock version that is supported (this value may or may not be the same as *`wVersion`*).

If *`wVersionRequested`* specifies a later version than the WinSock DLL supports, set *`wVersion`* and *`wHighVersion`* to the highest version that this WinSock supports. It is then up to the application to decide whether this WinSock's capabilities are adequate.

If *`wVersionRequested`* specifies an earlier version than the WinSock DLL supports, `WSAStartup()` returns a failure `code()`. The internal WinSock error code is set to WSAVERNOTSUPPORTED. To access the internal WinSock error code, use the `WSAGetLastError()` function outlined later in this chapter.

Retrieving Vendor Information and TCP/IP Stack Capabilities

The other capability of `WSAStartup()` is to provide to the calling application information about the underlying TCP/IP stack. We've examined the *`wVersion`* and *`wHighVersion`* variables of the `WSADATA` structure already. The remaining variables provide details of the WinSock implementation in use as follows:

- `szDescription` is a pointer to a null-terminated ASCII string that describes the WinSock implementation. This string may be up to 256 characters long and usually contains a reference to the WinSock vendor, whether it be Microsoft, Wollongong, Net Manage, FTP, or another vendor.
- `szSystemStatus` is a pointer to a null-terminated ASCII string that contains relevant status or configuration information.
- `iMaxSockets` is the maximum number of sockets that a single process can potentially open. Your application can use this number as a rough estimation of whether the WinSock DLL is usable by the application. It is not a guarantee that your application can allocate this number of sockets.
- `iMaxUdpDg` is the size, in bytes, of the largest UDP datagram that can be sent or received by the WinSock implementation. If this number is set to 0 (zero) there is no implied size limitation.
- `lpVendorInfo` is a pointer to a vendor-specific data structure. Because this data is vendor-specific, your program loses its stack independence if it makes use of this data.

WSACleanup

The `WSACleanup()` function is used to terminate an application's use of WinSock. For every call to `WSAStartup()` there has to be a matching call to `WSACleanup()`. `WSACleanup()` is usually called after your application's message loop has terminated. In an MFC application, the `ExitInstance()` member function of the `CWinApp` class provides a convenient location to call `WSACleanup()`. The prototype follows:

```
int PASCAL FAR WSACleanup(void);
```

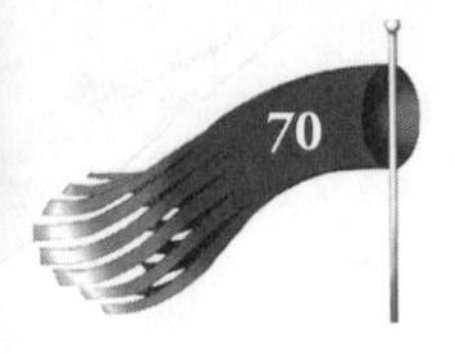

WSAGetLastError

The `WSAGetLastError()` function doesn't deal exclusively with startup or shutdown procedures, but it needs to be addressed early. Its function prototype looks like

```
int PASCAL FAR WSAGetLastError(void);
```

`WSAGetLastError()` returns the last WinSock error that occurred. In the MS-DOS or UNIX programming worlds, you're probably used to examining the *errno* variable, which is an application-specific global variable available in all programs. Because WinSock isn't really part of the operating system but is instead a later add-on, *errno* couldn't be used. As soon as a WinSock API call fails, you should call `WSAGetLastError()` to retrieve specific details of the error.

As an example, if `WSAStartup()` is called with a `wVersionRequested`, which is earlier than any WinSock API supported by the WinSock DLL, `WSAStartup()` returns an error indicator. Calling `WSAGetLastError()` immediately after the failed call to `WSAStartup()` reveals the WSAVERNTSUPPORTED error. The other possible error values generated by `WSAStartup()` are `WSASYSNOTREADY`, if the network subsystem is failing, and `WSAEINVAL`, if an invalid argument is passed.

Possible error values for `WSACleanup()` include `WSANOTINITIALIZED` if `WSAStartup()` wasn't called successfully, `WSAENETDOWN` if the network subsystem is failing, and `WSAEINPROGRESS` if a blocking WinSock operation is currently in progress.

Summary

This chapter discussed just the beginning of writing a WinSock application. Chapter 8, "Sample Applications," presents a program that uses the `WSADATA` structure in the call to `WSAStartup()` to present some useful information to the application user. The next few chapters will continue to present the mandatory WinSock functions useful to most applications.

6

Conversion and Database Functions

WinSock provides a set of procedures commonly referred to as the database functions. The duty of these database functions is to convert the host and service names that are used by humans into a format useable by the computer. The computers on an internetwork also require that certain data transmitted between them be in a common format. WinSock provides several conversion routines to fulfill this requirement.

NOTE

This chapter contains several small code samples. These aren't complete programs that run on their own but are presented instead to help clarify the textual description of the functions used in the sample. Study these examples so that you can use them in your own programs but don't worry about actual program implementation issues now. Later chapters will draw from these code snippets to produce complete programs.

Conversion Routines and Network Byte Ordering

There are several conditions under which a WinSock function should be called with a parameter stored in a particular format. An internetwork using WinSock is supposed to allow disparate computer systems to communicate. These different internetworked hosts are likely to have different hardware architectures based on the CPU used in the computer. They may store internal numerical data differently from one another. The way in which a CPU internally stores a number is called its byte ordering. To facilitate the different byte ordering used in different CPUs, WinSock provides a set of conversion functions. These conversion functions have the job of turning a host byte-ordered number into a number using the network byte-ordering scheme. Network byte ordering is the standard by which all TCP/IP connected computers must transmit certain data. In effect, the network byte-ordering sequence is the lowest common denominator of all internetworked computers.

There are four primary byte-order conversion routines. They handle the conversions to and from unsigned short integers and unsigned long integers.

Unsigned Short Integer Conversion

The `htons()` and `ntohs()` functions convert an unsigned short from host-to-network order and from network-to-host order, respectively. The prototypes look like

```
u_short PASCAL FAR htons(u_short hostshort);
u_short PASCAL FAR ntohs(u_short netshort);
```

`htons()` takes as input an unsigned short in its native host format and returns that number in network order. `ntohs()` takes as input an unsigned short in network order and returns that number in the native host format.

On an Intel 80×86 CPU, integers are stored with the least significant bit in the lower part of an integer's address space. Take the decimal number 43794 as an example. In hexadecimal notation this number is written as AB12. Suppose, also, that this value is stored at memory location *n*. On an Intel 80×86, the byte value at location *n* is 12 and the byte value at memory location *n* + 1 is AB. You can see that the least significant byte of the two-byte quantity is stored in the lower address space. This is the opposite of network byte ordering. The output of `htons(43794)` has AB in the lower address space and 12 stored in the higher address space of the two-byte quantity. On a different hardware platform, such as the Motorola 68000, the `ntohs()` function doesn't do any byte manipulation because the 68000's native byte ordering is the same as network byte ordering.

Unsigned Long Integer Conversion

The `htonl()` and `ntohl()` functions work like `htons()` and `ntohs()` except that they operate on four-byte unsigned longs rather than unsigned shorts. The prototypes look like the following:

```
u_long PASCAL FAR htons(u_long hostlong);
u_long PASCAL FAR ntohs(u_long netlong);
```

On an Intel 80×86 CPU, the decimal number 2870136116 is stored in memory, from lowest address space to highest, as hexadecimal 34 CD 12 AB. The output of `htonl(2870136116)` has AB in the lower address space, 12 stored in the next higher address space, and so on.

CAUTION

About byte ordering: Your program may run as expected under test conditions if the hosts involved in the test have the same native byte-ordering scheme. Problems may develop later if you ever try to connect your program to a host with a different byte-ordering scheme. As an example, say that you tested both a client application and a server application on an Intel 80×86 CPU. Everything may run fine even if you forget to use the conversion routines. Now, say that you move the server process over to a Motorola 68000-based Macintosh platform. The server "listens" on a well-known port. I'll use port number 427 as an example. In hexadecimal, that port is 01AB. The Macintosh server application is listening for connections to 01AB. If the 80×86-based client then tries to connect to port 427 without first calling the `htons()` conversion routine, it is really trying to connect to port AB01 hexadecimal, which is 43777 in decimal. Hence, the client never connects to the server process running on the Macintosh, or at least not the intended server process.

The functions that require their parameters to be in network byte order are so noted in the text accompanying each function's description.

Converting IP Addresses

WinSock provides another set of conversion functions that provide a translation between the ASCII representation of a dotted-decimal IP address and the internal 32-bit, byte-ordered number required by other WinSock functions.

Converting an IP Address String to Binary

`inet_addr()` converts a dotted-decimal IP address string into a number suitable for use as an Internet address. Its function prototype is as follows:

```
unsigned long PASCAL FAR inet_addr(const char FAR * cp);
```

`cp` is a pointer to a string representing an IP address in dotted-decimal notation. The `inet_addr()` function returns a binary representation of the Internet address given. This value is already in network byte order, so there is no need to call `htonl()`. If the `cp` string doesn't contain a valid IP address, `inet_addr()` returns `INADDR_NONE`. One possible cause for such an error is that the IP address has a component greater than 255. Remember that each of the four components of a dotted-decimal IP address represent one of four bytes of an unsigned long, therefore it's illegal to have any component with a value greater than 255 because the value of a byte must be between zero and 255 inclusive.

The following code fragment shows a typical call to `inet_addr()`. Of course, your real programs won't have hard-coded IP addresses; you'll most likely allow users to specify IP addresses when they configure your application.

```
u_long ulIPAddress = inet_addr("166.78.16.148");
```

The value of `ulIPAddress` after this code fragment has executed will be hexadecimal A64E1094. `inet_addr()` simply takes each component of the IP address and stores it in binary as one byte of the four-byte IP address. You don't need to specify all four parts of the IP address, though. `inet_addr()` can take an IP address in any of the following dotted-decimal notations: a.b.c.d, a.b.c, a.b, or a. The a.b.c.d value is a typical IP address as shown in the preceding code sample. If a quantity is omitted, the last defined quantity

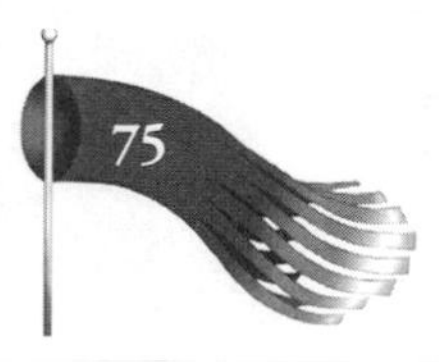

is simply extended to fill the remaining bytes to make a total of four bytes. For example, if the string passed to `inet_addr()` is "166.78.16", following the a.b.c format, the returned unsigned long is hexadecimal A64E0010.

Converting a Binary IP Address to a String

`inet_ntoa()` performs the opposite job of `inet_addr()`. Its function prototype is as follows:

```
char FAR * PASCAL FAR inet_ntoa(struct in_addr in);
```

`in` is a structure that contains an Internet host address. You'll see that some WinSock functions manipulate IP addresses as unsigned longs and others as `in_addr` structures. To remedy this difference, some byte copying is in order. This is shown in the following sample code. On success, the `inet_ntoa()` function returns a pointer to a string with a dotted-decimal representation of the IP address. On error, `NULL` is returned. A `NULL` value means that the IP address passed as the `in` parameter is invalid.

Following is a piece of somewhat contrived code:

```
// first get an unsigned long with a valid IP address
u_long ulIPAddress = inet_addr("166.78.16.148");

// copy the four bytes of the IP address into an in_addr structure
IN_ADDR in;
memcpy(&in, &ulIPAddress, 4);

// convert the IP address back into a string
char lpszIPAddress[16];
lstrcpy(lpszIPAddress, inet_ntoa(in));
```

I said the previous sample was contrived because of the way the binary IP address was retrieved. The binary IP address `ulIPAddress` is retrieved by using `inet_addr()` to convert an IP address string. In an actual program, the IP address on which you want to use `inet_ntoa()` will most likely come as the result of another WinSock call, not entered by the user or hard-coded; this part of the code is for demonstration purposes only. Once you have this unsigned long, it needs to be stored in an `in_addr` structure to be used by `inet_ntoa()`, so `memcpy()` is used. Next, the conversion function is called. The string pointer returned by `inet_ntoa()` is only temporary. It may be invalid after the next call to a WinSock function, so it is best to copy it into a variable in the application. A buffer of 16 bytes is allocated because this is the longest that a valid four-byte IP address will ever be (that is, "255.255.255.255" plus the terminating `NULL` character).

What's My Name?

Some applications need to know the name of the computer on which they are running. The `gethostname()` function provides this functionality. It was added to the WinSock

1.1 specification. The function's prototype looks like the following:

```
int PASCAL FAR gethostname(char FAR * name, int namelen);
```

`name` is a far pointer to a character array that will accept the null-terminated host name, and `namelen` is the size of that character array. The `gethostname()` function returns 0 (zero) on success and `SOCKET_ERROR` on failure. On a return value of `SOCKET_ERROR`, you can call `WSAGetLastError()` to determine the specifics of the problem. Possible error values include `WSAEFAULT` if the buffer was too small to accept the host name, `WSANOTINITIALIZED` if `WSAStartup()` wasn't called successfully, `WSAENETDOWN` if the network subsystem is failing, or `WSAEINPROGRESS` if a blocking WinSock operation is currently in progress.

The following code fragment shows a typical call to `gethostname()`:

```
#define HOST_NAME_LEN (50)
char lpszHostName[HOST_NAME_LEN];     // will accept the host name
char lpszMessage[100];                // informational message

if (gethostname(lpszHostName, HOST_NAME_LEN) == 0)
  wsprintf(lpszMessage, "This computer's name is %s", lpszHostName);
else
  wsprintf(lpszMessage, "gethostname() generated error %d",
   WSAGetLastError());

MessageBox(NULL, lpszMessage, "Info", MB_OK);
```

NOTE

The `name` populated by `gethostbyname()` may be a simple name or a fully qualified domain name. For example, my computer may be recognized as `goober` or `goober.ping.com`. It's up to those who implement WinSock to determine which format is returned. The only thing guaranteed about the `name` variable is that it can be parsed by the `gethostbyname()` function, which will be discussed later.

Host Name Resolution

Humans use a textual representation for the hosts to which their programs connect. The computer requires a host's address to be a 32-bit integer stored in a standardized way as described in the previous section on network byte ordering. Your program cannot connect to another computer until that computer's IP address is in the 32-bit format. To remedy this difference, your program can use either the `gethostbyname()` or `inet_addr()` functions. `gethostbyname()` is used if you know either the simple name or the fully qualified domain name. `inet_addr()` is used if you know the IP address.

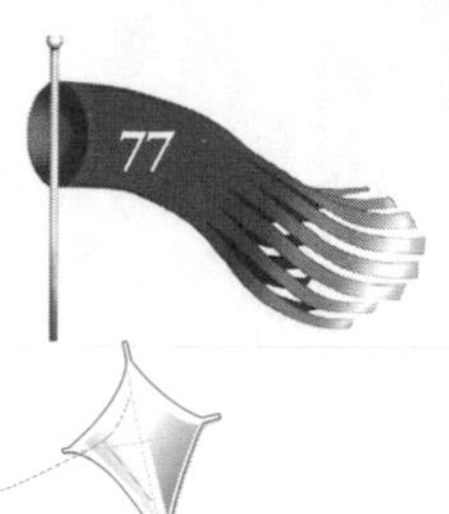

TIP

Most programs that have a configuration to select the host with which the program communicates enable the user to enter either a host name or an IP address. Your program should call `inet_addr()` first with the user's input. If this function returns successfully, your conversion job is finished; otherwise, you should call `gethostbyname()`, assuming that the user entered a host name.

Finding a Host's IP Address

The main duty of `gethostbyname()` is to take a host name and return its IP address. This function, and its asynchronous counterpart named `WSAAsyncGetHostByName()`, may perform a simple table lookup on a host file local to the computer on which the program is running, or it may send the request across the network to a name server. Figures 6.1 and 6.2 show the different means of host name resolution. The application programmer doesn't really know which method is used to resolve the host name and it usually isn't important, with one caveat, which is described in the section on `WSAAsyncGetHostByName()`. The function's prototype looks like the following:

```
struct hostent FAR * PASCAL FAR gethostbyname(const char FAR * name);
```

`name` is a far pointer to a null-terminated character array that contains the name of the computer about which you want host information. The `hostent` structure returned has the following format:

```
struct  hostent {
  char  FAR * h_name;             // official name of host
  char  FAR * FAR * h_aliases;    // alias list
  short h_addrtype;               // host address type
  short h_length;                 // length of address
  char  FAR * FAR * h_addr_list;  // list of addresses
#define h_addr  h_addr_list[0]    // address, for backward compatibility
};
```

On success, the `gethostbyname()` function returns a pointer to a `hostent` structure, and on failure, the function returns `NULL`. On a return value of `NULL`, you can call `WSAGetLastError()` to determine the specifics of the problem. Possible error values include the following: `WSANOTINITIALIZED` if `WSAStartup()` wasn't called successfully; `WSAENETDOWN` if the network subsystem is failing; `WSAHOST_NOT_FOUND` if the host name couldn't be resolved; `WSATRY_AGAIN` if the cause of the failure could be temporary, such as a name server being down; `WSANO_RECOVERY` if there was an unrecoverable error; `WSANO_DATA` if the host name is valid but no appropriate data could be found; `WSAEINPROGRESS` if a blocking WinSock operation is currently in progress; or `WSAEINTR` if the blocking call was canceled by `WSACancelBlockingCall()`.

TIP

About blocking versus asynchronous WinSock function calls: Certain WinSock functions are classified as blocking when their return times are indeterminate. If a program blocks on a function call in the nonpreemptive Windows 3.1 environment, the performance of the entire computer system may be affected. While the blocking function is in its blocking state, the message loop for the application doesn't receive any CPU time. Because this is unacceptable, the WinSock developers came up with a scheme whereby, under the nonpreemptive versions of Windows, a special message loop runs while a blocking function call is waiting to complete its operation. This ensures that the other programs on the computer get some CPU time.

Of course, the Windows NT environment, with its true preemptive multitasking capabilities, doesn't require this work-around, but it can be accessed for backward compatibility. Actually, even Windows NT can take advantage of this feature if you look at the thread level. Under Windows NT, a program may consist of one or more threads of execution. When a blocking call is executed, only the thread that made the blocking call is affected; the other threads of the program continue to get CPU time as do the other applications running on the computer. If this special message loop was running for the thread that called the blocking function, that thread could receive additional messages. WinSock has a default message loop but you can substitute your own using the `WSASetBlockingHook()` function. The only WinSock function that can be called safely from within this blocking hook function is `WSACancelBlockingCall()`. If this cancel function is executed by the special blocking hook function, the blocking WinSock function call will return `WSAEINTR`.

This book doesn't examine the use of this special blocking hook function because a much simpler and easily portable solution exists. This other solution involves the use of WinSock asynchronous functions. These functions begin with the WSAAsync prefix. They were designed specifically for the message-based Windows environment and provide a much "cleaner" solution to the preceding problem.

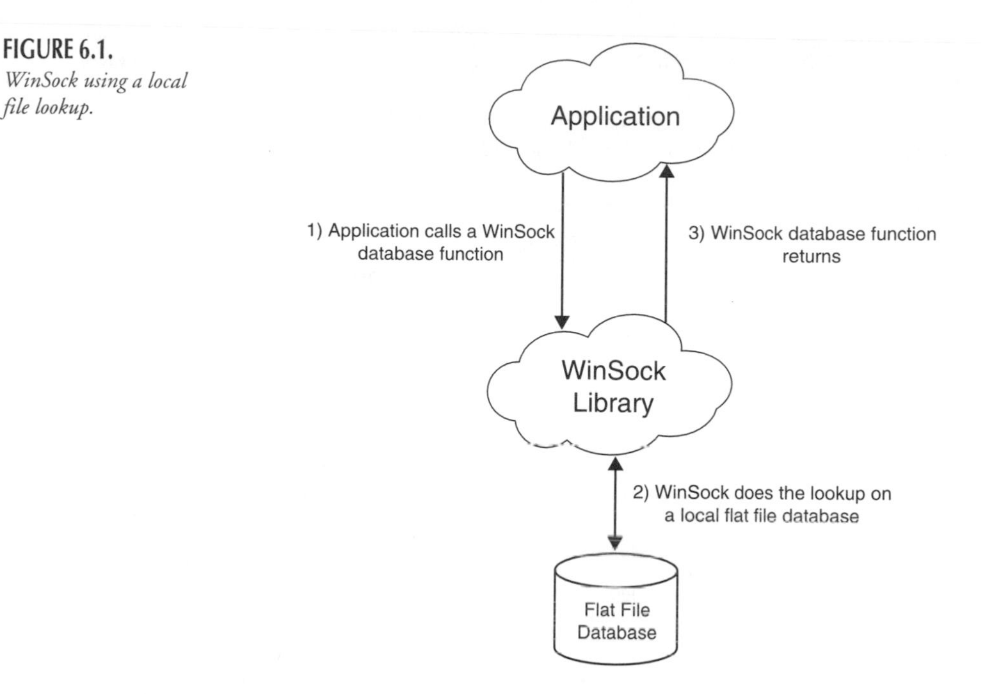

FIGURE 6.1.
WinSock using a local file lookup.

Using a couple of the functions described thus far, you can display the IP address of any host on your internetwork as well as find out your own machine's name and IP address. The following sample code fragment does just that:

```
#define HOST_NAME_LEN (50)
char lpszHostName[HOST_NAME_LEN];  // will accept the host name
char lpszMessage[100];             // informational message
char lpszIP[16];                   // IP address string
PHOSTENT phostent;                 // pointer to host entry structure
IN_ADDR in;                        // Internet address structure

// find the name of the machine this program is running on
if (gethostname(lpszHostName, HOST_NAME_LEN) != 0)
  wsprintf(lpszMessage, "gethostname() generated error %d",
   WSAGetLastError());
else
{
  // get the host entry structure for this machine
  if ((phostent = gethostbyname(lpszHostName)) == NULL)
    wsprintf(lpszMessage, "gethostbyname() generated error %d",
     WSAGetLastError());
  else
  {
    // copy the four byte IP address into a Internet address structure
    memcpy(&in, phostent->h_addr, 4);

    // format the results, converting the IP address into a string
    wsprintf(lpszMessage, "Host %s has IP address ", phostent->h_name);
    wsprintf(lpszIP, "%s", inet_ntoa(in));
```

```
    lstrcat(lpszMessage, lpszIP);
  }
}

MessageBox(NULL, lpszMessage, "Info", MB_OK);
```

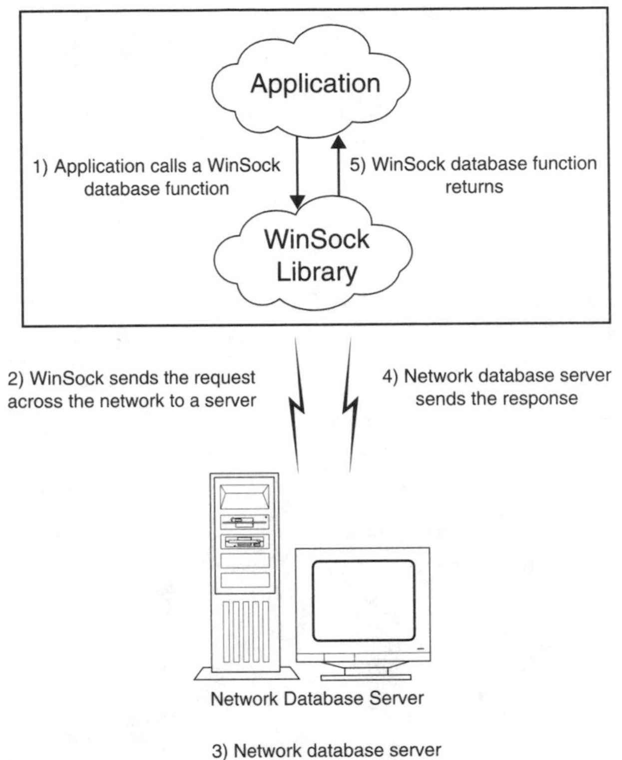

FIGURE 6.2.
WinSock using a networked database server.

Suppose that the computer on which this program runs is called "saturn." The call to `gethostname()` will set "saturn" as the host name, and that string will be copied into `lpszHostName`. Suppose also that this computer uses a host file for name resolution, as opposed to using a networked name server. One line of that host file might look like this:

```
166.78.16.200          saturn
```

`gethostbyname()` looks for "saturn" in the host file, finds the line on which it resides, and extracts the associated IP address. It then places all this information into a `hostent` host entry structure. The end result is the formatted message describing that "saturn" has an IP address of "166.78.16.200".

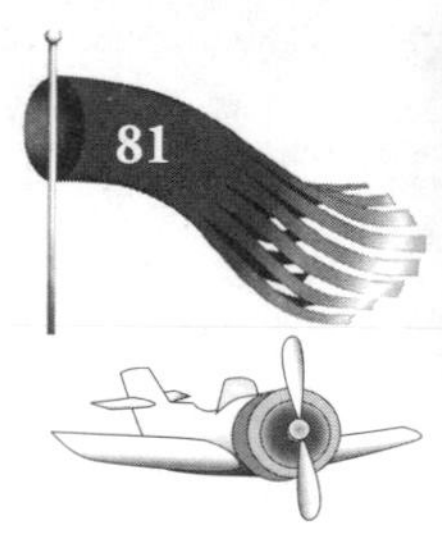

NOTE

Notice that in this sample, the IP address still had to be copied into an `in_addr` structure, but this time the source wasn't an unsigned long as it was in the `inet_ntoa()` sample. This time, the source of the IP address was the `hostent` host entry structure. The `h_addr` member variable of the `hostent` structure is a pointer to the first byte of the four-byte IP address, already stored in network byte order.

Asynchronously Finding a Host's IP Address

In the introduction to `gethostbyname()`, I said that there was one caveat with its use. In the getXbyY functions, one of which is `gethostbyname()`, the data retrieved might come from the local host or might come by way of a request over the network to a server of some kind. As soon as network communications is introduced into the picture, you have to be concerned with response times and the responsiveness of the application to the user while those network requests are taking place.

The `WSAAsyncGetHostByName()` function is the asynchronous version of `gethostbyname()`. It was added to WinSock to complement the Berkeley socket function for the message-passing architecture of Microsoft Windows. This function is described as asynchronous because calling the function doesn't suspend execution of the calling application, but instead allows the application to continue until the request generated by `WSAAsyncGetHostByName()` has completed. When `gethostbyname()` or any other getXbyY function is called, there is no guarantee when that function might return with a response. If the function generates a network operation, the response time is indeterminate. While that request is outstanding, your program is halted; the user can't move or close the window or even cancel the operation. Not only that, but in the nonpreemptive Windows 3.1 environment, other applications will suffer; the entire system will seem to come to a temporary, or not so temporary, halt. Using `WSAAsyncGetHostByName()` makes your application responsive to the user's input and doesn't adversely affect other applications running on the computer. Once the request has completed, a Windows message is posted to a window in the application. While the request is still outstanding (for example, if the networked domain name server is doing a database lookup and preparing to send the search results back over the network) the message loop in the calling application, as well as the message loops of the other applications running on the computer, continue to operate, making all the programs responsive to user manipulation.

NOTE

Practically speaking, if you know that the environment under which your program runs uses a local host's file to resolve host names, you don't need to bother with the extra overhead required to use the asynchronous versions of the getXbyY functions; the blocking functions will do fine because you know they will return immediately and won't cause any responsiveness problems for any running applications.

The function prototype for `WSAAsyncGetHostByName()` is as follows:

```
HANDLE PASCAL FAR WSAAsyncGetHostByName(HWND hWnd, u_int wMsg,
 const char FAR * name, char FAR * buf, int buflen);
```

`hWnd` is the handle to the window to which a message will be sent when `WSAAsyncGetHostByName()` has completed its asynchronous operation. `wMsg` is the message that will be posted to `hWnd` when the asynchronous operation is complete. `wMsg` is generally a user-defined message (that is, `WM_USER + 1`). `name` is a pointer to a string that contains the host name for which information is being requested (that is, "goober" or "goober.ping.com"). `buf` is a pointer to an area of memory that, on successful completion of the host name lookup, will contain the `hostent` structure for the desired host. Note that this buffer must be larger than the `hostent` structure itself, because WinSock uses the additional area to store related information. WinSock provides a defined value named `MAXGETHOSTSTRUCT`, which you can use as the size of the buffer. This size will ensure that there is enough space allocated. `buflen` is the size of the `buf` buffer. It should be `MAXGETHOSTSTRUCT` for safety's sake.

If the asynchronous operation is initiated successfully, the return value of `WSAAsyncGetHostByName()` is a handle to the asynchronous task. On failure of initialization, the function returns 0 (zero), and `WSAGetLastError()` should be called to find out the reason for the error. Possible error values include the following: `WSANOTINITIALIZED` if `WSAStartup()` wasn't called successfully; `WSAENETDOWN` if the network subsystem is failing; `WSAEWOULDBLOCK` if the function cannot be scheduled at this time due to a resource conflict within the specific WinSock implementation; or `WSAEINPROGRESS` if a blocking WinSock operation is currently in progress. Notice that the function's return value doesn't tell you whether the requested information was retrieved successfully; it only tells you whether the function was started properly.

The previous sample code, which displays the name and IP address of the machine on which the program runs, can be reworked to use the following asynchronous calls:

```
// global variables
#define WM_USER_GETHOSTBYNAME (WM_USER + 1)
#define HOST_NAME_LEN (50)
```

```
char lpszHostName[HOST_NAME_LEN];         // will accept the host name
char lpszMessage[100];                    // informational message
char lpszIP[16];                          // IP address string
PHOSTENT phostent;                        // pointer to host entry structure
char lpszHostEntryBuf[MAXGETHOSTSTRUCT]; // host entry structure
IN_ADDR in;                               // Internet address structure
HANDLE hGetHostByName;                    // handle of asynchronous request

// this function is [part of] the window procedure
long FAR PASCAL WndProc(HWND hWnd, UINT message, WPARAM wParam, LPARAM lParam)
{
  switch (message)
  {
    // check menu items
    case WM_COMMAND:
      // handle the menu item to get this host's name and IP address
      if (wParam == ID_GETHOSTBYNAME)
      {
        // find the name of the machine this program is running on
        if (gethostname(lpszHostName, HOST_NAME_LEN) != 0)
        {
          wsprintf(lpszMessage, "gethostname() generated error %d",
           WSAGetLastError());
          MessageBox(NULL, lpszMessage, "Info", MB_OK);
        }
        else
        {
          // get the host entry structure for this machine
          if ((hGetHostByName = WSAAsyncGetHostByName(hWnd,
           WM_USER_GETHOSTBYNAME, lpszHostName,
           lpszHostEntryBuf, MAXGETHOSTSTRUCT)) == 0)
          {
            wsprintf(lpszMessage, "WSAAsyncGetHostByName() generated error %d",
             WSAGetLastError());
            MessageBox(NULL, lpszMessage, "Info", MB_OK);
          }
        }
      }
      break;

    case WM_USER_GETHOSTBYNAME:
      // check for an error
      if (WSAGETASYNCERROR(lParam) != 0)
        MessageBox(NULL, "WSAAsyncGetHostByName() had an error", "Info", MB_OK);
      else
      {
        // assign a hostent host entry pointer to the buffer
        phostent = (PHOSTENT)lpszHostEntryBuf;

        // copy the four byte IP address into a Internet address structure
        memcpy(&in, phostent->h_addr, 4);

        // format the results, converting the IP address into a string
        wsprintf(lpszMessage, "Host %s has IP address ", phostent->h_name);
        wsprintf(lpszIP, "%s", inet_ntoa(in));
        lstrcat(lpszMessage, lpszIP);
        MessageBox(NULL, lpszMessage, "Info", MB_OK);
      }
```

```
        break;

      default:
        break;
    }
}
```

Note that the first thing done in the WM_USER_GETHOSTBYNAME message handler is a call to WSAASYNCERROR(). This is a macro that determines the success of the WSAAsyncGetHostByName() request. A value of 0 (zero) means everything is fine. Other possible values are any error messages in WINSOCK.H. If WSAASYNCERROR() returns error WSAENOBUFS, the buffer passed to WSAAsyncGetHostByName() to hold the hostent structure wasn't big enough. To be safe, use a buffer at least MAXGETHOSTSTRUCT bytes in size. Also, for your information, in the WM_USER_GETHOSTBYNAME message handler, wParam is the asynchronous task handle for the currently returning operation. This means that you could use the same WM_USER message for multiple, simultaneously outstanding asynchronous requests. You would then examine wParam to determine which specific operation was returning at that instance in time.

Doing It with Visual C++

This book is about the use of WinSock with Microsoft Visual C++ and the Microsoft Foundation Classes. The previous example was given in the "old-fashioned" SDK style as a way of introducing the first asynchronous function. The remaining samples in this book will be based primarily on Visual C++ and MFC. Using MFC, the preceding sample code could be implemented as follows.

First comes the class declaration. This example has a class named CMyWindow derived from the base class CFrameWnd. CFrameWnd is a class provided by MFC. This sample doesn't show the entire class declaration, only the pieces needed to replicate the previous SDK sample:

```
class CMyWindow : public CFrameWnd
{

...

  // member variables
#define HOST_NAME_LEN (50)
  char m_lpszHostName[HOST_NAME_LEN];        // will accept the host name
  char m_lpszMessage[100];                   // informational message
  char m_lpszIP[16];                         // IP address string
  PHOSTENT m_phostent;                       // pointer to host entry structure
  char m_lpszHostEntryBuf[MAXGETHOSTSTRUCT]; // host entry structure
  IN_ADDR m_in;                              // Internet address structure
  HANDLE m_hGetHostByName;                   // handle of asynchronous request

  // member functions in the message map
  //{{AFX_MSG(CMyWindow)
  afx_msg void OnDoAsyncGetHostByName();
```

```
  afx_msg LONG OnAsyncGetHostByName(WPARAM wParam, LPARAM lParam);
  //}}AFX_MSG
  DECLARE_MESSAGE_MAP()
};
```

One thing you'll notice is that all the variables that are global in the SDK sample are now encapsulated into the class in which they are used. This is just one of the benefits of the C++ object-oriented language. Note also that these variables, the class member variables, are preceded by the m_ prefix. Tagging member variables in this manner helps you recognize them more easily in the implementation of the class. The next section of the class declaration contains the prototypes for the functions that are in the window's message map. The message map is used by MFC to automate the routing of messages to their designated windows. It takes the place of the switch-case construct in a traditional SDK window procedure.

The implementation of the CMyWindow class begins with the message map for the window as follows:

```
#define WM_USER_ASYNCGETHOSTBYNAME (WM_USER + 1)

BEGIN_MESSAGE_MAP(CMyWindow, CFrameWnd)
  //{{AFX_MSG_MAP(CMyWindow)
  ON_COMMAND(ID_TEST_ASYNCGETHOSTBYNAME, OnDoAsyncGetHostByName)
  ON_MESSAGE(WM_USER_ASYNCGETHOSTBYNAME, OnAsyncGetHostByName)
  //}}AFX_MSG_MAP
END_MESSAGE_MAP()
```

The first entry in the message map is for a menu item that will launch the search. The ON_COMMAND macro automates the parsing of the WM_COMMAND message that is used in an SDK program. It matches up the appropriate menu ID, in this case ID_TEST_ASYNCGETHOSTBYNAME, and associates it with the OnDoAsyncGetHostByName() member function. When the user selects the menu item that has ID_TEST_ASYNCGETHOSTBYNAME as its identifier in the menu resource, the OnDoAsyncGetHostByName() function is called. That function is implemented as follows:

```
void CMyWindow::OnDoAsyncGetHostByName()
{
  // find the name of the machine this program is running on
  if (gethostname(m_lpszHostName, HOST_NAME_LEN) != 0)
  {
    wsprintf(m_lpszMessage, "gethostname() generated error %d",
     WSAGetLastError());
    MessageBox(m_lpszMessage, "Info");
  }
  else
  {
    // get the host entry structure for this machine
    if ((m_hGetHostByName = WSAAsyncGetHostByName(m_hWnd,
     WM_USER_ASYNCGETHOSTBYNAME, m_lpszHostName,
     m_lpszHostEntryBuf, MAXGETHOSTSTRUCT)) == 0)
    {
      wsprintf(m_lpszMessage, "WSAAsyncGetHostByName() generated error %d",
```

```
        WSAGetLastError());
      MessageBox(m_lpszMessage, "Info");
    }
  }
}
```

The second entry in the message map is for a user-defined message that indicates the asynchronous function has completed. The `ON_MESSAGE` macro automates the parsing of `WM_USER` messages that are used in an SDK program. It matches up a specific user-defined message, in this case `WM_USER_ASYNCGETHOSTBYNAME`, and associates it with the `OnAsyncGetHostByName()` member function. When the `WM_USER_ASYNCGETHOSTBYNAME` message is generated by WinSock on the completion of the asynchronous call, the `OnAsyncGetHostByName()` function is executed. That function is implemented as follows:

```
LONG CMyWindow::OnAsyncGetHostByName(WPARAM wParam, LPARAM lParam)
{
  // check for an error
  if (WSAGETASYNCERROR(lParam) != 0)
    MessageBox("WSAAsyncGetHostByName() had an error", "Info");
  else
  {
    // assign a hostent host entry pointer to the buffer
    m_phostent = (PHOSTENT)m_lpszHostEntryBuf;

    // copy the four byte IP address into a Internet address structure
    memcpy(&m_in, m_phostent->h_addr, 4);

    // format the results, converting the IP address into a string
    wsprintf(m_lpszMessage, "Host %s has IP address ", m_phostent->h_name);
    wsprintf(m_lpszIP, "%s", inet_ntoa(m_in));
    lstrcat(m_lpszMessage, m_lpszIP);
    MessageBox(m_lpszMessage, "Info");
  }

  return 0L;
}
```

Note that both `OnDoAsyncGetHostByName()` and `OnAsyncGetHostByName()` have an almost identical implementation to the SDK version of this sample.

NOTE

About message maps and the Visual C++ ClassWizard: ClassWizard associates message identifiers, such as menu items, with class member functions. It automatically inserts a skeletal function in the implementation file for the class. This is handy because ClassWizard "knows" the correct format for the function prototype. The programs in this book were developed using Visual C++ 1.5 and Visual C++ 1.1 32-Bit Edition. The versions of ClassWizard in these versions of Visual C++ do not support the automatic generation of message map entries for user-defined messages. This means that for any `WM_USER` messages you create,

you must manually insert the ON_MESSAGE macro into the message map, create a function prototype in the class definition, and create the member function from scratch.

Canceling an Outstanding Asynchronous Request

The handle returned by the asynchronous database functions, such as WSAAsyncGetHostByName(), can be used to terminate the database lookup. The WSACancelAsyncRequest() function performs this task. Its prototype is the following:

```
int PASCAL FAR WSACancelAsyncRequest(HANDLE hAsyncTaskHandle);
```

hAsyncTaskHandle is the handle to the asynchronous task you wish to abort. On success, this function returns 0 (zero). On failure, it returns SOCKET_ERROR, and WSAGetLastError() can be called. Possible errors include the following: WSANOTINITIALISED if WSAStartup() wasn't called successfully; WSAENETDOWN if the network subsystem is failing; WSAEINPROGRESS if a blocking WinSock operation is currently in progress; WSAEINVAL if the specified asynchronous task handle is invalid; or WSAEALREADY if the asynchronous routine being canceled has already completed. WSAEALREADY might result if the original operation has already completed and the resulting message has been processed or if the original operation has already completed but the resulting message is still waiting in the application's message queue.

By using WSACancelAsyncRequest() in your applications, you give users much greater control over the program. If users perform an operation that generates an asynchronous database call and the operation is taking an excruciatingly long time to complete, as it might when networked name servers are involved, it's nice to let users regain control of the program instead of being at its mercy.

IP Address Resolution

IP address resolution is the opposite of host name resolution. In host name resolution, using gethostbyname() or WSAAsyncGetHostByName(), the objective is to get the IP address when you know the host name. The goal of IP address resolution is to get the host name, and other host information, when all you know is its IP address. The gethostbyaddr() and WSAAsyncGetHostByName() functions are used to fulfill this goal. If you haven't yet, please read and get a full understanding of the gethostbyname() and WSAAsyncGetHostByName() functions; the remaining functions are used in a similar manner as those two functions, so the explanations for the following functions have been abbreviated.

Finding a Host Name When You Know Its IP Address

The main duty of `gethostbyaddr()` is to take the IP address of a host and return its name. This function, and its asynchronous counterpart named `WSAAsyncGetHostByAddr()`, might perform a simple table lookup on a host file local to the computer on which the program is running, or it might send the request across the network to a name server. The function's prototype looks like the following:

```
struct hostent FAR * PASCAL FAR gethostbyaddr(const char FAR * addr,
 int len, int type);
```

`addr` is a pointer to the IP address, in network byte order, of the computer about which you want host information. `len` is the length of the address to which `addr` points. In WinSock 1.1, the length is always four because this version of the specification supports only Internet style addressing. `type` must always be `PF_INET` for the same reason. The `gethostbyaddr()` function returns a pointer to a `hostent` host entry structure on success and `NULL` on failure. Upon a return value of `NULL`, you can call `WSAGetLastError()` to determine the specifics of the problem. Possible error values include the following: `WSANOTINITIALIZED` if `WSAStartup()` wasn't called successfully; `WSAENETDOWN` if the network subsystem is failing; `WSAHOST_NOT_FOUND` if the host name couldn't be resolved; `WSATRY_AGAIN` if the cause of the failure could be temporary, such as a name server being down; `WSANO_RECOVERY` if there was an unrecoverable error; `WSANO_DATA` if the IP address is valid but no appropriate data could be found; `WSAEINPROGRESS` if a blocking WinSock operation is currently in progress; or `WSAEINTR` if the blocking call was canceled by `WSACancelBlockingCall()`.

The following sample code fragment will find the host name that has the specified IP address:

```
u_long ulIPAddress = inet_addr("166.78.16.201");   // binary IP address
char lpszMessage[100];                            // informational message
char lpszIP[16];                                  // IP address string
PHOSTENT phostent;                                // pointer to host entry structure
IN_ADDR in;                                       // Internet address structure

// get the host entry structure for the specified IP address
if ((phostent = gethostbyaddr((char *)&ulIPAddress, 4, PF_INET)) == NULL)
  wsprintf(lpszMessage, "gethostbyaddr() generated error %d",
   WSAGetLastError());
else
{
  // copy the four byte IP address into an Internet address structure
  memcpy(&in, phostent->h_addr, 4);

  // format the results, converting the IP address into a string
  wsprintf(lpszMessage, "Host %s has IP address ", phostent->h_name);
  wsprintf(lpszIP, "%s", inet_ntoa(in));
  lstrcat(lpszMessage, lpszIP);
}
MessageBox(NULL, lpszMessage, "Info", MB_OK);
```

Suppose that the computer with IP address 166.78.16.201 is called "jupiter." Suppose also that this computer uses a host file for name resolution as opposed to a networked name server. One line of that host's file might look like this:

```
166.78.16.201          jupiter
```

`gethostbyaddr()` looks for the designated IP address in the host file, finds the line on which it resides, and extracts the associated host name. It then places all this information into a `hostent` host entry structure. The end result is the formatted message describing that "jupiter" has an IP address of "166.78.16.201".

NOTE

In the call to `gethostbyaddr()`, the IP address `ulIPAddress` had to be cast to a character pointer. ulIPAddress is an unsigned long (four bytes in size) that contains the binary IP address in network byte order. `gethostbyaddr()` expects a pointer to the first byte of that four quantity, so you take the address of the variable and cast it to a character pointer.

Asynchronously Finding a Host Name When You Know Its IP Address

The `WSAAsyncGetHostByAddr()` function is the asynchronous version of `gethostbyaddr()`. Its function prototype is as follows:

```
HANDLE PASCAL FAR WSAAsyncGetHostByAddr(HWND hWnd, u_int wMsg,
 const char FAR * addr, int len, int type, char FAR * buf, int buflen);
```

`hWnd` is the handle to the window to which a message will be sent when `WSAAsyncGetHostByAddr()` has completed its asynchronous operation. `wMsg` is the user-defined message that will be posted to `hWnd` when the asynchronous operation is complete. `addr` is a pointer to the IP address, in network byte order, of the computer about which you want host information. `len` is the length of the address to which `addr` points and is always 4 (four) for Internet addresses. `type` must always be `PF_INET` because WinSock 1.1 supports only Internet-style addressing. `buf` is a pointer to an area of memory that, upon successful completion of the address lookup, will contain the `hostent` structure for the desired host. This buffer must be large enough to store the `hostent` structure as well as other referenced data, therefore it should be at least `MAXGETHOSTSTRUCT` bytes long. `buflen` is the size of the `buf` buffer. It should be `MAXGETHOSTSTRUCT` for safety's sake.

If the asynchronous operation is initiated successfully, the return value of `WSAAsyncGetHostByAddr()` is a handle to the asynchronous task. On failure of initialization, the function returns 0 (zero) and `WSAGetLastError()` should be called to find out the reason for the error. Possible error values include the following: `WSANOTINITIALIZED` if `WSAStartup()` wasn't called successfully; `WSAENETDOWN` if the network subsystem is failing; `WSAEWOULDBLOCK` if the function cannot be scheduled at this time due to a resource conflict within the specific WinSock implementation; or `WSAEINPROGRESS` if a blocking WinSock operation is currently in progress. Note that the function's return value doesn't tell you whether the requested information was retrieved successfully; all it tells you is whether the function was started properly.

This function is used much like `WSAAsyncGetHostByName()`. Using an MFC implementation method to replicate the example given in the `gethostbyaddr()` example would have class declaration such as the following:

```
class CMyWindow : public CFrameWnd
{

...

  // member variables
  u_long m_ulIPAddress;                // binary IP address
  char m_lpszMessage[100];             // informational message
  char m_lpszIP[16];                   // IP address string
  PHOSTENT m_phostent;                 // pointer to host entry structure
  IN_ADDR m_in;                        // Internet address structure
  HANDLE m_hGetHostByAddr;             // handle of asynchronous request
  char m_lpszHostEntryBuf[MAXGETHOSTSTRUCT]; // host entry structure

  // member functions in the message map
  //{{AFX_MSG(CMyWindow)
  afx_msg void OnDoAsyncGetHostByAddr();
  afx_msg LONG OnAsyncGetHostByAddr(WPARAM wParam, LPARAM lParam);
  //}}AFX_MSG
  DECLARE_MESSAGE_MAP()
};
```

Note that the variables are now member variables of the class. The implementation of the `CMyWindow` class begins with the message map for the window:

```
#define WM_USER_ASYNCGETHOSTBYADDR (WM_USER + 2)

BEGIN_MESSAGE_MAP(CMyWindow, CFrameWnd)
  //{{AFX_MSG_MAP(CMyWindow)
  ON_COMMAND(ID_TEST_ASYNCGETHOSTBYADDR, OnDoAsyncGetHostByAddr)
  ON_MESSAGE(WM_USER_ASYNCGETHOSTBYADDR, OnAsyncGetHostByAddr)
  //}}AFX_MSG_MAP
END_MESSAGE_MAP()
```

The first entry in the message map is for a menu item that will launch the search. That function is implemented as follows:

```
void CMyWindow::OnDoAsyncGetHostByAddr()
{
  // get a binary IP address
  m_ulIPAddress = inet_addr("166.78.16.201");
```

```
  // get the host entry structure
  if ((m_hGetHostByAddr = WSAAsyncGetHostByAddr(m_hWnd,
   WM_USER_ASYNCGETHOSTBYADDR, (char *)&m_ulIPAddress, 4,
   PF_INET, m_lpszHostEntryBuf, MAXGETHOSTSTRUCT)) == 0)
  {
    wsprintf(m_lpszMessage, "WSAAsyncGetHostByAddr() generated error %d",
     WSAGetLastError());
    MessageBox(m_lpszMessage, "Info");
  }
}
```

In this example, the IP address is hard-coded; in production programs, values such as this should be user configurable. The second entry in the message map is for the user-defined message that indicates that the asynchronous function has completed. When the `WM_USER_ASYNCGETHOSTBYADDR` message is generated by WinSock upon the completion of the asynchronous call, the `OnAsyncGetHostByAddr()` function is executed. That function is implemented as follows:

```
LONG CMyWindow::OnAsyncGetHostByAddr(WPARAM wParam, LPARAM lParam)
{
  // check for an error
  if (WSAGETASYNCERROR(lParam) != 0)
    MessageBox("WSAAsyncGetHostByAddr() had an error", "Info");
  else
  {
    // assign a hostent host entry pointer to the buffer
    m_phostent = (PHOSTENT)m_lpszHostEntryBuf;

    // copy the four byte IP address into a Internet address structure
    memcpy(&m_in, m_phostent->h_addr, 4);

    // format the results, converting the IP address into a string
    wsprintf(m_lpszMessage, "Host %s has IP address ", m_phostent->h_name);
    wsprintf(m_lpszIP, "%s", inet_ntoa(m_in));
    lstrcat(m_lpszMessage, m_lpszIP);
    MessageBox(m_lpszMessage, "Info");
  }

  return 0L;
}
```

Note that the `OnAsyncGetHostByAddr()` member function is like `OnAsyncGetHostByName()`, with the only difference being the text in the error message. These functions are the same because each is manipulating a `hostent` host entry structure.

CAUTION

Don't forget to use the `WSAGETASYNCERROR()` macro to check for an error in your message handlers for the asynchronous calls.

Service Name Resolution

So far, you have seen how to retrieve a binary IP address, whether it be derived from a host name or the host's IP address. But the IP address of a host is only half of the equation when it comes to making a network connection between client and server applications; the port number provides the other half of the equation. When a computer is running a server application, it's said to be providing a service. Each service is uniquely identified by a well-known port number. The server program "listens" for connections on the well-known port and the client program opens a connection to that port. The port numbers must be unique to distinguish the many server programs that a host may provide. The port numbers must be well-known so that application programmers can request them by name. Figure 6.3 shows a host that is providing two services: port number 37 is acting as a time server over UDP, and port number 79 is acting as a finger server over TCP. Note that the ports out of which the clients connect are represented as question marks. Clients don't need to specify a port when they create their outbound sockets; the socket can be assigned a unique port at runtime by the TCP/IP stack.

FIGURE 6.3.
A host providing two services and two connecting clients.

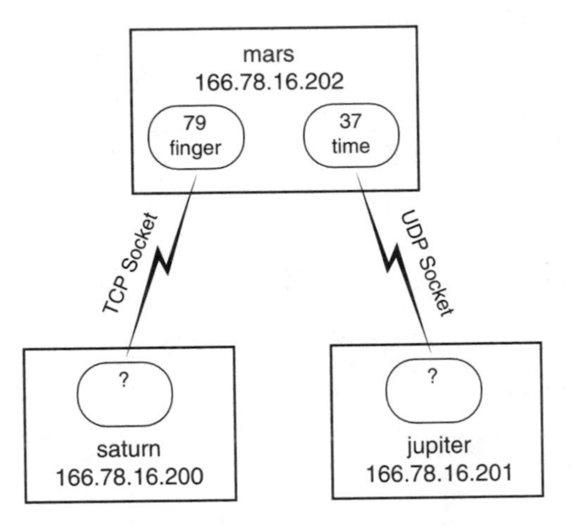

The `getservbyname()` and `WSAAsyncGetServByName()` functions are responsible for retrieving the port number when you know its service name. Using a service name in your program, as opposed to a port number, allows the user of your program to decide which port should be designated for the service your program is providing. Users appreciate this level of control. As the types of services users' computers provide, or the ways in which they're used, change over time, users have the flexibility of easily configuring their machines as they see fit.

The Services File

The service name to port translation is commonly supported by a flat file database called the services file. A partial listing of a common services file looks like the following:

```
# This file contains port numbers for well-known services
# as defined by RFC 1060 (Assigned Numbers).
#
# Format:
# <service name>  <port number>/<protocol>  [aliases...]   [#<comment>]

time              37/tcp    timserver
time              37/udp    timserver
finger            79/tcp
```

The lines preceded by a pound sign (#) are comments. Notice the reference to RFC 1060. This Internet Request for Comment outlines some standard well-known ports. This ensures that nobody creates a service that utilizes an already established port number. When you create your own custom servers, you need to allocate a port number between 1024 and 5000 exclusive. The ports from 1024 and below are reserved for universally well-known ports. Often, these ports are allocated to new services when someone invents the new service and distributes the specification through an RFC.

Following the header comment is the listed services. The left-most column contains the name of the service. The next column has the port number and transport-level protocol separated by a forward slash (/). The remaining columns contain aliases for the service. In the preceding example, the time service is recognized as "time" or "timeserver." The finger service has no aliases. The transport-level protocol field specifies either User Datagram Protocol or Transmission Control Protocol. This is the type of socket (datagram or stream) that must be used to communicate with the designated service. Note that the time service responds to port 37 on both a UDP and TCP connection. The port number/protocol pair provides for a unique correlation to a service within each transport protocol; this is to say that a service might respond to UDP port 100, and a completely different service might respond to TCP port 100. It's also possible for a specific service to respond to one UDP port and an entirely different TCP port.

TIP

For custom applications that you produce, it's usually sufficient to simply refer to a service number by its port number. This frees you from having to make an entry in the services table for your custom services. For the sake of flexibility, make your server and client applications configurable with respect to the port numbers they use. Allow the server to listen for connections on a configurable port and make sure that the port to which the client connects is also configurable. This will ensure an easy fix to the problem of having several different servers hard-coded to use the same port number. If your server program must run on a computer with another server that was written to use a hard-coded port number, you can change the server and client configuration to use an unused port. With this information hard-coded, the change requires a recompile of the applications.

Finding a Service's Port Number

The `getservbyname()` function gets service information corresponding to a specific service name and protocol. Its function prototype looks like the following:

```
struct servent FAR * PASCAL FAR getservbyname(const char FAR * name,
 const char FAR * proto);
```

`name` is a pointer to a string that contains the service for which you are searching. The service name is either the official service name or an alias. `proto` is a pointer to a string that contains the transport protocol to use; it's either "udp", "tcp", or `NULL`. A `NULL` `proto` will match on the first service in the services table that has the specified name, regardless of the protocol. The `servent` structure returned has the following format:

```
struct  servent {
  char  FAR * s_name;             // official service name
  char  FAR * FAR * s_aliases;    // alias list
  short s_port;                   // port #
  char  FAR * s_proto;            // protocol to use
};
```

A note on transport protocols: Protocol names are case sensitive. "TCP" is different from "tcp." Ensure that you are using the exact format as listed in your services file.

The `getservbyname()` function returns a pointer to a `servent` structure on success and `NULL` on failure. On a return value of `NULL`, you can call `WSAGetLastError()` to determine the specifics of the problem. Possible error values include the following: `WSANOTINITIALISED` if `WSAStartup()` wasn't called successfully; `WSAENETDOWN` if the network subsystem is failing; `WSANO_RECOVERY` if there was an unrecoverable error; `WSANO_DATA` if the service name is valid but no appropriate data could be found; `WSAEINPROGRESS` if a blocking WinSock operation is currently in progress; or `WSAEINTR` if the blocking call was canceled by `WSACancelBlockingCall()`.

This code fragment searches for the time service on a UDP transport connection:

```
PSERVENT pservent;           // pointer to service entry structure
char lpszMessage[100];       // informational message
char lpszPort[6];            // port number string
```

```
// get the service entry structure for the time service using UDP
if ((pservent = getservbyname("time", "udp")) == NULL)
  wsprintf(lpszMessage, "getservbyname() generated error %d",
   WSAGetLastError());
else
{
  // format the results
  wsprintf(lpszMessage, "Service %s using protocol %s has port ",
   pservent->s_name, pservent->s_proto);
  wsprintf(lpszPort, "%d", ntohs(pservent->s_port));
  lstrcat(lpszMessage, lpszPort);
}

MessageBox(NULL, lpszMessage, "Info", MB_OK);
```

The end result is the formatted message describing that the "time" service using the "udp" protocol has port 37. Notice that the port number, `pservent->s_port`, must be converted from network to host byte ordering.

If the sample was rewritten to not specify the transport protocol, the results would be different:

```
PSERVENT pservent;          // pointer to service entry structure
char lpszMessage[100];      // informational message
char lpszPort[6];           // port number string

// get the service entry structure for the time service
if ((pservent = getservbyname("time", NULL)) == NULL)
  wsprintf(lpszMessage, "getservbyname() generated error %d",
   WSAGetLastError());
else
{
  // format the results
  wsprintf(lpszMessage, "Service %s using protocol %s has port ",
   pservent->s_name, pservent->s_proto);
  wsprintf(lpszPort, "%d", ntohs(pservent->s_port));
  lstrcat(lpszMessage, lpszPort);
}

MessageBox(NULL, lpszMessage, "Info", MB_OK);
```

The end result of this sample is the formatted message describing that the "time" service using the "tcp" protocol has port 37. The TCP result is given because that entry appears first in the services file.

Asynchronously Finding a Service's Port Number

`WSAAsyncGetServByName()` is the asynchronous counterpart to `getservbyname()`. Its function prototype is as follows:

```
HANDLE PASCAL FAR WSAAsyncGetServByName(HWND hWnd, u_int wMsg,
 const char FAR * name, const char FAR * proto,
 char FAR * buf, int buflen);
```

hWnd is the handle to the window to which a message will be sent when WSAAsyncGetServByName() has completed its asynchronous operation. wMsg is the user-defined message that will be posted to hWnd when the asynchronous operation is complete. name is a pointer to a service name about which you want service information. proto is a pointer to a protocol name; it is "tcp", "udp", or NULL. If proto is NULL, the first matching service is returned. buf is a pointer to an area of memory that, on successful completion of the service lookup, will contain the servent structure for the desired service. This buffer must be large enough to store the servent structure as well as other referenced data; therefore, it should be at least MAXGETHOSTSTRUCT bytes long. buflen is the size of the buf buffer. It should be MAXGETHOSTSTRUCT for safety's sake.

If the asynchronous operation is initiated successfully, the return value of WSAAsyncGetServByName() is a handle to the asynchronous task. On failure of initialization, the function returns 0 (zero) and WSAGetLastError() should be called to find out the reason for the error. Possible error values include the following: WSANOTINITIALIZED if WSAStartup() wasn't called successfully; WSAENETDOWN if the network subsystem is failing; WSAEWOULDBLOCK if the function cannot be scheduled at this time due to a resource conflict within the specific WinSock implementation; or WSAEINPROGRESS if a blocking WinSock operation is currently in progress. The function's return value doesn't tell you whether the requested information was retrieved successfully; all it tells you is whether the function was started properly.

This function is used much like the asynchronous functions discussed earlier in this chapter. Using an MFC implementation method to replicate the example given in the getservbyname() example would have a class declaration like the following:

```
class CMyWindow : public CFrameWnd
{

...

  // member variables
  PSERVENT m_pservent;          // pointer to service entry structure
  char m_lpszMessage[100];      // informational message
  char m_lpszPort[6];           // port number string
  HANDLE m_hGetServByName;      // handle of asynchronous request
  char m_lpszServEntryBuf[MAXGETHOSTSTRUCT]; // service entry structure

  // member functions in the message map
  //{{AFX_MSG(CMyWindow)
  afx_msg void OnDoAsyncGetServByName();
  afx_msg LONG OnAsyncGetServByName(WPARAM wParam, LPARAM lParam);
  //}}AFX_MSG
  DECLARE_MESSAGE_MAP()
};
```

Notice that the variables are now member variables of the class. The implementation of the CMyWindow class begins with the message map for the window:

```
#define WM_USER_ASYNCGETSERVBYNAME (WM_USER + 3)
```

```
BEGIN_MESSAGE_MAP(CMyWindow, CFrameWnd)
  //{{AFX_MSG_MAP(CMyWindow)
  ON_COMMAND(ID_TEST_ASYNCGETSERVBYNAME, OnDoAsyncGetServByName)
  ON_MESSAGE(WM_USER_ASYNCGETSERVBYNAME, OnAsyncGetServByName)
  //}}AFX_MSG_MAP
END_MESSAGE_MAP()
```

The first entry in the message map is for a menu item that will launch the search. That function is implemented as follows:

```
void CMyWindow::OnDoAsyncGetServByName()
{
  // get the service entry structure for the time service using UDP
  if ((m_hGetServByName = WSAAsyncGetServByName(m_hWnd,
   WM_USER_ASYNCGETSERVBYNAME, "time", "udp",
   m_lpszServEntryBuf, MAXGETHOSTSTRUCT)) == 0)
  {
    wsprintf(m_lpszMessage, "WSAAsyncGetServByName() generated error %d",
     WSAGetLastError());
    MessageBox(m_lpszMessage, "Info");
  }
}
```

The second entry in the message map is for the user-defined message that indicates that the asynchronous function has completed. When the `WM_USER_ASYNCGETSERVBYNAME` message is generated by WinSock on the completion of the asynchronous call, the `OnAsyncGetServByName()` function is executed. That function is implemented as follows:

```
LONG CMyWindow::OnAsyncGetServByName(WPARAM wParam, LPARAM lParam)
{
  // check for an error
  if (WSAGETASYNCERROR(lParam) != 0)
    MessageBox("WSAAsyncGetServByName() had an error", "Info");
  else
  {
    // assign a servent service entry pointer to the buffer
    m_pservent = (PSERVENT)m_lpszServEntryBuf;

    // format the results
    wsprintf(m_lpszMessage, "Service %s using protocol %s has port ",
     m_pservent->s_name, m_pservent->s_proto);
    wsprintf(m_lpszPort, "%d", ntohs(m_pservent->s_port));
    lstrcat(m_lpszMessage, m_lpszPort);
    MessageBox(m_lpszMessage, "Info");
  }

  return 0L;
}
```

Port Resolution

Port resolution is the opposite of service name resolution. Its goal is, given a port number and transport protocol, to find the corresponding named service. The `getservbyport()` and `WSAAsyncGetServByPort()` functions fulfill this goal.

Finding a Service Name When You Know Its Port Number

The `getservbyport()` function gets service information corresponding to a specific port and protocol. Its function prototype looks like the following:

```
struct servent FAR * PASCAL FAR getservbyport(int port,
 const char FAR * proto);
```

`port` is the service port, in network byte order. `proto` is a pointer to a protocol name; it is "tcp", "udp", or `NULL`. If `proto` is `NULL`, the first matching service is returned. The `getservbyport()` function returns a pointer to a servent structure on success and `NULL` on failure. On a return value of `NULL`, you can call `WSAGetLastError()` to determine the specifics of the problem. Possible error values include the following: `WSANOTINITIALIZED` if `WSAStartup()` wasn't called successfully; `WSAENETDOWN` if the network subsystem is failing; `WSANO_RECOVERY` if there was an unrecoverable error; `WSANO_DATA` if the port number is valid but no appropriate data could be found; `WSAEINPROGRESS` if a blocking WinSock operation is currently in progress; or `WSAEINTR` if the blocking call was canceled by `WSACancelBlockingCall()`.

This code fragment searches for the service corresponding to port 37 on a UDP transport connection:

```
PSERVENT pservent;            // pointer to service entry structure
char lpszMessage[100];        // informational message
char lpszPort[6];             // port number string

// get the service entry structure for the port 37 service using UDP
if ((pservent = getservbyport(htons(37), "udp")) == NULL)
  wsprintf(lpszMessage, "getservbyport() generated error %d",
   WSAGetLastError());
else
{
  // format the results
  wsprintf(lpszMessage, "Service %s using protocol %s has port ",
   pservent->s_name, pservent->s_proto);
  wsprintf(lpszPort, "%d", ntohs(pservent->s_port));
  lstrcat(lpszMessage, lpszPort);
}

MessageBox(NULL, lpszMessage, "Info", MB_OK);
```

Note that the port number is converted to network byte order before it is passed to `getservbyport()`. The end result is the formatted message describing that port 37 using the "udp" transport protocol corresponds to the "time" service. Note the similarity between this sample and the one presented for `getservbyname()`.

Asynchronously Finding a Service Name When You Know Its Port Number

WSAAsyncGetServByPort() is the asynchronous counterpart to getservbyport(). Its function prototype is as follows:

```
HANDLE PASCAL FAR WSAAsyncGetServByPort(HWND hWnd, u_int wMsg,
 int port, const char FAR * proto, char FAR * buf, int buflen);
```

hWnd is the handle to the window to which a message will be sent when WSAAsyncGetServByName() has completed its asynchronous operation. wMsg is the user-defined message that will be posted to hWnd when the asynchronous operation is complete. port is the service port, in network byte order, of the service about which you want information. proto is a pointer to a protocol name; it is "tcp", "udp", or NULL. If proto is NULL, the first matching service is returned. buf is a pointer to an area of memory that, on successful completion of the service lookup, will contain the servent structure for the desired service. This buffer must be large enough to store the servent structure as well as other referenced data; therefore, it should be at least MAXGETHOSTSTRUCT bytes long. buflen is the size of the buf buffer. It should be MAXGETHOSTSTRUCT for safety's sake.

If the asynchronous operation is initiated successfully, the return value of WSAAsyncGetServByName() is a handle to the asynchronous task. On failure of initialization, the function returns 0 (zero) and WSAGetLastError() should be called to find out the reason for the error. Possible error values include the following: WSANOTINITIALIZED if WSAStartup() wasn't called successfully; WSAENETDOWN if the network subsystem is failing; WSAEWOULDBLOCK if the function cannot be scheduled at this time due to a resource conflict within the specific WinSock implementation; or WSAEINPROGRESS if a blocking WinSock operation is currently in progress. The function's return value doesn't tell you whether the requested information was retrieved successfully; all it tells you is whether the function was started properly.

This function is used much like the other asynchronous functions discussed thus far. Using an MFC implementation method to replicate the example given in the getservbyport() example would have a class declaration like the following:

```
class CMyWindow : public CFrameWnd
{

...

  // member variables
  PSERVENT m_pservent;          // pointer to service entry structure
  char m_lpszMessage[100];      // informational message
  char m_lpszPort[6];           // port number string
  HANDLE m_hGetServByPort;      // handle of asynchronous request
  char m_lpszServEntryBuf[MAXGETHOSTSTRUCT]; // service entry structure
```

```
  // member functions in the message map
  //{{AFX_MSG(CMyWindow)
  afx_msg void OnDoAsyncGetServByPort();
  afx_msg LONG OnAsyncGetServByPort(WPARAM wParam, LPARAM lParam);
  //}}AFX_MSG
  DECLARE_MESSAGE_MAP()
};
```

Notice that the variables are now member variables of the class. The implementation of the `CMyWindow` class begins with the message map for the window:

```
#define WM_USER_ASYNCGETSERVBYPORT (WM_USER + 4)

BEGIN_MESSAGE_MAP(CMyWindow, CFrameWnd)
  //{{AFX_MSG_MAP(CMyWindow)
  ON_COMMAND(ID_TEST_ASYNCGETSERVBYPORT, OnDoAsyncGetServByPort)
  ON_MESSAGE(WM_USER_ASYNCGETSERVBYPORT, OnAsyncGetServByPort)
  //}}AFX_MSG_MAP
END_MESSAGE_MAP()
```

The first entry in the message map is for a menu item that will launch the search. That function is implemented as follows:

```
void CMyWindow::OnDoAsyncGetServByPort()
{
  // get the service entry structure for the port 37 service using UDP
  if ((m_hGetServByPort = WSAAsyncGetServByPort(m_hWnd,
   WM_USER_ASYNCGETSERVBYNAME, htons(37), "udp",
   m_lpszServEntryBuf, MAXGETHOSTSTRUCT)) == 0)
  {
    wsprintf(m_lpszMessage, "WSAAsyncGetServByPort() generated error %d",
     WSAGetLastError());
    MessageBox(m_lpszMessage, "Info");
  }
}
```

The second entry in the message map is for the user-defined message that indicates the asynchronous function has completed. When the `WM_USER_ASYNCGETSERVBYPORT` message is generated by WinSock on completion of the asynchronous call, the `OnAsyncGetServByPort()` function is executed. That function is implemented as follows:

```
LONG CMyWindow::OnAsyncGetServByPort(WPARAM wParam, LPARAM lParam)
{
  // check for an error
  if (WSAGETASYNCERROR(lParam) != 0)
    MessageBox("WSAAsyncGetServByPort() had an error", "Info");
  else
  {
    // assign a servent service entry pointer to the buffer
    m_pservent = (PSERVENT)m_lpszServEntryBuf;

    // format the results
    wsprintf(m_lpszMessage, "Service %s using protocol %s has port ",
     m_pservent->s_name, m_pservent->s_proto);
    wsprintf(m_lpszPort, "%d", ntohs(m_pservent->s_port));
    lstrcat(m_lpszMessage, m_lpszPort);
    MessageBox(m_lpszMessage, "Info");
```

```
    }

    return 0L;
}
```

Summary

This chapter examined the many conversion and database functions provided by WinSock. There are more such functions but the most commonly used ones were presented here. Chapter 8, "Sample Applications," contains a complete application that uses several of these functions.

The next chapter discusses the functions necessary for creating a socket, connecting through sockets, and sending data back and forth through a socket. With that knowledge, you'll be ready to write fully functional WinSock applications.

7

Socket Functions

The preceding two chapters show how to initialize the WinSock library and how to resolve host names and services. This chapter discusses the remaining WinSock functions necessary to make a truly useful networked application. Among these functions are the following: `socket()` to create an end-point of communication, `bind()` to give the end-point a name, `listen()` to listen for incoming connections, `accept()` to accept a connection, `send()` and `sendto()` to send data, and `recv()` and `recvfrom()` to receive data.

Figure 7.1 shows the flow of WinSock function calls for a client and server using TCP. Figure 7.2 shows a similar flow of WinSock function calls, but this time for a client and server using UDP.

FIGURE 7.1.
Client/server WinSock function flow using TCP.

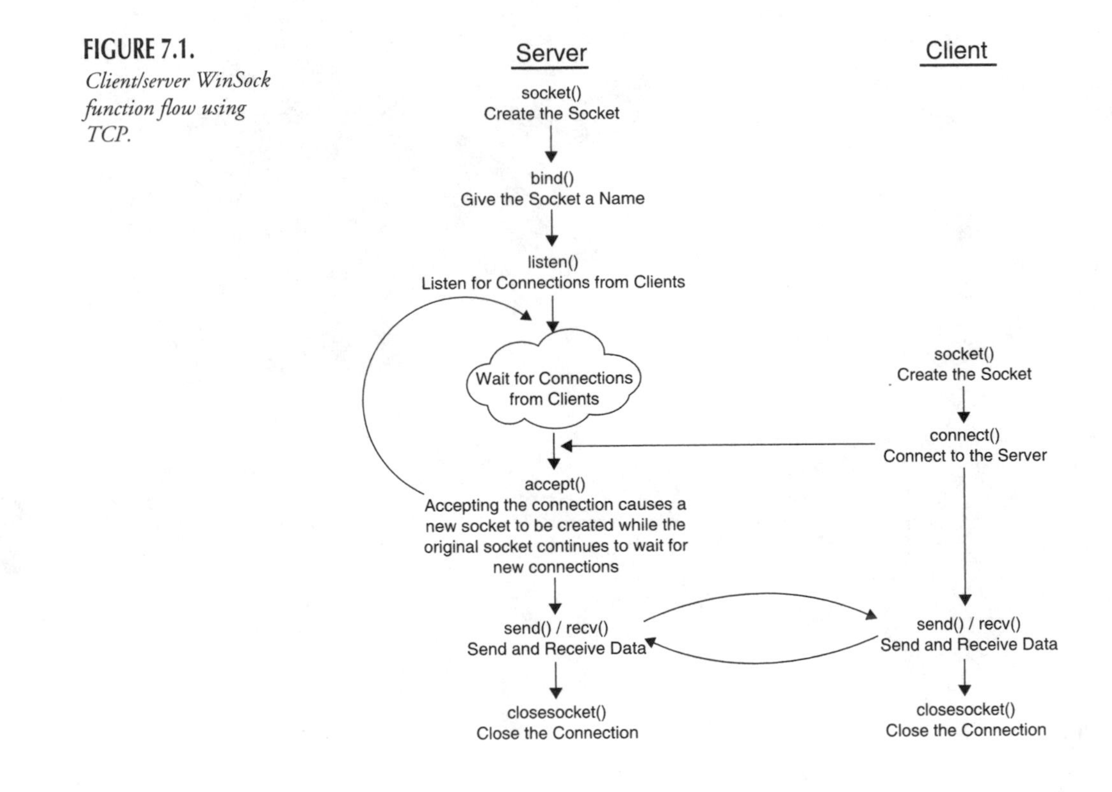

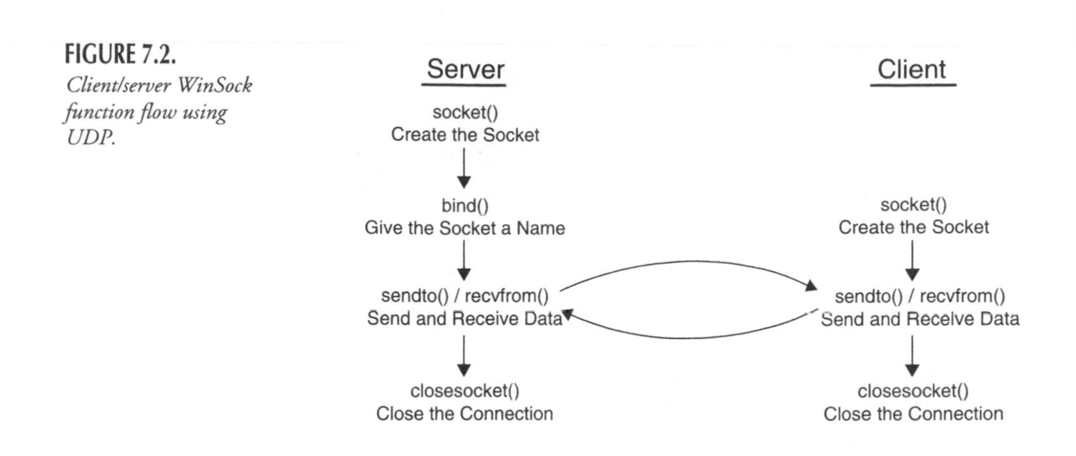

FIGURE 7.2.
Client/server WinSock function flow using UDP.

Creating an End-Point of Communication

The `socket()` function creates an end-point of communication called a *socket*. Its function prototype is as follows:

```
SOCKET PASCAL FAR socket(int af, int type, int protocol);
```

`af` specifies the address family this socket uses. WinSock 1.1 supports only the `AF_INET`, or Internet address family format. `type` is the type specification for the socket. For most applications, this value is either `SOCK_STREAM`, for a connection-oriented byte stream, or `SOCK_DGRAM`, for connectionless datagram service. `protocol` is the particular protocol to use and is usually set to 0 (zero), which lets `socket()` use a default value. The protocol can be defaulted because the address family (`af`) and socket type (`type`) combination already uniquely describe a socket's protocol. If the family is `AF_INET` and the socket type is `SOCK_DGRAM`, the protocol must be UDP. Likewise, if the family is `AF_INET` and the socket type is `SOCK_STREAM`, the protocol must be TCP.

On success, `socket()` returns a socket descriptor. On failure, `INVALID_SOCKET` is returned and `WSAGetLastError()` should be called to find out the reason for the error. Possible error values include the following: `WSANOTINITIALIZED` if `WSAStartup()` wasn't called successfully; `WSAENETDOWN` if the network subsystem is failing; `WSAEAFNOSUPPORT` if the address family specified by `af` isn't supported; `WSAEINPROGRESS` if a blocking WinSock operation is currently in progress; `WSAEMFILE` if there are no more free socket descriptors; `WSAENOBUFS` if no buffer space can be created; `WSAEPROTONOSUPPORT` if the protocol specified by `protocol` isn't supported; `WSAEPROTOTYPE` if the protocol is the wrong type for this socket; or `WSAESOCKTNOSUPPORT` if the socket type specified by `type` isn't supported in the address family specified by `af`.

CAUTION

Several of the preceding error messages returned by `WSAGetLastError()` make reference to unsupported address families, socket types, or protocols. These parameters have several interdependencies that, if not arranged properly, can result in error. For example, a socket with the `AF_INET` address family, `SOCK_STREAM` type, and UDP protocol is impossible because the UDP protocol can't support a byte stream. This book uses two basic sockets. Both have the `AF_INET` address family specifier. One socket has type `SOCK_STREAM`, and the other has type `SOCK_DGRAM`. The protocol is left as 0 (zero) to let the `socket()` function use the default. It figures out this default by examining the address family and socket type. `AF_INET` and `SOCK_STREAM` default to TCP. `AF_INET` and `SOCK_DGRAM` default to UDP.

Example Call to *socket()*

The following code sample shows a call to the `socket()` function to create a stream socket:

```
SOCKET s;                          // socket descriptor
char lpszMessage[100];             // informational message

s = socket(AF_INET, SOCK_STREAM, 0);

if (s == INVALID_SOCKET)
  wsprintf(lpszMessage, "socket() generated error %d",
   WSAGetLastError());
else
  lstrcpy(lpszMessage, "socket() succeeded");

MessageBox(NULL, lpszMessage, "Info", MB_OK);
```

Notice that the protocol field was set to 0 (zero) to allow `socket()` to use a default value generated from the address family and socket type combination.

Stream Versus Datagram

A socket, generally speaking, is of the stream or datagram variety and has either `SOCK_STREAM` or `SOCK_DGRAM`, respectively, as its type specifier in the call to `socket()`. You have to make a choice about which type is more appropriate for your application.

The stream socket supports a connection-oriented, reliable byte stream. Data is guaranteed to arrive in the order it was sent and without any duplication. The stream socket sees the data flow as a continuous, bidirectional stream of bytes with no record boundaries.

The datagram socket supports unconnected, unreliable packet transmission. Data may not arrive in the order it was sent, it may be duplicated, or it may not arrive at all. The datagram socket sees the data flow as a sequence of packets with record boundaries preserved.

Data Flow Behavior

A simple example illustrates the difference between stream and datagram data flow. Suppose that the following two strings were sent to a receiving socket using two separate calls to `send()` or `sendto()`: "This book is about" and "programming with WinSock".

For a stream socket, created with type `SOCK_STREAM`, the application doesn't see these two strings as two separate records; record boundaries are lost. If the receiving socket does a `recv()` on this socket with a buffer size of ten bytes, the first `recv()` returns `"This book "`, the second returns `"is about p"`, the third returns `"rogramming"`, the fourth returns `" with WinS"`, and the fifth returns `"ock"`.

For a datagram socket, created with type `SOCK_DGRAM`, the application sees these two strings as two separate records; record boundaries are preserved. If the receiving socket does a `recvfrom()` on this socket with a buffer size of 10 bytes, the first `recvfrom()` returns `"This book "` and the second returns `"programmin"`. The remaining portion of each of these strings is lost.

From this example, you can see that streams and datagrams are appropriate for different tasks. For something inherently byte-stream oriented, such as a terminal emulator, streams are more appropriate. For something inherently record oriented, such as database record retrieval, datagrams may be more appropriate. But there is a trade-off in either scenario. The use of datagrams means that you may have to include some sort of ack/nack communication (acknowledgment/negative acknowledgment) in your application because the protocol does not do this for you. On the other hand, the use of streams means that you may have to keep track of record boundaries in your application.

Stream-Oriented Client/Server Communication

Stream-oriented, client/server communication, using socket type `SOCK_STREAM`, is more complicated than datagram-oriented communication; both the server and client applications must perform several extra steps that are unnecessary using datagrams. By explaining the more involved stream scenario first, I hope to ease the understanding of the datagram scenario presented later.

How a Server Accepts a Connection from a Client

In a server, the stream socket is bound to a well-known name. Then the server application listens for connections on that socket. When a client connects to the server, the server accepts the new connection. At this point, data transfer begins.

Giving the Socket a Name

Creating a socket does little more than allocate a socket descriptor for your application from the list of available descriptors. To make it useful, you need to give the socket a name. The `bind()` function does this. Its prototype is as follows:

```
int PASCAL FAR bind(SOCKET s, const struct sockaddr FAR *addr, int namelen);
```

`s` is the socket descriptor returned by `socket()`. `addr` is a pointer to the address, or name, to assign to the socket. `namelen` is the length of the structure `addr` points to.

On success, `bind()` returns 0 (zero). On failure, `SOCKET_ERROR` is returned and `WSAGetLastError()` should be called to find out the reason for the error. Possible error values include `WSANOTINITIALIZED` if `WSAStartup()` wasn't called successfully; `WSAENETDOWN` if the network subsystem is failing; `WSAEADDRINUSE` if the address specified by `addr` is already in use; `WSAEFAULT` if `namelen` is too small; `WSAEINPROGRESS` if a blocking WinSock call is currently in progress; `WSAEAFNOSUPORT` if the address family specified in the structure `addr` points to isn't supported by this protocol; `WSAEINVAL` if the socket is already bound to an address; `WSAENOBUFS` if no buffer space can be created; or `WSAENOTSOCK` if the socket descriptor `s` is invalid.

The `sockaddr` structure is defined as follows:

```
struct sockaddr
{
  u_short sa_family;    // address family
  char    sa_data[14];  // up to 14 bytes of direct address
};
```

The format of `sa_data` depends on the address family. In WinSock 1.1, only the Internet addressing format is supported. For this reason, the `sockaddr_in` structure is provided. Use it rather than `sockaddr` when calling `bind()`. The format of the `sockaddr_in` structure follows:

```
struct sockaddr_in
{
  short   sin_family;          // address family
  u_short sin_port;            // service port
  struct  in_addr sin_addr;    // Internet address
  char    sin_zero[8];         // filler
};
```

sin_family must be AF_INET for WinSock 1.1; this value matches the af argument in the call to socket(). sin_port is the port number, in network byte order, on which your server application provides its service. sin_addr is an in_addr structure that contains the IP address, in network byte order, on which your server will listen for connections. The in_addr structure is used to provide three different ways of examining the IP address: as four bytes, as two shorts, or as one long. The format of in_addr is as follows:

```
struct in_addr
{
  union
  {
    struct { u_char s_b1, s_b2, s_b3, s_b4; } S_un_b;
    struct { u_short s_w1,s_w2; } S_un_w;
    u_long S_addr;
  } S_un;

#define s_addr  S_un.S_addr       // can be used for most tcp & ip code
#define s_host  S_un.S_un_b.s_b2 // host on imp
#define s_net   S_un.S_un_b.s_b1 // network
#define s_imp   S_un.S_un_w.s_w2 // imp
#define s_impno S_un.S_un_b.s_b4 // imp #
#define s_lh    S_un.S_un_b.s_b3 // logical host
};
```

Notice the definition of s_addr. This will be the most common way of accessing the IP address, as an unsigned long in network byte order, because the database and conversion routines manipulate the IP address similarly. The remaining field of the sockaddr_in structure, sin_zero, is provided as a filler to buffer the remaining eight bytes that are allotted for an address (2 byte port + 4 byte IP address + 8 byte filler = 14 bytes total).

Following is an example of using bind():

```
SOCKET s;                          // socket descriptor
char lpszMessage[100];             // informational message
SOCKADDR_IN addr;                  // Internet address

// create a stream socket
s = socket(AF_INET, SOCK_STREAM, 0);
if (s != INVALID_SOCKET)
{
  // fill out the socket's address information
  addr.sin_family = AF_INET;
  addr.sin_port = htons(1050);
  addr.sin_addr.s_addr = htonl(INADDR_ANY);

  // bind the socket to its address
  if (bind(s, (LPSOCKADDR)&addr, sizeof(addr)) == SOCKET_ERROR)
  {
    wsprintf(lpszMessage, " bind() generated error %d",
     WSAGetLastError());
    MessageBox(NULL, lpszMessage, "Info", MB_OK);
  }
  else
    ...
}
```

Notice the assignment of addr.sin_port to htons(1050). This tells you that this server application listens for connections on port 1050. You also could use the getservbyname() or WSAAsyncGetServByName() functions, as in the following example, to assign a port number:

```
LPSERVENT pservent;              // pointer to service entry structure
pservent = getservbyname("daytime", "tcp");
if (pservent != NULL)
  addr.sin_port = pservent->s_port; // already in network byte order
```

The next line in the sample is the assignment of addr.sin_addr.s_addr, the actual IP address. In this sample, the IP address is set to htonl(INADDR_ANY). This tells you that this server listens for connections on any network to which the host is connected.

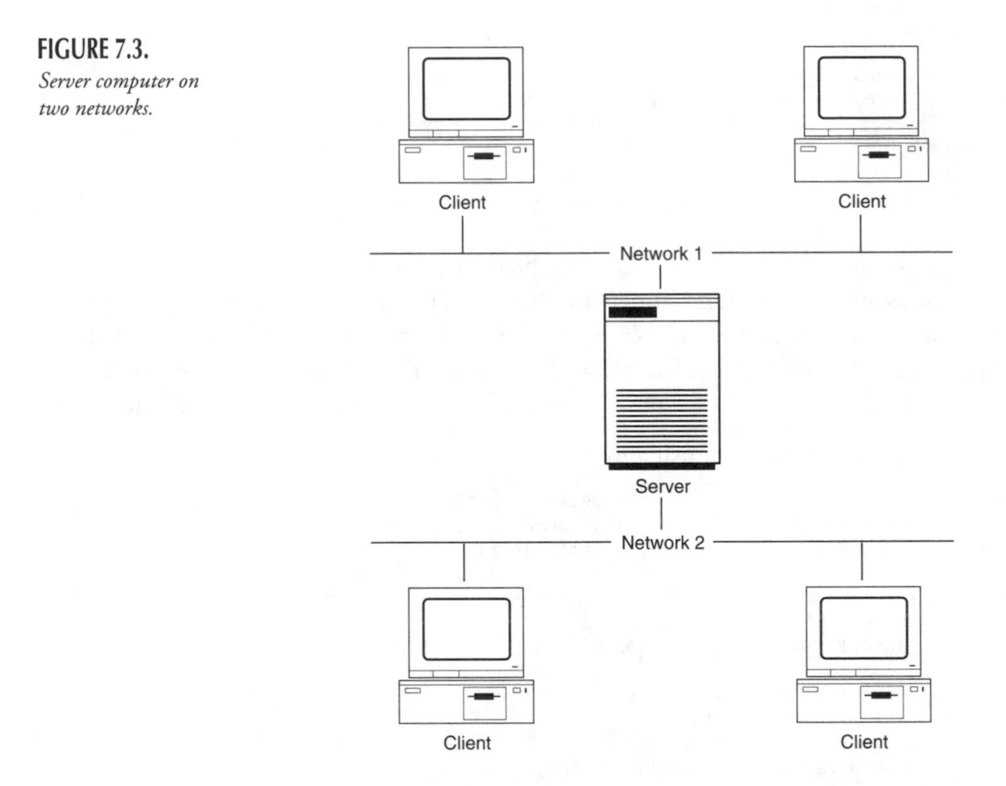

FIGURE 7.3.
Server computer on two networks.

In most server applications, the name bound to a socket has its IP address set to INADDR_ANY. This tells WinSock that you are willing to accept requests from any network to which the host is connected. The only time this is an issue is if the host running your server application has more than one IP address assigned to it. For example, this might be the case if the host has two Ethernet cards as shown in Figure 7.3. One Ethernet card is assigned one IP address (say 166.78.16.200) and the other Ethernet card has a

different IP address (say 166.78.16.201). In this case, you may want to place a limit whereby clients can connect through only one IP address or the other, but not both. In this case you do something like the following:

```
addr.sin_addr.s_addr = inet_addr("166.78.16.200");
```

One last thing to note about this code sample is the call to `bind()` itself. The `addr` parameter's address must be cast to a long pointer to a `sockaddr` structure (`LPSOCKADDR`) because `addr` is a `sockaddr_in` structure (`SOCKADDR_IN`).

Listen for Connections

Now that you can name a socket, you can put it to real use by listening for connections to that socket from client applications. The `listen()` function does this. Its prototype is as follows:

```
int PASCAL FAR listen(SOCKET s, int backlog);
```

`s` is the socket descriptor on which to listen for connections. `backlog` is a count of pending connections that may be queued up before the server application processes them. `backlog` must be between one and five, inclusively.

On success, `listen()` returns 0 (zero). On failure, `SOCKET_ERROR` is returned and `WSAGetLastError()` should be called to find out the reason for the error. Possible error values include: `WSANOTINITIALIZED` if `WSAStartup()` wasn't called successfully; `WSAENETDOWN` if the network subsystem is failing; `WSAEADDRINUSE` if the address specified by `addr` is already in use; `WSAEINPROGRESS` if a blocking WinSock call is currently in progress; `WSAEINVAL` if the socket hasn't been bound to an address using `bind()` or the socket is already connected; `WSAEISCONN` if the socket is already connected; `WSAEMFILE` if there are no more free file descriptors; `WSAENOBUFS` if no buffer space can be created; `WSAENOTSOCK` if the socket descriptor `s` is invalid; or `WSAEOPNOTSUPP` if the socket `s` doesn't support the `listen()` operation (this could happen if socket `s` is of type `SOCK_DGRAM`).

NOTE

Backlog acts as a safety net by preventing the WinSock layer from allocating lots of resources. Suppose that your server application is very slow and can process client connections only once every five seconds. Suppose also that the socket has a backlog of three. If four clients try to connect to the server socket within five seconds, the fourth client attempt will generate a `WSAECONNREFUSED` error at the client side.

Following is a code snippet showing the use of the `listen()` function:

```
SOCKET s;                          // socket descriptor
char lpszMessage[100];             // informational message
SOCKADDR_IN addr;                  // Internet address

// create a stream socket
s = socket(AF_INET, SOCK_STREAM, 0);
if (s != INVALID_SOCKET)
{
  // fill out the socket's address information
  addr.sin_family = AF_INET;
  addr.sin_port = htons(1050);
  addr.sin_addr.s_addr = htonl(INADDR_ANY);

  // bind the socket to its address
  if (bind(s, (LPSOCKADDR)&addr, sizeof(addr)) != SOCKET_ERROR)
  {
    // listen for connections (queueing up to three)
    if (listen(s, 3) == SOCKET_ERROR)
    {
      wsprintf(lpszMessage, "listen() generated error %d",
       WSAGetLastError());
      MessageBox(lpszMessage, "Info");
    }
    else
      ...
  }
}
```

Accept a Connection

Now you have a named socket listening for connections. The next thing for a server to do is accept a connection from a client. The `accept()` function does this. Its prototype is as follows:

```
SOCKET PASCAL FAR accept(SOCKET s, struct sockaddr FAR *addr,
 int FAR *addrlen);
```

`s` is the socket descriptor on which to accept a connection request. `addr` is a pointer to a `sockaddr` structure that will accept the address of the connecting client. You may pass `NULL` for this parameter or a pointer to a `sockaddr_in` structure, as in the `bind()` example. `addrlen` is a pointer that will accept the actual length of the address structure in `addr`. If `addr` is NULL, `addrlen` can also be `NULL`; otherwise, the value pointed to by `addrlen` should initially contain the length of the structure pointed to by `addr`. This is more clearly explained in the following examples.

On success, `accept()` returns a socket descriptor. This returned socket descriptor is the one used for communication with the client; the original socket `s` passed in the call to `accept()` remains available to accept additional connections. On failure, `INVALID_SOCKET` is returned, and `WSAGetLastError()` should be called to find out the reason for the error. Possible error values include: `WSANOTINITIALIZED` if `WSAStartup()` wasn't called

successfully; WSAENETDOWN if the network subsystem is failing; WSAEFAULT if addrlen is too small; WSAEINTR if the blocking call was canceled; WSAEINPROGRESS if a blocking WinSock call is currently in progress; WSAEINVAL if listen() wasn't called before accept(); WSAEFILE if the queue is empty and there are no descriptors available; WSAENOBUFS if no buffer space can be created; WSAENOTSOCK if the socket descriptor s is invalid; WSAEOPNOTSUPP if the socket s does not support the accept() operation (this could happen if socket s is of type SOCK_DGRAM); or WSAEWOULDBLOCK if the socket is marked as nonblocking and no connections are present to be accepted.

Following is a code snippet that shows the accept() call in use:

```
SOCKET s;                        // socket descriptor
SOCKET clientS;                  // client socket descriptor
char lpszMessage[100];           // informational message
SOCKADDR_IN addr;                // Internet address
SOCKADDR_IN clientAddr;          // Internet address
IN_ADDR clientIn;                // IP address
int nClientAddrLen;

// create a stream socket
s = socket(AF_INET, SOCK_STREAM, 0);
if (s != INVALID_SOCKET)
{
  // fill out the socket's address information
  addr.sin_family = AF_INET;
  addr.sin_port = htons(1050);
  addr.sin_addr.s_addr = htonl(INADDR_ANY);

  // bind the socket to its address
  if (bind(s, (LPSOCKADDR)&addr, sizeof(addr)) != SOCKET_ERROR)
  {
    // listen for connections (queueing up to three)
    if (listen(s, 3) != SOCKET_ERROR)
    {
      // set the size of the client address structure
      nClientAddrLen = sizeof(clientAddr);

      // accept a connection
      clientS = accept(s, (LPSOCKADDR)&clientAddr, &nClientAddrLen);
      if (clientS == INVALID_SOCKET)
      {
        wsprintf(lpszMessage, " accept() generated error %d",
         WSAGetLastError());
        MessageBox(lpszMessage, "Info");
      }
      else
      {
        // copy the four byte IP address into an IP address structure
        memcpy(&clientIn, &clientAddr.sin_addr.s_addr, 4);

        // print an informational message
        wsprintf(lpszMessage,
         "accept() ok: client IP address is %s, port is %d",
         inet_ntoa(clientIn), ntohs(clientAddr.sin_port));
```

```
        MessageBox(lpszMessage, "Info");

        ...
      }
}
  }
}
```

In this example, the `accept()` function is called with a pointer to a `sockaddr_in` structure and a pointer to an integer containing the length of the `sockaddr_in` structure. When the `accept()` function successfully returns, the `sockaddr_in` structure contains the address information of the connecting client. As noted previously, you can pass `NULL` for these two parameters and no client information will be conveyed to the accepting server application. The alternative method of discovering details about the connecting client is to use the `getpeername()` function. Its prototype is as follows:

```
int PASCAL FAR getpeername(SOCKET s,
 struct sockaddr FAR *name, int FAR * namelen);
```

Its parameters are the same as those of `accept()` except that the socket `s` is the socket descriptor that's returned by `accept()`, not the socket descriptor that's used to listen for connections. The other difference is that the function prototype uses `name` and `namelen` rather than `addr` and `addrlen`, respectively. The inconsistent use of the terms *name* and *address* is a problem with some WinSock functions.

On success, `getpeername()` returns 0 (zero). On error, `SOCKET_ERROR` is returned and `WSAGetLastError()` should be called to find out the reason for the error. Possible error values include: `WSANOTINITIALIZED` if `WSAStartup()` wasn't called successfully; `WSAENETDOWN` if the network subsystem is failing; `WSAEFAULT` if `namelen` is too small; `WSAEINPROGRESS` if a blocking WinSock call is currently in progress; `WSAENOTSOCK` if the socket descriptor `s` is invalid; or `WSAENOTCONN` if the socket isn't connected to a client.

To use this function you do something like this:

```
...

      // accept a connection
      clientS = accept(s, NULL, NULL);
      if (clientS == INVALID_SOCKET)
      {
        wsprintf(lpszMessage, "accept() generated error %d",
         WSAGetLastError());
        MessageBox(lpszMessage, "Info");
      }
      else
      {
        if (getpeername(clientS,
         (LPSOCKADDR)&clientAddr, &nClientAddrLen)) == SOCKET_ERROR)
        {
          wsprintf(lpszMessage, "getpeername() generated error %d",
           WSAGetLastError());
          MessageBox(lpszMessage, "Info");
```

```
        }
        else
        {
          // copy the four byte IP address into an IP address structure
          memcpy(&clientIn, &clientAddr.sin_addr.s_addr, 4);

          // print an informational message
          wsprintf(lpszMessage,
           "client IP address is %s, port is %d",
           inet_ntoa(clientIn), ntohs(clientAddr.sin_port));
          MessageBox(lpszMessage, "Info");

          ...
        }
      }
...
```

What If No Clients Are Trying to Connect?

In the previous example no mention was made of what the outcome of the code segment is if there is no client trying to connect to the server when the server executes the `accept()` function. In this scenario, the server application blocks, waiting for a client connection. This is similar to what happens with the `getXbyY` functions discussed in an earlier chapter. And just as there is a work-around for the `getXbyY` problem, using the `WSAAsyncGetXByY` functions, there is an answer to the `accept()` problem as well. The solution lies in using nonblocking sockets. By default, a socket created with `socket()` is in blocking mode. There are two methods for putting the socket into nonblocking mode.

Doing It the Berkeley Way

The Berkeley method of using nonblocking sockets involves two functions: `ioctl()` and `select()`. `ioctl()` is the UNIX function to perform input/output control on a file descriptor or socket. Because a WinSock socket descriptor may not be a true operating system file descriptor, `ioctl()` can't be used, so `ioctlsocket()` is provided instead. `select()` is used to determine the status of one or more sockets.

The use of `ioctlsocket()` to convert a socket to nonblocking mode looks like this:

```
// put socket s into nonblocking mode
u_long ulCmdArg = 1;    // 1 for nonblocking, 0 for blocking
ioctlsocket(s, FIONBIO, &ulCmdArg);
```

Once a socket is in its nonblocking mode, calling a normally blocking function simply returns `WSAEWOULDBLOCK` if the function can't immediately complete, as in the following example.

```
// put socket s into nonblocking mode
u_long ulCmdArg = 1;    // 1 for nonblocking, 0 for blocking
ioctlsocket(s, FIONBIO, &ulCmdArg);
```

```
SOCKET clientS;
clientS = accept(s, NULL, NULL);
if (clientS == INVALID_SOCKET)
{
  int nError = WSAGetLastError();

  // if there is no client waiting to connect to this server,
  // nError will be WSAEWOULDBLOCK

}
```

Your server application could simply call `accept()` periodically until the call succeeded, or you could use the `select()` call to query the status of the socket. The `select()` function checks the readability, writeability, and exception status of one or more sockets. Even the most die-hard UNIX or Berkeley sockets supporter probably agrees that the use of `select()` is fairly unintuitive. As one example, if `select()` tells you that a socket is readable, that could mean the socket is ready to connect to a client, or it could mean there is some data sent by a client ready to be read. To use `select()` in a Windows program would require that it be called periodically, as the result of a timer or every time through the application's message loop. No matter what, its use doesn't fit well within the message-driven architecture of Windows. Thankfully, WinSock provides a more "Windows native" method of performing nonblocking socket operations.

Doing It the Windows Way

WinSock provides a function called `WSAAsyncSelect()` to solve the problem of blocking socket function calls. It is a much more natural solution to the problem than using `ioctlsocket()` and `select()`. It works by sending a Windows message to notify a window of a socket event. Its prototype is as follows:

```
int PASCAL FAR WSAAsyncSelect(SOCKET s, HWND hWnd,
 u_int wMsg, long lEvent);
```

`s` is the socket descriptor for which event notification is required. `hWnd` is the Window handle that should receive a message when an event occurs on the socket. `wMsg` is the message to be received by `hWnd` when a socket event occurs on socket `s`. It is usually a user-defined message (`WM_USER` + n). `lEvent` is a bitmask that specifies the events in which the application is interested.

`WSAAsyncSelect()` returns 0 (zero) on success and `SOCKET_ERROR` on failure. On failure, `WSAGetLastError()` should be called. Possible error values include the following: `WSANOTINITIALIZED` if `WSAStartup()` wasn't called successfully; `WSAENETDOWN` if the network subsystem is failing; `WSAEINPROGRESS` if a blocking WinSock call is currently in progress; or `WSAEINVAL` if one of the parameters is invalid.

TIP

Calling `WSAAsyncSelect()` automatically puts the socket into a nonblocking state. There is no need to use `ioctlsocket()` to do this first.

`WSAAsyncSelect()` is capable of monitoring several socket events. Table 7.1 lists these events, which are represented by `lEvent` in the function prototype.

Table 7.1. `WSAAsyncSelect()` **Events.**

Event	*Meaning*
`FD_READ`	Socket ready for reading
`FD_WRITE`	Socket ready for writing
`FD_OOB`	Out-of-band data ready for reading on socket
`FD_ACCEPT`	Socket ready for accepting a new incoming connection
`FD_CONNECT`	Connection on socket completed
`FD_CLOSE`	Connection on socket has been closed

The `lEvent` parameter is constructed by doing a logical OR on the events in which you're interested. For example, the following code will post a `WM_USER + 1` message to the window handle specified by `hWnd` when there is an incoming connection to socket `s` or when socket `s` has data to be read:

```
long lEvent = FD_ACCEPT ¦ FD_READ;
WSAAsyncSelect(s, hWnd, WM_USER + 1, lEvent);
```

TIP

Issuing `WSAAsyncSelect()` for a socket cancels any previous `WSAAsyncSelect()` for the same socket. You can't do separate calls like this:

```
WSAAsyncSelect(s, hWnd, WM_USER + 1, FD_ACCEPT);

WSAAsyncSelect(s, hWnd, WM_USER + 1, FD_READ);
```

The preceding code will ignore FD_ACCEPT events; only FD_READ events will be posted as message `WM_USER + 1`.

You also can't use separate calls to `WSAAsyncSelect()` to assign different messages to the different events for a specific socket. For example, the following code is incorrect:

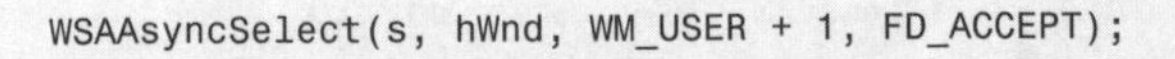

```
WSAAsyncSelect(s, hWnd, WM_USER + 1, FD_ACCEPT);

WSAAsyncSelect(s, hWnd, WM_USER + 2, FD_READ);
```

The FD_ACCEPT event will never generate `WM_USER + 1`. Only FD_READ will generate a message (`WM_USER + 2`).

To cancel all event notifications, call `WSAAsyncSelect()` with wMsg and lEvent set to 0 (zero), as in the following:

```
WSAAsyncSelect(s, hWnd, 0, 0L);
```

You can see that there are six events you can express interest in. This section is about how a server accepts a connection from a client, so that's the area of `WSAAsyncSelect()` on which I'll concentrate. Please note that other sections of this chapter use `WSAAsyncSelect()` to monitor the sending and receiving of data, as well as other events. The basic use of `WSAAsyncSelect()` is the same for all events, so I'll give a full description of an appropriate message handler here.

The `FD_ACCEPT` event is generated whenever a listening socket has a client wishing to make a connection. An example of calling `WSAAsyncSelect()` from within a Visual C++ MFC program follows.

```
BOOL CServerWindow::StartListening()
{
  // m_s is the socket descriptor which is a member
  // variable of the CServerWindow class

  // m_s has already been created and bound to a name

  // listen for connections
  if (listen(m_s, 3) == SOCKET_ERROR)
    return FALSE;

  // get asycnchronous event notification of accept
  // to this object's window (m_hWnd)
  if (WSAAsyncSelect(m_s, m_hWnd, WM_USER + 1, FD_ACCEPT) == SOCKET_ERROR)
    return FALSE;

  return TRUE;
}
```

You also need a member function in `CServerWindow` to handle the `WM_USER + 1` message that's generated when a client connection is requested of socket `m_s`:

```
BEGIN_MESSAGE_MAP(CServerWindow, CFrameWnd)
  //{{AFX_MSG_MAP(CServerWindow)
  ...
  ON_MESSAGE(WM_USER + 1, OnAsyncSelect)
...
```

```
  //}}AFX_MSG_MAP
END_MESSAGE_MAP()

LONG CServerWindow::OnAsyncSelect(WPARAM wParam, LPARAM lParam)
{
  // wParam is the socket descriptor
  // lParam is a status or error indicator

  // check for an error
  if (WSAGETSELECTERROR(lParam) != 0)
    return 0L;

  // what event are we being notified of?
  if (WSAGETSELECTEVENT(lParam) == FD_ACCEPT)
  {
    // m_clientS is defined as SOCKET in the CServerWindow class declaration
    m_clientS = accept(m_s, NULL, NULL);
    if (m_clientS == INVALID_SOCKET)
    {
      int nError = WSAGetLastError();
      if (nError == WSAEWOULDBLOCK)
        // There really isn't a client ready to connect.
        // This error should never occur for the FD_ACCEPT event
        // so it should be treated just like this event
        // notification function hadn't been called.
        ;
      else
        // some other error
        ;
    }
  }
}
```

Notice the call to `WSAGETSELECTERROR`. This is a macro provided in WINSOCK.H, which is called to determine whether there is an error in the asynchronous event. It returns 0 (zero) on success and an error value on failure. For the `FD_ACCEPT` event notification message, the error could be `WSAENETDOWN`, which means the network subsystem is down.

Also note that the `WSAGETSELECTEVENT` macro is called to determine the event that triggered this message handler even though the only way the `CServerWindow::OnAsyncSelect()` function is called is if the `FD_ACCEPT` event occurs. This macro will be used in later sample programs where the class's member function handles several WinSock events for a particular socket.

If for some reason the `CServerWindow::OnAsyncSelect()` function is called with the `FD_ACCEPT` event but there is no client trying to connect to this server application, `accept()` returns `INVALID_SOCKET`. Calling `WSAGetLastError()` will return `WSAEWOULDBLOCK`, which tells you that this function is set up for nonblocking mode and if it weren't, it would block.

How Clients Connect to Servers

You have now seen how a server creates a socket, gives it a name, listens for connections, and accepts connections from clients. This section explains what a client does to connect to a server application.

Giving the Socket a Default Name

After the call to `socket()`, the `bind()` function may be used to give the socket a name. This step might be necessary because calling `socket()` simply reserves a socket descriptor. By naming the socket with `bind()`, you give the socket a port, out of which it communicates with a server.

The use of `bind()` to give a client socket a default name is shown here:

```
SOCKET s;                          // socket descriptor
char lpszMessage[100];             // informational message
SOCKADDR_IN addr;                  // Internet address

// create a stream socket
s = socket(AF_INET, SOCK_STREAM, 0);
if (s != INVALID_SOCKET)
{
  // fill out the socket's address information
  addr.sin_family = AF_INET;
  addr.sin_port = 0;     // let WinSock assign a port
  addr.sin_addr.s_addr = htonl(INADDR_ANY);

  // bind the socket to its address
  if (bind(s, (LPSOCKADDR)&addr, sizeof(addr)) == SOCKET_ERROR)
  {
    wsprintf(lpszMessage, " bind() generated error %d",
     WSAGetLastError());
    MessageBox(NULL, lpszMessage, "Info", MB_OK);
  }
  else
    ...
}
```

Note that `addr.sin_port` is assigned 0 (zero). This allows WinSock to assign any unused port it sees fit. This is in contrast to a server socket, which needs to listen for connections on a specific port. It really doesn't matter which port a client uses. But if you do want to know which port a socket was assigned, you can use the `getsockname()` function. Its function prototype is as follows:

```
int PASCAL FAR getsockname(SOCKET s,
 struct sockaddr FAR *name, int FAR * namelen);
```

It is used much like getpeername(). An example call to getsockname() is listed here:

```
SOCKET s;                         // socket descriptor
char lpszMessage[100];            // informational message
SOCKADDR_IN addr;                 // Internet address used by bind()
SOCKADDR_IN addrAssigned;         // Internet address assigned by bind()
int nAddrAssignedLen = sizeof(addrAssigned);

// create a stream socket
s = socket(AF_INET, SOCK_STREAM, 0);
if (s != INVALID_SOCKET)
{
  // fill out the socket's address information
  addr.sin_family = AF_INET;
  addr.sin_port = 0;              // let WinSock assign a port
  addr.sin_addr.s_addr = htonl(INADDR_ANY);

  // bind the socket to its address
  if (bind(s, (LPSOCKADDR)&addr, sizeof(addr)) != SOCKET_ERROR)
  {
    // find out what port was assigned by WinSock
    if (getsockname(s, (LPSOCKADDR)&addrAssigned, &nAddrAssignedLen) == 0)
      // now addrAssigned.sin_port contains the port number
      // that WinSock assigned to this client port
      ...

  }
}
```

In this example, as in the server example, the socket's IP address is set to INADDR_ANY. This means that the socket can use any network interface the computer has. This use is fine for most instances. It may be necessary to specify a particular address if the computer on which the client application runs is connected to more than one network through more than one network interface. Figure 7.4 shows one possible scenario. The client computer in Figure 7.4 has two IP addresses; suppose that they are 166.12.34.101 and 166.12.34.102. If you want the client limited to going through only one network interface, you can do the following instead of using INADDR_ANY:

```
addr.sin_addr.s_addr = inet_addr("166.12.34.101");
```

Connecting to a Server

A client connects to a server using the connect() function. Its prototype is as follows:

```
int PASCAL FAR connect(SOCKET s,
 const struct sockaddr FAR *name, int namelen);
```

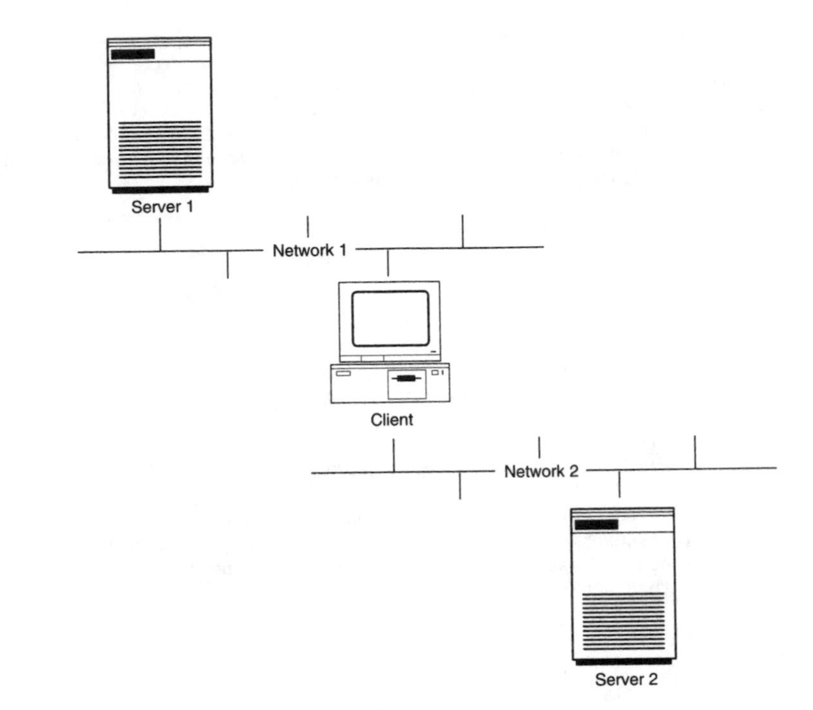

FIGURE 7.4.
Client computer on two networks.

`s` is the socket to use for the connection. `name` is the address of the server to connect to. It is always a `sockaddr_in` Internet address structure for WinSock 1.1. `namelen` is the length of the `name` parameter.

On success, `connect()` returns 0 (zero). On failure, it returns `SOCKET_ERROR` and `WSAGetLastError()` should be called to find out the cause of the error. Possible error values include the following: `WSANOTINITIALIZED` if WinSock hasn't been successfully initialized with a call to `WSAStartup()`; `WSAENETDOWN` if the network subsystem is failing; `WSAEADDRINUSE` if the address is already in use; `WSAEINTR` if the blocking call was canceled with `WSACancelBlockingCall()`; `WSAEINPROGRESS` if a blocking WinSock call is in progress; `WSAEADDRNOTAVAIL` if the address specified by `addr` isn't available; `WSAENOSUPPORT` if the addresses in the specified family can't be used with this socket; `WSAECONNREFUSED` if the server forcefully refused the connection attempt; `WSAEDESTADDREQ` if `name` isn't specified; `WSAEFAULT` if `namelen` is invalid; `WSAEINVAL` if socket `s` isn't bound to an address; `WSAEISCONN` if socket `s` is already connected; `WSAEMFILE` if there are no free file descriptors; `WSAENETUNREACH` if the network can't be reached from this host at this time; `WSAENOBUFS` if no buffer space is available; `WSAENOTSOCK` if socket `s` isn't a valid socket descriptor; `WSAETIMEDOUT` if the attempt to connect timed out; or `WSAEWOULDBLOCK` if socket `s` is marked as nonblocking and this connection can't be completed immediately.

An example of using connect() is shown here:

```
SOCKET s;                          // socket descriptor
char lpszMessage[100];             // informational message
SOCKADDR_IN addr;                  // Internet address used by bind()
SOCKADDR_IN addrServer;

...
// s is a socket that has been bound to a default address
...

// fill out the address information of the server application
// (the server has IP address 166.34.56.100 and listens on port 1050)
addrServer.sin_family = AF_INET;
addrServer.sin_port = htons(1050);
addrServer.sin_addr.s_addr = inet_addr("166.34.56.100");

if (connect(s, (LPSOCKADDR)&addrServer, sizeof(addrServer)) == SOCKET_ERROR)
  // error
```

What if the Server Isn't Listening?

The connect() call suffers from the same problem as accept(). What happens if the server to which the client application is trying to connect isn't listening for connections? Using a blocking socket, the connect() function won't return until the server accepts the connection. If the server never accepts the connection request, the client application remains hung until the WSAETIMEDOUT error is generated; the client's message loop never executes. To battle this problem, the WSAAsyncSelect() function is used. The event of importance in this scenario is FD_CONNECT. The following example code shows how WSAAsyncSelect() might be called in a Visual C++ MFC program:

```
BOOL CClientWindow::DoConnect()
{
  // m_s is the socket descriptor which is a member
  // variable of the CClientWindow class

  // m_s has already been created and bound to a default name

  // fill out the address information of the server application
  // (the server has IP address 166.34.56.100 and listens on port 1050)
  m_addrServer.sin_family = AF_INET;
  m_addrServer.sin_port = htons(1050);
  m_addrServer.sin_addr.s_addr = inet_addr("166.34.56.100");

  // get asycnchronous event notification of
  // connect to this object's window (m_hWnd)
  if (WSAAsyncSelect(m_s, m_hWnd, WM_USER + 1, FD_CONNECT) ==
   SOCKET_ERROR)
  {
    // error ...
  }
```

```
   // make the connection
   if (connect(m_s, (LPSOCKADDR)&m_addrServer, sizeof(m_addrServer)) ==
    SOCKET_ERROR)
   {
     int nError = WSAGetLastError();
     if (nError == WSAEWOULDBLOCK)
     {
       // this is ok...just wait for async notice
     }
     else
     {
       // some other error
     }
   }
}
```

You also need a member function in `CClientWindow` to handle the `WM_USER + 1` message that's generated when a client connection is completed:

```
BEGIN_MESSAGE_MAP(CClientWindow, CFrameWnd)
  //{{AFX_MSG_MAP(CClientWindow)
  ...
  ON_MESSAGE(WM_USER + 1, OnAsyncSelect)
...
  //}}AFX_MSG_MAP
END_MESSAGE_MAP()

LONG CClientWindow::OnAsyncSelect(WPARAM wParam, LPARAM lParam)
{
  // wParam is the socket descriptor
  // lParam is a status or error indicator

  // check for an error
  if (WSAGETSELECTERROR(lParam) != 0)
    return 0L;

  // what event are we being notified of?
  if (WSAGETSELECTEVENT(lParam) == FD_CONNECT)
  {
    // you now know that the m_s socket is connected to the server
  }
}
```

This message handler follows the same format as the `CServerWindow::OnAsyncSelect()` function. First, check for an error using the `WSAGETSELECTERROR` macro. Next, use `WSAGETSELECTEVENT` to determine which event caused this message handle to be called. The `FD_CONNECT` event tells us the client socket is connected to the server.

Sending and Receiving Data on a Stream Socket

You have now seen how a server accepts a connection and how a client makes a connection. Once the client and server sockets are connected, data can be sent and received.

The `send()` and `recv()` functions are used to send and receive stream data, respectively. These two functions can also operate on datagrams, but this discussion is limited to their use with respect to stream sockets.

Sending Data

Sending data over a stream socket involves the use of WinSock's `send()` function. Its prototype is as follows:

```
int PASCAL FAR send(SOCKET s, const char FAR * buf, int len, int flags);
```

`s` is the connected socket to send data over. `buf` is a pointer to a buffer containing the data to be transmitted. `len` is the number of bytes in `buf`. `flags` specifies the way in which the `send()` call is made. `flags` can be any of the following logically ORed together: 0 (zero) for no special send options, `MSG_DONTROUTE` if the data shouldn't be subject to routing, and `MSG_OOB` to send out-of-band data.

On success, `send()` returns the number of bytes sent. This could range from 1 (one) to `len`. On failure, `SOCKET_ERROR` is returned and `WSAGetLastError()` specifies the following: `WSANOTINITIALIZED` if WinSock wasn't initialized with `WSAStartup()`; `WSAENETDOWN` if the network subsystem is failing; `WSAEACCESS` if the address is a broadcast address but the appropriate flag wasn't set; `WSAEINTR` if the blocking call was canceled with `WSACancelBlockingCall()`; `WSAEINPROGRESS` if a blocking call is in progress; `WSAEFAULT` if `buf` isn't in a valid part of the user address space; `WSAENETRESET` if the connection needs to be reset; `WSAENOBUFS` if there is a internal WinSock buffer deadlock; `WSAENOTCONN` if the socket `s` isn't connected; `WSAENOTSOCK` if the socket `s` isn't a valid socket descriptor; `WSAEOPNOTSUPP` if `MSG_OOB` was specified by `flags` but the socket `s` isn't a stream socket; `WSAESHUTDOWN` if the socket `s` has been shutdown; `WSAEWOULDBLOCK` if the socket `s` is marked as nonblocking and the `send()` would block; `WSAEMSGSIZE` if socket `s` is a datagram socket and the buffer is too large; `WSAEINVAL` if the socket `s` hasn't been bound; `WSAECONNABORTED` if the virtual circuit was aborted due to timeout or other failure; or `WSAECONNRESET` if the virtual circuit was reset by the remote side.

NOTE

Out-of-band (OOB) data can be thought of as a logically independent transmission channel associated with each pair of connected stream sockets. Out-of-band data is delivered to the user independently of normal stream data.

Unfortunately, there are two conflicting interpretations of out-of-band implementation. Internet RFC 793 introduced the concept of out-of-band data and RFC 1122 provided the host requirements. The problem arises because the Berkeley implementation of out-of-band data handling does not follow RFC 1122. Most TCP/IP stack providers document their implementation so that you know which they use: BSD or RFC 1122. Because of this difference of opinion, it is best not to use out-of-band data in your applications. Of course, if your application must interoperate with an existing client or server, perhaps running on a UNIX computer, you have no choice.

The following demonstrates a typical call to `send()`:

```
SOCKET s;               // socket to communicate over
char pszBuf[100];       // buffer to send
int nBufLen;            // number of bytes in buffer to send
int nBytesSent;         // bytes sent
int nError;             // error status

// create, bind, and connect socket s ...

lstrcpy(pszBuf, "Hello, World!");
nBufLen = lstrlen(pszBuf);

nBytesSent = send(s, pszBuf, nBufLen, 0);
if (nBytesSent == SOCKET_ERROR)
{
  nError = WSAGetLastError();
}
else
{
  // nBytesSent is the number of bytes successfully sent
}
```

The `send()` function has the same problem with blocking as the `accept()`, `connect()`, and `getXbyY` functions. If none of the data can be sent for some reason—because the receiving socket has too much incoming data spooled up, for example—`send()` blocks waiting for the receiver to read the spooled up data. While `send()` is blocking, the user loses control over your application. To prevent this problem, the `WSAAsyncSelect()` function is used to put the socket into nonblocking send mode. The event of interest in this scenario is `FD_WRITE`. An `FD_WRITE` message is posted when a socket is first connected with `connect()` or accepted with `accept()`, and then after a `send()` fails with `WSAEWOULDBLOCK` and buffer space becomes available. Therefore, an application can assume that sends are possible starting from the first `FD_WRITE` message and lasting until a send returns `WSAEWOULDBLOCK`. After such a failure, the application will be notified that sends are again possible with a new `FD_WRITE` message.

A Visual C++ MFC example makes this more understandable. Following is a function to make a connection with a server. Note that this example is looking at this problem from the client's perspective, but a server uses the same techniques. The following code is similar to the `connect()` example except that it calls `WSAAsyncSelect()` with both `FD_CONNECT` and `FD_WRITE`.

```
BOOL CClientWindow::DoConnect()
{
  // m_s is the socket descriptor which is a member
  // variable of the CClientWindow class

  // m_s has already been created and bound to a default name

  // m_addrServer is the address of the server and has
  // already been assigned

  // get asycnchronous event notification of connect
  // and writeability to this object's window (m_hWnd)
  if (WSAAsyncSelect(m_s, m_hWnd, WM_USER + 1, FD_CONNECT ¦ FD_WRITE) ==
   SOCKET_ERROR)
  {
    // error ...
  }

  // make the connection
  if (connect(m_s, (LPSOCKADDR)&m_addrServer, sizeof(m_addrServer)) ==
   SOCKET_ERROR)
  {
    int nError = WSAGetLastError();
    if (nError != WSAEWOULDBLOCK)
    {
      // a real error ...
    }
  }
}
```

You also need a member function in `CClientWindow` to handle the `WM_USER + 1` message that's generated when a client connection is completed and when the socket is writeable.

```
BEGIN_MESSAGE_MAP(CClientWindow, CFrameWnd)
  //{{AFX_MSG_MAP(CClientWindow)
  ...
  ON_MESSAGE(WM_USER + 1, OnAsyncSelect)
...
  //}}AFX_MSG_MAP
END_MESSAGE_MAP()

LONG CMainFrame::OnAsyncSelect(WPARAM wParam, LPARAM lParam)
{
  int nError;                        // error status
  int nBytesSent;                    // bytes sent
  static char *pszBuf, *pszBufTmp;   // buffer to send
  static int nBufLen;                // length of buffer

  // check for an error
  if (WSAGETSELECTERROR(lParam) != 0)
```

```
{
  // ...
  return 0L;
}

// what event are we being notified of?
switch (WSAGETSELECTEVENT(lParam))
{
  case FD_CONNECT:
    // client made a connection

    // allocate some buffer space and fill
    // it with useful data to send
    nBufLen = 5000;
    pszBuf = (char *)malloc(nBufLen);
    if (pszBuf == NULL)
      nBufLen = 0;
    else
    {
      // this temporary pointer will be used
      // to move through the buffer
      pszBufTmp = pszBuf;

      // fill the buffer with some useful data to send ...
    }

    break; // case FD_CONNECT

  case FD_WRITE:
    // client can send data now

    // is there any data to send?
    if (nBufLen > 0)
    {
      // send as many bytes as possible
      do
      {
        // send data in 100 byte chunks
        if (nBufLen < 100)
          nBytesSent = send(m_s, pszBufTmp, nBufLen, 0);
        else
          nBytesSent = send(m_s, pszBufTmp, 100, 0);

        if (nBytesSent == SOCKET_ERROR)
        {
          nError = WSAGetLastError();
          if (nError == WSAEWOULDBLOCK)
            // ok, we'll get another FD_WRITE eventually
          else
            // a real error ...
        }
        else
        {
          // advance the pointer and decrement the byte count
          pszBufTmp += nBytesSent;
          nBufLen -= nBytesSent;

          if (nBufLen == 0)
```

```
                free(pszBuf);
            }
        }
        while ((nBytesSent != SOCKET_ERROR) && (nBufLen > 0));
    }

    break; // case FD_WRITE

  } // switch

  return 0L;
}
```

Notice that the asynchronous select message handler, `CClientWindow::OnAsyncSelect()`, handles multiple WinSock events, so a `switch` statement is used. As soon as the client's connect succeeds, the `FD_CONNECT` message is sent, telling you that the socket is connected. Immediately after that, the `FD_WRITE` message is sent, telling you that the socket is writeable. In this example, there is only one call to `WSAAsyncSelect()` done in `CClientWindow::DoConnect()`. This single call registers interest in both the `FD_CONNECT` and the `FD_WRITE` events. You also could use two separate calls. The first call, in the `DoConnect()` member function, could simply register interest in `FD_CONNECT`. Then, in the `OnAsyncSelect()` member function's handling of `FD_CONNECT`, you could call `WSAAsyncSelect()` expressing interest in just the `FD_WRITE` event. Either technique gives the same result.

In this example, a buffer is allocated and filled with data to send in response to the `FD_CONNECT` event. The `FD_WRITE` handler sends the data in 100-byte pieces until the entire buffer is transmitted. I used 100-byte buffers in this example so that you could see the `do-while` loop in action. This loop is executed as long as there are bytes to send and there are no errors. If you get a `WSAEWOULDBLOCK` error, it doesn't pose a problem because the `FD_WRITE` handler will be called again as soon as the network subsystem can do it. Thanks to the use of the static variables, when the `FD_WRITE` handler gets called again, the rest of the buffer is sent from where it left off.

Receiving Data

Sending is just half the battle. This section describes receiving data using the `recv()` function. Its prototype is as follows:

```
int PASCAL FAR recv(SOCKET s, char FAR * buf, int len, int flags);
```

`s` is the connected socket from which to receive data. `buf` is a pointer to a buffer that will receive the data. `len` is the size of `buf`. `flags` specifies the way in which the `recv()` call is made. `flags` can be any of the following logically ORed together: 0 (zero) for no special receive options, `MSG_PEEK` to copy the data to `buf` but not remove it from the internal WinSock queues, and `MSG_OOB` to process out-of-band data. On success, `recv()` returns the number of bytes of received. This could range from 0 (zero) to `len`.

A return value of 0 (zero) means the connection has been closed. On failure, SOCKET_ERROR is returned and WSAGetLastError() specifies: WSANOTINITIALIZED if WinSock wasn't initialized with WSAStartup(); WSAENETDOWN if the network subsystem is failing; WSAEINTR if the blocking call was canceled with WSACancelBlockingCall(); WSAEINPROGRESS if a blocking call is in progress; WSAENOTCONN if the socket s isn't connected; WSAENOTSOCK if the socket s isn't a valid socket descriptor; WSAEOPNOTSUPP if MSG_OOB was specified by flags but the socket s isn't a stream socket; WSAESHUTDOWN if the socket s has been shutdown; WSAEWOULDBLOCK if the socket s is marked as nonblocking and the recv() would block; WSAEMSGSIZE if socket s is a datagram socket and the datagram was too large for buf; WSAEINVAL if the socket s hasn't been bound; WSAECONNABORTED if the virtual circuit was aborted due to timeout or other failure; WSAECONNRESET if the virtual circuit was reset by the remote side.

The following demonstrates a typical call to recv():

```
SOCKET s;                // socket to communicate over
#define BUFSIZE (100)    // receive buffer size
char pszBuf[BUFSIZE];    // buffer to receive data
int nBytesRecv;          // number of bytes received
int nError;              // error status

// create, bind, and connect socket s ...

nBytesRecv = recv(s, pszBuf, BUFSIZE, 0);
if (nBytesRecv == SOCKET_ERROR)
{
  nError = WSAGetLastError();
}
else
{
  // nBytesRecv is the number of bytes successfully received
}
```

The recv() function has the same problem with blocking as the accept(), connect(), getXbyY, and send() functions. If there is no data waiting to be received, recv() blocks waiting for the sender to send some data. While recv() is blocking, the user loses control over your application. To prevent this problem, the WSAAsyncSelect() function is used to put the socket into nonblocking receive mode. The event of interest in this scenario is FD_READ. An FD_READ message is posted when a socket has data available to be read.

FD_READ works differently from FD_WRITE. For FD_WRITE, you get a single FD_WRITE when the socket is first connected. You must then send data until the send() results in a WSAEWOULDBLOCK error. You won't get another FD_WRITE message until the condition that generated the WSAEWOULDBLOCK is cleared up. With FD_READ, you get the first FD_READ when data first arrives. If you then do a recv() and there is still more data waiting to be received, you will receive another FD_READ event notification. For example, suppose that the TCP/IP layer receives 100 bytes of data on a socket and WinSock posts a FD_READ

message to the appropriate window. If the application calls `recv()` with a buffer size of only 50, the first 50 bytes are returned in the buffer, and WinSock posts another `FD_READ` message to let the application know there is data still waiting to be read.

A Visual C++ MFC example makes this more understandable. Following is a function to make a connection with a server. Note that this example is looking at this problem from the client's perspective but a server uses the same techniques. The following code is similar to the `connect()` example.

```
BOOL CClientWindow::DoConnect()
{
  // m_s is the socket descriptor which is a member
  // variable of the CClientWindow class

  // m_s has already been created and bound to a default name

  // m_addrServer is the address of the server and has
  // already been assigned

  // get asycnchronous event notification of connect
  if (WSAAsyncSelect(m_s, m_hWnd, WM_USER + 1, FD_CONNECT) ==
   SOCKET_ERROR)
  {
    // error ...
  }

  // make the connection
  if (connect(m_s, (LPSOCKADDR)&m_addrServer, sizeof(m_addrServer)) ==
   SOCKET_ERROR)
  {
    int nError = WSAGetLastError();
    if (nError != WSAEWOULDBLOCK)
    {
      // a real error ...
    }
  }
}
```

You also need a member function in `CClientWindow` to handle the `WM_USER + 1` message that's generated when a client connection is completed and when the socket is readable:

```
BEGIN_MESSAGE_MAP(CClientWindow, CFrameWnd)
  //{{AFX_MSG_MAP(CClientWindow)
  ...
  ON_MESSAGE(WM_USER + 1, OnAsyncSelect)
...
  //}}AFX_MSG_MAP
END_MESSAGE_MAP()

LONG CMainFrame::OnAsyncSelect(WPARAM wParam, LPARAM lParam)
{
#define BUFSIZE (100)
  char pszBuf[BUFSIZE];          // receive buffer
  int nError;                    // error status
  int nBytesRecv;                // bytes received
```

```
  // check for an error
  if (WSAGETSELECTERROR(lParam) != 0)
  {
    // ...
    return 0L;
  }

  // what event are we being notified of?
  switch (WSAGETSELECTEVENT(lParam))
  {
    case FD_CONNECT:
      // client made a connection

      // get notices of readability
      if (WSAAsyncSelect(m_s, m_hWnd, WM_USER + 1, FD_READ) ==
       SOCKET_ERROR)
      {
        // error ...
      }

      break; // case FD_CONNECT

    case FD_READ:
      // client can receive data now

      nBytesRecv = recv(m_s, pszBuf, BUFSIZE, 0);
      if (nBytesRecv == SOCKET_ERROR)
      {
        nError = WSAGetLastError();
        if (nError == WSAEWOULDBLOCK)
          // this should never happen but handle it anyway
          // so it is differentiated from a real error
        else
          // a real error ...
      }
      else
      {
        // got some data ...
      }

      break; // case FD_READ

  } // switch

  return 0L;
}
```

Notice that the asynchronous select message handler, `CClientWindow::OnAsyncSelect()`, handles multiple WinSock events, so a `switch` statement is used. As soon as the client's connect succeeds, the `FD_CONNECT` message is sent, telling us that the socket is connected. This example uses two separate calls to `WSAAsyncSelect()`. The first call, in the `DoConnect()` member function, simply registers interest in `FD_CONNECT`. Then, in the `OnAsyncSelect()` member function's handling of `FD_CONNECT`, `WSAAsyncSelect()` is called again, this time expressing interest in just the `FD_READ` event.

Out-of-band data is received similarly to regular in-line data, unless the socket is configured to receive out-of-band data in-line. When a socket is configured this way, out-of-band data's urgency loses its effectiveness. Assuming that a socket isn't receiving out-of-band data in-line, the only differences to the preceding code would be as follows. The line that registers interest in the FD_READ event is expanded to read:

```
if (WSAAsyncSelect(m_s, m_hWnd, WM_USER + 1, FD_READ ¦ FD_OOB) ==
 SOCKET_ERROR)
{
  // error ...
}
```

You also need a FD_OOB handler in the CMainFrame::OnAsyncSelect() function. It is identical to the FD_READ event handler except the call to recv() is as follows:

```
nBytesRecv = recv(m_s, pszBuf, BUFSIZE, MSG_OOB);
```

Datagram-Oriented Client/Server Communication

Datagram-oriented client/server communication, using socket type SOCK_DGRAM, is simpler than the stream-oriented communication described in the preceding section. A server doesn't need to listen for and accept connections from clients, and a client doesn't need to connect to a server. Instead, each piece of data is individually addressed.

How a Server Prepares for Communication

In the stream environment, a server must create a socket, bind the socket to a well-known name, listen for connections on the socket, and accept connections on the socket. In the datagram environment, a server must only create a socket and bind the socket to a well-known name.

Creating the socket is exactly like the stream counterpart except that SOCK_DGRAM is specified rather than SOCK_STREAM:

```
SOCKET s;
s = socket(AF_INET, SOCK_DGRAM, 0);
```

The last step in preparing a server for communication is binding the socket to a well-known name. This procedure is identical to that of the stream socket:

```
SOCKADDR_IN addr;
int nError;

addr.sin_family = AF_INET;
addr.sin_port = htons(2050);
addr.sin_addr.s_addr = htonl(INADDR_ANY);
```

```
if (bind(s, (LPSOCKADDR)&addr, sizeof(addr)) == SOCKET_ERROR)
{
  nError = WSAGetLastError();
  // ...
}
```

In this code snippet, the server is preparing to receive data on port 2050, from any network interface the host has available.

How a Client Prepares for Communication

In the stream environment, a client must create a socket, fill out an Internet address structure of the server, and connect to the server. In the datagram environment, a client must only create a socket. After that, an Internet address structure is used for each communication.

Sending Datagram Data

To send a datagram, use the `sendto()` function. Its prototype is as follows:

```
int PASCAL FAR sendto(SOCKET s, const char FAR * buf, int len, int flags,
 const struct sockaddr FAR *to, int tolen);
```

`s` is the socket to send on. `buf` is a pointer to the data to send. `len` is the length of the `buf` buffer. `flags` specifies the way in which `sendto()` is called. `flags` can be any of the following logically ORed together: 0 (zero) for no special send options, `MSG_DONTROUTE` if the data shouldn't be subject to routing, and `MSG_OOB` to send out-of-band data. `to` is a pointer to the Internet address of the intended receiver. For WinSock 1.1, `to` must be a `sockaddr_in` structure. `tolen` is the length of the `to` parameter.

On success, `sendto()` returns the number of bytes sent. On failure, `SOCKET_ERROR` is returned and `WSAGetLastError()` should be called. Possible error values are the following: `WSANOTINITIALIZED` if WinSock wasn't initialized with `WSAStartup()`; `WSAENETDOWN` if the network subsystem is failing; `WSAEACCESS` if the address is a broadcast address but the appropriate flag was not set; `WSAEINTR` if the blocking call was canceled with `WSACancelBlockingCall()`; `WSAEINPROGRESS` if a blocking call is in progress; `WSAEFAULT` if `buf` or `to` are not in a valid part of the user address space or if `to` is too small to hold a `sockaddr` structure; `WSAENETRESET` if the connection needs to be reset; `WSAENOBUFS` if there is a internal WinSock buffer deadlock; `WSAENOTCONN` if the socket `s` isn't connected (for `SOCK_STREAM` only); `WSAENOTSOCK` if the socket `s` isn't a valid socket descriptor; `WSAEOPNOTSUPP` if `MSG_OOB` was specified by `flags` but the socket `s` isn't a stream socket; `WSAESHUTDOWN` if the socket `s` has been shutdown; `WSAEWOULDBLOCK` if the socket `s` is marked as nonblocking and the `sendto()` would block; `WSAEMSGSIZE` if socket `s` is a datagram socket and the `buf` buffer is larger than the maximum supported by the particular WinSock implementation; `WSAECONNABORTED` if the virtual circuit was aborted due to timeout or other failure; `WSAECONNRESET` if the virtual circuit was reset by the remote

side; WSAEADDRNOTAVAIL if the address specified by to isn't available from the local machine; WSAENOSUPPORT if the addresses in the specified family can't be used with this socket; WSAEDESTADDRREQ if a destination address is required; or WSAENETUNREACH if the network can't be reached from this host at this time.

CAUTION

The WSAEMSGSIZE error will result if you try to send too large a datagram. This maximum is WinSock vendor dependent. To find out the maximum size for your particular WinSock implementation, examine the iMaxUdpDg variable in the WSAData structure that was passed to WSAStartup().

Here is an example of using the sendto() function:

```
SOCKET s;
SOCKADDR_IN addr;
#define BUFSIZE (100)
char pszBuf[BUFSIZE];
int nBufLen;
int nBytesSent;
int nError;

s = socket(AF_INET, SOCK_DGRAM, 0);
if (s == INVALID_SOCKET)
{
  nError = WSAGetLastError();
  // ...
}
else
{
  // fill out the address of the recipient
  addr.sin_family = AF_INET;
  addr.sin_port = htons(2050);
  addr.sin_addr.s_addr = inet_addr("166.78.16.150");

  // assign some data to send
  lstrcpy(pszBuf, "Hello, World!");
  nBufLen = lstrlen(pszBuf);

  // send the datagram
  nBytesSent = sendto(s, pszBuf, nBufLen, 0, (LPSOCKADDR)&addr, sizeof(addr));
  if (nBytesSent == SOCKET_ERROR)
  {
    nError = WSAGetLastError();
    // ...
  }
  else
  {
    // data was sent
  }

  closesocket(s);
}
```

In this example, data is sent to port 2050 on the host with IP address 166.78.16.150. Notice that no connection was established before transmission.

One of the capabilities of datagram sockets (SOCK_DGRAM) is that they can be sent to multiple recipients with one call to sendto(). This is accomplished by specifying the INADDR_BROADCAST address, as in the following:

```
addr.sin_addr.s_addr = htonl(INADDR_BROADCAST);
```

By default, a socket doesn't support broadcast transmission. If you try to send to the INADDR_BROADCAST address, you get the WSAEACCESS error. To remedy this, use the setsockopt() function, as in the following:

```
BOOL bBroadcast = TRUE;    // TRUE = enable, FALSE = disable
setsockopt(s, SOL_SOCKET, SO_BROADCAST,
(LPSTR)&bBroadcast, sizeof(bBroadcast));
```

sendto() may block, so you can use WSAAsyncSelect(), just as it was used for stream communication, by expressing interest in the FD_WRITE event.

Receiving Datagram Data

To receive a datagram, use the recvfrom() function. Its prototype is as follows:

```
int PASCAL FAR recvfrom(SOCKET s, char FAR * buf, int len, int flags,
 struct sockaddr FAR *from, int FAR * fromlen);
```

s is the socket descriptor to use for communication. buf is a buffer to accept the incoming data. len is the size of buf. flags specifies the way recvfrom() is made. flags can be any of the following logically ORed together: 0 (zero) for no special receive options, MSG_PEEK to peek at the incoming data by copying it into buf but not removing it from the input queue, and MSG_OOB to receive out-of-band data (for streams only). from is an optional pointer to a sockaddr_in structure, which will contain the address of the sending socket upon return of recvfrom(). fromlen is an optional pointer to the length of from. fromlen should be initialized to the size of sockaddr_in before it is used.

On success, recvfrom() returns the number of bytes received. On failure, SOCKET_ERROR is returned and WSAGetLastError() should be called. Possible error values are as follows: WSANOTINITIALIZED if WinSock wasn't initialized with WSAStartup(); WSAENETDOWN if the network subsystem is failing; WSAEINTR if the blocking call was canceled with WSACancelBlockingCall(); WSAEINPROGRESS if a blocking call is in progress; WSAEFAULT if fromlen is too small to hold a sockaddr structure; WSAEINVAL if socket s isn't bound; WSAENOTCONN if the socket s isn't connected (for SOCK_STREAM only); WSAENOTSOCK if the socket s isn't a valid socket descriptor; WSAEOPNOTSUPP if MSG_OOB was specified by flags but the socket s isn't a stream socket; WSAESHUTDOWN if the socket s has been shutdown; WSAEWOULDBLOCK if the socket s is marked as nonblocking and the sendto() would block;

WSAEMSGSIZE if socket s is a datagram socket and the data was too large to fit into buf (the data is truncated); WSAECONNABORTED if the virtual circuit was aborted due to timeout or other failure; or WSAECONNRESET if the virtual circuit was reset by the remote side.

Here is an example of using the recvfrom() function in a datagram server application:

```
char pszMessage[100];    // informational message
SOCKET s;                // socket to receive data on
SOCKADDR_IN addr;        // address of the socket
#define BUFSIZE (100)    // receive buffer size
char pszBuf[BUFSIZE];    // receive buffer
int nBytesRecv;          // number of bytes received
int nError;              // error code
SOCKADDR_IN addrFrom;    // address of sender
int nAddrFromLen = sizeof(addrFrom);  // lengh of sender structure
IN_ADDR inFrom;          // IP address of sender

s = socket(AF_INET, SOCK_DGRAM, 0);
if (s == INVALID_SOCKET)
{
  nError = WSAGetLastError();
  // ...
}
else
{
  // fill out the name this server will read data from
  addr.sin_family = AF_INET;
  addr.sin_port = htons(2050);
  addr.sin_addr.s_addr = htonl(INADDR_ANY);

  // bind the name to the socket
  if (bind(s, (LPSOCKADDR)&addr, sizeof(addr)) == SOCKET_ERROR)
  {
    nError = WSAGetLastError();
    // ...
  }
  else
  {
    nBytesRecv = recvfrom(s, pszBuf, 100, 0,
     (LPSOCKADDR)&addrFrom, &nAddrFromLen);
    if (nBytesRecv == SOCKET_ERROR)
    {
      nError = WSAGetLastError();
      // ...
    }
    else
    {
      // got some data ...

      // copy the four byte IP address into an IP address structure
      memcpy(&inFrom, &addrFrom.sin_addr.s_addr, 4);

      // print an informational message
      wsprintf(pszMessage,
       "server received %d bytes from %s, port is %d",
       nBytesRecv, inet_ntoa(inFrom), ntohs(addrFrom.sin_port));
```

```
        MessageBox(pszMessage, "Datagram Server Info");
      }
    }

    closesocket(s);
}
```

Note that in this example the optional from parameter was provided. This gives the receiver the ability to send data back to the sender. This is demonstrated in the next chapter's datagram example program.

As with the sendto() function, the recvfrom() function may block. Use WSAAsyncSelect() with the FD_READ event to solve this problem. Implementation is similar to that of the stream example.

Closing a Socket

The previous sections explain how network applications create sockets and communicate through them. The last thing to do is close the socket. The closesocket() function's prototype is as follows:

```
int PASCAL FAR closesocket(SOCKET s);
```

s is the socket to close. On success, it returns 0 (zero). On failure, SOCKET_ERROR is returned and WSAGetLastError() reveals the following: WSANOTINITIALIZED if WinSock wasn't initialized with WSAStartup(); WSAENETDOWN if the network subsystem is failing; WSAEINTR if the blocking call was canceled with WSACancelBlockingCall(); WSAEINPROGRESS if a blocking call is in progress; WSAENOTSOCK if the socket s isn't a valid socket descriptor; or WSAEWOULDBLOCK if the socket s is marked as nonblocking and the closesocket() would block.

There are several variables that determine the closing characteristics of a socket. These characteristics are determined by the socket's linger options as set with setsockopt() (see Table 7.2).

Table 7.2. Linger Behavior on closesocket().

Option	*Interval*	*Type of Close*	*Wait for Close?*
SO_LINGER	Zero	Hard	No
SO_LINGER	Nonzero	Graceful	Yes
SO_DONTLINGER	Don't care	Graceful	No

If SO_LINGER is set with a zero timeout interval, closesocket() isn't blocked, even if queued data has not yet been sent or acknowledged. This is called a hard close because the socket is closed immediately and any unsent data is lost. Any recv() call on the remote side of the circuit can fail with WSAECONNRESET.

If SO_LINGER is set with a nonzero timeout interval, the closesocket() call blocks until the remaining data has been sent or until the timeout expires. This is called a graceful disconnect. Note that if the socket is set to nonblocking and SO_LINGER is set to a nonzero timeout, the call to closesocket() will fail with an error of WSAEWOULDBLOCK.

If SO_DONTLINGER is set on a stream socket, the closesocket() call will return immediately. However, any data queued for transmission will be sent, if possible, before the underlying socket is closed. This is also called a graceful disconnect. Note that in this case, the WinSock implementation may not release the socket and other resources for an arbitrary period, which may affect applications that expect to use all available sockets.

To set the linger options of a socket, use setsockopt(). The following three code segments demonstrate the three entries in Table 7.2.

```
// Option     Interval  Type of Close  Wait for Close?
// SO_LINGER  Zero      Hard           No
LINGER ling;
ling.l_onoff = 1;  // linger on
ling.l_linger = 0; // timeout in seconds
setsockopt(s, SOL_SOCKET, SO_LINGER, (LPSTR)&ling, sizeof(ling));

// Option     Interval  Type of Close  Wait for Close?
// SO_LINGER  Non-zero  Graceful       Yes
LINGER ling;
ling.l_onoff = 1;  // linger on
ling.l_linger = 5; // timeout in seconds
setsockopt(s, SOL_SOCKET, SO_LINGER, (LPSTR)&ling, sizeof(ling));

// Option         Interval    Type of Close  Wait for Close?
// SO_DONTLINGER  Don't care  Graceful       No
LINGER ling;
ling.l_onoff = 0;  // linger off
ling.l_linger = 0; // timeout in seconds
setsockopt(s, SOL_SOCKET, SO_LINGER, (LPSTR)&ling, sizeof(ling));
```

If your application wants to know when the socket has been closed, use WSAAsyncSelect() and specify the FD_CLOSE event. If WSAGETSELECTERROR returns 0 (zero) for the FD_CLOSE event, the socket was closed gracefully. An error value of WSAECONNRESET tells you the socket was abortively disconnected.

Summary

This chapter discussed the socket related functions necessary to make a client/server application, using both datagrams and streams. Stream communication is complicated by the need to make the connection between the client and server, but this trade-off provides for a robust communication path. Although datagram communication is easy to initiate, it is limited by its inherent unreliability.

The next chapter develops four sample applications that use the functions discussed in this chapter. These sample chapters provide the cohesion between this chapter's disparate presentation of several WinSock functions.

8

Sample Applications

This chapter presents four sample programs that make use of the WinSock functions described in the preceding three chapters. The first sample initializes WinSock and offers you a dialog box to view specifics about the WinSock implementation on which the program is running. The second sample application gives you access to WinSock database functions, in both their blocking and nonblocking modes of operation. The third and fourth samples are composed of two programs each: a client that sends either datagrams or stream data and a server that receives them and sends them back to the client.

Maintaining 16-Bit and 32-Bit Projects

With the help of the Microsoft Foundation Class library, it's very easy to maintain the same source code for both a 16-bit executable and a 32-bit executable. Unfortunately, maintaining the Visual C++ projects for these different executable versions isn't as easy. The project files (makefiles) for 16-bit Visual C++ 1.5 and 32-bit Visual C++ 1.1 aren't compatible; you must maintain two separate projects.

The easiest way to do this is to use the Visual C++ product that you like best (16-bit or 32-bit) to create a project and then create a makefile for the other environment. As an example, suppose that a project named PROJ is initially developed with the 16-bit compiler. The Visual C++ 16-bit project file is called PROJ.MAK. After program development is far enough along, rename the PROJ.MAK file to PROJ.M16 and remove all temporary files in the project's directory (for example, *.OBJ and *.RES). Next, launch 32-bit Visual C++ and select New... from the Project menu. Add all of the source needed to build the project, as well as any libraries it needs to link with. Call this new project PROJ as well. Use this project file to build the 32-bit version. When you wish to switch back to the 16-bit environment, rename PROJ.MAK to PROJ.M32 and then copy PROJ.M16 to PROJ.MAK.

If you're wondering why not just use different project names such as PROJ16.MAK and PROJ32.MAK, the answer lies in Visual C++ and its associated tools, such as App Studio and ClassWizard. These tools use the project file's name when determining what other files are named. This makes it difficult to use App Studio and ClassWizard effectively. This limitation also makes it difficult to use separate directories for the projects, as in \PROJ\16BIT\PROJ.MAK and \PROJ\32BIT\PROJ.MAK.

To simplify the procedure of switching between 16-bit and 32-bit project files, a couple of batch files are used. The batch file shown in Listing 8.1 is used to select which project file to use. Note that this batch file should be used only when you're prepared to build the project under the new compiler, because all of the object files and other temporary files are removed by running the script.

Listing 8.1. USE.BAT batch file.

```
@ECHO OFF
REM Replace PROJ with the actual project name

IF "%1"=="16" GOTO USE
IF "%1"=="32" GOTO USE

ECHO Directions for use: USE 16 or USE 32
GOTO END

:USE
IF NOT EXIST PROJ.M%1 GOTO NOFILE
DEL *.APS
DEL *.BSC
DEL *.CLW
DEL *.EXE
DEL *.OBJ
DEL *.PCH
DEL *.PDB
DEL *.RES
DEL *.SBR
DEL *.VCW
DEL *.WSP
COPY PROJ.M%1 PROJ.MAK
GOTO END

:NOFILE
ECHO %1-bit project file does not exist
GOTO END

:END
```

The batch file shown in Listing 8.2 is a script used to save the project file to the appropriate 16-bit or 32-bit makefile. Be careful when using this batch file because you could accidentally write over the 16-bit makefile with the 32-bit version, and vice versa. For example, don't run 32-bit Visual C++, exit Visual C++, and then run SAVE 16. This will cause you to lose the 16-bit project file.

Listing 8.2. SAVE.BAT batch file.

```
@ECHO OFF
REM Replace PROJ with the actual project name

IF "%1"=="16" GOTO USE
IF "%1"=="32" GOTO USE

ECHO Directions for use: SAVE 16 or SAVE 32
GOTO END

:USE
```

continues

Listing 8.2. continued

```
ECHO Are you sure you are saving the correct version?
ECHO Press CTRL-C to abort this procedure
PAUSE
COPY PROJ.MAK PROJ.M%1

:END
```

Using these two batch files to support 16-bit and 32-bit project makefiles gives you the flexibility of using either development environment with the same source code.

CAUTION

16-bit Visual C++ users: The WINVER.H header file shipped with Visual C++ 1.1 32-bit edition is named VER.H in Visual C++ 1.5. This header file is for the support of version information and is included in the RC2 file created by AppWizard. One possible solution would be to use an `ifdef` in the RC2 file, as in

```
#ifdef _WIN32
#include "winver.h"
#else
#include "ver.h"
#endif
```

Apparently, though, the Visual C++ resource compiler doesn't interpret preprocessor directives as you might expect when they appear in an RC2 file. The solution I use is to copy VER.H to WINVER.H in the 16-bit Visual C++'s include directory (that is, C:\MSVC\INCLUDE).

The sample programs in this book rely on WINVER.H's existence. If you don't copy VER.H to WINVER.H, you'll receive a compile error about not finding WINVER.H.

Reference the Microsoft Knowledgebase article Q103719 dated January 20, 1994, for more details on migrating 16-bit makefiles to 32-bit.

WinSock TCP/IP Stack Information

This program, WSINFO, allows you to view the details of the WinSock TCP/IP stack that the computer is running. It uses the following WinSock functions: `WSAStartup()`, `WSACleanup()`, and `WSAGetLastError()`. This program is generated using Visual C++'s AppWizard feature, which creates a skeleton application from which to build upon. This book isn't geared toward the beginning Visual C++ programmer, so only the first sample program is worked through step by step.

The first step in producing this program is to use AppWizard to generate a skeletal application. This application uses the Single Document Interface rather than the Multiple Document Interface. There's no need for any special features such as a toolbar, printing and print preview, context-sensitive help, or Object Linking and Embedding. This application is very simple in comparison to most. Use WSINFO as the project name.

After AppWizard has finished its magic, edit WSINFO.H. This file contains the class declaration for the application class `CWsinfoApp`. Add the following publicly accessible member variables to the class:

```
WSADATA m_wsaData;        // WinSock information
BOOL m_bWinSockOK;        // TRUE if WinSock startup succeeded
int m_nWinSockError;      // WinSock error code
```

`m_wsaData` contains the WinSock information returned by `WSAStartup()`. `m_bWinSockOK` is TRUE if WinSock startup succeeded; it's FALSE otherwise. `m_nWinSockError` contains the error code if WinSock startup failed. The WSINFO.H file is also a good place to include the WINSOCK.H header file because WSINFO.H is included in the other source files of the project. Add the `ExitInstance()` function to the class. This function is called when the application exits, allowing us a good opportunity to shutdown WinSock.

At this point, the `CWsinfoApp` class looks like the following:

```
class CWsinfoApp : public CWinApp
{
public:
  WSADATA m_wsaData;        // WinSock information
  BOOL m_bWinSockOK;        // TRUE if WinSock startup succeeded
  int m_nWinSockError;      // WinSock error code

public:
  CWsinfoApp();

// Overrides
  virtual BOOL InitInstance();
  virtual int ExitInstance();
```

```
// Implementation

  //{{AFX_MSG(CWsinfoApp)
  afx_msg void OnAppAbout();
  //}}AFX_MSG
  DECLARE_MESSAGE_MAP()
};
```

Edit the WSINFO.CPP file to modify the `InitInstance()` and `ExitInstance()` CWsinfoApp class member functions. In `InitInstance()`, `WSAStartup()` is called. When modifications to `InitInstance()` are completed, it looks like the following:

```
BOOL CWsinfoApp::InitInstance()
{
  // WinSock startup
  // If WSAStartup() is successful, we still
  // need to check the version numbers.

  WORD wVersionRequired = MAKEWORD(1, 1);  // WinSock 1.1 required
  m_bWinSockOK = FALSE;                    // not OK
  m_nWinSockError = 0;                     // no WinSock error
  if (WSAStartup(wVersionRequired, &m_wsaData) == 0)
  {
    if (wVersionRequired == m_wsaData.wVersion)
      m_bWinSockOK = TRUE;
    else
      WSACleanup();
  }
  else
    m_nWinSockError = WSAGetLastError();

  // Standard initialization
  // If you are not using these features and wish to reduce the size
  //  of your final executable, you should remove from the following
  //  the specific initialization routines you do not need.

  SetDialogBkColor();         // set dialog background color to gray
  LoadStdProfileSettings();   // Load standard INI file options (including MRU)

  // Register the application's document templates.  Document templates
  //  serve as the connection between documents, frame windows and views.

  AddDocTemplate(new CSingleDocTemplate(IDR_MAINFRAME,
      RUNTIME_CLASS(CWsinfoDoc),
      RUNTIME_CLASS(CMainFrame),     // main SDI frame window
      RUNTIME_CLASS(CWsinfoView)));


  // create a new (empty) document
  OnFileNew();

  if (m_lpCmdLine[0] != '\0')
  {
    // TODO: add command line processing here
  }

  return TRUE;
}
```

In `ExitInstance()`, `WSACleanup()` is called. When modifications to `ExitInstance()` are completed, it looks like the following:

```
int CWsinfoApp::ExitInstance()
{
  // WinSock cleanup
  // If WinSock was started successfully, it must be shutdown.

  if (m_bWinSockOK)
    WSACleanup();

  // call the base class' member function

  return CWinApp::ExitInstance();
}
```

Note that the base class's `ExitInstance()` function is called to allow for the default processing of this event.

Now use App Studio to create a dialog box resource. This dialog box is used to display the information contained in the `WSADATA` structure that's defined in the application's class. Give the dialog box a caption of "WinSock Information" and an ID of IDD_DIALOG_WINSOCK_INFO. By default, App Studio includes an OK and Cancel button in a dialog; remove the Cancel button because this dialog box is for informational purposes only and its return value is simply ignored. To display the data stored in the `WSADATA` structure, we need several fields. This example uses EDIT controls to display this information. Each EDIT control is preceded by a STATIC text control, which acts as a label. Create five `EDIT` controls aligned vertically with the following names: `IDC_EDIT_VERSION`, `IDC_EDIT_DESCRIPTION`, `IDC_EDIT_STATUS`, `IDC_EDIT_MAXIMUM_SOCKETS`, and `IDC_EDIT_MAXIMUM_DATAGRAM_SIZE`.

From within App Studio and with the "WinSock Information" dialog box selected, run ClassWizard to create a class associated with this dialog resource. Name the class `CWinSockInfoDlg` with a base class of `CDialog`. Change the name of the source files that ClassWizard creates for this class to INFODLG.CPP and INFODLG.H.

After the class is created, use ClassWizard to create a function to handle the dialog box initialization phase. With the `CWinSockInfoDlg` class name selected, select `CWinSockInfoDlg` under ClassWizard's Object ID list. When you do this, a whole bunch of stuff will fill the Messages section of the ClassWizard window. These are the Windows messages that may be sent to the `CWinSockInfoDlg` class. Scroll down to the `WM_INITDIALOG` message and then click on the Add Function button. ClassWizard automatically generates a stub function called`OnInitDialog()`.

Exit App Studio and edit the INFODLG.CPP file. Add code to populate the fields of the dialog box with the information stored in the `WSADATA` structure. The `WSADATA` structure is a public member variable of the `CWsinfoApp` class, so you can access it from the

`CWinSockInfoDlg` class by getting a pointer to the application object. The `AfxGetApp()` function is used for this purpose. The `OnInitDialog()` function should look like this when you're done:

```
BOOL CWinSockInfoDlg::OnInitDialog()
{
  CDialog::OnInitDialog();

  // initialize the fields of the dialog box

  CWsinfoApp *pApp = (CWsinfoApp *)AfxGetApp(); // pointer to app
  LPWSADATA pWsaData = &(pApp->m_wsaData);      // pointer to app's WinSock info
  char pszMsg[100];                             // buffer to use for formatting

  wsprintf(pszMsg, "%d.%d",
   (int)(HIBYTE(pWsaData->wVersion)), (int)(LOBYTE(pWsaData->wVersion)));
  SetDlgItemText(IDC_EDIT_VERSION, pszMsg);
  SetDlgItemText(IDC_EDIT_DESCRIPTION, pWsaData->szDescription);
  SetDlgItemText(IDC_EDIT_STATUS, pWsaData->szSystemStatus);
  wsprintf(pszMsg, "%u", pWsaData->iMaxSockets);
  SetDlgItemText(IDC_EDIT_MAXIMUM_SOCKETS, pszMsg);
  wsprintf(pszMsg, "%u", pWsaData->iMaxUdpDg);
  SetDlgItemText(IDC_EDIT_MAXIMUM_DATAGRAM_SIZE, pszMsg);

  return TRUE;  // return TRUE  unless you set the focus to a control
}
```

Now you have enough code to start WinSock and to populate an informational dialog box. The only thing missing is a way to launch the dialog box. Start App Studio and edit the menu resource. Add a menu item under the Help selection with a caption of "WinSock Information" and an ID of `ID_WINSOCK_INFO`. Run the ClassWizard to generate a function for the `ID_WINSOCK_INFO` message. Select `CWsinfoApp` for the class name, and then scroll through the object IDs until you reach `ID_WINSOCK_INFO`. In the message section, select COMMAND and then click the Add Function button. Use `OnWinsockInfo` as the function name to handle this menu item being selected. The code for the `OnWinsockInfo` member function looks like the following:

```
void CWsinfoApp::OnWinsockInfo()
{
  // If WinSock startup was successful, display an informational
  // dialog box; otherwise, display an error message

  if (m_bWinSockOK)
  {
    CWinSockInfoDlg dlg;
    dlg.DoModal();
  }
  else
  {
    char pszError[100];
    if (m_nWinSockError)
      wsprintf(pszError, "WinSock startup failed with error %d",
       m_nWinSockError);
    else
```

```
        lstrcpy(pszError, "WinSock does not meet version requirements");

      AfxMessageBox(pszError);
    }
}
```

The only thing remaining before compiling and running the program is to change the linker options so that WINSOCK.LIB or WSOCK32.LIB is linked in for the 16-bit or 32-bit version, respectively.

Figure 8.1 shows the WinSock Information menu item about to be selected. Figure 8.2 shows the result running on Windows NT using the WinSock TCP/IP stack supplied by Microsoft.

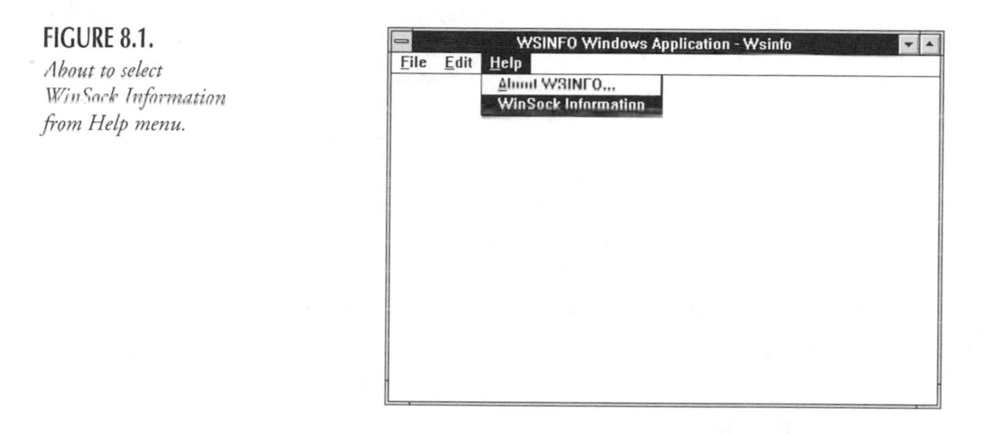

FIGURE 8.1.
About to select WinSock Information from Help menu.

FIGURE 8.2.
WinSock Information for the Windows NT TCP/IP Stack.

You may want to use the `CWinSockInfoDlg` class in applications you develop. It can be very useful as a debugging aid.

WinSock Database Test Application

This program, DBTST, allows you to execute WinSock database lookups for hosts and services. It uses the following WinSock functions: `WSAStartup()`, `WSACleanup()`, `WSAGetLastError()`, `WSACancelAsyncRequest()`, `WSAAsyncGetHostByName()`, `WSAAsyncGetHostByAddr()`, `gethostbyname()`, `gethostbyaddr()`, `WSAAsyncGetServByName()`, `WSAAsyncGetServByPort()`, `getservbybname()`, `getservbyport()`, and `ntohs()`. This program is created from scratch without the benefit of AppWizard. Visual C++ project files are utilized.

Extra steps must be taken when creating programs from scratch, as opposed to letting AppWizard do the grunt work. The benefit of creating a program from scratch is that you don't have to deal with possibly unneeded features such as documents and views. This approach is closer to doing things the old SDK way, but it still benefits from the Microsoft Foundation Classes.

The first source files to look at are STDAFX.H and STDAFX.CPP. These files support the precompiled header feature. By including STDAFX.H in each implementation file (that is, *.CPP), there's no need to include the mandatory Windows and MFC header files in each. STDAFX.H and STDAFX.CPP are shown in Listings 8.3 and 8.4, respectively. You must configure the compiler's precompiled header compiler option to use this feature.

Listing 8.3. STDAFX.H for DBTST.

```
#include <afxwin.h>
#include <winsock.h>
```

Listing 8.4. STDAFX.CPP for DBTST.

```
#include "stdafx.h"
```

The next files of interest implement the application object `CTheApp`. `CTheApp` is derived from the MFC class `CWinApp`. The class declaration is in DBTST.H, shown in Listing 8.5. The class is implemented in DBTST.CPP and is shown in Listing 8.6. Note that the WinSock startup isn't as robust as in the WSINFO example; there are no error messages displayed on error, for example. Instead, the application simply exits immediately if WinSock can't be initialized.

Listing 8.5. DBTST.H for DBTST.

```
#ifndef __DBTST_H__
#define __DBTST_H__

#include "resource.h"

////////////////////////////////////////////////////////////////////////////
// CTheApp class declaration
//
class CTheApp : public CWinApp
{
private:
  WSADATA m_WsaData;  // WinSock data structure

public:
  BOOL InitInstance();
  int ExitInstance();
};

#endif // __DBTST_H__
```

Listing 8.6. DBTST.CPP for DBTST.

```
////////////////////////////////////////////////////////////////////////////
// CTheApp implementation file
//

#include "stdafx.h"
#include "dbtst.h"
#include "mainwnd.h"

////////////////////////////////////////////////////////////////////////////
// Creating a CTheApp object starts the application running
//
CTheApp NEAR TheApp;

////////////////////////////////////////////////////////////////////////////
// CTheApp::InitInstance
//
// When the CTheApp object is created, this member function is
// automatically called. WinSock is initiated here. The main window
// of the application is created and shown here.
//
BOOL CTheApp::InitInstance()
{
  if (WSAStartup(MAKEWORD(1, 1), &m_WsaData) != 0)
    return FALSE;

  m_pMainWnd = new CMainWindow();
  m_pMainWnd->ShowWindow(m_nCmdShow);
  m_pMainWnd->UpdateWindow();
```

continues

Listing 8.6. continued

```
  return TRUE;
}

////////////////////////////////////////////////////////////////////////////
// CTheApp::ExitInstance
//
// When the application is closed, shutdown WinSock.
//
int CTheApp::ExitInstance()
{
  WSACleanup();

  return CWinApp::ExitInstance();
}
```

This application can look up either host or service information. To support this, two dialog boxes are used. The host dialog box is implemented in the `CHostDlg` class. This class is created using App Studio and ClassWizard. The class declaration file (HOST.H) is shown in Listing 8.7. Listing 8.8 shows the class implementation file (HOST.CPP). `CHostDlg` has as a public member variable a `CString` object named `m_stringHost`. This variable contains the string the user enters into the dialog box's single EDIT control. The dialog box has three buttons: Asynchronous, Blocking, and Cancel. If the user presses the Asynchronous button, IDC_BUTTON_ASYNC is returned to the caller, signaling that the user wants the database lookup to be carried out asynchronously. Likewise, IDC_BUTTON_BLOCKING is returned when the Blocking button is pressed. Pressing Cancel aborts the lookup.

Listing 8.7. HOST.H for DBTST.

```
////////////////////////////////////////////////////////////////////////////
// CHostDlg dialog
//
class CHostDlg : public CDialog
{
// Construction
public:
  CHostDlg(CWnd* pParent = NULL); // standard constructor

// Dialog Data
  //{{AFX_DATA(CHostDlg)
  enum { IDD = IDD_HOST };
  CString m_stringHost;
  //}}AFX_DATA

// Implementation
protected:
  virtual void DoDataExchange(CDataExchange* pDX);  // DDX/DDV support
```

```
   // Generated message map functions
   //{{AFX_MSG(CHostDlg)
   afx_msg void OnClickedButtonAsync();
   afx_msg void OnClickedButtonBlocking();
   //}}AFX_MSG
   DECLARE_MESSAGE_MAP()
};
```

Listing 8.8. HOST.CPP for DBTST.

```
// host.cpp : implementation file
//

#include "stdafx.h"
#include "dbtst.h"
#include "host.h"

#ifdef _DEBUG
#undef THIS_FILE
static char BASED_CODE THIS_FILE[] = __FILE__;
#endif

/////////////////////////////////////////////////////////////////////////////
// CHostDlg dialog

CHostDlg::CHostDlg(CWnd* pParent /*=NULL*/)
   : CDialog(CHostDlg::IDD, pParent)
{
   //{{AFX_DATA_INIT(CHostDlg)
   m_stringHost = "";
   //}}AFX_DATA_INIT
}

void CHostDlg::DoDataExchange(CDataExchange* pDX)
{
   CDialog::DoDataExchange(pDX);
   //{{AFX_DATA_MAP(CHostDlg)
   DDX_Text(pDX, IDC_EDIT_HOST, m_stringHost);
   //}}AFX_DATA_MAP
}

BEGIN_MESSAGE_MAP(CHostDlg, CDialog)
   //{{AFX_MSG_MAP(CHostDlg)
   ON_BN_CLICKED(IDC_BUTTON_ASYNC, OnClickedButtonAsync)
   ON_BN_CLICKED(IDC_BUTTON_BLOCKING, OnClickedButtonBlocking)
   //}}AFX_MSG_MAP
END_MESSAGE_MAP()

/////////////////////////////////////////////////////////////////////////////
// CHostDlg message handlers

void CHostDlg::OnClickedButtonAsync()
{
   UpdateData(TRUE);
```

continues

Listing 8.8. continued

```
  EndDialog(IDC_BUTTON_ASYNC);
}

void CHostDlg::OnClickedButtonBlocking()
{
  UpdateData(TRUE);
  EndDialog(IDC_BUTTON_BLOCKING);
}
```

The dialog box to prompt for which service to look up is implemented as the `CServiceDlg` class. The source code for this dialog box is in the SERVICE.H and SERVICE.CPP files shown in Listings 8.9 and 8.10, respectively. The code follows a similar format as the `CHostDlg` class except that there are two data entry fields in the services dialog: service and protocol.

Listing 8.9. SERVICE.H for DBTST.

```
/////////////////////////////////////////////////////////////////////////////
// CServiceDlg dialog
//
class CServiceDlg : public CDialog
{
// Construction
public:
  CServiceDlg(CWnd* pParent = NULL);  // standard constructor

// Dialog Data
  //{{AFX_DATA(CServiceDlg)
  enum { IDD = IDD_SERVICE };
  CString m_stringService;
  CString m_stringProtocol;
  //}}AFX_DATA

// Implementation
protected:
  virtual void DoDataExchange(CDataExchange* pDX);  // DDX/DDV support

  // Generated message map functions
  //{{AFX_MSG(CServiceDlg)
  afx_msg void OnClickedButtonAsync();
  afx_msg void OnClickedButtonBlocking();
  //}}AFX_MSG
  DECLARE_MESSAGE_MAP()
};
```

Listing 8.10. SERVICE.CPP for DBTST.

```
// service.cpp : implementation file
//

#include "stdafx.h"
#include "dbtst.h"
#include "service.h"

#ifdef _DEBUG
#undef THIS_FILE
static char BASED_CODE THIS_FILE[] = __FILE__;
#endif

/////////////////////////////////////////////////////////////////////////////
// CServiceDlg dialog

CServiceDlg::CServiceDlg(CWnd* pParent /*=NULL*/)
  : CDialog(CServiceDlg::IDD, pParent)
{
  //{{AFX_DATA_INIT(CServiceDlg)
  m_stringService = "";
  m_stringProtocol = "";
  //}}AFX_DATA_INIT
}

void CServiceDlg::DoDataExchange(CDataExchange* pDX)
{
  CDialog::DoDataExchange(pDX);
  //{{AFX_DATA_MAP(CServiceDlg)
  DDX_Text(pDX, IDC_EDIT_SERVICE, m_stringService);
  DDX_Text(pDX, IDC_EDIT_PROTOCOL, m_stringProtocol);
  //}}AFX_DATA_MAP
}

BEGIN_MESSAGE_MAP(CServiceDlg, CDialog)
  //{{AFX_MSG_MAP(CServiceDlg)
  ON_BN_CLICKED(IDC_BUTTON_ASYNC, OnClickedButtonAsync)
  ON_BN_CLICKED(IDC_BUTTON_BLOCKING, OnClickedButtonBlocking)
  //}}AFX_MSG_MAP
END_MESSAGE_MAP()

/////////////////////////////////////////////////////////////////////////////
// CServiceDlg message handlers

void CServiceDlg::OnClickedButtonAsync()
{
  UpdateData(TRUE);
  EndDialog(IDC_BUTTON_ASYNC);
}

void CServiceDlg::OnClickedButtonBlocking()
{
  UpdateData(TRUE);
  EndDialog(IDC_BUTTON_BLOCKING);
}
```

The class that does most of the work in this sample program is `CMainWindow`, derived from the MFC class `CFrameWnd`. It's this class that actually creates the window, provides the menu, and calls the WinSock database functions. Its header file is shown in Listing 8.11. Several private member variables are used to support database lookup.

Listing 8.11. MAINWND.H for DBTST.

```
#ifndef __MAINWND_H__
#define __MAINWND_H__

#define USER_INPUT_BUF_LEN   (100)

/////////////////////////////////////////////////////////////////////////////
// CMainWindow class declaration
//
class CMainWindow : public CFrameWnd
{
private:
  // variables to support host lookup
  HANDLE m_hAsyncHost;                   // async request handle
  char m_achHostEnt[MAXGETHOSTSTRUCT];   // hostent buffer for async call
  char m_lpszHost[USER_INPUT_BUF_LEN];   // host name or IP address
  PHOSTENT m_pHostEnt;                   // pointer to host entry structure
  IN_ADDR m_in;                          // Internet address structure
  u_long m_ulIPAddress;                  // Internet address

  // variables to support service lookup
  HANDLE m_hAsyncService;                    // async request handle
  char m_achServEnt[MAXGETHOSTSTRUCT];       // servent buffer for async call
  char m_lpszService[USER_INPUT_BUF_LEN];    // service name or port number
  char m_lpszProtocol[USER_INPUT_BUF_LEN];   // transport protocol
  PSERVENT m_pServEnt;                       // pointer to service entry structure
  short m_nPort;                             // port number

public:
  CMainWindow();

  //{{AFX_MSG(CMainWindow)
  afx_msg void OnHost();
  afx_msg LONG OnAsyncHost(WPARAM wParam, LPARAM lParam);
  afx_msg void OnCancelHost();
  afx_msg void OnService();
  afx_msg LONG OnAsyncService(WPARAM wParam, LPARAM lParam);
  afx_msg void OnCancelService();
  //}}AFX_MSG
  DECLARE_MESSAGE_MAP()
};

/////////////////////////////////////////////////////////////////////////////
// User defined messages used in CMainWindow's message map
//
#define WM_USER_ASYNC_HOST_LOOKUP    (WM_USER + 1)
#define WM_USER_ASYNC_SERVICE_LOOKUP (WM_USER + 2)

#endif // __MAINWND_H__
```

The CMainWindow class is implemented in the MAINWND.CPP file shown in Listing 8.12. The CMainWindow object is created by CTheApp. The constructor for this class creates a window, loads a keyboard accelerator, and initializes the asynchronous database call handles.

When the user selects Host Lookup from the Test menu, the OnHost() member function is called due to MFC's message-mapping facility. A dialog box is presented (CHostDlg) to prompt for a host name or dotted-decimal IP address. inet_addr() is called to see whether what the user entered is a host name or an IP address. Next, OnHost() checks to see whether the user wants to do a blocking or nonblocking lookup. If a blocking lookup is selected, gethostbyname() or gethostbyaddr() is called, depending on the results of the inet_addr() call discussed earlier. Note that while this lookup is taking place, the application's menu is inaccessible. If a nonblocking lookup is selected, WSAGetHostByName() or WSAGetHostByAddr() is called, telling WinSock to notify the CMainWindow object's window handle with a WM_USER_ASYNC_HOST_LOOKUP message. While the nonblocking lookup is taking place, the program remains fully responsive to the user's input. If the user wishes to cancel the lookup before it returns, Cancel Host Lookup is chosen from the Test menu, or the keyboard accelerator Ctrl-H is used. If the lookup is allowed to complete, the OnAsyncHost() member function is called automatically as the result of the WM_USER_ASYNC_HOST_LOOKUP message being posted by WinSock.

The service lookup is done in a similar manner as the host lookup.

Listing 8.12. MAINWND.CPP for DBTST.

```
#include "stdafx.h"
#include "dbtst.h"
#include "mainwnd.h"
#include "host.h"
#include "service.h"

/////////////////////////////////////////////////////////////////////////////
// CMainWindow message map
//
BEGIN_MESSAGE_MAP(CMainWindow, CFrameWnd)
  //{{AFX_MSG_MAP(CMainWindow)
  ON_COMMAND(IDM_HOST, OnHost)
  ON_MESSAGE(WM_USER_ASYNC_HOST_LOOKUP, OnAsyncHost)
  ON_COMMAND(IDM_CANCEL_HOST, OnCancelHost)
  ON_COMMAND(IDM_SERVICE, OnService)
  ON_MESSAGE(WM_USER_ASYNC_SERVICE_LOOKUP, OnAsyncService)
  ON_COMMAND(IDM_CANCEL_SERVICE, OnCancelService)
  //}}AFX_MSG_MAP
END_MESSAGE_MAP()

/////////////////////////////////////////////////////////////////////////////
// CMainWindow::CMainWindow constructor
```

continues

Listing 8.12. continued

```
//
// Create the window with the appropriate style, size, menu, etc.
//
CMainWindow::CMainWindow()
{
  LoadAccelTable("MainAccelTable");

  Create(NULL, "WinSock Database Test Application",
   WS_OVERLAPPEDWINDOW, rectDefault, NULL, "MainMenu");

  // initialize the asynchronous request handles so we
  // know if there is any outstanding request
  m_hAsyncHost = m_hAsyncService = 0;
}

/////////////////////////////////////////////////////////////////////////////
// CMainWindow::OnHost
//
// Called when the Test ¦ Host Lookup menu item is selected.
//
void CMainWindow::OnHost()
{
  char lpszMessage[100];    // informational message

  // prompt the user for host information
  CHostDlg dlg;
  int nStatus = dlg.DoModal();
  if (nStatus != IDCANCEL)
  {
    // copy the host information the user entered into a member variable
    if (dlg.m_stringHost.GetLength() < USER_INPUT_BUF_LEN)
      lstrcpy(m_lpszHost, dlg.m_stringHost);
    else
    {
      MessageBox("Host name or IP address was too long", "Host Lookup");
      return;
    }

    // see if the user entered a dotted-decimal IP address
    m_ulIPAddress = inet_addr(m_lpszHost);

    if (nStatus == IDC_BUTTON_ASYNC)
    {
      // do an asynchronous host lookup

      if (m_hAsyncHost != 0)
        MessageBox("Asynchronous host lookup already in progress", "Host Lookup");
      else
      {
        if (m_ulIPAddress == INADDR_NONE)
          m_hAsyncHost = WSAAsyncGetHostByName(m_hWnd, WM_USER_ASYNC_HOST_LOOKUP,
           m_lpszHost, m_achHostEnt, MAXGETHOSTSTRUCT);
        else
          m_hAsyncHost = WSAAsyncGetHostByAddr(m_hWnd, WM_USER_ASYNC_HOST_LOOKUP,
           (char *)&m_ulIPAddress, 4, PF_INET, m_achHostEnt, MAXGETHOSTSTRUCT);
```

```
        if (m_hAsyncHost == 0)
        {
          wsprintf(lpszMessage, "Host lookup failed (WinSock error %d)",
           WSAGetLastError());

          MessageBox(lpszMessage, "Host Lookup");
        }
      }
    }
    else
    {
      // do a blocking host lookup

      if (m_ulIPAddress == INADDR_NONE)
        m_pHostEnt = gethostbyname(m_lpszHost);
      else
        m_pHostEnt = gethostbyaddr((char *)&m_ulIPAddress, 4, PF_INET);

      if (m_pHostEnt == NULL)
        wsprintf(lpszMessage, "Host lookup failed (WinSock error %d)",
         WSAGetLastError());
      else
      {
        // copy the four byte IP address into an Internet address structure
        memcpy(&m_in, m_pHostEnt->h_addr, 4);

        // format the results, converting the IP address into a string
        wsprintf(lpszMessage, "Host %s has IP address %s",
         m_pHostEnt->h_name, inet_ntoa(m_in));
      }

      MessageBox(lpszMessage, "Host Lookup");
    }
  }
}

/////////////////////////////////////////////////////////////////////////////
// CMainWindow::OnAsyncHost
//
// Called when the asynchronous lookup is done.
//
LONG CMainWindow::OnAsyncHost(WPARAM wParam, LPARAM lParam)
{
  char lpszMessage[100];   // informational message

  // check for an error
  if (WSAGETASYNCERROR(lParam) != 0)
    wsprintf(lpszMessage,
     "Host lookup failed (WinSock error %d)",
     WSAGETASYNCERROR(lParam));
  else
  {
    // assign a hostent host entry pointer to the buffer
    m_pHostEnt = (PHOSTENT)m_achHostEnt;

    // copy the four byte IP address into an Internet address structure
    memcpy(&m_in, m_pHostEnt->h_addr, 4);
```

continues

Listing 8.12. continued

```
    // format the results, converting the IP address into a string
    wsprintf(lpszMessage, "Host %s has IP address %s",
     m_pHostEnt->h_name, inet_ntoa(m_in));
  }

  m_hAsyncHost = 0;
  MessageBox(lpszMessage, "Host Lookup");

  return 0L;
}

/////////////////////////////////////////////////////////////////////////////
// CMainWindow::OnCancelHost
//
// Called when the Test ¦ Cancel Host Lookup menu item is selected.
//
void CMainWindow::OnCancelHost()
{
  char lpszMessage[100];   // informational message

  // see if there is an outstanding asynchronous request
  if (m_hAsyncHost == 0)
    lstrcpy(lpszMessage, "No asynchronous host lookup in progress");
  else
  {
    // cancel the asynchronouos request

    if (WSACancelAsyncRequest(m_hAsyncHost) != 0)
      wsprintf(lpszMessage, "Cancel asynchronous host lookup failed (WinSock error
%d)",
       WSAGetLastError());
    else
      lstrcpy(lpszMessage, "Asynchronous host lookup canceled");

    m_hAsyncHost = 0;
  }

  MessageBox(lpszMessage, "Host Lookup");
}

/////////////////////////////////////////////////////////////////////////////
// CMainWindow::OnService
//
// Called when the Test ¦ Service Lookup menu item is selected.
//
void CMainWindow::OnService()
{
  char lpszMessage[100];   // informational message

  // prompt the user for service information
  CServiceDlg dlg;
  int nStatus = dlg.DoModal();
  if (nStatus == IDCANCEL)
    return;
```

```
  // copy the service name or port number if its format is legal
  int nServiceLen = dlg.m_stringService.GetLength();
  if ((nServiceLen > USER_INPUT_BUF_LEN) || (nServiceLen == 0))
  {
    MessageBox("Service name or port number is either too long or unspecified",
"Service Lookup");
    return;
  }
  lstrcpy(m_lpszService, dlg.m_stringService);

  // see if the user entered a port number
  m_nPort = atoi(m_lpszService);
  m_nPort = htons(m_nPort);

  // copy the transport protocol
  static char *lpszProtocol;
  int nProtocolLen = dlg.m_stringProtocol.GetLength();
  if (nProtocolLen > USER_INPUT_BUF_LEN)
  {
    MessageBox("Protocol name is too long", "Service Lookup");
    return;
  }
  if (nProtocolLen > 0)
  {
    lstrcpy(m_lpszProtocol, dlg.m_stringProtocol);
    lpszProtocol = m_lpszProtocol;
  }
  else
    lpszProtocol = NULL;   // protocol wasn't specifiy so NULL gets passed

  if (nStatus == IDC_BUTTON_ASYNC)
  {
    // do an asynchronous service lookup

    if (m_hAsyncService != 0)
      MessageBox("Asynchronous service lookup already in progress", "Service Lookup");
    else
    {
      if (m_nPort == 0)
        m_hAsyncService = WSAAsyncGetServByName(m_hWnd, WM_USER_ASYNC_SERVICE_LOOKUP,
         m_lpszService, lpszProtocol, m_achServEnt, MAXGETHOSTSTRUCT);
      else
        m_hAsyncService = WSAAsyncGetServByPort(m_hWnd, WM_USER_ASYNC_SERVICE_LOOKUP,
         m_nPort, lpszProtocol, m_achHostEnt, MAXGETHOSTSTRUCT);

      if (m_hAsyncService == 0)
      {
        wsprintf(lpszMessage, "Service lookup failed (WinSock error %d)",
         WSAGetLastError());

        MessageBox(lpszMessage, "Service Lookup");
      }
    }
  }
  else
  {
    // do a blocking service lookup
```

continues

Listing 8.12. continued

```
    if (m_nPort == 0)
      m_pServEnt = getservbyname(m_lpszService, lpszProtocol);
    else
      m_pServEnt = getservbyport(m_nPort, lpszProtocol);

    if (m_pServEnt == NULL)
      wsprintf(lpszMessage, "Service lookup failed (WinSock error %d)",
       WSAGetLastError());
    else
      // format the results, converting the port to host byte order
      wsprintf(lpszMessage, "%s service using protocol %s has port %d",
       m_pServEnt->s_name, m_pServEnt->s_proto, ntohs(m_pServEnt->s_port));

    MessageBox(lpszMessage, "Service Lookup");
  }
}

/////////////////////////////////////////////////////////////////////////////
// CMainWindow::OnAsyncService
//
// Called when the asynchronous lookup is done.
//
LONG CMainWindow::OnAsyncService(WPARAM wParam, LPARAM lParam)
{
  char lpszMessage[100];    // informational message

  // check for an error
  if (WSAGETASYNCERROR(lParam) != 0)
    wsprintf(lpszMessage,
     "Service lookup failed (WinSock error %d)",
     WSAGETASYNCERROR(lParam));
  else
  {
    // assign a servent host entry pointer to the buffer
    m_pServEnt = (PSERVENT)m_achServEnt;

    // format the results, converting the port to host byte order
    wsprintf(lpszMessage, "%s service using protocol %s has port %d",
     m_pServEnt->s_name, m_pServEnt->s_proto, ntohs(m_pServEnt->s_port));
  }

  m_hAsyncService = 0;
  MessageBox(lpszMessage, "Service Lookup");

  return 0L;
}

/////////////////////////////////////////////////////////////////////////////
// CMainWindow::OnCancelService
//
// Called when the Test ¦ Cancel Service Lookup menu item is selected.
//
void CMainWindow::OnCancelService()
{
  char lpszMessage[100];    // informational message
```

```
  // see if there is an outstanding asynchronous request
  if (m_hAsyncService == 0)
    lstrcpy(lpszMessage, "No asynchronous service lookup in progress");
  else
  {
    // cancel the asynchronouos request

    if (WSACancelAsyncRequest(m_hAsyncService) != 0)
      wsprintf(lpszMessage, "Cancel asynchronous service lookup failed (WinSock error
%d)",
        WSAGetLastError());
    else
      lstrcpy(lpszMessage, "Asynchronous service lookup canceled");

    m_hAsyncService = 0;
  }

  MessageBox(lpszMessage, "Service Lookup");
}
```

An example execution of DBTST is shown in Figures 8.3 through 8.7. Figure 8.3 shows the menu of the DBTST application. Figure 8.4 shows entering host information, and Figure 8.5 shows the outcome of the host lookup. Figure 8.6 shows entering service information, and Figure 8.7 shows the results of the service lookup. You may want to keep this application close by, as it comes in very handy when you need to quickly know a host's IP address.

FIGURE 8.3.
DBTST menu items.

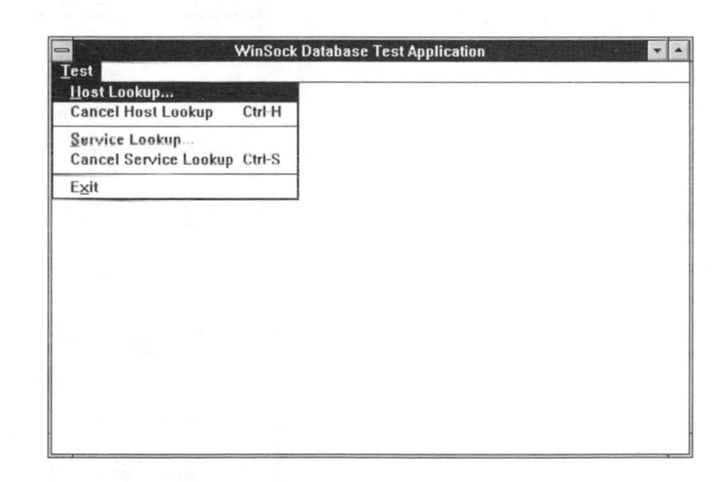

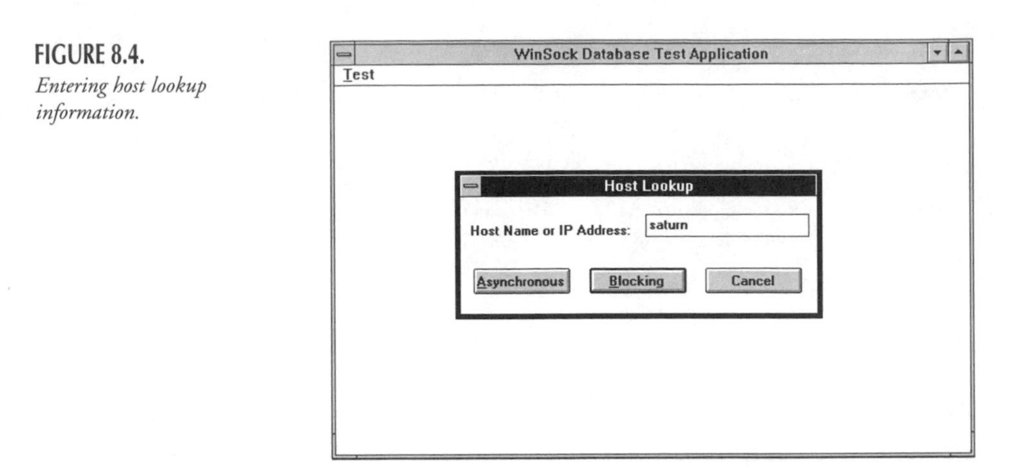

FIGURE 8.4.
Entering host lookup information.

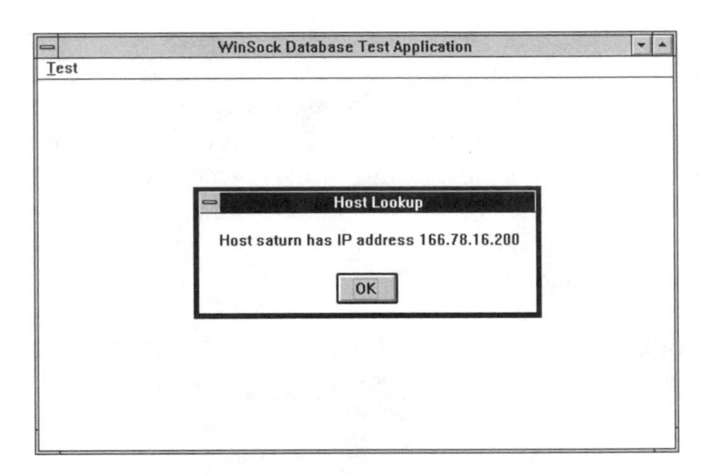

FIGURE 8.5.
Results of host lookup.

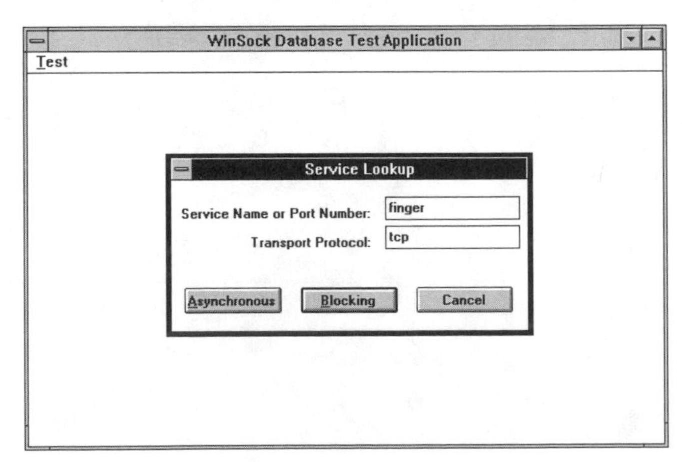

FIGURE 8.6.
Entering service lookup information.

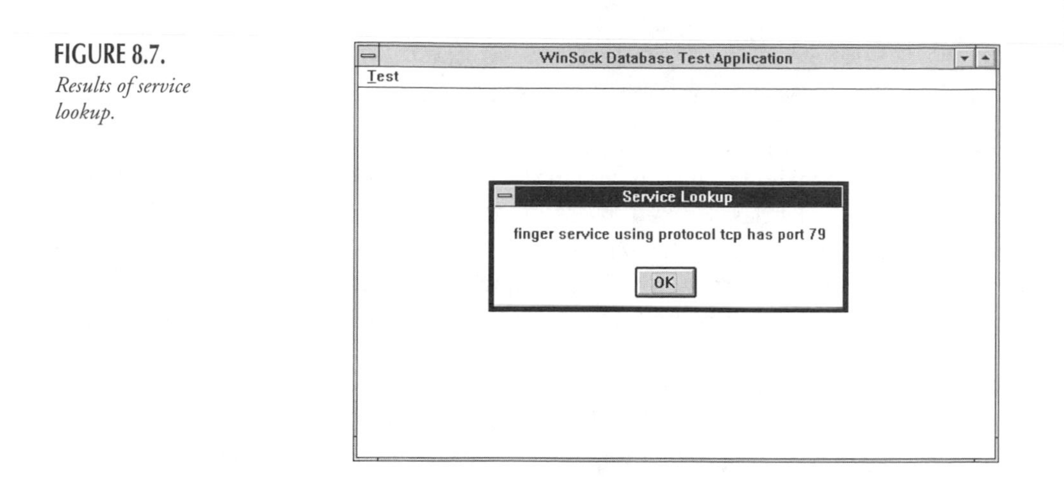

FIGURE 8.7.
Results of service lookup.

Datagram Echo Client and Server

These programs, DESERV and DECLIENT, demonstrate the use of nonblocking datagram sockets. They use the following WinSock functions: `WSAStartup()`, `WSACleanup()`, `WSAGetLastError()`, `socket()`, `closesocket()`, `bind()`, `WSAAsyncSelect()`, `sendto()`, `recvfrom()`, `getsockname()`, `ntohs()`, and `inet_ntoa()`. The DESERV server application receives data and sends it back to the client. The DECLIENT client application sends data to the server and receives the echoed reply.

Datagram Echo Server DESERV

These programs are generated using Visual C++'s AppWizard feature. The WINSOCK.H header file is included in the STDAFX.H precompiled header file, as shown in Listing 8.13. STDAFX.H is included by the source modules of the project, so WinSock functions and structures are always available.

Listing 8.13. STDAFX.H for DESERV.

```
// stdafx.h : include file for standard system include files,
//  or project specific include files that are used frequently, but
//    are changed infrequently
//

#include <afxwin.h>      // MFC core and standard components
#include <afxext.h>      // MFC extensions
#include <winsock.h>     // Windows Sockets
```

Like the WSINFO example, DESERV uses the application object to start and stop WinSock in `CDeservApp::InitInstance()` and `CDeservApp::ExitInstance()`, respectively.

DESERV uses the Single Document Interface of window management. AppWizard creates a default view class derived from the MFC class `CView`, but this class isn't used by the application. Instead, a `CFormView` derived object is used. Using a `CFormView` means first using App Studio to create a dialog box resource. A dialog box is created that has a static text label and a list box that's used for status messages. Generally speaking, a dialog box resource is created and ClassWizard is used to create a class derived from `CDialog`. Because you want this dialog box resource to be the program's main interface, ClassWizard is used to create a class derived from `CFormView`. But first, the dialog box resource must have its flags set appropriately. Specifically, the style is child, the border is none, the visible flag is unchecked, and the Caption is left blank. Figure 8.8 shows the style portion of the dialog properties for the dialog box resource used as DESERV's main window.

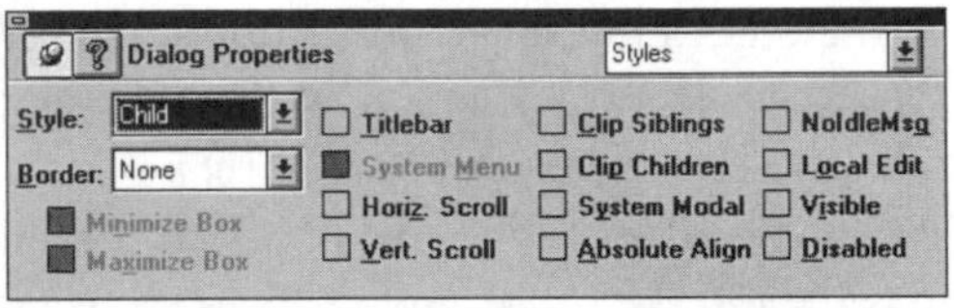

FIGURE 8.8.
Style properties for DESERV's main window dialog resource.

A change is made to the application object `CDeservApp` so that it uses this view rather than the default view generated by AppWizard. The default implementation of `CDeservApp::InitInstance()` has a call to `AddDocTemplate()` that looks like the following:

```
AddDocTemplate(new CSingleDocTemplate(IDR_MAINFRAME,
 RUNTIME_CLASS(CDeservDoc),
 RUNTIME_CLASS(CMainFrame),      // main SDI frame window
 RUNTIME_CLASS(CDeservView)));
```

It needs to look as follows:

```
AddDocTemplate(new CSingleDocTemplate(IDR_MAINFRAME,
 RUNTIME_CLASS(CDeservDoc),
 RUNTIME_CLASS(CMainFrame),      // main SDI frame window
 RUNTIME_CLASS(CMainView)));
```

The `CFormView` derived object is named `CMainView` and its header file is shown in Listing 8.14. Notice the member variables `m_s` and `m_addr`, and the function `OnAsyncSelect()`. `OnAsyncSelect()` is added to the class by hand because ClassWizard doesn't support user-defined messages.

Listing 8.14. MAINVIEW.H for DESERV.

```
// mainview.h : header file
//

/////////////////////////////////////////////////////////////////////////////
// CMainView form view

#ifndef __AFXEXT_H__
#include <afxext.h>
#endif

class CMainView : public CFormView
{
  DECLARE_DYNCREATE(CMainView)

public:
  SOCKET m_s;            // socket to receive from
  SOCKADDR_IN m_addr;    // address of socket

protected:
  CMainView();       // protected constructor used by dynamic creation

// Form Data
public:
  //{{AFX_DATA(CMainView)
  enum { IDD = IDD_DIALOG_MAIN };
    // NOTE: the ClassWizard will add data members here
  //}}AFX_DATA

// Attributes
public:

// Operations
public:

// Implementation
protected:
  virtual ~CMainView();
  virtual void DoDataExchange(CDataExchange* pDX);  // DDX/DDV support
  virtual void OnInitialUpdate();
  // Generated message map functions
  //{{AFX_MSG(CMainView)
  afx_msg LONG OnAsyncSelect(WPARAM wParam, LPARAM lParam);
  //}}AFX_MSG
  DECLARE_MESSAGE_MAP()
};

/////////////////////////////////////////////////////////////////////////////

#define WM_USER_ASYNC_SELECT (WM_USER + 1)
```

The implementation of the CMainView object is shown in Listing 8.15. This object performs most of the work for the DESERV application. CMainView::OnInitialUpdate() is called soon after the object is created. This function is responsible for creating a socket, binding it to a name (with the port assigned by WinSock), and waiting for data to arrive. When data is ready to be received or data can be sent, the CMainView::OnAsyncSelect() member function is called due to the message mapping of the user-defined message WM_USER_ASYNC_SELECT.

Listing 8.15. MAINVIEW.CPP for DESERV.

```
// mainview.cpp : implementation file
//

#include "stdafx.h"
#include "deserv.h"
#include "mainview.h"

#ifdef _DEBUG
#undef THIS_FILE
static char BASED_CODE THIS_FILE[] = __FILE__;
#endif

/////////////////////////////////////////////////////////////////////////////
// CMainView

IMPLEMENT_DYNCREATE(CMainView, CFormView)

CMainView::CMainView()
  : CFormView(CMainView::IDD)
{
  m_s = INVALID_SOCKET;  // initialize socket to invalid handle

  //{{AFX_DATA_INIT(CMainView)
    // NOTE: the ClassWizard will add member initialization here
  //}}AFX_DATA_INIT
}

CMainView::~CMainView()
{
  // if the socket was opened successfully, close it

  if (m_s != INVALID_SOCKET)
  {
    closesocket(m_s);
    m_s = INVALID_SOCKET;
  }
}

void CMainView::DoDataExchange(CDataExchange* pDX)
{
  CFormView::DoDataExchange(pDX);
  //{{AFX_DATA_MAP(CMainView)
    // NOTE: the ClassWizard will add DDX and DDV calls here
  //}}AFX_DATA_MAP
```

```
}

void CMainView::OnInitialUpdate()
{
  char pszMessage[100]; // informational message

  // get pointer to list box used for status messages

  CListBox *plb = (CListBox *)GetDlgItem(IDC_LIST_STATUS);

  // create the socket and prepare it
  // for receiving data

  plb->InsertString(0, "Initializing...");

  m_s = socket(AF_INET, SOCK_DGRAM, 0);
  if (m_s == INVALID_SOCKET)
    plb->InsertString(0, "Datagram echo server could not create socket");
  else
  {
    // bind the socket, allowing WinSock to assign the service port

    m_addr.sin_family = AF_INET;                    // Internet address family
    m_addr.sin_port = 0;                            // let WinSock assign a port
    m_addr.sin_addr.s_addr = htonl(INADDR_ANY);  // any network interface

    if (bind(m_s, (LPSOCKADDR)&m_addr, sizeof(m_addr)) == SOCKET_ERROR)
      plb->InsertString(0, "Datagram echo server could not bind socket");
    else
    {
      // find out the port number WinSock assigned

      SOCKADDR_IN addr;
      int nAddrLen = sizeof(addr);

      if (getsockname(m_s, (LPSOCKADDR)&addr, &nAddrLen) == SOCKET_ERROR)
        plb->InsertString(0, "Datagram echo server could not get socket's port");
      else
      {
        wsprintf(pszMessage, "Datagram echo server using port %d",
         ntohs(addr.sin_port));
        plb->InsertString(0, pszMessage);

        // do the asynchronous select to wait for data

        if (WSAAsyncSelect(m_s, m_hWnd, WM_USER_ASYNC_SELECT,
         FD_READ | FD_WRITE) == SOCKET_ERROR)
          plb->InsertString(0, "Datagram echo server could not do async select");
      }
    }
  }
}

BEGIN_MESSAGE_MAP(CMainView, CFormView)
  //{{AFX_MSG_MAP(CMainView)
  ON_MESSAGE(WM_USER_ASYNC_SELECT, OnAsyncSelect)
  //}}AFX_MSG_MAP
```

continues

Listing 8.15. continued

```
END_MESSAGE_MAP()

/////////////////////////////////////////////////////////////////////////////
// CMainView message handlers

/////////////////////////////////////////////////////////////////////////////
// CMainView::OnAsyncSelect()
//
// Receives data from a client and echoes the data back to the sending client.
// While there is data yet to be sent back to the sending client, the server
// will not receive any more data. (a single data buffer is used for
// incoming and outgoing data)
//
LONG CMainView::OnAsyncSelect(WPARAM wParam, LPARAM lParam)
{
  char pszMessage[100];          // informational message
  static char pBuf[101];         // send/recv buffer
  int nBytesRecv;                // number of bytes received
  int nBytesSent;                // number of bytes sent
  static int nBytesToSend = 0;   // number of bytes to send
  int nError;                    // WinSock error
  static SOCKADDR_IN addrFrom;   // address of client
  static int nAddrFromLen = sizeof(addrFrom); // length of client address struct
  static IN_ADDR inFrom;         // IP address of client

  // get pointer to list box used for status messages
  CListBox *plb = (CListBox *)GetDlgItem(IDC_LIST_STATUS);

  // check for an error
  if (WSAGETSELECTERROR(lParam) != 0)
  {
    wsprintf(pszMessage, "Datagrem echo server async select got error %d",
     WSAGETSELECTERROR(lParam));
    plb->InsertString(0, pszMessage);
    return 0L;
  }

  // what event are we being notified of?
  switch (WSAGETSELECTEVENT(lParam))
  {
    case FD_WRITE:
      // echo the data back to the client

      plb->InsertString(0, "FD_WRITE");

      // are there bytes to send?
      if (nBytesToSend != 0)
      {
        // send the data
        nBytesSent = sendto(m_s, pBuf, nBytesToSend, 0,
         (LPSOCKADDR)&addrFrom, nAddrFromLen);

        // check for send error
        if (nBytesSent == SOCKET_ERROR)
        {
          // if the error is just that the send would block,
```

```
      // don't do anything...we'll get another FD_WRITE soon
      nError = WSAGetLastError();
      if (nError != WSAEWOULDBLOCK)
      {
        wsprintf(pszMessage, "Error %d sending data to %s, %d",
         nError, inet_ntoa(inFrom), ntohs(addrFrom.sin_port));
        plb->InsertString(0, pszMessage);

        nBytesToSend = 0;

        // just in case the FD_READ was called but it didn't read
        // because the buffer still contained data to send
        PostMessage(WM_USER_ASYNC_SELECT, m_s, WSAMAKESELECTREPLY(FD_READ, 0));
      }
    }
    else
    {
      wsprintf(pszMessage, "Data sent (%s) to %s, %d",
       pBuf, inet_ntoa(inFrom), ntohs(addrFrom.sin_port));
      plb->InsertString(0, pszMessage);
      nBytesToSend = 0;
    }
  }
  break;

case FD_READ:
  // receive data back from a client

  plb->InsertString(0, "FD_READ");

  // if there are still bytes waiting to be sent back (echoed)
  // to the client, don't do anything here (the FD_WRITE handler will
  // generate FD_READ when it is through with sending)
  if (nBytesToSend == 0)
  {
    // receive data
    nBytesRecv = recvfrom(m_s, pBuf, 100, 0, (LPSOCKADDR)&addrFrom, &nAddrFromLen);

    // check for receive error
    if (nBytesRecv == SOCKET_ERROR)
    {
      // if the error is just that the receive would block,
      // don't do anything...we'll get another FD_READ soon
      nError = WSAGetLastError();
      if (nError != WSAEWOULDBLOCK)
      {
        wsprintf(pszMessage, "Error %d receiving data", nError);
        plb->InsertString(0, pszMessage);
      }
    }
    else
    {
      // save sending client's IP address
      memcpy(&inFrom, &addrFrom.sin_addr.s_addr, 4);

      nBytesToSend = nBytesRecv;
```

continues

Listing 8.15. continued

```
          pBuf[nBytesToSend] = '\0';
          wsprintf(pszMessage, "Data received (%s) from %s, %d",
           pBuf, inet_ntoa(inFrom), ntohs(addrFrom.sin_port));
          plb->InsertString(0, pszMessage);

          // just in case the FD_WRITE was called but it didn't have
          // any data to send at that time (it has data to send now)
          PostMessage(WM_USER_ASYNC_SELECT, m_s, WSAMAKESELECTREPLY(FD_WRITE, 0));
        }
      }
      break;

    default:
      break;
  }

  return 0L;
}
```

Datagram Echo Client DECLIENT

The datagram echo client, DECLIENT, follows the same basic outline as DESERV. It also uses a `CFormView` object as its main interface. The primary difference lies in the implementation of the `CMainView` object.

The header file for the `CMainView` object is shown in Listing 8.16. Its implementation is shown in Listing 8.17. This object performs most of the work for the DECLIENT application. `CMainView::OnInitialUpdate()` is called soon after the object is created. This function is responsible for creating a socket, waiting to send and receive data, and setting a timer to be used for sending data. When data is ready to be received or data can be sent, the `CMainView::OnAsyncSelect()` member function is called due to the message mapping of the user-defined message WM_USER_ASYNC_SELECT. The `CMainView::OnTimer()` function is called every five seconds to format a string to send to the echo server.

Listing 8.16. MAINVIEW.H for DECLIENT.

```
// mainview.h : header file
//

/////////////////////////////////////////////////////////////////////////////
// CMainView form view

#ifndef __AFXEXT_H__
#include <afxext.h>
#endif
```

```
class CMainView : public CFormView
{
  DECLARE_DYNCREATE(CMainView)

public:
  SOCKET m_s;           // socket
  SOCKADDR_IN m_addr;   // address to send to
  IN_ADDR m_in;         // IP address of address to send to
  int m_nBytesToSend;   // number of bytes to send
  char m_pBuf[101];     // buffer to send

protected:
  CMainView();      // protected constructor used by dynamic creation

// Form Data
public:
  //{{AFX_DATA(CMainView)
  enum { IDD = IDD_DIALOG_MAIN };
    // NOTE: the ClassWizard will add data members here
  //}}AFX_DATA

// Attributes
public:

// Operations
public:

// Implementation
protected:
  virtual ~CMainView();
  virtual void DoDataExchange(CDataExchange* pDX);  // DDX/DDV support
  virtual void OnInitialUpdate();
  // Generated message map functions
  //{{AFX_MSG(CMainView)
  afx_msg LONG OnAsyncSelect(WPARAM wParam, LPARAM lParam);
  afx_msg void OnTimer(UINT nIDEvent);
  //}}AFX_MSG
  DECLARE_MESSAGE_MAP()
};

/////////////////////////////////////////////////////////////////////////////

#define WM_USER_ASYNC_SELECT (WM_USER + 1)
```

Listing 8.17. MAINVIEW.CPP for DECLIENT.

```
// mainview.cpp : implementation file
//

#include "stdafx.h"
#include "declient.h"
#include "mainview.h"
#include "servdlg.h"
```

continues

Listing 8.17. continued

```
#ifdef _DEBUG
#undef THIS_FILE
static char BASED_CODE THIS_FILE[] = __FILE__;
#endif

/////////////////////////////////////////////////////////////////////////////
// CMainView

IMPLEMENT_DYNCREATE(CMainView, CFormView)

CMainView::CMainView()
  : CFormView(CMainView::IDD)
{
  m_s = INVALID_SOCKET;  // initialize socket to invalid handle

  //{{AFX_DATA_INIT(CMainView)
    // NOTE: the ClassWizard will add member initialization here
  //}}AFX_DATA_INIT
}

CMainView::~CMainView()
{
  // if the socket was opened successfully, close it

  if (m_s != INVALID_SOCKET)
  {
    closesocket(m_s);
    m_s = INVALID_SOCKET;
  }
}

void CMainView::DoDataExchange(CDataExchange* pDX)
{
  CFormView::DoDataExchange(pDX);
  //{{AFX_DATA_MAP(CMainView)
    // NOTE: the ClassWizard will add DDX and DDV calls here
  //}}AFX_DATA_MAP
}


BEGIN_MESSAGE_MAP(CMainView, CFormView)
  //{{AFX_MSG_MAP(CMainView)
  ON_MESSAGE(WM_USER_ASYNC_SELECT, OnAsyncSelect)
  ON_WM_TIMER()
  //}}AFX_MSG_MAP
END_MESSAGE_MAP()

/////////////////////////////////////////////////////////////////////////////
// CMainView message handlers

void CMainView::OnInitialUpdate()
{
  // get pointer to list box used for status messages
  CListBox *plb = (CListBox *)GetDlgItem(IDC_LIST_STATUS);

  // prompt for server information (IP and port)
```

```
  CServerDlg dlg;
  if (dlg.DoModal() == IDCANCEL)
    return;

  plb->InsertString(0, "Initializing...");

  // create the socket
  m_s = socket(AF_INET, SOCK_DGRAM, 0);
  if (m_s == INVALID_SOCKET)
    plb->InsertString(0, "Datagram echo client could not create socket");
  else
  {
    // fill out the server's address
    m_addr.sin_family = AF_INET;
    m_addr.sin_port = htons(atoi(dlg.m_stringPort));
    m_addr.sin_addr.s_addr = inet_addr(dlg.m_stringIP);

    // save sending client's IP address
    memcpy(&m_in, &m_addr.sin_addr.s_addr, 4);

    // do the asynchronous select to wait for data
    if (WSAAsyncSelect(m_s, m_hWnd, WM_USER_ASYNC_SELECT,
     FD_READ | FD_WRITE) == SOCKET_ERROR)
      plb->InsertString(0, "Datagram echo client could not do async select");
    else
      SetTimer(1, 5000, NULL);
  }
}

////////////////////////////////////////////////////////////////////////////
// CMainView::OnAsyncSelect()
//
LONG CMainView::OnAsyncSelect(WPARAM wParam, LPARAM lParam)
{
  char pszMessage[100];         // informational message
  static char pBuf[101];        // send/recv buffer
  int nBytesRecv;               // number of bytes received
  int nBytesSent;               // number of bytes sent
  int nError;                   // WinSock error

  // get pointer to list box used for status messages
  CListBox *plb = (CListBox *)GetDlgItem(IDC_LIST_STATUS);

  // check for an error
  if (WSAGETSELECTERROR(lParam) != 0)
  {
    wsprintf(pszMessage, "Datagrem echo client async select got error %d",
     WSAGETSELECTERROR(lParam));
    plb->InsertString(0, pszMessage);
    return 0L;
  }

  // what event are we being notified of?
  switch (WSAGETSELECTEVENT(lParam))
  {
    case FD_WRITE:
      plb->InsertString(0, "FD_WRITE");
```

continues

Listing 8.17. continued

```
        // is there any data to send?
        if (m_nBytesToSend != 0)
        {
          // send the data
          nBytesSent = sendto(m_s, m_pBuf, m_nBytesToSend, 0,
           (LPSOCKADDR)&m_addr, sizeof(m_addr));

          // check for send error
          if (nBytesSent == SOCKET_ERROR)
          {
            // if the error is just that the send would block,
            // don't do anything...we'll get another FD_WRITE soon
            nError = WSAGetLastError();
            if (nError != WSAEWOULDBLOCK);
            {
              wsprintf(pszMessage, "Error %d sending data to %s, %d",
               nError, inet_ntoa(m_in), ntohs(m_addr.sin_port));
              plb->InsertString(0, pszMessage);

              m_nBytesToSend = 0;
            }
          }
          else
          {
            wsprintf(pszMessage, "Data sent (%s) to %s, %d",
             m_pBuf, inet_ntoa(m_in), ntohs(m_addr.sin_port));
            plb->InsertString(0, pszMessage);

            m_nBytesToSend = 0;
          }
        }
        break;

      case FD_READ:
        plb->InsertString(0, "FD_READ");

        // receive data
        nBytesRecv = recvfrom(m_s, pBuf, 100, 0, NULL, NULL);

        // check for receive error
        if (nBytesRecv == SOCKET_ERROR)
        {
          // if the error is just that the receive would block,
          // don't do anything...we'll get another FD_READ soon
          nError = WSAGetLastError();
          if (nError != WSAEWOULDBLOCK)
          {
            wsprintf(pszMessage, "Error %d receiving data", nError);
            plb->InsertString(0, pszMessage);
          }
        }
        else
        {
          pBuf[nBytesRecv] = '\0';
          wsprintf(pszMessage, "Data received (%s) from %s, %d",
```

```
          pBuf, inet_ntoa(m_in), ntohs(m_addr.sin_port));
        plb->InsertString(0, pszMessage);
      }
      break;

    default:
      break;
  }

  return 0L;
}

/////////////////////////////////////////////////////////////////////////////
// CMainView::OnTimer()
//
// Timer to generate a string to send. Won't send
// unless the previous string is completely sent.
//
void CMainView::OnTimer(UINT nIDEvent)
{
  static int nSendCount = 1;   //

  if (m_nBytesToSend == 0)
  {
    wsprintf(m_pBuf, "Hello %d", nSendCount);
    ++nSendCount;
    m_nBytesToSend = lstrlen(m_pBuf);
    PostMessage(WM_USER_ASYNC_SELECT, m_s, WSAMAKESELECTREPLY(FD_WRITE, 0));
  }

  CFormView::OnTimer(nIDEvent);
}
```

Running the Datagram Echo Server and Client

A sample sequence of events of running the datagram echo server and client is as follows:

Run DESERV. It displays on which port it's waiting for data to arrive.

Run DECLIENT on the same or a different computer. It prompts for the IP address and port DESERV is using.

In five seconds the timer will trigger in DECLIENT, causing `CMainView::OnTimer()` to get called. No bytes are waiting to be sent yet, so the outgoing buffer is filled and a WinSock `FD_WRITE` message is faked to trigger the sending of the data. This has to be done because the real `FD_WRITE` may have been missed or it may have occurred when there was nothing to send yet.

`CMainView::OnAsyncSelect()` is called in DECLIENT with an FD_WRITE event. There are bytes to be sent, so an attempt to transmit them to the datagram echo server is made. If the attempt succeeds and bytes are written, the number of bytes to send is reset to 0 (zero). If there was an error sending but the error was simply that the send would block, the count of bytes to send is retained because you'll get a real `FD_WRITE` eventually.

Assuming that DECLIENT sends a buffer, `CMainView::OnAsyncSelect()` is called in DESERV with an `FD_READ` notice. If the data is read successfully, a byte count is recorded, the originator of the data is noted, and a fake `FD_WRITE` message is generated to force the sending of the just-received data back to the originator (DECLIENT).

`CMainView::OnAsyncSelect()` is called in DESERV with an `FD_WRITE` event. There are bytes to be sent, so an attempt to transmit them to the datagram echo client is made. If the attempt succeeds and bytes are written, the number of bytes to send is reset to 0 (zero). If there was an error sending but the error was simply that the send would block, the count of bytes to send is retained because you'll get a real `FD_WRITE` eventually.

Assuming that DESERV sends a buffer, `CMainView::OnAsyncSelect()` is called in DECLIENT with an `FD_READ` notice and the client reads the echoed data.

Another timer goes off in DECLIENT and the process repeats.

Figure 8.9 shows DESERV and DECLIENT running on the same computer, which has the IP address 166.78.16.150. The server and client were assigned ports 1059 and 1060, respectively. Notice that after each application initialized, it received an `FD_WRITE` notification. WinSock is simply telling the application that the socket is in a writeable state. The applications ignore the message unless they have bytes to send.

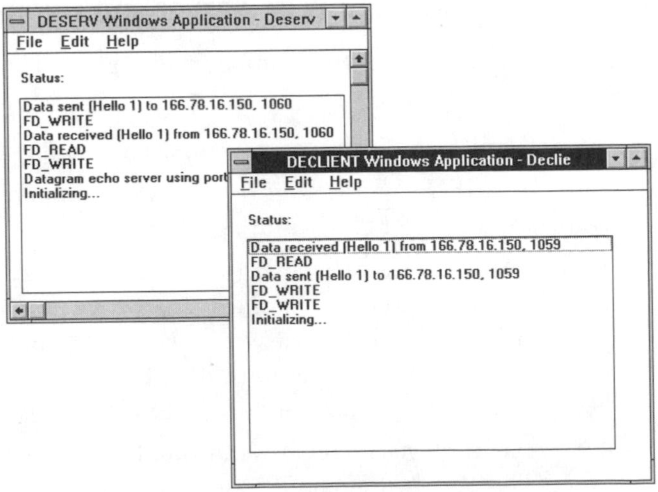

FIGURE 8.9.
DESERV and DECLIENT running on the same computer.

Stream Echo Client and Server

These programs, SESERV and SECLIENT, demonstrate the use of nonblocking stream sockets. They use the following WinSock functions: `WSAStartup()`, `WSACleanup()`, `WSAGetLastError()`, `socket()`, `closesocket()`, `bind()`, `connect()`, `accept()`, `WSAAsyncSelect()`, `send()`, `recv()`, `getsockname()`, `ntohs()`, and `inet_ntoa()`. The SESERV server application accepts a connection from a client, receives data, and sends the data back to the client. The SECLIENT client application connects to the server, sends data to the server, and receives the echoed reply.

Stream Echo Server SESERV

These programs are generated using Visual C++'s AppWizard feature. Implementation is similar to DESERV, with the primary difference being in the `CMainView` object. `CMainView`'s header is shown in Listing 8.18. Listing 8.19 shows the implementation of the `CMainView` object. When `CMainView::OnInitialUpdate()` is called, soon after the `CMainView` object is created, it creates a socket, binds it to a name, and waits for a connection request. When a connection is requested, data is ready to be received, or data can be sent, the `CMainView::OnAsyncSelect()` member function is called due to the message mapping of the user-defined message WM_USER_ASYNC_SELECT. This stream socket server application communicates with only one client at a time due to the single `m_sClient` variable in the `CMainView` class. Once `m_sClient` is connected, all other requests to connect are ignored until the connection is closed by the originating client.

Listing 8.18. MAINVIEW.H for SESERV.

```
// mainview.h : header file
//

/////////////////////////////////////////////////////////////////////////////
// CMainView form view

#ifndef __AFXEXT_H__
#include <afxext.h>
#endif

class CMainView : public CFormView
{
  DECLARE_DYNCREATE(CMainView)

public:
  SOCKET m_s;            // socket to listen for connections on
  SOCKADDR_IN m_addr;    // address of socket to listen on
  SOCKET m_sClient;      // socket to client
```

continues

Listing 8.18. continued

```
protected:
  CMainView();      // protected constructor used by dynamic creation

// Form Data
public:
  //{{AFX_DATA(CMainView)
  enum { IDD = IDD_DIALOG_MAIN };
    // NOTE: the ClassWizard will add data members here
  //}}AFX_DATA

// Attributes
public:

// Operations
public:

// Implementation
protected:
  virtual ~CMainView();
  virtual void DoDataExchange(CDataExchange* pDX);  // DDX/DDV support
  virtual void OnInitialUpdate();
  // Generated message map functions
  //{{AFX_MSG(CMainView)
  afx_msg LONG OnAsyncSelect(WPARAM wParam, LPARAM lParam);
  //}}AFX_MSG
  DECLARE_MESSAGE_MAP()
};

/////////////////////////////////////////////////////////////////////////////

#define WM_USER_ASYNC_SELECT (WM_USER + 1)
```

Listing 8.19. MAINVIEW.CPP for SESERV.

```
// mainview.cpp : implementation file
//

#include "stdafx.h"
#include "seserv.h"
#include "mainview.h"

#ifdef _DEBUG
#undef THIS_FILE
static char BASED_CODE THIS_FILE[] = __FILE__;
#endif

/////////////////////////////////////////////////////////////////////////////
// CMainView

IMPLEMENT_DYNCREATE(CMainView, CFormView)

CMainView::CMainView()
```

```
  : CFormView(CMainView::IDD)
{
  m_s = m_sClient = INVALID_SOCKET;  // initialize socket to invalid handle

  //{{AFX_DATA_INIT(CMainView)
    // NOTE: the ClassWizard will add member initialization here
  //}}AFX_DATA_INIT
}

CMainView::~CMainView()
{
  // if the socket was opened successfully, close it

  if (m_s != INVALID_SOCKET)
  {
    closesocket(m_s);
    m_s = INVALID_SOCKET;
  }
  if (m_sClient != INVALID_SOCKET)
  {
    closesocket(m_sClient);
    m_sClient = INVALID_SOCKET;
  }
}

void CMainView::DoDataExchange(CDataExchange* pDX)
{
  CFormView::DoDataExchange(pDX);
  //{{AFX_DATA_MAP(CMainView)
    // NOTE: the ClassWizard will add DDX and DDV calls here
  //}}AFX_DATA_MAP
}

void CMainView::OnInitialUpdate()
{
  char pszMessage[100]; // informational message

  // get pointer to list box used for status messages

  CListBox *plb = (CListBox *)GetDlgItem(IDC_LIST_STATUS);

  // create the socket and prepare it
  // for receiving data

  plb->InsertString(0, "Initializing...");

  m_s = socket(AF_INET, SOCK_STREAM, 0);
  if (m_s == INVALID_SOCKET)
    plb->InsertString(0, "Stream echo server could not create socket");
  else
  {
    // bind the socket, allowing WinSock to assign the service port

    m_addr.sin_family = AF_INET;                    // Internet address family
    m_addr.sin_port = 0;                            // let WinSock assign a port
    m_addr.sin_addr.s_addr = htonl(INADDR_ANY);  // any network interface
```

continues

Listing 8.19. continued

```
    if (bind(m_s, (LPSOCKADDR)&m_addr, sizeof(m_addr)) == SOCKET_ERROR)
      plb->InsertString(0, "Stream echo server could not bind socket");
    else
    {
      // find out the port number WinSock assigned

      SOCKADDR_IN addr;
      int nAddrLen = sizeof(addr);

      if (getsockname(m_s, (LPSOCKADDR)&addr, &nAddrLen) == SOCKET_ERROR)
        plb->InsertString(0, "Stream echo server could not get socket's port");
      else
      {
        wsprintf(pszMessage, "Stream echo server using port %d",
         ntohs(addr.sin_port));
        plb->InsertString(0, pszMessage);

        // do the asynchronous select to wait for a connection

        if (WSAAsyncSelect(m_s, m_hWnd, WM_USER_ASYNC_SELECT, FD_ACCEPT) ==
         SOCKET_ERROR)
          plb->InsertString(0, "Stream echo server could not do async select");
        else
        {
          // listen for connections

          if (listen(m_s, 3) == SOCKET_ERROR)
            plb->InsertString(0, "Stream echo server could not listen");
        }
      }
    }
  }
}

BEGIN_MESSAGE_MAP(CMainView, CFormView)
  //{{AFX_MSG_MAP(CMainView)
  ON_MESSAGE(WM_USER_ASYNC_SELECT, OnAsyncSelect)
  //}}AFX_MSG_MAP
END_MESSAGE_MAP()

/////////////////////////////////////////////////////////////////////////////
// CMainView message handlers

/////////////////////////////////////////////////////////////////////////////
// CMainView::OnAsyncSelect()
//
// Receives data from a client and echoes the data back to the sending client.
// While there is data yet to be sent back to the sending client, the server
// will not receive any more data. (A single data buffer is used for
// incoming and outgoing data)
//
LONG CMainView::OnAsyncSelect(WPARAM wParam, LPARAM lParam)
{
  char pszMessage[100];        // informational message
  static char pBuf[101];       // send/recv buffer
```

```
int nBytesRecv;              // number of bytes received
int nBytesSent;              // number of bytes sent
static int nTotalBytesToSend;// total number of bytes to send
static int nBytesToSend = 0; // number of bytes to send
int nError;                  // WinSock error
static SOCKADDR_IN addrFrom; // address of client
static int nAddrFromLen = sizeof(addrFrom); // length of client address struct
static IN_ADDR inFrom;       // IP address of client

// get pointer to list box used for status messages
CListBox *plb = (CListBox *)GetDlgItem(IDC_LIST_STATUS);

// check for an error
if (WSAGETSELECTERROR(lParam) != 0)
{
  wsprintf(pszMessage, "Stream echo server async select got error %d",
   WSAGETSELECTERROR(lParam));
  plb->InsertString(0, pszMessage);
  return 0L;
}

// what event are we being notified of?
switch (WSAGETSELECTEVENT(lParam))
{
  case FD_ACCEPT:
    // if we don't have a connection yet, accept the new connection

    if (m_sClient == INVALID_SOCKET)
    {
      m_sClient = accept(m_s, (LPSOCKADDR)&addrFrom, &nAddrFromLen);
      if (m_sClient == INVALID_SOCKET)
      {
        nError = WSAGetLastError();
        if (nError != WSAEWOULDBLOCK)
        {
          wsprintf(pszMessage, "Error %d accepting connection",
           nError);
          plb->InsertString(0, pszMessage);
        }
      }
      else
      {
        // copy the four byte IP address into an IP address structure
        memcpy(&inFrom, &addrFrom.sin_addr.s_addr, 4);

        wsprintf(pszMessage, "Connection accepted from %s, %d",
         inet_ntoa(inFrom), ntohs(addrFrom.sin_port));
        plb->InsertString(0, pszMessage);
      }

      WSAAsyncSelect(m_sClient, m_hWnd, WM_USER_ASYNC_SELECT,
       FD_READ | FD_WRITE | FD_CLOSE);
    }
    else
      plb->InsertString(0, "Busy: refused connection");
    break;
```

continues

Listing 8.19. continued

```
    case FD_CLOSE:
      // close the client socket

      closesocket(m_sClient);
      m_sClient = INVALID_SOCKET;
      plb->InsertString(0, "Client closed connection");
      break;

    case FD_WRITE:
      // echo the data back to the client

      plb->InsertString(0, "FD_WRITE");

      // are there bytes to send?
      if (nBytesToSend != 0)
      {
        // send the data
        nBytesSent = send(m_sClient, &pBuf[nTotalBytesToSend - nBytesToSend],
         nBytesToSend, 0);

        // check for send error
        if (nBytesSent == SOCKET_ERROR)
        {
          // if the error is just that the send would block,
          // don't do anything...we'll get another FD_WRITE soon
          nError = WSAGetLastError();
          if (nError != WSAEWOULDBLOCK)
          {
            wsprintf(pszMessage, "Error %d sending data to %s, %d",
             nError, inet_ntoa(inFrom), ntohs(addrFrom.sin_port));
            plb->InsertString(0, pszMessage);

            nBytesToSend = nTotalBytesToSend = 0;
          }
        }
        else
        {
          wsprintf(pszMessage, "Data sent (%s) to %s, %d",
           pBuf, inet_ntoa(inFrom), ntohs(addrFrom.sin_port));
          plb->InsertString(0, pszMessage);

          nBytesToSend = nBytesToSend - nBytesSent;
          if (nBytesToSend == 0)
            nTotalBytesToSend = 0;;
          else
            // there are more bytes to send so we'll trigger
            // the FD_WRITE event again
            PostMessage(WM_USER_ASYNC_SELECT, m_s,
             WSAMAKESELECTREPLY(FD_WRITE, 0));
        }

        // just in case the FD_READ was called but it didn't read
        // because the buffer still contained data to send
        if (nBytesToSend == 0)
          PostMessage(WM_USER_ASYNC_SELECT, m_sClient,
```

```
            WSAMAKESELECTREPLY(FD_READ, 0));
        }
        break;

      case FD_READ:
        // receive data back from a client

        plb->InsertString(0, "FD_READ");

        // if there are still bytes waiting to be sent back (echoed)
        // to the client, don't do anything here (the FD_WRITE handler will
        // generate FD_READ when it is through with sending)
        if (nBytesToSend == 0)
        {
          // receive data
          nBytesRecv = recv(m_sClient, pBuf, 100, 0);

          // check for receive error
          if (nBytesRecv == SOCKET_ERROR)
          {
            // if the error is just that the receive would block,
            // don't do anything...we'll get another FD_READ soon
            nError = WSAGetLastError();
            if (nError != WSAEWOULDBLOCK)
            {
              wsprintf(pszMessage, "Error %d receiving data", nError);
              plb->InsertString(0, pszMessage);
            }
          }
          else
          {
            nBytesToSend = nTotalBytesToSend = nBytesRecv;

            pBuf[nBytesToSend] = '\0';
            wsprintf(pszMessage, "Data received (%s) from %s, %d",
             pBuf, inet_ntoa(inFrom), ntohs(addrFrom.sin_port));
            plb->InsertString(0, pszMessage);

            // just in case the FD_WRITE was called but it didn't have
            // any data to send at that time (it has data to send now)
            PostMessage(WM_USER_ASYNC_SELECT, m_sClient,
             WSAMAKESELECTREPLY(FD_WRITE, 0));
          }
        }
        break;

      default:
        break;
    }

    return 0L;
}
```

Stream Echo Client SECLIENT

The stream echo client, SECLIENT, follows the same basic outline as DECLIENT. The primary difference lies in the implementation of the `CMainView` object. The header file for the `CMainView` object is shown in Listing 8.20. Its implementation is shown in Listing 8.21. This object performs most of the work for the SECLIENT application. `CMainView::OnInitialUpdate()` is called soon after the object is created. This function is responsible for creating a socket, connecting to the server, waiting to send and receive data, and setting a timer to be used for sending data. When the connection with the server is made, data is ready to be received, or data can be sent, the `CMainView::OnAsyncSelect()` member function is called due to the message mapping of the user-defined message WM_USER_ASYNC_SELECT. The `CMainView::OnTimer()` function is called every five seconds to format a string to send to the echo server.

Listing 8.20. MAINVIEW.H for SECLIENT.

```
// mainview.h : header file
//

/////////////////////////////////////////////////////////////////////////////
// CMainView form view

#ifndef __AFXEXT_H__
#include <afxext.h>
#endif

class CMainView : public CFormView
{
  DECLARE_DYNCREATE(CMainView)

public:
  SOCKET m_s;             // socket
  SOCKADDR_IN m_addr;     // address of server
  IN_ADDR m_in;           // IP address of server
  int m_nBytesToSend;     // bytes left to send in the buffer
  int m_nTotalBytesToSend; // total bytes in the buffer
  char m_pBuf[101];         // buffer to send

protected:
  CMainView();       // protected constructor used by dynamic creation

// Form Data
public:
  //{{AFX_DATA(CMainView)
  enum { IDD = IDD_DIALOG_MAIN };
    // NOTE: the ClassWizard will add data members here
  //}}AFX_DATA

// Attributes
public:
```

```
// Operations
public:

// Implementation
protected:
  virtual ~CMainView();
  virtual void DoDataExchange(CDataExchange* pDX);  // DDX/DDV support
  virtual void OnInitialUpdate();
  // Generated message map functions
  //{{AFX_MSG(CMainView)
  afx_msg LONG OnAsyncSelect(WPARAM wParam, LPARAM lParam);
  afx_msg void OnTimer(UINT nIDEvent);
  //}}AFX_MSG
  DECLARE_MESSAGE_MAP()
};

/////////////////////////////////////////////////////////////////////////////

#define WM_USER_ASYNC_SELECT (WM_USER + 1)
```

Listing 8.21. MAINVIEW.CPP for SECLIENT.

```
// mainview.cpp : implementation file
//

#include "stdafx.h"
#include "seclient.h"
#include "mainview.h"
#include "servdlg.h"

#ifdef _DEBUG
#undef THIS_FILE
static char BASED_CODE THIS_FILE[] = __FILE__;
#endif

/////////////////////////////////////////////////////////////////////////////
// CMainView

IMPLEMENT_DYNCREATE(CMainView, CFormView)

CMainView::CMainView()
  : CFormView(CMainView::IDD)
{
  m_s = INVALID_SOCKET;  // initialize socket to invalid handle

  //{{AFX_DATA_INIT(CMainView)
    // NOTE: the ClassWizard will add member initialization here
  //}}AFX_DATA_INIT
}

CMainView::~CMainView()
{
  // if the socket was opened successfully, close it
```

continues

Listing 8.21. continued

```
  if (m_s != INVALID_SOCKET)
  {
    closesocket(m_s);
    m_s = INVALID_SOCKET;
  }
}

void CMainView::DoDataExchange(CDataExchange* pDX)
{
  CFormView::DoDataExchange(pDX);
  //{{AFX_DATA_MAP(CMainView)
    // NOTE: the ClassWizard will add DDX and DDV calls here
  //}}AFX_DATA_MAP
}


BEGIN_MESSAGE_MAP(CMainView, CFormView)
  //{{AFX_MSG_MAP(CMainView)
  ON_MESSAGE(WM_USER_ASYNC_SELECT, OnAsyncSelect)
  ON_WM_TIMER()
  //}}AFX_MSG_MAP
END_MESSAGE_MAP()

/////////////////////////////////////////////////////////////////////////////
// CMainView message handlers

void CMainView::OnInitialUpdate()
{
  // get pointer to list box used for status messages
  CListBox *plb = (CListBox *)GetDlgItem(IDC_LIST_STATUS);

  // prompt for server information (IP and port)
  CServerDlg dlg;
  if (dlg.DoModal() == IDCANCEL)
    return;

  plb->InsertString(0, "Initializing...");

  // create the socket
  m_s = socket(AF_INET, SOCK_STREAM, 0);
  if (m_s == INVALID_SOCKET)
    plb->InsertString(0, "Stream echo client could not create socket");
  else
  {
    // fill out the server's address
    m_addr.sin_family = AF_INET;
    m_addr.sin_port = htons(atoi(dlg.m_stringPort));
    m_addr.sin_addr.s_addr = inet_addr(dlg.m_stringIP);

    // save sending client's IP address
    memcpy(&m_in, &m_addr.sin_addr.s_addr, 4);

    // do the asynchronous select to wait for data
    if (WSAAsyncSelect(m_s, m_hWnd, WM_USER_ASYNC_SELECT, FD_CONNECT) ==
     SOCKET_ERROR)
      plb->InsertString(0, "Stream echo client could not do async select");
```

```
    else
    {
      // try to make the connection
      // if it doesn't succeed it may still be ok as long
      // as the error was that the connection would block
      if (connect(m_s, (LPSOCKADDR)&m_addr, sizeof(m_addr)) == SOCKET_ERROR)
      {
        int nError = WSAGetLastError();
        if (nError != WSAEWOULDBLOCK)
          plb->InsertString(0, "Stream echo client could not connect");
      }
      SetTimer(1, 5000, NULL);
    }
  }
}

//////////////////////////////////////////////////////////////////////////////
// CMainView::OnAsyncSelect()
//
LONG CMainView::OnAsyncSelect(WPARAM wParam, LPARAM lParam)
{
  char pszMessage[100];         // informational message
  static char pBuf[101];        // send/recv buffer
  int nBytesRecv;               // number of bytes received
  int nBytesSent;               // number of bytes sent
  int nError;                   // WinSock error

  // get pointer to list box used for status messages
  CListBox *plb = (CListBox *)GetDlgItem(IDC_LIST_STATUS);

  // check for an error
  if (WSAGETSELECTERROR(lParam) != 0)
  {
    wsprintf(pszMessage, "Datagrem echo client async select got error %d",
     WSAGETSELECTERROR(lParam));
    plb->InsertString(0, pszMessage);
    return 0L;
  }

  // what event are we being notified of?
  switch (WSAGETSELECTEVENT(lParam))
  {
    case FD_CONNECT:
      // the connection has been completed

      plb->InsertString(0, "Stream echo client connected");

      if (WSAAsyncSelect(m_s, m_hWnd, WM_USER_ASYNC_SELECT,
       FD_READ | FD_WRITE | FD_CLOSE) == SOCKET_ERROR)
        plb->InsertString(0, "Stream echo client could not do async select");
      break;

    case FD_CLOSE:
      // close the socket

      closesocket(m_s);
      m_s = INVALID_SOCKET;
```

continues

Listing 8.21. continued

```
      plb->InsertString(0, "Server closed connection");
      break;

    case FD_WRITE:
      plb->InsertString(0, "FD_WRITE");

      // is there any data to send?
      if (m_nBytesToSend != 0)
      {
        // send the data
        nBytesSent = send(m_s, &m_pBuf[m_nTotalBytesToSend - m_nBytesToSend],
         m_nBytesToSend, 0);

        // check for send error
        if (nBytesSent == SOCKET_ERROR)
        {
          // if the error is just that the send would block,
          // don't do anything...we'll get another FD_WRITE soon
          nError = WSAGetLastError();
          if (nError != WSAEWOULDBLOCK);
          {
            wsprintf(pszMessage, "Error %d sending data to %s, %d",
             nError, inet_ntoa(m_in), ntohs(m_addr.sin_port));
            plb->InsertString(0, pszMessage);

            m_nBytesToSend = m_nTotalBytesToSend = 0;
          }
        }
        else
        {
          wsprintf(pszMessage, "Data sent (%s) to %s, %d",
           m_pBuf, inet_ntoa(m_in), ntohs(m_addr.sin_port));
          plb->InsertString(0, pszMessage);

          m_nBytesToSend = m_nBytesToSend - nBytesSent;
          if (m_nBytesToSend == 0)
            m_nTotalBytesToSend = 0;;
          else
            // there are more bytes to send so we'll trigger
            // the FD_WRITE event again
            PostMessage(WM_USER_ASYNC_SELECT, m_s,
             WSAMAKESELECTREPLY(FD_WRITE, 0));
        }
      }
      break;

    case FD_READ:
      plb->InsertString(0, "FD_READ");

      // receive data
      nBytesRecv = recv(m_s, pBuf, 100, 0);

      // check for receive error
      if (nBytesRecv == SOCKET_ERROR)
      {
```

```
        // if the error is just that the receive would block,
        // don't do anything...we'll get another FD_READ soon
        nError = WSAGetLastError();
        if (nError != WSAEWOULDBLOCK)
        {
          wsprintf(pszMessage, "Error %d receiving data", nError);
          plb->InsertString(0, pszMessage);
        }
      }
      else
      {
        pBuf[nBytesRecv] = '\0';
        wsprintf(pszMessage, "Data received (%s) from %s, %d",
         pBuf, inet_ntoa(m_in), ntohs(m_addr.sin_port));
        plb->InsertString(0, pszMessage);
      }
      break;

    default:
      break;
  }

  return 0L;
}

/////////////////////////////////////////////////////////////////////////////
// CMainView::OnTimer()
//
// Timer to generate a string to send. Won't send
// unless the previous string is completely sent.
//
void CMainView::OnTimer(UINT nIDEvent)
{
  static int nSendCount = 1;   //

  if (m_nBytesToSend == 0)
  {
    wsprintf(m_pBuf, "Hello %d", nSendCount);
    ++nSendCount;
    m_nBytesToSend = m_nTotalBytesToSend = lstrlen(m_pBuf);
    PostMessage(WM_USER_ASYNC_SELECT, m_s, WSAMAKESELECTREPLY(FD_WRITE, 0));
  }

  CFormView::OnTimer(nIDEvent);
}
```

Running the Stream Echo Server and Client

A sample sequence of events of running the stream echo server and client is as follows:

Run SESERV. It displays on which port it's listening for connections.

Run SECLIENT on the same or a different computer. It prompts for the IP address and port SESERV is using. A connection is attempted and eventually succeeds. SECLIENT's `CMainView::OnAsyncSelect()` is called with the `FD_CONNECT` event.

SESERV's `CMainView::OnAsyncSelect()` is called with the `FD_ACCEPT` event and, if the `m_sClient` socket isn't yet connected, a connection is made.

In five seconds the timer will trigger in SECLIENT, causing `CMainView::OnTimer()` to get called. No bytes are waiting to be sent yet, so the outgoing buffer is filled and a WinSock `FD_WRITE` message is faked to trigger the sending of the data. This has to be done because the real `FD_WRITE` may have been missed or it may have occurred when there was nothing to send yet.

`CMainView::OnAsyncSelect()` is called in SECLIENT with an `FD_WRITE` event. There are bytes to be sent, so an attempt to transmit them to the stream echo server is made. If the attempt succeeds, the number of bytes remaining to be sent is reduced. If there was an error sending but the error was simply that the send would block, the count of bytes to send is retained because you'll get a real `FD_WRITE` eventually. If all the bytes to be sent can't be transmitted in a single call to `send()` (unlikely given the size of the data in the sample), `FD_WRITE` events will continue to be generated and the byte count will be reduced until it's eventually 0 (zero).

Assuming that SECLIENT sends a buffer, `CMainView::OnAsyncSelect()` is called in SESERV with an `FD_READ` notice. SESERV only has one buffer for both incoming and outgoing data, so `FD_READ` is ignored if there are any bytes still to be echoed back to the client. If the data is read successfully, a byte count is recorded and a fake `FD_WRITE` message is generated to force the sending of the just-received data back to the originator (SECLIENT).

`CMainView::OnAsyncSelect()` is called in SESERV with an `FD_WRITE` event. There are bytes to be sent, so an attempt to transmit them to the stream echo client is made. If the attempt succeeds and bytes are written, the number of bytes yet to send is reduced by however many bytes were successfully written. If there was an error sending but the error was simply that the send would block, the count of bytes to send is retained because you'll get a real `FD_WRITE` eventually. Several `FD_WRITE` events may be generated until the entire buffer is echoed (although this is highly unlikely in this example, given the small buffer size).

Assuming that SESERV sends a buffer, `CMainView::OnAsyncSelect()` is called in SECLIENT with an `FD_READ` notice and the client reads the echoed data.

Another timer goes off in SECLIENT and the process repeats.

Figure 8.10 shows SESERV and SECLIENT running on the same computer, which has the IP address 166.78.16.150. The server and client were assigned ports 1067 and 1068, respectively. Notice the additional status messages regarding connections as compared to the datagram-based sample.

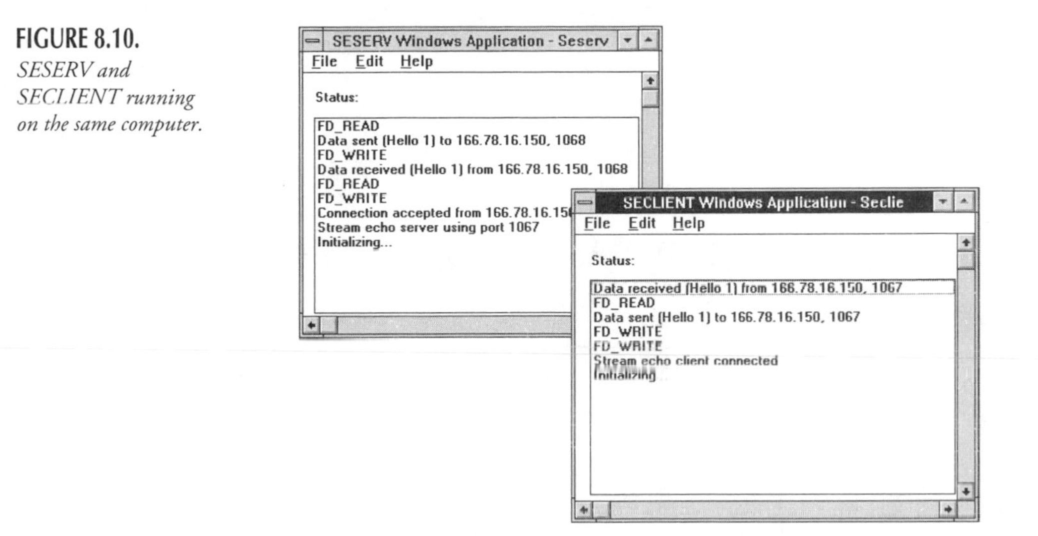

FIGURE 8.10.
SESERV and SECLIENT running on the same computer.

Summary

This chapter demonstrates the use of many important WinSock functions in complete applications. Functions are demonstrated that initialize WinSock, provide detailed information about the WinSock TCP/IP stack on the computer, do database lookups, and transfer data over stream and datagram sockets.

Several enhancements could be made to the programs explained here to make them more robust. One modification you may want to explore on your own is the capability to enter a host name, rather than simply an IP address, into the DECLIENT and SECLIENT applications. Try using `WSAAsyncGetHostByName()` for this purpose, but don't forget to call `inet_addr()` first just in case the user did enter an IP address.

Chapters 9 through 13 introduce several C++ classes that encapsulate WinSock functionality and make it even easier to write networked applications.

III

WinSock Class Library

9
Design Goals

The previous chapter examined several sample programs that utilize WinSock functions. You may notice that the applications are "littered" with WinSock-specific function calls. Although that style of programming may have been considered satisfactory a few years ago, today's object-oriented concepts and languages allow applications to better isolate explicit functionality, such as networking.

The remainder of this book presents a framework upon which networked applications are built, along with several sample applications that use the framework. This framework is built as a set of C++ classes.

Objectives

The objectives of generating a class library to manage WinSock network communication are similar to the objectives that object-oriented programming has, including simplification, generalization, and encapsulation. When designing the class library, you shouldn't think of how to incorporate all of the WinSock functions into a class; you should instead look at it from the application's perspective and ask, "What does an application need to do?"

You can see from the previous sample programs that networked applications perform relatively few functions. Don't confuse functions with function calls, though. The WinSock functionality used most often is the following:

- Start and stop WinSock.
- Resolve names humans like to use into a format useable by the computer.
- Create an end-point of communication and optionally assign a name to it.
- Destroy an end-point.
- Listen for and accept connections to an end-point.
- Connect to an end-point.
- Send and receive data to and from an end-point.

Essentially, that is all the functionality WinSock provides to an application. Of course, the devil is in the details. The objective of the class library is to hide these details from the application. This allows the application to be developed and debugged separately from the networking portion. The networking portion, the WinSock class library, is developed and debugged until it's fully functional. The application can then use the class library as a simple black box; feed a certain input into the black box and get a certain output from it.

Judging from the functionality list, a good class breakdown might have three classes:

- Start, stop, and retrieve information on WinSock
- Datagram socket (send to and receive from)
- Stream socket (listen, accept, connect, send, and receive)

Encapsulation

The class library encapsulates many of the details required to effectively use WinSock. Looking at the previous samples, you can see the need for several variables, many of which are used once and then discarded. The class library encapsulates these variables and only exposes to the application those that are essential.

Simplification

The class library also has a goal of simplifying the application's access to network functionality. Part of that simplification is handled by the encapsulation of variables and functions in the class, and another part comes from exposing only what is absolutely necessary to the application. The class library hides the intricacies of performing certain functions. For example, examine the very common WinSock functionality of sending stream data. In the previous samples, the application had to know when it was able to send more data. It also had to keep track of how much of the data was left to send in the buffer after each successful, but partial, send. By using the class library, the application can simply perform a send on a piece of data and the object keeps track of when data can be sent and how much of the data remains to be sent. The object may then notify the application when it has completed the send, but in the meantime, the application divorces itself from the details of sending the data.

Generalization

Designing a class library mandates that the functionality be generalized. These classes may be base classes for some future derived classes. They must be general enough to not prevent their use as base classes, but they must also have enough functionality to be useful right away.

Compromises

To maintain the generality of the class, some compromises are made. When considering what the compromises are, you must look back to the list that describes the WinSock functionality of which an application takes advantage.

As an example of a compromise that could be made, look at a sample server application. The two servers presented in the preceding chapter, DESERV and SESERV, didn't specify which port they operated on. Instead, they let WinSock assign one dynamically. In this case, the matching client program needed to know this port number before it could communicate with the server. It's much more common that the port to which a service is assigned is hard-coded or entered into the services file on the hosts, allowing the port number to be resolved by its name. With this in mind, a compromise could be made mandating that a server socket specify either a port number or a service name; letting WinSock decide whether the port number could be prevented. This compromise simplifies both the server and client, and hence the class library itself.

Implementation Details

The entire WinSock class library, composed of several classes, is implemented in the CWINSOCK.CPP file with CWINSOCK.H containing the class declarations. This source file is simply added to each project that requires WinSock functionality. This is in contrast to creating a dynamic link library that is then linked to the application. If you want to create a DLL out of the WinSock classes, you have to use a Microsoft Foundation Class Extension DLL because some of the WinSock classes are derived from MFC classes. The creation of such a DLL is beyond the scope of this book, but documentation on how to do so is available from Microsoft sources such as the Developer Network CD.

The actual code for the WinSock class libraries follows the convention used in the Microsoft Foundation Class library. All class names begin with a capital *C*, as in:

```
class CWinSock
```

All class member variables begin with the `m_` prefix. The Hungarian naming convention is appended after the `m_` prefix but before the actual variable name. For example, an integer containing the length of a buffer might look like the following:

```
int m_nBufLen;
```

This naming convention should ensure quick, easy recognition and understanding of WinSock class references in your applications.

Summary

This chapter introduces the notion of a WinSock class library, including its requirements and possible limitations. Chapters 10 through 13 describe several classes that compose the WinSock class library. These classes are then used in fully functional programs in Chapters 14 through 16.

10
CWinSock

This chapter discusses the `CWinSock` class.

This class is responsible for initializing the WinSock subsystem, shutting down WinSock, and retrieving WinSock TCP/IP stack information.

The class declaration is as follows:

```
/////////////////////////////////////////////////////////////////////////////
// CWinSock
//
class CWinSock
{
private:
  WORD m_wVersionRequired;   // WinSock version required by application
  int m_nLastError;          // last WinSock error
  WSADATA m_wsaData;         // WinSock information

public:
  CWinSock(WORD wVersionRequired = MAKEWORD(1, 1));
  int Startup();
  int Shutdown();
  void Information(LPWSADATA pwsaData);
  int LastError() { return m_nLastError; }
};
```

The class contains three private member variables, which are inaccessible outside the class implementation.

CWinSock Constructor

The constructor for the CWinSock object simply initializes two member variables. The `m_wVersionRequired` variable is the WinSock version that's required by the application. It's passed into the constructor by the application. If this parameter is not supplied, it defaults to version 1.1. The class' constructor looks like the following:

```
/////////////////////////////////////////////////////////////////////////////
// CWinSock constructor
//
// Constructs the CWinSock object. Initializes member variables
//
CWinSock::CWinSock(WORD wVersionRequired/*= MAKEWORD(1, 1)*/)
{
  // initialize member variables
  m_wVersionRequired = wVersionRequired;
  m_nLastError = 0;
}
```

CWinSock::Startup()

The `Startup()` member function actually initializes the WinSock subsystem. It must be called before any other WinSock data manipulation functions are called. If an error

occurs during initialization, the function returns the CWINSOCK_WINSOCK_ERROR error code and the m_nLastError member variable contains the actual WinSock error. Its implementation looks like the following:

```
/////////////////////////////////////////////////////////////////////////////
// CWinSock::Startup()
//
// Start the WinSock sub-system.
//
int CWinSock::Startup()
{
  int nStatus = CWINSOCK_NOERROR;

  m_nLastError = WSAStartup(m_wVersionRequired, &m_WSAData);

  if (m_nLastError != 0)
    nStatus = CWINSOCK_WINSOCK_ERROR;

  return nStatus;
}
```

CWinSock::Shutdown()

The Shutdown() member function cleans up the WinSock subsystem. If an error occurs during shutdown, the function returns the CWINSOCK_WINSOCK_ERROR error code and the m_nLastError member variable contains the actual WinSock error. Its implementation looks like the following:

```
/////////////////////////////////////////////////////////////////////////////
// CWinSock::Shutdown()
//
// Shutdown the WinSock sub-system.
//
int CWinSock::Shutdown()
{
  int nStatus = CWINSOCK_NOERROR;

  if (WSACleanup() != 0)
  {
    m_nLastError = WSAGetLastError();
    nStatus = CWINSOCK_WINSOCK_ERROR;
  }

  return nStatus;
}
```

CWinSock::Information()

The Information() member function copies the WinSock TCP/IP stack informational structure to a WSADATA structure passed in by the calling application. This gives the application access to some interesting data, such as the vendor information string, without you having to worry about the application wrongly modifying the m_wsaData member variable. Its implementation looks like the following:

```
/////////////////////////////////////////////////////////////////////////////
// CWinSock::Information()
//
// Copy the WinSock information structure.
//
void CWinSock::Information(LPWSADATA pwsaData)
{
  memcpy(pwsaData, &m_wsaData, sizeof(WSADATA));
}
```

CWinSock::LastError()

The LastError() member function is implemented as an in-line function. It simply returns the m_nLastError value that contains the last WinSock error message generated by the CWinSock object.

Summary

This chapter describes the simplest of the WinSock classes, but also the class that must appear in any application that expects to use WinSock in a data-handling capacity. The next chapter describes a class that handles datagram socket communications.

11 CDatagramSocket

This chapter discusses the `CDatagramSocket` class. This class simplifies an application's interaction with a datagram socket. This class is responsible for creating a datagram socket, optionally binding the socket to a name, sending and receiving data, and destroying the socket.

The class declaration is as follows:

```
/////////////////////////////////////////////////////////////////////////////
// CDatagramSocket
//
class CDatagramSocket : public CWnd
{
private:
  CWnd *m_pParentWnd;       // window to receive event notification
  UINT m_uMsg;              // message to send to m_pParentWnd on event
  SOCKET m_s;               // socket handle
  SOCKADDR_IN m_sinLocal;   // name bound to socket m_s
  int m_nLastError;         // last WinSock error
  BOOL m_bServer;           // TRUE if socket m_s is bound to a name
  CPtrList m_listWrite;     // data waiting to be sent
  CPtrList m_listRead;      // data read

public:
  CDatagramSocket(CWnd *pParentWnd, UINT uMsg);
  virtual ~CDatagramSocket();
  int CreateSocket(int nLocalPort);
  int CreateSocket(LPSTR pszLocalService = NULL);
  int DestroySocket();
  int Write(int nLen, LPVOID pData, LPSTR pszRemoteName, int nRemotePort);
  int Write(int nLen, LPVOID pData, LPSTR pszRemoteName, LPSTR pszRemoteService);
  int Write(int nLen, LPVOID pData, LPSOCKADDR_IN psinRemote);
  LPVOID Read(LPINT pnLen, LPSOCKADDR_IN psinRemote = NULL);
  int LastError() { return m_nLastError; }

private:
  void InitVars(BOOL bInitLastError = TRUE);
  LONG HandleRead(WPARAM wParam, LPARAM lParam);
  LONG HandleWrite(WPARAM wParam, LPARAM lParam);

  // message map functions
protected:
  //{{AFX_MSG(CStreamSocket)
  //}}AFX_MSG
  LONG OnWinSockEvent(WPARAM wParam, LPARAM lParam);
  DECLARE_MESSAGE_MAP()
};
```

The class contains several private member variables that are inaccessible outside of the class implementation. Of particular interest are the `m_listWrite` and `m_listRead` member variables. These `CPtrObject`-derived objects maintain pointers to the incoming and outgoing data. The data maintained by these lists has the following structure:

```
// structure used for datagram socket read/write queue
typedef struct tagDATAGRAMDATA
{
```

```
  LPVOID      pData;
  int         nLen;
  SOCKADDR_IN sin;
} DATAGRAMDATA, FAR * LPDATAGRAMDATA;
```

CDatagramSocket Constructor

The constructor for the `CDatagramSocket` object initializes the class' member variables. The `m_pParentWnd` variable is the window object that's creating this datagram socket object. This parameter is required because the `CDatagramSocket` object uses Windows messaging to communicate certain status information back to the object's user. Similarly, the `m_uMsg` variable is the actual Windows message that `m_pParentWnd` receives when the datagram socket needs to notify the application of certain information. The class' constructor looks like:

```
/////////////////////////////////////////////////////////////////////////////
// CDatagramSocket constructor
//
// Constructs the CDatagramSocket object. Initializes member variables
//
CDatagramSocket::CDatagramSocket(CWnd *pParentWnd, UINT uMsg)
{
  // initialize member variables
  m_pParentWnd = pParentWnd;
  ASSERT(m_pParentWnd != NULL);
  m_uMsg = uMsg;
  ASSERT(m_uMsg != 0);
  InitVars();
}
```

CDatagramSocket::InitVars()

The `InitVars()` member function initializes several private member variables. Its implementation looks like the following:

```
/////////////////////////////////////////////////////////////////////////////
// CDatagramSocket::InitVars()
//
// Initialize class member variables.
//
void CDatagramSocket::InitVars(BOOL bInitLastError/*= TRUE*/)
{
  if (bInitLastError)
    m_nLastError = 0;

  m_s = INVALID_SOCKET;
  memset(&m_sinLocal, 0, sizeof(m_sinLocal));
  m_bServer = FALSE;
}
```

CDatagramSocket::CreateSocket()

The `CreateSocket()` member function creates a hidden window that's used for WinSock messages (that is, `FD_READ` and `FD_WRITE`). This function also creates a datagram socket and optionally binds the socket to a name. There are two implementations of the `CreateSocket()` member function. One implementation takes an integer parameter representing the port number, in host byte order, that should be bound to the socket. The other version of `CreateSocket()` accepts a string containing the numerical port number or service name to bind to the socket, or `NULL`. If `NULL` is specified, or if the function is called with no parameter at all, the socket is not bound to a name. Generally speaking, the parameter is specified only for server type sockets.

The version of `CreateSocket()` that accepts an integer port number simply converts the integer into a string and calls the other version of `CreateSocket()`. It's implemented as follows:

```
/////////////////////////////////////////////////////////////////////////////
// CDatagramSocket::CreateSocket()
//
// Create a hidden window that will receive asynchronous messages
// from WinSock.  Also creates a socket and optionally binds it to
// a name if the socket is a server socket.
//
// This version of the CreateSocket() function takes a
// port number, in host order, as input.  A port number
// should only be specified if the socket is to be bound
// to a certain port.  If you don't care which port is
// assigned to the socket, just call CreateSocket() without
// any parameter, causing CreateSocket(NULL) to be called.
//
int CDatagramSocket::CreateSocket(int nLocalPort)
{
  // if this version of the function is being called,
  // a valid port number must be specified
  if (nLocalPort <= 0)
    return CWINSOCK_PROGRAMMING_ERROR;

  // convert the port number into a string and
  // call the version of CreateSocket() which
  // accepts a string
  char pszLocalService[18];
  _itoa(nLocalPort, pszLocalService, 10);
  return CreateSocket(pszLocalService);
}
```

The version of `CreateSocket()` that accepts a string port number or service name is implemented in the code that follows. If the datagram socket need not be bound to a specific port number or service name, simply call this function with no parameter. The C++ default argument feature will pass `NULL` to the function, triggering `CreateSocket()` to not bind the socket.

```
/////////////////////////////////////////////////////////////////////////////
// CDatagramSocket::CreateSocket()
//
// Create a hidden window that will receive asynchronous messages
// from WinSock.  Also creates a socket and optionally binds it to
// a name if the socket is a server socket.
//
// This version of the CreateSocket() function takes a
// string containing a service name or port number.
// A parameter should only be specified if the socket is to be
// bound to a certain port.  If you don't care which port is
// assigned to the socket, just call CreateSocket() without
// any parameter, causing CreateSocket(NULL) to be called.
//
int CDatagramSocket::CreateSocket(LPSTR pszLocalService/*= NULL*/)
{
  int nStatus = CWINSOCK_NOERROR;

  while (1)
  {
    // Make sure the socket isn't already created.
    // If the socket handle is valid, return from this
    // function right away so the existing parameters of
    // the object are not tampered with.
    if (m_s != INVALID_SOCKET)
      return CWINSOCK_PROGRAMMING_ERROR;

    InitVars();

    // create the hidden window
    RECT rect;
    rect.left = 0;
    rect.top = 0;
    rect.right = 100;
    rect.bottom = 100;
    if (Create(NULL, NULL, WS_OVERLAPPEDWINDOW, rect, m_pParentWnd, 0) == 0)
    {
      nStatus = CWINSOCK_WINDOWS_ERROR;
      break;
    }

    // create the socket
    m_s = socket(PF_INET, SOCK_DGRAM, 0);
    if (m_s == INVALID_SOCKET)
    {
      m_nLastError = WSAGetLastError();
      nStatus = CWINSOCK_WINSOCK_ERROR;
      DestroyWindow();
      break;
    }

    // If pszLocalService is not NULL, this is a server socket
    // that will accept data on the specified port.
    if (pszLocalService != NULL)
    {
      // this socket is bound to a port number
      // so set the server flag
      m_bServer = TRUE;
```

```
      // assign the address family
      m_sinLocal.sin_family = AF_INET;

      // assign the service port (may have to do a database lookup
      // if a service port number was not specified)
      m_sinLocal.sin_port = htons(atoi(pszLocalService));
      if (m_sinLocal.sin_port == 0)
      {
        LPSERVENT pSent = getservbyname(pszLocalService, "udp");
        if (pSent == NULL)
        {
          m_nLastError = WSAGetLastError();
          nStatus = CWINSOCK_WINSOCK_ERROR;
          closesocket(m_s);
          DestroyWindow();
          break;
        }
        m_sinLocal.sin_port = pSent->s_port;
      }

      // assign the IP address
      m_sinLocal.sin_addr.s_addr = htonl(INADDR_ANY);

      // bind the server socket to the name containing the port
      if (bind(m_s, (LPSOCKADDR)&m_sinLocal, sizeof(m_sinLocal)) == SOCKET_ERROR)
      {
        m_nLastError = WSAGetLastError();
        nStatus = CWINSOCK_WINSOCK_ERROR;
        closesocket(m_s);
        DestroyWindow();
        break;
      }
    }

    // start asynchronous event notification
    long lEvent = FD_READ | FD_WRITE;
    if (WSAAsyncSelect(m_s, m_hWnd, CWINSOCK_EVENT_NOTIFICATION, lEvent) ==
     SOCKET_ERROR)
    {
      m_nLastError = WSAGetLastError();
      nStatus = CWINSOCK_WINSOCK_ERROR;
      closesocket(m_s);
      DestroySocket();
      break;
    }

    break;
  }

  // if anything failed in this function, set the
  // socket variables appropriately
  if (nStatus != CWINSOCK_NOERROR)
    InitVars(FALSE);

  return nStatus;
}
```

CDatagramSocket::Write()

The Write() member function writes data to the specified destination host and port. The data is not immediately sent out the socket, though. Instead, the data, its length, and the data's destination address are added to the write queue. The data is not sent until the datagram socket receives the FD_WRITE message from the WinSock subsystem, notifying it that sending is now possible.

Because the data is not sent immediately, the data specified by the data pointer must not be deallocated or reused until the window that owns the datagram socket receives the m_uMsg message with wParam set to CWINSOCK_DONE_WRITING or CWINSOCK_ERROR_WRITING. When this message is received by the application window, lParam is the pointer to the data sent. At this point, the data specified by the pointer can be freed or reused. If the Write() function fails immediately, denoted by the function returning something other than CWINSOCK_NOERROR, the data pointer may be freed or reused (the m_uMsg write message will never be received for this data pointer).

There are three implementations of the Write() member function. All three functions have parameters that specify the number of bytes to send and a pointer to the data. The remaining function parameters vary depending on how you call Write(). Write() returns CWINSOCK_NOERROR on success.

One implementation takes a string containing the dotted-decimal IP address of the destination or the destination host name, and an integer parameter representing the port number, in host byte order. This version of Write() simply converts the integer to a string and calls another version of the function that's designed to accept a string containing the port number or service name.

```
/////////////////////////////////////////////////////////////////////////////
// CDatagramSocket::Write()
//
// Write data to the socket specified by the name and port.
//
// This version of the Write() function takes an integer
// representing the length of the data to send, a pointer
// to the data to send, a pointer to a string representing
// the host name to send the data to, and an integer
// representing the port number to send to.
//
// The data pointed to by pData must remain valid until either
// the Write() function returns with an error, or the
// write's completion is notified by the m_uMsg being sent
// to the window that owns this datagram object with wParam set
// to CWINSOCK_DONE_WRITING or CWINSOCK_ERROR_WRITING.
//
int CDatagramSocket::Write(int nLen, LPVOID pData,
 LPSTR pszRemoteName, int nRemotePort)
```

```
{
  // convert the port number into a string and
  // call the version of Write() which accepts
  // a string service name or number
  char pszRemoteService[18];
  _itoa(nRemotePort, pszRemoteService, 10);
  return Write(nLen, pData, pszRemoteName, pszRemoteService);
}
```

The second implementation of `Write()` takes a string containing the dotted-decimal IP address of the destination or the destination host name, and a string containing either a port number or service name. This version of `Write()` converts the two strings into a `SOCKADDR_IN` Internet address structure and calls another version of the `Write()` function.

```
/////////////////////////////////////////////////////////////////////////////
// CDatagramSocket::Write()
//
// Write data to the socket specified by the name and service
// name or number.
//
// This version of the Write() function takes an integer
// representing the length of the data to send, a pointer
// to the data to send, a pointer to a string representing
// the host name to send the data to, and a string representing
// the service name or port number to send the data to.
//
// The data pointed to by pData must remain valid until either
// the Write() function returns with an error, or the
// write's completion is notified by the m_uMsg being sent
// to the window that owns this datagram object with wParam set
// to CWINSOCK_DONE_WRITING or CWINSOCK_ERROR_WRITING.
//
int CDatagramSocket::Write(int nLen, LPVOID pData,
 LPSTR pszRemoteName, LPSTR pszRemoteService)
{
  int nStatus = CWINSOCK_NOERROR; // error status
  LPHOSTENT pHent;                // pointer to host entry structure
  LPSERVENT pSent;                // pointer to service entry structure
  SOCKADDR_IN sinRemote;          // Internet address of destination

  while (1)
  {
    // assign the address family
    sinRemote.sin_family = AF_INET;

    // assign the service port (may have to do a database lookup
    // if a service port number was not specified)
    sinRemote.sin_port = htons(atoi(pszRemoteService));
    if (sinRemote.sin_port == 0)
    {
      pSent = getservbyname(pszRemoteService, "udp");
      if (pSent == NULL)
      {
        m_nLastError = WSAGetLastError();
        nStatus = CWINSOCK_WINSOCK_ERROR;
        break;
```

```
        }
        sinRemote.sin_port = pSent->s_port;
      }

      // assign the IP address (may have to do a database lookup
      // if a dotted decimal IP address was not specified)
      sinRemote.sin_addr.s_addr = inet_addr(pszRemoteName);
      if (sinRemote.sin_addr.s_addr == INADDR_NONE)
      {
        pHent = gethostbyname(pszRemoteName);
        if (pHent == NULL)
        {
          m_nLastError = WSAGetLastError();
          nStatus = CWINSOCK_WINSOCK_ERROR;
          break;
        }
        sinRemote.sin_addr.s_addr = *(u_long *)pHent->h_addr;
      }

      // call the version of Write() that takes an
      // Internet address structure
      return Write(nLen, pData, &sinRemote);
    }

    return nStatus;
}
```

The third implementation of `Write()` takes a pointer to an Internet address structure representing the data's destination. This is the function that does the actual work of adding the data to the write queue. After the data, its length, and the destination address are added to the write queue, a message is posted to the datagram object to trigger the sending of the data. This message is normally sent by the WinSock subsystem whenever it's safe to send data out the socket. But when the last message arrived from the WinSock subsystem, there might not have been any data in the write queue that was waiting to be sent. Faking the WinSock `FD_WRITE` event causes the socket to check the write queue and send the first piece of data waiting to be sent.

```
/////////////////////////////////////////////////////////////////////////////
// CDatagramSocket::Write()
//
// Write data to the socket specified by the Internet address.
//
// This version of the Write() function takes an integer
// representing the length of the data to send, a pointer
// to the data to send, and a pointer to an Internet address
// structure to send the data to.
//
// The data pointed to by pData must remain valid until either
// the Write() function returns with an error, or the
// write's completion is notified by the m_uMsg being sent
// to the window that owns this datagram object with wParam set
// to CWINSOCK_DONE_WRITING or CWINSOCK_ERROR_WRITING.
//
int CDatagramSocket::Write(int nLen, LPVOID pData,
 LPSOCKADDR_IN psinRemote)
```

```
{
  int nStatus = CWINSOCK_NOERROR;

  while (1)
  {
    // dynamically allocate a structure to hold the
    // data pointer, the data's length, and the destination address
    LPDATAGRAMDATA pDatagramData = new DATAGRAMDATA;
    if (pDatagramData == NULL)
    {
      nStatus = CWINSOCK_WINDOWS_ERROR;
      break;
    }
    pDatagramData->pData = pData;
    pDatagramData->nLen = nLen;
    memcpy(&(pDatagramData->sin), psinRemote, sizeof(SOCKADDR_IN));

    // add the data to the list
    TRY
    {
      m_listWrite.AddTail(pDatagramData);
    }
    CATCH (CMemoryException, e)
    {
      nStatus = CWINSOCK_WINDOWS_ERROR;
      break;
    }
    END_CATCH

    // trigger the FD_WRITE handler to try to send
    PostMessage(CWINSOCK_EVENT_NOTIFICATION, m_s, WSAMAKESELECTREPLY(FD_WRITE, 0));
    break;
  }

  return nStatus;
}
```

CDatagramSocket::Read()

The `Read()` member function retrieves data that was sent to the socket. The application may call `Read()` when the window that owns the datagram socket receives the `m_uMsg` message with `wParam` set to `CWINSOCK_DONE_READING`. When this message is received by the application window, `lParam` is the number of `Read()` function calls that can be executed (that is, `lParam` is the number of datagram packets presently stored in the read queue). The `Read()` function takes a pointer to an integer (`pnLen`) and, optionally, a pointer to a `SOCKADDR_IN` structure (`psinRemote`). Upon successful completion of `Read()`, a pointer to the data is returned and the integer pointed to by `pnLen` contains the number of bytes in the datagram returned. If a pointer was supplied for the `psinRemote` parameter, the address of the sender of the data is returned. On error, `NULL` is returned.

```
/////////////////////////////////////////////////////////////////////////////
// CDatagramSocket::Read()
```

```
//
// Read data that has been received by the socket.
//
// This function takes a pointer to an integer that will be filled
// with the length of the data read and an optional pointer
// to an Internet address structure that will be filled with
// the address of the sender of the data.
//
// A pointer to the data is returned on success.  The application
// using this object must free this pointer.  NULL is returned on failure.
//
LPVOID CDatagramSocket::Read(LPINT pnLen, LPSOCKADDR_IN psinRemote/*= NULL*/)
{
  LPVOID pData = NULL;

  // check to see if there is data to retrieve
  if (!m_listRead.IsEmpty())
  {
    // remove the stream data from the list
    LPDATAGRAMDATA pDatagramData = (LPDATAGRAMDATA)m_listRead.RemoveHead();
    pData = pDatagramData->pData;
    *pnLen = pDatagramData->nLen;
    if (psinRemote != NULL)
      memcpy(psinRemote, &(pDatagramData->sin), sizeof(SOCKADDR_IN));
    delete pDatagramData;
  }

  return pData;
}
```

CDatagramSocket::OnWinSockEvent()

The `OnWinSockEvent()` member function handles the asynchronous event notification messages sent by the WinSock subsystem. The WinSock events of interest are `FD_READ` and `FD_WRITE`. Interest in these events is registered by the call to `WSAAsyncSelect()` in the `CreateSocket()` member function. The Microsoft Foundation Class message map facility is used to map the `CWINSOCK_EVENT_NOTIFICATION` message to the `OnWinSockEvent()` function. The message map looks like the following:

```
// message map
BEGIN_MESSAGE_MAP(CDatagramSocket, CWnd)
  //{{AFX_MSG_MAP(CDatagramSocket)
  //}}AFX_MSG_MAP
  ON_MESSAGE(CWINSOCK_EVENT_NOTIFICATION, OnWinSockEvent)
END_MESSAGE_MAP()
```

The code for `OnWinSockEvent()` follows. It simply checks for errors and, if there are none, calls an appropriate message handler.

```
/////////////////////////////////////////////////////////////////////////////
// CDatagramSocket::OnWinSockEvent()
//
// Called when there is an asynchronous event on the socket.
//
```

```
LONG CDatagramSocket::OnWinSockEvent(WPARAM wParam, LPARAM lParam)
{
  // check for an error
  if (WSAGETSELECTERROR(lParam) != 0)
    return 0L;

  // what event are we being notified of?
  switch (WSAGETSELECTEVENT(lParam))
  {
    case FD_READ:
      return HandleRead(wParam, lParam);
      break;
    case FD_WRITE:
      return HandleWrite(wParam, lParam);
      break;
    default:
      // this should never happen
      ASSERT(0);
      break;
  }

  return 0L;
}
```

CDatagramSocket::HandleRead()

The `HandleRead()` member function handles the asynchronous `FD_READ` event notification messages sent by the WinSock subsystem. This function is called when WinSock thinks a read from the socket will succeed. The first portion of this function allocates memory for the datagram data structure. A `recvfrom()` is then attempted. If the receive is successful, the data is added to the read queue. If everything goes OK, the `m_uMsg` message is posted to the application window that owns this datagram socket object, with `wParam` set to `CWINSOCK_DONE_READING` and `lParam` set to the number of datagrams waiting to be read. When the application receives this message, it should call the `Read()` member function. If there is an error in receiving the datagram, `wParam` is set to `CWINSOCK_ERROR_READING`.

```
/////////////////////////////////////////////////////////////////////////////
// CDatagramSocket::HandleRead()
//
// Called when there is an asynchronous read event on the socket.
//
// If the read was successful, the data, its length, and the address
// of the sender of the data, are stored in the read queue. Upon
// a successful read, the application window using this object is
// then notified with the m_uMsg message (wParam set to
// CWINSOCK_DONE_READING; lParam set to the number of data chunks
// in the read queue).  At this point, the application should call
// Read(). If the read fails for some reason, the m_uMsg is sent
// with wParam set to CWINSOCK_ERROR_READING.
//
LONG CDatagramSocket::HandleRead(WPARAM wParam, LPARAM lParam)
```

```
{
  while (1)
  {
    // allocate memory for incoming data
    LPVOID pData = malloc(READ_BUF_LEN);
    LPDATAGRAMDATA pDatagramData = new DATAGRAMDATA;
    if ((pData == NULL) || (pDatagramData == NULL))
    {
      // free anything that was allocated
      if (pData != NULL)
        free(pData);
      pData = NULL;
      if (pDatagramData != NULL)
        delete pDatagramData;
      pDatagramData = NULL;

      // tell the parent that a possible data read failed
      m_pParentWnd->PostMessage(m_uMsg, CWINSOCK_ERROR_READING);

      // fake the event to try again
      PostMessage(CWINSOCK_EVENT_NOTIFICATION, m_s,
       WSAMAKESELECTREPLY(FD_READ, 0));

      break;
    }

    // receive data
    int nAddrLen = sizeof(SOCKADDR_IN);
    int nBytesRead = recvfrom(m_s, (LPSTR)pData, READ_BUF_LEN, 0,
     (LPSOCKADDR)&(pDatagramData->sin), &nAddrLen);
    if (nBytesRead == SOCKET_ERROR)
    {
      // free memory for incoming data
      free(pData);
      pData = NULL;
      delete pDatagramData;
      pDatagramData = NULL;

      // if the error is just that the read would block,
      // don't do anything; we'll get another FD_READ soon
      m_nLastError = WSAGetLastError();
      if (m_nLastError == WSAEWOULDBLOCK)
        m_nLastError = 0;
      else
        // tell the parent that a data read failed
        m_pParentWnd->PostMessage(m_uMsg, CWINSOCK_ERROR_READING);

      break;
    }

    // add the data to the list
    pDatagramData->pData = pData;
    pDatagramData->nLen = nBytesRead;
    TRY
    {
      m_listRead.AddTail(pDatagramData);
    }
    CATCH (CMemoryException, e)
```

```
    {
      free(pData);
      pData = NULL;
      delete pDatagramData;
      pDatagramData = NULL;
      // tell the parent that a data read failed
      m_pParentWnd->PostMessage(m_uMsg, CWINSOCK_ERROR_READING);
      break;
    }
    END_CATCH

    // tell the parent that data has been read
    m_pParentWnd->PostMessage(m_uMsg, CWINSOCK_DONE_READING,
     (LPARAM)m_listRead.GetCount());

    break;
  }

  return 0L;
}
```

CDatagramSocket::HandleWrite()

The `HandleWrite()` member function handles the asynchronous `FD_WRITE` event notification messages sent by the WinSock subsystem. This function is called when WinSock thinks a write out of the socket will succeed. The first portion of this socket checks to see whether there is any data waiting to be sent from the write queue. This queue is added to by the application calling the `Write()` member function. If there is data in the write queue, a `sendto()` is attempted. If the `sendto()` would block, the data is retained to have another send attempted at a later time. If the `sendto()` fails with an error other than `WSAEWOULDBLOCK`, the data is removed from the write queue and the `m_uMsg` message is sent to the application window with `wParam` set to `CWINSOCK_ERROR_WRITING` and `lParam` the pointer to the data that was unsuccessfully sent. If the `sendto()` succeeds, `wParam` is `CWINSOCK_DONE_WRITING` and `lParam` is the data pointer. When the application receives this message notification, it's safe to free or reuse the storage space pointed to by the pointer returned in `lParam`.

```
/////////////////////////////////////////////////////////////////////////////
// CDatagramSocket::HandleWrite()
//
// Called when there is an asynchronous write event on the socket.
//
// If there is data in the write queue waiting to be sent,
// a WinSock send is attempted. If the send is successful,
// a m_uMsg message is sent to the application window with
// wParam set to CWINSOCK_DONE_WRITING and lParam set to the
// address of the data that was sent. On send failure,
// wParam is set to CWINSOCK_ERROR_WRITING and lParam set to
// the address of the data which couldn't be sent. In either
// case, the application may free the pointer pointing to
// the data or reuse that data buffer.
```

```
//
LONG CDatagramSocket::HandleWrite(WPARAM wParam, LPARAM lParam)
{
  while (1)
  {
    // check to see if there is any data to send
    if (m_listWrite.IsEmpty())
      break;

    // get pointers to data, data length, and destination address
    LPDATAGRAMDATA pDatagramData = (LPDATAGRAMDATA)m_listWrite.GetHead();
    LPVOID pData = pDatagramData->pData;
    int nLen = pDatagramData->nLen;
    SOCKADDR_IN sin;
    memcpy(&sin, &(pDatagramData->sin), sizeof(SOCKADDR_IN));

    // send the data
    BOOL bRemove = FALSE;       // remove data from queue?
    int nBytesSent = sendto(m_s, (LPCSTR)pData, nLen, 0,
     (LPSOCKADDR)&sin, sizeof(SOCKADDR_IN));
    if (nBytesSent == SOCKET_ERROR)
    {
      // if the error is just that the send would block,
      // don't do anything; we'll get another FD_WRITE soon
      m_nLastError = WSAGetLastError();
      if (m_nLastError == WSAEWOULDBLOCK)
        m_nLastError = 0;
      else
      {
        bRemove = TRUE;
        m_pParentWnd->PostMessage(m_uMsg, CWINSOCK_ERROR_WRITING,
         (LPARAM)pData);
      }
    }
    else
    {
      // if data was sent, we must still check to see
      // if all the bytes were sent
      bRemove = TRUE;
      if (nBytesSent == nLen)
        m_pParentWnd->PostMessage(m_uMsg, CWINSOCK_DONE_WRITING,
         (LPARAM)pData);
      else
        m_pParentWnd->PostMessage(m_uMsg, CWINSOCK_ERROR_WRITING,
         (LPARAM)pData);
    }

    // if the data was sent or there was a real
    // error, remove the data from the queue
    if (bRemove)
    {
      delete pDatagramData;
      m_listWrite.RemoveHead();
    }

    // if there is more data to send, trigger this FD_WRITE handler
    if (!m_listWrite.IsEmpty())
      PostMessage(CWINSOCK_EVENT_NOTIFICATION, m_s,
```

```
        WSAMAKESELECTREPLY(FD_WRITE, 0));

      break;
    }

  return 0L;
}
```

CDatagramSocket::DestroySocket()

The `DestroySocket()` member function removes any data queued up on the read or write queues, closes the socket, and destroys the hidden window that's used for WinSock messages. It's implemented as follows:

```
/////////////////////////////////////////////////////////////////////////////
// CDatagramSocket::DestroySocket()
//
// Close the socket, remove any queued data,
// and destroy the hidden window.
//
int CDatagramSocket::DestroySocket()
{
  int nStatus = CWINSOCK_NOERROR;

  // make sure the socket is valid
  if (m_s == INVALID_SOCKET)
    nStatus = CWINSOCK_PROGRAMMING_ERROR;
  else
  {
    // remove any data in the write queue
    while (!m_listWrite.IsEmpty())
    {
      LPDATAGRAMDATA pDatagramData = (LPDATAGRAMDATA)m_listWrite.RemoveHead();
      LPVOID pData = pDatagramData->pData;
      delete pDatagramData;

      m_pParentWnd->PostMessage(m_uMsg, CWINSOCK_ERROR_WRITING,
       (LPARAM)pData);
    }

    // remove any data in the read queue
    while (!m_listRead.IsEmpty())
    {
      LPDATAGRAMDATA pDatagramData = (LPDATAGRAMDATA)m_listRead.RemoveHead();
      free(pDatagramData->pData);
      delete pDatagramData;
    }

    // close the socket and initialize variables
    closesocket(m_s);
    InitVars();

    // destroy the hidden window
    DestroyWindow();
```

```
  }

  return nStatus;
}
```

CDatagramSocket::LastError()

The `LastError()` member function is implemented as an in-line function. It simply returns the `m_nLastError` value that contains the last WinSock error message generated by the `CDatagramSocket` object. This function should be called whenever a `CDatagramSocket` member function returns `CWINSOCK_WINSOCK_ERROR`.

Application Responsibility

The goal of this object is to enable the rapid development of a networked application using datagram sockets. The public interface to the `CDatagramSocket` object consists of the following functions: `CreateSocket()`, `DestroySocket()`, `Read()`, `Write()`, and `LastError()`.

The application must provide a certain level of support for the datagram object. The application must provide a message handler to receive messages sent from the object. Also, the datagram object's constructor requires a pointer to the application window object and a message. A sample call to a datagram object constructor looks like the following:

```
pdg = new CDatagramSocket(this, WM_USER + 1);
```

An entry must be made in the message map to associate the `WM_USER + 1` message to an application member function.

```
BEGIN_MESSAGE_MAP(CMainFrame, CFrameWnd)
  //{{AFX_MSG_MAP(CMainFrame)
  //}}AFX_MSG_MAP
  ON_MESSAGE(WM_USER + 1, OnWinSockEvent)
END_MESSAGE_MAP()
```

The function that handles the `WM_USER + 1` message, `OnWinSockEvent` in this case, must have handlers for four different `wParam` values. In the following code snippet, `m_pdg` is a member variable of the `CMainFrame` class, which points to a `CDatagramSocket` object. The following code may be used as a template for your datagram socket object message handler:

```
LONG CMainFrame::OnWinSockEvent(WPARAM wParam, LPARAM lParam)
{
  LPVOID pDataWritten;
  LPVOID pDataRead;
  int nLen;
```

```
SOCKADDR_IN sin;

switch (wParam)
{
  case CWINSOCK_DONE_WRITING:
    // lParam = pointer to data that was sent
    pDataWritten = (LPVOID)lParam;
    // the data storage space pointed to by pDataWritten
    // may now be freed or reused
    break;
  case CWINSOCK_ERROR_WRITING:
    // lParam = pointer to data that generated error sending
    pDataWritten = (LPVOID)lParam;
    // the data storage space pointed to by pDataWritten
    // may now be freed or reused
    break;
  case CWINSOCK_DONE_READING:
    // lParam = # data chunks in queue
    pDataRead = m_pdg->Read(&nLen, &sin);
    // the data storage space pointed to by pDataRead
    // may be freed after your processing is complete
    break;
  case CWINSOCK_ERROR_READING:
    break;
  default:
    break;
}

return 0L;
}
```

Allocating the datagram socket object doesn't make the socket available for communication. The `CreateSocket()` member function must be called first. If the socket is to act as a server, it must be bound to a specific port or service name. To do that, call the function in one of the following ways:

```
int nPort;
char pszServiceName[100];
int nStatus;

...assign port or service name...

nStatus = m_pdg->CreateSocket(nPort);
nStatus = m_pdg->CreateSocket(pszServiceName);
```

If this socket isn't a server, simply call `CreateSocket()`, as in:

```
nStatus = m_pdg->CreateSocket();
```

To send data, the application must provide the number of bytes to send, a pointer to the data, and the destination specifier. The data must remain allocated until the message handler discussed previously receives a message with `wParam` set to `CWINSOCK_DONE_WRITING` or `CWINSOCK_ERROR_WRITING`. In this case, `lParam` is the pointer

initially passed to `Write()`. The data may also be deallocated if `Write()` returns an error value. There are several options for the destination specifier. The following code shows the many ways of calling `Write()`:

```
int nLen;
LPVOID pData;
char pszHostName[100];
char pszHostIP[100];
int nPort;
char pszServiceName[100];
SOCKADDR_IN sin;
int nStatus;

... allocate data buffer and assign destination specifiers...

nStatus = m_pdg->Write(nLen, pData, pszHostName, nPort);
nStatus = m_pdg->Write(nLen, pData, pszHostIP, nPort);
nStatus = m_pdg->Write(nLen, pData, pszHostName, pszServiceName);
nStatus = m_pdg->Write(nLen, pData, pszHostIP, pszServiceName);
nStatus = m_pdg->Write(nLen, pData, &sin);
```

You also have an option with the way the data buffer is allocated. You may allocate one buffer that gets continually reused. You know when it's safe to reuse the buffer when the write notification message comes in with `wParam` set to `CWINSOCK_DONE_WRITING` or `CWINSOCK_ERROR_WRITING`. The other option you have is to allocate a new buffer whenever you want to send. In this case you would simply free each buffer when the `CWINSOCK_DONE_WRITING` or `CWINSOCK_ERROR_WRITING` message arrives.

To receive data, the application must provide a pointer to an integer to retrieve the number of bytes read. A pointer to a `SOCKADDR_IN` structure can optionally be provided to retrieve the address of the datagram's sender. The `Read()` function returns a pointer to the data or `NULL` on error. `Read()` should be called when the message handler is activated with `wParam` set to `CWINSOCK_DONE_READING`. Following are the two ways to call `Read()`:

```
LPVOID pDataRead;
int nLen;
SOCKADDR_IN sin;

pDataRead = m_pdg->Read(&nLen);
pDataRead = m_pdg->Read(&nLen, &sin);
```

It's the application's responsibility to free the pointer returned by `Read()`.

To end the use of the datagram socket object, call `DestroySocket()`, as in:

```
int nStatus;
nStatus = m_pdg->DestroySocket();
```

Summary

This chapter describes a class to manipulate a datagram socket. The goal of this object is to enable the rapid development of a networked application using datagram communication. The next chapter describes a class that handles stream socket communications. Chapters 14 and 15 use the `CDatagramSocket` object in complete programs.

12

CStreamSocket

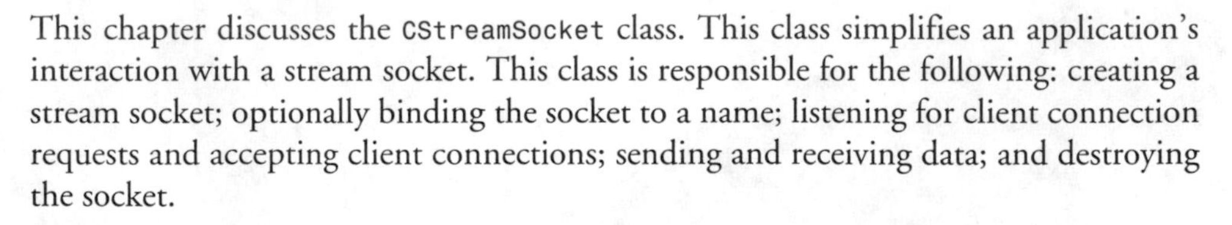

This chapter discusses the CStreamSocket class. This class simplifies an application's interaction with a stream socket. This class is responsible for the following: creating a stream socket; optionally binding the socket to a name; listening for client connection requests and accepting client connections; sending and receiving data; and destroying the socket.

The class declaration is as follows:

```
/////////////////////////////////////////////////////////////////////////////
// CStreamSocket
//
class CStreamSocket : public CWnd
{
private:
  CWnd *m_pParentWnd;        // window to receive event notification
  UINT m_uMsg;               // message to send to m_pParentWnd on event
  SOCKET m_s;                // socket handle
  SOCKADDR_IN m_sinLocal;    // name bound to socket m_s
  SOCKADDR_IN m_sinRemote;   // name on other side of m_s
  int m_nLastError;          // last WinSock error
  BOOL m_bServer;            // TRUE if socket m_s is bound to a name
  CPtrList m_listWrite;      // data waiting to be sent
  CPtrList m_listRead;       // data read

public:
  CStreamSocket(CWnd *pParentWnd, UINT uMsg);
  virtual ~CStreamSocket();
  int CreateSocket(int nLocalPort);
  int CreateSocket(LPSTR pszLocalService = NULL);
  int DestroySocket();
  int Connect(LPSTR pszRemoteName, int nRemotePort);
  int Connect(LPSTR pszRemoteName, LPSTR pszRemoteService);
  int Connect(LPSOCKADDR_IN psinRemote);
  int Accept(CStreamSocket *pStreamSocket);
  int Write(int nLen, LPVOID pData);
  LPVOID Read(LPINT pnLen);
  int GetPeerName(LPSOCKADDR_IN psinRemote);
  int LastError() { return m_nLastError; }

private:
  void InitVars(BOOL bInitLastError = TRUE);
  LONG HandleRead(WPARAM wParam, LPARAM lParam);
  LONG HandleWrite(WPARAM wParam, LPARAM lParam);

  // message map functions
protected:
  //{{AFX_MSG(CStreamSocket)
  //}}AFX_MSG
  LONG OnWinSockEvent(WPARAM wParam, LPARAM lParam);
  DECLARE_MESSAGE_MAP()
};
```

The class contains several private member variables that are inaccessible outside of the class implementation. Of particular interest are the m_listWrite and m_listRead

member variables. These CPtrObject-derived objects maintain pointers to the incoming and outgoing data. The data maintained by these lists has the following structure:

```
// structure used for stream socket read/write queue
typedef struct tagSTREAMDATA
{
  LPVOID pData;
  int    nLen;
} STREAMDATA, FAR * LPSTREAMDATA;
```

CStreamSocket Constructor

The constructor for the CStreamSocket object initializes the class' member variables. The m_pParentWnd variable is the window object that's creating this stream socket object. This parameter is required because the CStreamSocket object uses Windows messaging to communicate certain status information back to the object's user. Similarly, the m_uMsg variable is the actual Windows message that m_pParentWnd receives when the stream socket needs to notify the application of certain information. The class' constructor looks like the following:

```
/////////////////////////////////////////////////////////////////////////////
// CStreamSocket constructor()
//
// Constructs the CStreamSocket object. Initializes member variables
//
CStreamSocket::CStreamSocket(CWnd *pParentWnd, UINT uMsg)
{
  m_pParentWnd = pParentWnd;
  ASSERT(m_pParentWnd != NULL);
  m_uMsg = uMsg;
  ASSERT(m_uMsg != 0);
  InitVars();
}
```

CStreamSocket::InitVars()

The InitVars() member function initializes several private member variables. Its implementation looks like the following:

```
/////////////////////////////////////////////////////////////////////////////
// CStreamSocket::InitVars()
//
// Initialize class member variables.
//
void CStreamSocket::InitVars(BOOL bInitLastError/*= TRUE*/)
{
  if (bInitLastError)
    m_nLastError = 0;

  m_s = INVALID_SOCKET;
```

```
  memset(&m_sinLocal, 0, sizeof(SOCKADDR_IN));
  memset(&m_sinRemote, 0, sizeof(SOCKADDR_IN));
  m_bServer = FALSE;
}
```

CStreamSocket::CreateSocket()

The `CreateSocket()` member function creates a hidden window that's used for WinSock messages (that is, FD_READ, FD_WRITE, FD_ACCEPT, FD_CONNECT, and FD_CLOSE). This function also creates a stream socket and optionally binds the socket to a name. There are two implementations of the `CreateSocket()` member function. One implementation takes an integer parameter representing the port number, in host byte order, that should be bound to the socket. The other version of `CreateSocket()` accepts a string containing the numerical port number or service name to bind to the socket, or NULL. If NULL is specified, or if the function is called with no parameter at all, the socket is not bound to a name. This parameter is only specified for server type sockets.

The version of `CreateSocket()` that accepts an integer port number simply converts the integer into a string and calls the other version of `CreateSocket()`. It's implemented as follows:

```
/////////////////////////////////////////////////////////////////////////////
// CStreamSocket::CreateSocket()
//
// Create a hidden window that will receive asynchronous messages
// from WinSock.  Also creates a socket and optionally binds it to
// a name if the socket is a server socket.
//
// This version of the CreateSocket() function takes a
// port number, in host order, as input.  A port number
// should only be specified if the socket is to be bound
// to a certain port.  If you don't care which port is
// assigned to the socket, just call CreateSocket() without
// any parameter, causing CreateSocket(NULL) to be called.
//
int CStreamSocket::CreateSocket(int nLocalPort)
{
  // if this version of the function is being called,
  // a valid port number must be specified
  if (nLocalPort <= 0)
    return CWINSOCK_PROGRAMMING_ERROR;

  // convert the port number into a string and
  // call the version of CreateSocket() which
  // accepts a string
  char pszLocalService[18];
  _itoa(nLocalPort, pszLocalService, 10);
  return CreateSocket(pszLocalService);
}
```

The version of `CreateSocket()` that accepts a string port number or service name is implemented in the code that follows. If the stream socket need not be bound to a specific port number or service name, simply call this function with no parameter. The C++ default argument feature will pass `NULL` to the function, triggering `CreateSocket()` to not bind the socket.

```
/////////////////////////////////////////////////////////////////////////////
// CStreamSocket::CreateSocket()
//
// Create a hidden window that will receive asynchronous messages
// from WinSock.  Also creates a socket and optionally binds it to
// a name if the socket is a server socket.
//
// This version of the CreateSocket() function takes a
// string containing a service name or port number.
// A parameter should only be specified if the socket is to be
// bound to a certain port.  If you don't care which port is
// assigned to the socket, just call CreateSocket() without
// any parameter, causing CreateSocket(NULL) to be called.
//
int CStreamSocket::CreateSocket(LPSTR pszLocalService/*= NULL*/)
{
  int nStatus = CWINSOCK_NOERROR;

  while (1)
  {
    // Make sure the socket isn't already created.
    // If the socket handle is valid, return from this
    // function right away so the existing parameters of
    // the object are not tampered with.
    if (m_s != INVALID_SOCKET)
      return CWINSOCK_PROGRAMMING_ERROR;

    InitVars();

    // create the hidden window
    RECT rect;
    rect.left = 0;
    rect.top = 0;
    rect.right = 100;
    rect.bottom = 100;
    if (Create(NULL, NULL, WS_OVERLAPPEDWINDOW, rect, m_pParentWnd, 0) == 0)
    {
      nStatus = CWINSOCK_WINDOWS_ERROR;
      break;
    }

    // create the socket
    m_s = socket(PF_INET, SOCK_STREAM, 0);
    if (m_s == INVALID_SOCKET)
    {
      m_nLastError = WSAGetLastError();
      nStatus = CWINSOCK_WINSOCK_ERROR;
      DestroyWindow();
      break;
    }
```

```
// If pszLocalService is not NULL, this is a server socket
// that will accept data on the specified port.
if (pszLocalService != NULL)
{
  // this socket is bound to a port number
  // so set the server flag
  m_bServer = TRUE;

  // assign the address family
  m_sinLocal.sin_family = AF_INET;

  // assign the service port (may have to do a database lookup
  // if a service port number was not specified)
  m_sinLocal.sin_port = htons(atoi(pszLocalService));
  if (m_sinLocal.sin_port == 0)
  {
    LPSERVENT pSent = getservbyname(pszLocalService, "tcp");
    if (pSent == NULL)
    {
      m_nLastError = WSAGetLastError();
      nStatus = CWINSOCK_WINSOCK_ERROR;
      closesocket(m_s);
      DestroyWindow();
      break;
    }
    m_sinLocal.sin_port = pSent->s_port;
  }

  // assign the IP address
  m_sinLocal.sin_addr.s_addr = htonl(INADDR_ANY);

  // bind the server socket to the name containing the port
  if (bind(m_s, (LPSOCKADDR)&m_sinLocal, sizeof(SOCKADDR_IN)) == SOCKET_ERROR)
  {
    m_nLastError = WSAGetLastError();
    nStatus = CWINSOCK_WINSOCK_ERROR;
    closesocket(m_s);
    DestroyWindow();
    break;
  }
}

// start asynchronous event notification
long lEvent;
if (m_bServer)
  lEvent = FD_READ | FD_WRITE | FD_ACCEPT | FD_CLOSE;
else
  lEvent = FD_READ | FD_WRITE | FD_CONNECT | FD_CLOSE;
if (WSAAsyncSelect(m_s, m_hWnd, CWINSOCK_EVENT_NOTIFICATION, lEvent) ==
 SOCKET_ERROR)
{
  m_nLastError = WSAGetLastError();
  nStatus = CWINSOCK_WINSOCK_ERROR;
  closesocket(m_s);
  DestroySocket();
  break;
}
```

```
    // if this is a server, listen for client connections
    if (m_bServer)
    {
      if (listen(m_s, 3) == SOCKET_ERROR)
      {
        m_nLastError = WSAGetLastError();
        nStatus = CWINSOCK_WINSOCK_ERROR;
        closesocket(m_s);
        DestroySocket();
        break;
      }
    }

    break;
  }

  // if anything failed in this function, set the
  // socket variables appropriately
  if (nStatus != CWINSOCK_NOERROR)
    InitVars(FALSE);

  return nStatus;
}
```

CStreamSocket::Connect()

The `Connect()` member function is used by client sockets to connect to a server. There are three implementations of `Connect()` that specify the server address in different ways.

One implementation takes a string containing the dotted-decimal IP address of the destination or the destination host name, and an integer parameter representing the port number, in host byte order. This version of `Connect()` simply converts the integer to a string and calls another version of the function that's designed to accept a string containing the port number or service name.

```
/////////////////////////////////////////////////////////////////////////////
// CStreamSocket::Connect()
//
// Connect the client socket to a server specified by the name and port.
//
// This version of the Connect() function takes a pointer to a
// string representing the host name to send the data to and
// an integer representing the port number to connect to.
//
int CStreamSocket::Connect(LPSTR pszRemoteName, int nRemotePort)
{
  // convert the port number into a string and
  // call the version of Connect() which accepts
  // a string service name or number
  char pszRemoteService[18];
  _itoa(nRemotePort, pszRemoteService, 10);
  return Connect(pszRemoteName, pszRemoteService);
}
```

The second implementation of `Connect()` takes a string containing the dotted-decimal IP address of the destination or the destination host name, and a string containing either a port number or service name. This version of `Connect()` converts the two strings into a `SOCKADDR_IN` Internet address structure and calls another version of the `Connect()` function.

```
/////////////////////////////////////////////////////////////////////////////
// CStreamSocket::Connect()
//
// Connect the client socket to a server specified by the name and
// service name or port.
//
// This version of the Connect() function takes a pointer to a
// string representing the host name to send the data to and
// an integer representing the service name or port number to
// connect to.
//
int CStreamSocket::Connect(LPSTR pszRemoteName, LPSTR pszRemoteService)
{
  int nStatus = CWINSOCK_NOERROR; // error status
  LPHOSTENT pHent;                // pointer to host entry structure
  LPSERVENT pSent;                // pointer to service entry structure
  SOCKADDR_IN sinRemote;          // Internet address of destination

  while (1)
  {
    // assign the address family
    sinRemote.sin_family = AF_INET;

    // assign the service port (may have to do a database lookup
    // if a service port number was not specified)
    sinRemote.sin_port = htons(atoi(pszRemoteService));
    if (sinRemote.sin_port == 0)
    {
      pSent = getservbyname(pszRemoteService, "tcp");
      if (pSent == NULL)
      {
        m_nLastError = WSAGetLastError();
        nStatus = CWINSOCK_WINSOCK_ERROR;
        break;
      }
      sinRemote.sin_port = pSent->s_port;
    }

    // assign the IP address (may have to do a database lookup
    // if a dotted decimal IP address was not specified)
    sinRemote.sin_addr.s_addr = inet_addr(pszRemoteName);
    if (sinRemote.sin_addr.s_addr == INADDR_NONE)
    {
      pHent = gethostbyname(pszRemoteName);
      if (pHent == NULL)
      {
        m_nLastError = WSAGetLastError();
        nStatus = CWINSOCK_WINSOCK_ERROR;
        break;
      }
      sinRemote.sin_addr.s_addr = *(u_long *)pHent->h_addr;
```

```
    }

    // call the version of Connect() that takes an
    // Internet address structure
    return Connect(&sinRemote);
  }

  return nStatus;
}
```

The third implementation of `Connect()` takes a pointer to an Internet address structure representing the server. This is the function that does the actual work of connecting to the server. When the asynchronous connect operation succeeds, a `CWINSOCK_YOU_ARE_CONNECTED` message is sent to the parent of the `CStreamSocket` object.

```
/////////////////////////////////////////////////////////////////////////////
// CStreamSocket::Connect()
//
// Connect the client socket to a server specified by the
// Internet address.
//
// This version of the Connect() function takes a pointer
// to an Internet address structure to connect to.
//
int CStreamSocket::Connect(LPSOCKADDR_IN psinRemote)
{
  int nStatus = CWINSOCK_NOERROR;

  while (1)
  {
    // only clients should call connect
    if (m_bServer)
    {
      nStatus = CWINSOCK_PROGRAMMING_ERROR;
      break;
    }

    // copy the Internet address of the remote server to connect to
    memcpy(&m_sinRemote, psinRemote, sizeof(SOCKADDR_IN));

    // attempt the asynchronous connect
    if (connect(m_s, (LPSOCKADDR)&m_sinRemote, sizeof(SOCKADDR_IN)) ==
     SOCKET_ERROR)
    {
      m_nLastError = WSAGetLastError();
      if (m_nLastError == WSAEWOULDBLOCK)
        m_nLastError = 0;
      else
        nStatus = CWINSOCK_WINSOCK_ERROR;
      break;
    }

    break;
  }

  return nStatus;
}
```

CStreamSocket::Accept()

The `Accept()` member function is used by server sockets to accept a client connection request. `Accept()` is called when the parent who owns the server `CStreamSocket` object receives the `CWINSOCK_READY_TO_ACCEPT_CONNECTION` message. `Accept()` takes a pointer to another `CStreamSocket` object. It's this object that's used for data transfer between the client and server. The original server socket remains available for listening for more client connection requests.

```
/////////////////////////////////////////////////////////////////////////////
// CStreamSocket::Accept()
//
// Accept a connection request from a client.
//
// This function takes a pointer to a CStreamSocket object. This
// pointer will become the newly connected socket.
//
int CStreamSocket::Accept(CStreamSocket *pStreamSocket)
{
  int nStatus = CWINSOCK_NOERROR;

  while (1)
  {
    // must have valid CStreamSocket object pointer passed in
    if (pStreamSocket == NULL)
    {
      ASSERT(0);
      nStatus = CWINSOCK_PROGRAMMING_ERROR;
      break;
    }

    // only servers should call accept
    if (!m_bServer)
    {
      nStatus = CWINSOCK_PROGRAMMING_ERROR;
      break;
    }

    // Make sure the socket isn't already created.
    // If the socket handle is valid, return from this
    // function right away so the existing parameters of
    // the object are not tampered with.
    if (pStreamSocket->m_s != INVALID_SOCKET)
      return CWINSOCK_PROGRAMMING_ERROR;

    pStreamSocket->InitVars();

    // create the hidden window
    RECT rect;
    rect.left = 0;
    rect.top = 0;
    rect.right = 100;
    rect.bottom = 100;
    if (pStreamSocket->Create(NULL, NULL, WS_OVERLAPPEDWINDOW, rect,
     pStreamSocket->m_pParentWnd, 0) == 0)
```

```
    {
      nStatus = CWINSOCK_WINDOWS_ERROR;
      break;
    }

    // accept the client connection
    pStreamSocket->m_s = accept(m_s, NULL, NULL);
    if (pStreamSocket->m_s == INVALID_SOCKET)
    {
      m_nLastError = WSAGetLastError();
      nStatus = CWINSOCK_WINSOCK_ERROR;
      pStreamSocket->DestroyWindow();
      break;
    }

    // start asynchronous event notification
    long lEvent;
    lEvent = FD_READ ¦ FD_WRITE ¦ FD_CONNECT ¦ FD_CLOSE;
    if (WSAAsyncSelect(pStreamSocket->m_s, pStreamSocket->m_hWnd,
     CWINSOCK_EVENT_NOTIFICATION, lEvent) == SOCKET_ERROR)
    {
      m_nLastError = WSAGetLastError();
      nStatus = CWINSOCK_WINSOCK_ERROR;
      closesocket(pStreamSocket->m_s);
      pStreamSocket->DestroySocket();
      break;
    }

    break;
  }

  // if anything failed in this function, set the
  // socket variables appropriately
  if (nStatus == CWINSOCK_WINSOCK_ERROR)
    pStreamSocket->InitVars(FALSE);
  else if (nStatus == CWINSOCK_NOERROR)
    // notify the parent if the connection was accepted successfully
    pStreamSocket->m_pParentWnd->PostMessage(m_uMsg,
     CWINSOCK_YOU_ARE_CONNECTED);

  return nStatus;
}
```

CStreamSocket::GetPeerName()

The `GetPeerName()` member function is used to find the Internet address at the other end of a connected stream socket. This is a useful function for servers that may wish to log the names of the clients that use its services.

```
/////////////////////////////////////////////////////////////////////////////
// CStreamSocket::GetPeerName()
//
// Copies the Internet address of the other end of the socket
// connection into the pointer provided.
// Useful for server's to use after an Accept().
//
```

```
int CStreamSocket::GetPeerName(LPSOCKADDR_IN psinRemote)
{
  int nStatus = CWINSOCK_NOERROR;
  int nLen = sizeof(SOCKADDR_IN);

  // make sure the listening socket doesn't call this function
  if (m_bServer)
    nStatus = CWINSOCK_PROGRAMMING_ERROR;
  else if (getpeername(m_s, (LPSOCKADDR)psinRemote, &nLen) == SOCKET_ERROR)
  {
    m_nLastError = WSAGetLastError();
    nStatus = CWINSOCK_WINSOCK_ERROR;
  }

  return (nStatus);
}
```

CStreamSocket::Write()

The `Write()` member function writes data to the connected socket. The data is not immediately sent out the socket, though. Instead, the data is added to the write queue. The data is not sent until the stream socket receives the `FD_WRITE` message from the WinSock subsystem, notifying it that sending is now possible.

Because the data is not sent immediately, the data specified by the data pointer must not be deallocated or reused until the window that owns the stream socket receives the `m_uMsg` message with `wParam` set to `CWINSOCK_DONE_WRITING` or `CWINSOCK_ERROR_WRITING`. When this message is received by the application window, `lParam` is the pointer to the data sent. At this point, the data specified by the pointer can be freed or reused. If the `Write()` function fails immediately, denoted by the function returning something other than `CWINSOCK_NOERROR`, the data pointer may be freed or reused (the `m_uMsg` write message will never be received for this data pointer).

`Write()` takes parameters that specify the number of bytes to send and a pointer to the data. After the data and its length are added to the write queue, a message is posted to the stream object to trigger the sending of the data. This message is normally sent by the WinSock subsystem whenever it's safe to send data out the socket. But when the last message arrived from the WinSock subsystem, there may not have been any data in the write queue that was waiting to be sent. Faking the WinSock `FD_WRITE` event causes the socket to check the write queue and send the first piece of data waiting to be sent.

```
/////////////////////////////////////////////////////////////////////////////
// CStreamSocket::Write()
//
// Write data to the socket..
//
// This function takes an integer representing the length of the
// data to send and a pointer to the data to send.
//
```

```
// The data pointed to by pData must remain valid until either
// the Write() function returns with an error, or the
// write's completion is notified by the m_uMsg being sent
// to the window that owns this stream object with wParam set
// to CWINSOCK_DONE_WRITING or CWINSOCK_ERROR_WRITING.
//
int CStreamSocket::Write(int nLen, LPVOID pData)
{
  int nStatus = CWINSOCK_NOERROR;

  while (1)
  {
    // dynamically allocate a structure to hold the
    // data pointer and the data's length
    LPSTREAMDATA pStreamData = new STREAMDATA;
    if (pStreamData == NULL)
    {
      nStatus = CWINSOCK_WINDOWS_ERROR;
      break;
    }
    pStreamData->pData = pData;
    pStreamData->nLen = nLen;

    // add the data to the list
    TRY
    {
      m_listWrite.AddTail(pStreamData);
    }
    CATCH (CMemoryException, e)
    {
      delete pStreamData;
      nStatus = CWINSOCK_WINDOWS_ERROR;
      break;
    }
    END_CATCH

    // trigger the FD_WRITE handler to try to send
    PostMessage(CWINSOCK_EVENT_NOTIFICATION, m_s, WSAMAKESELECTREPLY(FD_WRITE, 0));
    break;
  }

  return nStatus;
}
```

CStreamSocket::Read()

The `Read()` member function retrieves data that was sent to the socket. The application may call `Read()` when the window that owns the stream socket receives the `m_uMsg` message with `wParam` set to `CWINSOCK_DONE_READING`. When this message is received by the application window, `lParam` is the number of `Read()` function calls that may be executed (that is, `lParam` is the number of data buffers presently stored in the read queue). The `Read()` function takes a pointer to an integer (`pnLen`). Upon successful completion of `Read()`, a pointer to the data is returned and the integer pointed to by `pnLen` contains the number of bytes in the data buffer returned. On error, `NULL` is returned.

```
/////////////////////////////////////////////////////////////////////////////
// CStreamSocket::Read()
//
// Read data that has been received by the socket.
//
// This function takes a pointer to an integer that will be filled
// with the length of the data read.
//
// A pointer to the data is returned on success.  The application
// using this object must free this pointer.  NULL is returned on failure.
//
LPVOID CStreamSocket::Read(LPINT pnLen)
{
  LPVOID pData = NULL;

  // check to see if there is data to retrieve
  if (!m_listRead.IsEmpty())
  {
    // remove the stream data from the list
    LPSTREAMDATA pStreamData = (LPSTREAMDATA)m_listRead.RemoveHead();
    pData = pStreamData->pData;
    *pnLen = pStreamData->nLen;
    delete pStreamData;
  }

  return pData;
}
```

CStreamSocket::OnWinSockEvent()

The `OnWinSockEvent()` member function handles the asynchronous event notification messages sent by the WinSock subsystem. The WinSock events of interest are `FD_READ`, `FD_WRITE`, and `FD_CLOSE`. If the socket is a server, interest is also expressed in the `FD_ACCEPT` event. For clients, `FD_CONNECT` is the additional event of interest. Interest in these events is registered by the call to `WSAAsyncSelect()` in the `CreateSocket()` member function. The Microsoft Foundation Class message map facility is used to map the `CWINSOCK_EVENT_NOTIFICATION` message to the `OnWinSockEvent()` function. The message map looks like the following:

```
// message map
BEGIN_MESSAGE_MAP(CStreamSocket, CWnd)
  //{{AFX_MSG_MAP(CStreamSocket)
  //}}AFX_MSG_MAP
  ON_MESSAGE(CWINSOCK_EVENT_NOTIFICATION, OnWinSockEvent)
END_MESSAGE_MAP()
```

`OnWinSockEvent()` checks for errors and, if there are none, executes an appropriate message handler. For the `FD_ACCEPT`, `FD_CONNECT`, and `FD_CLOSE` events, a message is simply relayed to the parent of the stream object. Before the `FD_CLOSE` message is relayed to the

application by the sending of the `CWINSOCK_LOST_CONNECTION` message, a check is made for additional data arriving on the socket. The `CWINSOCK_LOST_CONNECTION` message isn't sent to the application until all queued data is received and processed.

```
/////////////////////////////////////////////////////////////////////////////
// CStreamSocket::OnWinSockEvent()
//
// Called when there is an asynchronous event on the socket.
//
LONG CStreamSocket::OnWinSockEvent(WPARAM wParam, LPARAM lParam)
{
  // check for an error
  if (WSAGETSELECTERROR(lParam) != 0)
    return 0L;

  // what event are we being notified of?
  switch (WSAGETSELECTEVENT(lParam))
  {
    case FD_READ:
      return HandleRead(wParam, lParam);
      break;
    case FD_WRITE:
      return HandleWrite(wParam, lParam);
      break;
    case FD_ACCEPT:
      // tell the parent window that a client would like to connect
      // to the server socket
      m_pParentWnd->PostMessage(m_uMsg, CWINSOCK_READY_TO_ACCEPT_CONNECTION);
      break;
    case FD_CONNECT:
      // tell the parent window that the socket has connected
      m_pParentWnd->PostMessage(m_uMsg, CWINSOCK_YOU_ARE_CONNECTED);
      break;
    case FD_CLOSE:
      // check for more data queued on the socket
      // (don't tell the application that the socket is closed
      // until all data has been read and notification has been posted)
      if (HandleRead(wParam, lParam))
      {
        // fake the close event to try again
        PostMessage(CWINSOCK_EVENT_NOTIFICATION, wParam, lParam);
        break;
      }

      // tell the parent window that the socket is closed
      m_pParentWnd->PostMessage(m_uMsg, CWINSOCK_LOST_CONNECTION);
      break;
    default:
      // this should never happen
      ASSERT(0);
      break;
  }

  return 0L;
}
```

CStreamSocket::HandleRead()

The `HandleRead()` member function handles the asynchronous `FD_READ` event notification messages sent by the WinSock subsystem. This function is called when WinSock thinks a read from the socket will succeed. The first portion of this function allocates memory for the data and the data's length. A `recv()` is then attempted. If the receive is successful, the data is added to the read queue. If everything goes OK, the `m_uMsg` message is posted to the application window that owns this stream socket object, with `wParam` set to `CWINSOCK_DONE_READING` and `lParam` set to the number of data buffers waiting to be read. When the application receives this message, it should call the `Read()` member function. If there is an error in receiving the data, `wParam` is set to `CWINSOCK_ERROR_READING`. If data is received and the `CWINSOCK_DONE_READING` message is sent to the application, a 1 is returned by `HandleRead()`, otherwise, 0 is returned. This differentiation is used by `OnWinSockEvent()`'s `FD_CLOSE` handler to let it know when all data received on the socket is completely processed.

```
/////////////////////////////////////////////////////////////////////////////
// CStreamSocket::HandleRead()
//
// Called when there is an asynchronous read event on the socket.
//
// If the read was successful, the data and its length are stored
// in the read queue.  Upon a successful read, the application
// window using this object is then notified with the m_uMsg message
// (wParam set to CWINSOCK_DONE_READING; lParam set to the number of
// data chunks in the read queue).  At this point, the application
// should call Read(). If the read fails for some reason, the m_uMsg
// is sent with wParam set to CWINSOCK_ERROR_READING.
//
LONG CStreamSocket::HandleRead(WPARAM wParam, LPARAM lParam)
{
  while (1)
  {
    // allocate memory for incoming data
    LPVOID pData = malloc(READ_BUF_LEN);
    LPSTREAMDATA pStreamData = new STREAMDATA;
    if ((pData == NULL) || (pStreamData == NULL))
    {
      // free anything that was allocated
      if (pData != NULL)
        free(pData);
      pData = NULL;
      if (pStreamData != NULL)
        delete pStreamData;
      pStreamData = NULL;

      // tell the parent that a possible data read failed
      m_pParentWnd->PostMessage(m_uMsg, CWINSOCK_ERROR_READING);

      // fake the event to try again
      PostMessage(CWINSOCK_EVENT_NOTIFICATION, m_s,
       WSAMAKESELECTREPLY(FD_READ, 0));
```

```
    break;
  }

  // receive data
  int nBytesRead = recv(m_s, (LPSTR)pData, READ_BUF_LEN, 0);
  if (nBytesRead == SOCKET_ERROR)
  {
    // free memory for incoming data
    free(pData);
    pData = NULL;
    delete pStreamData;
    pStreamData = NULL;

    // if the error is just that the read would block,
    // don't do anything; we'll get another FD_READ soon
    m_nLastError = WSAGetLastError();
    if (m_nLastError == WSAEWOULDBLOCK)
      m_nLastError = 0;
    else
      // tell the parent that a data read failed
      m_pParentWnd->PostMessage(m_uMsg, CWINSOCK_ERROR_READING);

    break;
  }

  // make sure some data was read
  if (nBytesRead == 0)
  {
    // free memory for incoming data
    free(pData);
    pData = NULL;
    delete pStreamData;
    pStreamData = NULL;

    break;
  }

  // add the data to the list
  pStreamData->pData = pData;
  pStreamData->nLen = nBytesRead;
  TRY
  {
    m_listRead.AddTail(pStreamData);
  }
  CATCH (CMemoryException, e)
  {
    free(pData);
    pData = NULL;
    delete pStreamData;
    pStreamData = NULL;
    // tell the parent that a data read failed
    m_pParentWnd->PostMessage(m_uMsg, CWINSOCK_ERROR_READING);
    break;
  }
  END_CATCH

  // tell the parent that data has been read
```

```
    m_pParentWnd->PostMessage(m_uMsg, CWINSOCK_DONE_READING,
     (LPARAM)m_listRead.GetCount());

    // 1 is returned if there is data so CStreamSocket::OnWinSockEvent()'s
    // FD_CLOSE handler will know when the socket can really be closed
    return 1L;

    break;
  }

  return 0L;
}
```

CStreamSocket::HandleWrite()

The `HandleWrite()` member function handles the asynchronous `FD_WRITE` event notification messages sent by the WinSock subsystem. This function is called when WinSock thinks a write out of the socket will succeed. The first portion of this socket checks to see whether there is any data waiting to be sent from the write queue. This queue is added to by the application calling the `Write()` member function. If there is data in the write queue, a `send()` is attempted. If the `send()` would block, the data is retained to have another send attempted at a later time. If the `send()` fails with an error other than `WSAEWOULDBLOCK`, the data is removed from the write queue and the `m_uMsg` message is sent to the application window with `wParam` set to `CWINSOCK_ERROR_WRITING` and `lParam` the pointer to the data that was unsuccessfully sent. If the `send()` succeeds but not all of the bytes are sent, a pointer into the buffer is retained until the next time `HandleWrite()` is executed. When the entire buffer is successfully sent, `wParam` is set to `CWINSOCK_DONE_WRITING` and `lParam` is the data pointer. When the application receives this message notification, it's safe to free or reuse the storage space pointed to by the pointer returned in `lParam`.

```
/////////////////////////////////////////////////////////////////////////////
// CStreamSocket::HandleWrite()
//
// Called when there is an asynchronous write event on the socket.
//
// If there is data in the write queue waiting to be sent,
// a WinSock send is attempted.  If the send is successful,
// a m_uMsg message is sent to the application window with
// wParam set to CWINSOCK_DONE_WRITING and lParam set to the
// address of the data that was sent.  On send failure,
// wParam is set to CWINSOCK_ERROR_WRITING and lParam set to
// the address of the data which couldn't be sent.  In either
// case, the application may free the pointer pointing to
// the data or reuse that data buffer.  It is possible for the
// entire amount of data to not be sent in one call to send().
// In this case, an attempt is made to send the remaining portion
// of that block of data the next time HandleWrite() is invoked.
//
//
```

```
LONG CStreamSocket::HandleWrite(WPARAM wParam, LPARAM lParam)
{
  LPSTREAMDATA pStreamData;             // pointer to stream data structure
  LPVOID pData;                         // pointer to buffer to send
  int nLen;                             // total length of buffer to send
  static LPVOID pDataRemaining = NULL; // pointer into buffer to send
  static int nLenRemaining = 0;         // number of bytes left to send

  while (1)
  {
    // check to see if there is any data to send
    if (m_listWrite.IsEmpty())
      break;

    // if we are not in the middle of another buffer send,
    // get data and data length from the write queue
    pStreamData = (LPSTREAMDATA)m_listWrite.GetHead(); // not RemoveHead()
    pData = pStreamData->pData;
    nLen = pStreamData->nLen;
    if (pDataRemaining == NULL)
    {
      pDataRemaining = pData;
      nLenRemaining = nLen;
    }

    // send the data
    BOOL bRemove = FALSE;       // remove data from queue?
    int nBytesSent = send(m_s, (LPCSTR)pDataRemaining, nLenRemaining, 0);
    if (nBytesSent == SOCKET_ERROR)
    {
      // if the error is just that the send would block,
      // don't do anything; we'll get another FD_WRITE soon
      m_nLastError = WSAGetLastError();
      if (m_nLastError == WSAEWOULDBLOCK)
        m_nLastError = 0;
      else
      {
        bRemove = TRUE;
        m_pParentWnd->PostMessage(m_uMsg, CWINSOCK_ERROR_WRITING,
         (LPARAM)pData);
      }
    }
    else
    {
      // if data was sent, we must still check to see
      // if all the bytes were sent
      if (nBytesSent == nLenRemaining)
      {
        bRemove = TRUE;
        m_pParentWnd->PostMessage(m_uMsg, CWINSOCK_DONE_WRITING,
         (LPARAM)pData);
      }
      else
      {
        // the complete buffer was not sent so adjust
        // these values accordingly
        pDataRemaining = (LPVOID)((LPCSTR)pDataRemaining + nBytesSent);
        nLenRemaining = nLenRemaining - nBytesSent;
      }
```

```
    }

    // if the data was completely sent or there was
    // a real error, remove the data from the queue
    if (bRemove)
    {
      delete pStreamData;
      m_listWrite.RemoveHead();
      pDataRemaining = NULL;
      nLenRemaining = 0;
    }

    // if there is more data to send, trigger this FD_WRITE handler
    if (!m_listWrite.IsEmpty())
      PostMessage(CWINSOCK_EVENT_NOTIFICATION, m_s,
       WSAMAKESELECTREPLY(FD_WRITE, 0));

    break;
  }

  return 0L;
}
```

CStreamSocket::DestroySocket()

The `DestroySocket()` member function removes any data queued up on the read or write queues, closes the socket, and destroys the hidden window that's used for WinSock messages. It's implemented as follows:

```
/////////////////////////////////////////////////////////////////////////////
// CStreamSocket::DestroySocket()
//
// Close the socket, remove any queued data,
// and destroy the hidden window.
//
int CStreamSocket::DestroySocket()
{
  int nStatus = CWINSOCK_NOERROR;

  // make sure the socket is valid
  if (m_s == INVALID_SOCKET)
    nStatus = CWINSOCK_PROGRAMMING_ERROR;
  else
  {
    // remove any data in the write queue
    while (!m_listWrite.IsEmpty())
    {
      LPSTREAMDATA pStreamData = (LPSTREAMDATA)m_listWrite.RemoveHead();
      LPVOID pData = pStreamData->pData;
      delete pStreamData;

      m_pParentWnd->PostMessage(m_uMsg, CWINSOCK_ERROR_WRITING,
       (LPARAM)pData);
    }
```

```
    // remove any data in the read queue
    while (!m_listRead.IsEmpty())
    {
      LPSTREAMDATA pStreamData = (LPSTREAMDATA)m_listRead.RemoveHead();
      free(pStreamData->pData);
      delete pStreamData;
    }

    // close the socket and initialize variables
    closesocket(m_s);
    InitVars();

    // destroy the hidden window
    DestroyWindow();
  }

  return nStatus;
}
```

CStreamSocket::LastError()

The `LastError()` member function is implemented as an in-line function. It simply returns the `m_nLastError` value that contains the last WinSock error message generated by the `CStreamSocket` object. This function should be called whenever a `CStreamSocket` member function returns `CWINSOCK_WINSOCK_ERROR`.

Application Responsibility

The goal of this object is to enable the rapid development of a networked application using stream sockets. The public interface to the `CStreamSocket` object consists of the following functions: `CreateSocket()`, `DestroySocket()`, `Read()`, `Write()`, `Connect()`, `Accept()`, `GetPeerName()`, and `LastError()`.

The application must provide a certain level of support for the stream object. The application must provide a message handler to receive messages sent from the object. Also, the stream object's constructor requires a pointer to the application window object and a message. A sample call to a stream object constructor looks like the following:

```
ps = new CStreamSocket(this, WM_USER + 1);
```

An entry must be made in the message map to associate the `WM_USER + 1` message to an application member function.

```
BEGIN_MESSAGE_MAP(CMainFrame, CFrameWnd)
  //{{AFX_MSG_MAP(CMainFrame)
  //}}AFX_MSG_MAP
  ON_MESSAGE(WM_USER + 1, OnWinSockEvent)
END_MESSAGE_MAP()
```

The function that handles the `WM_USER + 1` message, `OnWinSockEvent` in this case, must have handlers for six different `wParam` values. In the following code snippet, `m_ps` is a member variable of the `CMainFrame` class that points to a `CStreamSocket` object. The following code may be used as a template for your stream socket object message handler:

```
LONG CMainFrame::OnWinSockEvent(WPARAM wParam, LPARAM lParam)
{
  LPVOID pDataWritten;
  LPVOID pDataRead;
  int nLen;

  switch (wParam)
  {
    case CWINSOCK_DONE_WRITING:
      // lParam = pointer to data that was sent
      pDataWritten = (LPVOID)lParam;
      // the data storage space pointed to by pDataWritten
      // may now be freed or reused
      break;
    case CWINSOCK_ERROR_WRITING:
      // lParam = pointer to data that generated error sending
      pDataWritten = (LPVOID)lParam;
      // the data storage space pointed to by pDataWritten
      // may now be freed or reused
      break;
    case CWINSOCK_DONE_READING:
      // lParam = # data chunks in queue
      pDataRead = m_ps->Read(&nLen);
      // the data storage space pointed to by pDataRead
      // may be freed after your processing is complete
      break;
    case CWINSOCK_ERROR_READING:
      break;
    case CWINSOCK_LOST_CONNECTION:
      // the other side of the socket closed the connection
      break;

    // the following handler is required for a client only
    case CWINSOCK_YOU_ARE_CONNECTED:
      break;

    // the following handler is required for a server only
    case CWINSOCK_READY_TO_ACCEPT_CONNECTION:
      // Accept() may now be called
      break;

    default:
      break;
  }

  return 0L;
}
```

Allocating the stream socket object doesn't make the socket available for communication. The `CreateSocket()` member function must be called first. If the socket is to act

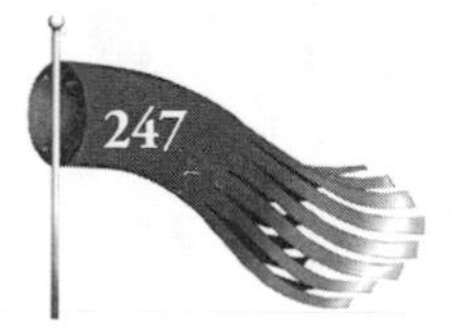

as a server, it must be bound to a specific port or service name. To do that, call the function in one of the following ways:

```
int nPort;
char pszServiceName[100];
int nStatus;

...assign port or service name...

nStatus = m_ps->CreateSocket(nPort);
nStatus = m_ps->CreateSocket(pszServiceName);
```

If this socket isn't a server, simply call `CreateSocket()`, as in:

```
nStatus = m_ps->CreateSocket();
```

A client must connect to a server before it can send or receive data. A connection is made by specifying a host specifier. There are five possible ways to call `Connect()`:

```
char pszHostName[100];
char pszHostIP[100];
int nPort;
char pszServiceName[100];
SOCKADDR_IN sin;
int nStatus;

...assign destination specifiers...

nStatus = m_ps->Connect(pszHostName, nPort);
nStatus = m_ps->Connect(pszHostIP, nPort);
nStatus = m_ps->Connect(pszHostName, pszServiceName);
nStatus = m_ps->Connect(pszHostIP, pszServiceName);
nStatus = m_ps->Connect(&sin);
```

A server must accept a connection from a client before data transfer can take place. When a connection is accepted, a new `CStreamSocket` object is used. The `Accept()` member function is called in response to the `CWINSOCK_READY_TO_ACCEPT_CONNECTION` message from the server stream socket:

```
CStreamSocket *psClient; // will communicate with the client
int nStatus;

psClient = new CStreamSocket(this, WM_USER + 2);

// m_ps is the server socket
nStatus = m_ps->Accept(psClient);
```

If a server wishes to know the Internet address of the client on the other side of an accepted connection, `GetPeerName()` is used. This function is called from the socket passed to the `Accept()` call, as in:

```
SOCKADDR_IN sin; // address of client on other side of socket
int nStatus;

nStatus = psClient->GetPeerName(&sin);
```

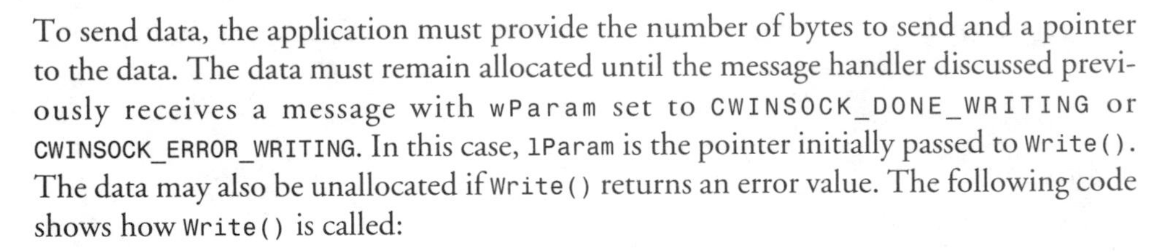

To send data, the application must provide the number of bytes to send and a pointer to the data. The data must remain allocated until the message handler discussed previously receives a message with `wParam` set to `CWINSOCK_DONE_WRITING` or `CWINSOCK_ERROR_WRITING`. In this case, `lParam` is the pointer initially passed to `Write()`. The data may also be unallocated if `Write()` returns an error value. The following code shows how `Write()` is called:

```
int nLen;
LPVOID pData;
int nStatus;

... allocate data buffer ...

nStatus = m_ps->Write(nLen, pData);
```

You have an option with the way the data buffer is allocated. You may allocate one buffer that gets continually reused. You know that it's safe to reuse the buffer when the write notification message comes in with `wParam` set to `CWINSOCK_DONE_WRITING` or `CWINSOCK_ERROR_WRITING`. The other option you have is to allocate a new buffer whenever you want to send. In this case you would simply free each buffer when the `CWINSOCK_DONE_WRITING` or `CWINSOCK_ERROR_WRITING` message arrives.

To receive data, the application must provide a pointer to an integer to retrieve the number of bytes read. The `Read()` function returns a pointer to the data or `NULL` on error. `Read()` should be called when the message handler is activated with `wParam` set to `CWINSOCK_DONE_READING`. Following are the two ways to call `Read()`:

```
LPVOID pDataRead;
int nLen;

pDataRead = m_ps->Read(&nLen);
```

It's the application's responsibility to free the pointer returned by `Read()`.

To end the use of the stream socket object, call `DestroySocket()`, as in:

```
int nStatus;
nStatus = m_ps->DestroySocket();
```

Summary

This chapter describes a class to manipulate a stream socket. The goal of this object is to enable the rapid development of a networked application using stream communication. The next chapter wraps up the class library. Chapters 14 through 16 use the `CStreamSocket` object in fully functional programs.

13

Bringing It All Together

This chapter discusses the last pieces of the WinSock class library, including a function to display a WinSock error message.

CWinSockErrorBox()

One thing that is missing thus far is a function to display an error message with a textual description of the actual WinSock error. The `CWinSockErrorBox()` function does just that.

The first parameter to `CWinSockErrorBox()` is an integer representing the WinSock error as returned by `WSAGetLastError()`. The second parameter is an optional pointer to a string that contains additional information you would like to present to the user.

The prototype for the function is as follows:

```
void CWinSockErrorBox(int nError, LPSTR pszMessage = NULL);
```

The `CWinSockErrorBox()` function is implemented as follows:

```
/////////////////////////////////////////////////////////////////////////////
// CWinSockErrorBox
//
void CWinSockErrorBox(int nError, LPSTR pszMessage/*= NULL*/)
{
#define ERROR_BUF_LEN (1000)
  char pszError[ERROR_BUF_LEN];

  wsprintf(pszError, "WinSock error %d: ", nError);

  switch (nError)
  {
    case WSAEINTR:
      lstrcat(pszError, "Interrupted system call");
      break;
    case WSAEBADF:
      lstrcat(pszError, "Bad file number");
      break;
    case WSAEACCES:
      lstrcat(pszError, "Permission denied");
      break;
    case WSAEFAULT:
      lstrcat(pszError, "Bad address");
      break;
    case WSAEINVAL:
      lstrcat(pszError, "Invalid argument");
      break;
    case WSAEMFILE:
      lstrcat(pszError, "Too many open files");
      break;
    case WSAEWOULDBLOCK:
      lstrcat(pszError, "Operation would block");
      break;
```

```
case WSAEINPROGRESS:
  lstrcat(pszError, "Operation now in progress");
  break;
case WSAEALREADY:
  lstrcat(pszError, "Operation already in progress");
  break;
case WSAENOTSOCK:
  lstrcat(pszError, "Socket operation on non-socket");
  break;
case WSAEDESTADDRREQ:
  lstrcat(pszError, "Destination address required");
  break;
case WSAEMSGSIZE:
  lstrcat(pszError, "Message too long");
  break;
case WSAEPROTOTYPE:
  lstrcat(pszError, "Protocol wrong type for socket");
  break;
case WSAENOPROTOOPT:
  lstrcat(pszError, "Protocol not available");
  break;
case WSAEPROTONOSUPPORT:
  lstrcat(pszError, "Protocol not supported");
  break;
case WSAESOCKTNOSUPPORT:
  lstrcat(pszError, "Socket type not supported");
  break;
case WSAEOPNOTSUPP:
  lstrcat(pszError, "Operation not supported on socket");
  break;
case WSAEPFNOSUPPORT:
  lstrcat(pszError, "Protocol family not supported");
  break;
case WSAEAFNOSUPPORT:
  lstrcat(pszError, "Address family not supported by protocol family");
  break;
case WSAEADDRINUSE:
  lstrcat(pszError, "Address already in use");
  break;
case WSAEADDRNOTAVAIL:
  lstrcat(pszError, "Can't assign requested address");
  break;
case WSAENETDOWN:
  lstrcat(pszError, "Network is down");
  break;
case WSAENETUNREACH:
  lstrcat(pszError, "Network is unreachable");
  break;
case WSAENETRESET:
  lstrcat(pszError, "Network dropped connection on reset");
  break;
case WSAECONNABORTED:
  lstrcat(pszError, "Software caused connection abort");
  break;
case WSAECONNRESET:
  lstrcat(pszError, "Connection reset by peer");
  break;
```

```
case WSAENOBUFS:
  lstrcat(pszError, "No buffer space available");
  break;
case WSAEISCONN:
  lstrcat(pszError, "Socket is already connected");
  break;
case WSAENOTCONN:
  lstrcat(pszError, "Socket is not connected");
  break;
case WSAESHUTDOWN:
  lstrcat(pszError, "Can't send after socket shutdown");
  break;
case WSAETOOMANYREFS:
  lstrcat(pszError, "Too many references: can't splice");
  break;
case WSAETIMEDOUT:
  lstrcat(pszError, "Connection timed out");
  break;
case WSAECONNREFUSED:
  lstrcat(pszError, "Connection refused");
  break;
case WSAELOOP:
  lstrcat(pszError, "Too many levels of symbolic links");
  break;
case WSAENAMETOOLONG:
  lstrcat(pszError, "File name too long");
  break;
case WSAEHOSTDOWN:
  lstrcat(pszError, "Host is down");
  break;
case WSAEHOSTUNREACH:
  lstrcat(pszError, "No route to host");
  break;
case WSAENOTEMPTY:
  lstrcat(pszError, "Directory not empty");
  break;
case WSAEPROCLIM:
  lstrcat(pszError, "Too many processes");
  break;
case WSAEUSERS:
  lstrcat(pszError, "Too many users");
  break;
case WSAEDQUOT:
  lstrcat(pszError, "Disc quota exceeded");
  break;
case WSAESTALE:
  lstrcat(pszError, "Stale NFS file handle");
  break;
case WSAEREMOTE:
  lstrcat(pszError, "Too many levels of remote in path");
  break;
case WSAEDISCON:
  lstrcat(pszError, "Disconnect");
  break;
case WSASYSNOTREADY:
  lstrcat(pszError, "Network sub-system is unusable");
  break;
case WSAVERNOTSUPPORTED:
  lstrcat(pszError, "WinSock DLL cannot support this application");
```

```
      break;
    case WSANOTINITIALISED:
      lstrcat(pszError, "WinSock not initialized");
      break;
    case WSAHOST_NOT_FOUND:
      lstrcat(pszError, "Host not found");
      break;
    case WSATRY_AGAIN:
      lstrcat(pszError, "Non-authoritative host not found");
      break;
    case WSANO_RECOVERY:
      lstrcat(pszError, "Non-recoverable error");
      break;
    case WSANO_DATA:
      lstrcat(pszError, "Valid name, no data record of requested type");
      break;
    default:
      lstrcpy(pszError, "Not a WinSock error");
      break;
  }

  lstrcat(pszError, "\n");

  int n = lstrlen(pszError);
  if (pszMessage != NULL)
    n += lstrlen(pszMessage);
  if ((pszMessage != NULL) && (n < ERROR_BUF_LEN))
    lstrcat(pszError, pszMessage);

  AfxMessageBox(pszError);
}
```

If the WinSock error is `WSANOTINITIALISED`, the result of the following code looks like Figure 13.1:

```
if (...WinSock function fails...)
  CWinSockErrorBox(WSAGetLastError());
```

Supplying the second parameter to `CWinSockErrorBox()`, as in the following sample, results in that shown in Figure 13.2:

```
if (...WinSock function fails...)
  CWinSockErrorBox(WSAGetLastError(),
    "Contact your software distributor for technical support");
```

FIGURE 13.1.
CWinSockErrorBox().

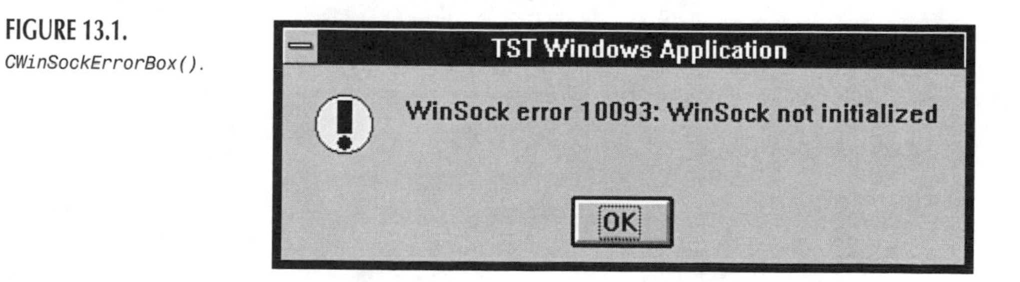

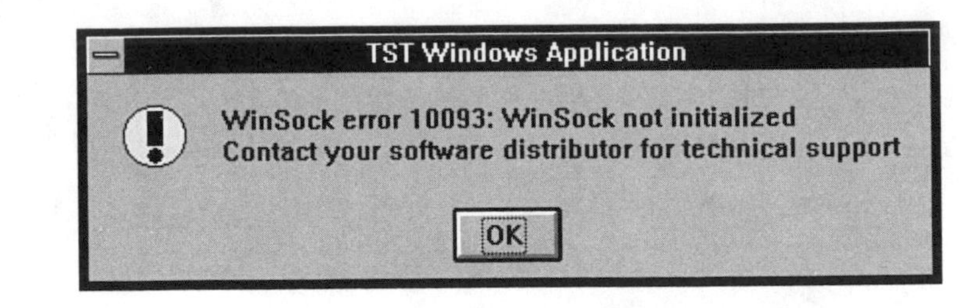

FIGURE 13.2.
`CWinSockErrorBox()` with second parameter.

Implementation Details

The error message strings that are copied into pszError within the large switch statement consume a significant amount of DGROUP space in your application. If you get compiler errors referring to DGROUP space, consider moving these error message strings into the string table of your project's resource file. You can then use the `LoadString()` function to retrieve the appropriate text.

As discussed in Chapter 9, "Design Goals," the three classes (`CWinSock`, `CDatagramSocket`, and `CStreamSocket`) and the `CWinSockErrorBox()` function are implemented in the CWINSOCK.CPP file. The class and function prototypes are contained in the CWINSOCK.H file. The CWINSOCK.CPP source file is simply added to each project that requires WinSock functionality.

Summary

This chapter wraps up the WinSock class library. The remaining chapters of the book examine several sample programs that make use of the class library developed in Chapters 9 through 13.

IV

Programming with the WinSock Class Library

14

Sample Applications

This chapter presents the reimplementation of two of the samples described in Chapter 8, "Sample Applications." This time, the WinSock class library, developed in the preceding chapters, is used rather than the raw WinSock API. The two samples are composed of two programs each: a client that sends either datagrams or stream data, and a server that receives them and sends them back to the client.

Datagram Echo Client and Server

These programs, CDESRV and CDECLNT, demonstrate the use of the `CDatagramSocket` object. The CDESRV server application receives data and sends it back to the client. The CDECLNT client application sends data to the server and receives the echoed reply. These programs are generated using Visual C++'s AppWizard feature.

Datagram Echo Server CDESRV

As in the DESERV program described in Chapter 8, this sample uses a `CFormView`-derived object named `CMainView` as its primary user interface. The `CMainView` header file is shown in Listing 14.1. The `m_pWinSock` member variable controls the starting and stopping of the WinSock subsystem for this program. The `m_pDatagram` member variable is a pointer to the datagram socket object that receives data from clients. The `OnDatagram()` member function receives status information for the datagram socket object. It's triggered by the `WM_USER_DATAGRAM` user-defined message.

Listing 14.1. MAINVIEW.H for CDESRV.

```
// mainview.h : header file
//

/////////////////////////////////////////////////////////////////////////////
// CMainView form view

#ifndef __AFXEXT_H__
#include <afxext.h>
#endif

#include "cwinsock.h"    // Windows Sockets classes

class CMainView : public CFormView
{
  DECLARE_DYNCREATE(CMainView)

private:
  CWinSock * m_pWinSock;          // WinSock sub-system startup/.shutdown
  CDatagramSocket * m_pDatagram; // Datagram socket to receive from

protected:
```

```
  CMainView();       // protected constructor used by dynamic creation

// Form Data
public:
  //{{AFX_DATA(CMainView)
  enum { IDD = IDD_DIALOG_MAIN };
    // NOTE: the ClassWizard will add data members here
  //}}AFX_DATA

// Attributes
public:

// Operations
public:

// Implementation
protected:
  virtual ~CMainView();
  virtual void DoDataExchange(CDataExchange* pDX);  // DDX/DDV support
  virtual void OnInitialUpdate();
  // Generated message map functions
  //{{AFX_MSG(CMainView)
  afx_msg LONG OnDatagram(WPARAM wParam, LPARAM lParam);
  //}}AFX_MSG
  DECLARE_MESSAGE_MAP()
};

/////////////////////////////////////////////////////////////////////////////

#define WM_USER_DATAGRAM (WM_USER + 1)
```

The implementation of the `CMainView` object is shown in Listing 14.2. This object performs most of the work for the CDESRV application. `OnInitialUpdate()` is called soon after the object is created. This function is responsible for starting the WinSock subsystem and creating a server datagram socket that waits for data to arrive on port 2000. When data is ready to be received on the socket, the `OnDatagram()` member function is triggered with `wParam` set to `CWINSOCK_DONE_READING`. Data is read and a write attempt is made to echo the data back to the client. When the write finishes, `OnDatagram()` is called with `wParam` set to `CWINSOCK_DONE_WRITING`. At this point, the data pointer is freed. When the server application is closed, `CMainView`'s destructor is called, destroying the datagram socket object and shutting down the WinSock subsystem.

Listing 14.2. MAINVIEW.CPP for CDESRV.

```
// mainview.cpp : implementation file
//

#include "stdafx.h"
#include "cdesrv.h"
#include "mainview.h"
```

continues

Listing 14.2. continued

```
#ifdef _DEBUG
#undef THIS_FILE
static char BASED_CODE THIS_FILE[] = __FILE__;
#endif

/////////////////////////////////////////////////////////////////////////////
// CMainView

IMPLEMENT_DYNCREATE(CMainView, CFormView)

CMainView::CMainView()
  : CFormView(CMainView::IDD)
{
  //{{AFX_DATA_INIT(CMainView)
    // NOTE: the ClassWizard will add member initialization here
  //}}AFX_DATA_INIT

  // initialize class variables

  m_pWinSock = NULL;
  m_pDatagram = NULL;
}

CMainView::~CMainView()
{
  // free the datagram and WinSock objects

  if (m_pDatagram)
  {
    m_pDatagram->DestroySocket();
    delete m_pDatagram;
    m_pDatagram = NULL;
  }

  if (m_pWinSock)
  {
    m_pWinSock->Shutdown();
    delete m_pWinSock;
    m_pWinSock = NULL;
  }
}

void CMainView::DoDataExchange(CDataExchange* pDX)
{
  CFormView::DoDataExchange(pDX);
  //{{AFX_DATA_MAP(CMainView)
    // NOTE: the ClassWizard will add DDX and DDV calls here
  //}}AFX_DATA_MAP
}

void CMainView::OnInitialUpdate()
{
  // get pointer to list box used for status messages

  CListBox *plb = (CListBox *)GetDlgItem(IDC_LIST_STATUS);
```

```
  // initialize the WinSock object

  m_pWinSock = new CWinSock;
  if (m_pWinSock->Startup() == CWINSOCK_NOERROR)
    plb->InsertString(0, "WinSock initialized");
  else
  {
    plb->InsertString(0, "WinSock initialization failed");
    delete m_pWinSock;
    m_pWinSock = NULL;
    return;
  }

  // initialize the datagram socket object

  m_pDatagram = new CDatagramSocket(this, WM_USER_DATAGRAM);
  if (m_pDatagram->CreateSocket(2000) == CWINSOCK_NOERROR)
    plb->InsertString(0, "Datagram created (port 2000)");
  else
  {
    plb->InsertString(0, "Datagram creation failed");
    delete m_pDatagram;
    m_pDatagram = NULL;
  }
}

BEGIN_MESSAGE_MAP(CMainView, CFormView)
  //{{AFX_MSG_MAP(CMainView)
  ON_MESSAGE(WM_USER_DATAGRAM, OnDatagram)
  //}}AFX_MSG_MAP
END_MESSAGE_MAP()

/////////////////////////////////////////////////////////////////////////////
// CMainView message handlers

/////////////////////////////////////////////////////////////////////////////
// CMainView::OnDatagram()
//
// Receives messages from the datagram object.
//
LONG CMainView::OnDatagram(WPARAM wParam, LPARAM lParam)
{
  LPVOID pDataWritten;  // pointer to data that is completely written
  LPVOID pDataRead;     // pointer to data just read
  int nLen;             // length
  SOCKADDR_IN sin;      // Internet address of data's sender
  IN_ADDR in;           // IP address of data's sender
  char pszMessage[1000];// informational message

  // get pointer to list box used for status messages
  CListBox *plb = (CListBox *)GetDlgItem(IDC_LIST_STATUS);

  switch (wParam)
  {
    case CWINSOCK_DONE_WRITING:
      // lParam = pointer to data that was sent
      pDataWritten = (LPVOID)lParam;
      wsprintf(pszMessage, "Data sent (%s)", pDataWritten);
```

continues

Listing 14.2. continued

```
      plb->InsertString(0, pszMessage);
      free(pDataWritten);
      break;

    case CWINSOCK_ERROR_WRITING:
      // lParam = pointer to data that generated error sending
      pDataWritten = (LPVOID)lParam;
      wsprintf(pszMessage, "Error sending data (%s)", pDataWritten);
      plb->InsertString(0, pszMessage);
      free(pDataWritten);
      break;

    case CWINSOCK_DONE_READING:
      // lParam = # data chunks in queue
      pDataRead = m_pDatagram->Read(&nLen, &sin);
      // display informational message (data must be NULL terminated)
      memcpy(&in, &sin.sin_addr.s_addr, 4);
      wsprintf(pszMessage, "Data received (%s) from %s, %d",
       pDataRead, inet_ntoa(in), ntohs(sin.sin_port));
      plb->InsertString(0, pszMessage);

      // echo the data back to the sender
      if (m_pDatagram->Write(nLen, pDataRead, &sin) != CWINSOCK_NOERROR)
      {
        wsprintf(pszMessage, "Error sending data (%s)", pDataRead);
        plb->InsertString(0, pszMessage);
        free(pDataRead);
      }

      break;

    case CWINSOCK_ERROR_READING:
      break;

    default:
      break;
  }

  return 0L;
}
```

Datagram Echo Client CDECLNT

The datagram echo client, CDECLNT, is a reimplementation of the DECLIENT program described in Chapter 8. It uses a `CFormView`-derived object as its main interface. The header file for the `CMainView` object is shown in Listing 14.3. Its implementation is shown in Listing 14.4. This object performs most of the work for the CDECLNT application. `OnInitialUpdate()` is called soon after the object is created. This function is responsible for starting the WinSock subsystem, creating a client datagram socket, prompting for the host name or IP address of the CDESRV datagram echo server, and setting a five-second interval timer used for data writes. When the timer goes off, `OnTimer()` is called. If there is no data waiting to be sent, denoted by the first byte of the outgoing buffer `m_pszBuf` containing a `NULL`, an outgoing data stream is formatted and the datagram socket object's `Write()` member function is called to send data to port 2000 on the designated server. When the write completes, `OnDatagram()` is called with `wParam` set to `CWINSOCK_DONE_WRITING`. The first byte of `m_pszBuf` is set to `NULL` to indicate that the buffer is available. This buffer usage method is in contrast to dynamically allocating and freeing memory. The `CMainView` object is continually waiting for its previously sent data to be echoed back. When data arrives on the datagram socket, `OnDatagram()` is triggered with `wParam` set to `CWINSOCK_DONE_READING`. The data is read and the read buffer is then freed. When the client application is closed, `CMainView`'s destructor is called, destroying the datagram socket object and shutting down the WinSock subsystem.

Listing 14.3. MAINVIEW.H for CDECLNT.

```
// mainview.h : header file
//

/////////////////////////////////////////////////////////////////////////////
// CMainView form view

#ifndef __AFXEXT_H__
#include <afxext.h>
#endif

#include "cwinsock.h"    // Windows Sockets classes

class CMainView : public CFormView
{
  DECLARE_DYNCREATE(CMainView)

private:
  CWinSock * m_pWinSock;          // WinSock sub-system startup/.shutdown
  CDatagramSocket * m_pDatagram; // Datagram socket to receive from
  char m_pszBuf[100];             // buffer to send
  char m_pszServer[100];          // host name or IP address of datagram server

protected:
  CMainView();       // protected constructor used by dynamic creation

// Form Data
public:
  //{{AFX_DATA(CMainView)
  enum { IDD = IDD_DIALOG_MAIN };
    // NOTE: the ClassWizard will add data members here
  //}}AFX_DATA

// Attributes
```

continues

Listing 14.3. continued

```
public:

// Operations
public:

// Implementation
protected:
  virtual ~CMainView();
  virtual void DoDataExchange(CDataExchange* pDX);  // DDX/DDV support
  virtual void OnInitialUpdate();
  // Generated message map functions
  //{{AFX_MSG(CMainView)
  afx_msg LONG OnDatagram(WPARAM wParam, LPARAM lParam);
  afx_msg void OnTimer(UINT nIDEvent);
  //}}AFX_MSG
  DECLARE_MESSAGE_MAP()
};

/////////////////////////////////////////////////////////////////////////////

#define WM_USER_DATAGRAM (WM_USER + 1)
```

Listing 14.4. MAINVIEW.CPP for CDECLNT.

```
// mainview.cpp : implementation file
//

#include "stdafx.h"
#include "cdeclnt.h"
#include "mainview.h"
#include "servdlg.h"

#ifdef _DEBUG
#undef THIS_FILE
static char BASED_CODE THIS_FILE[] = __FILE__;
#endif

/////////////////////////////////////////////////////////////////////////////
// CMainView

IMPLEMENT_DYNCREATE(CMainView, CFormView)

CMainView::CMainView()
  : CFormView(CMainView::IDD)
{
  //{{AFX_DATA_INIT(CMainView)
    // NOTE: the ClassWizard will add member initialization here
  //}}AFX_DATA_INIT

  // initialize class variables

  m_pWinSock = NULL;
  m_pDatagram = NULL;
```

```
  (*m_pszBuf) = '\0';
}

CMainView::~CMainView()
{
  // free the datagram and WinSock objects

  if (m_pDatagram)
  {
    m_pDatagram->DestroySocket();
    delete m_pDatagram;
    m_pDatagram = NULL;
  }

  if (m_pWinSock)
  {
    m_pWinSock->Shutdown();
    delete m_pWinSock;
    m_pWinSock = NULL;
  }
}

void CMainView::DoDataExchange(CDataExchange* pDX)
{
  CFormView::DoDataExchange(pDX);
  //{{AFX_DATA_MAP(CMainView)
    // NOTE: the ClassWizard will add DDX and DDV calls here
  //}}AFX_DATA_MAP
}

void CMainView::OnInitialUpdate()
{
  // start the timer used to trigger the socket writes

  SetTimer(1, 5000, NULL);   // 5 second timer

  // get pointer to list box used for status messages

  CListBox *plb = (CListBox *)GetDlgItem(IDC_LIST_STATUS);

  // initialize the WinSock object

  m_pWinSock = new CWinSock;
  if (m_pWinSock->Startup() == CWINSOCK_NOERROR)
    plb->InsertString(0, "WinSock initialized");
  else
  {
    plb->InsertString(0, "WinSock initialization failed");
    delete m_pWinSock;
    m_pWinSock = NULL;
    return;
  }

  // prompt for server information
  // (host name or IP address of datagram server)

  while (1)
```

continues

Listing 14.4. continued

```
  {
    CServerDlg dlg;
    dlg.DoModal();
    if (dlg.m_stringServer.GetLength() < sizeof(m_pszServer))
    {
      lstrcpy(m_pszServer, dlg.m_stringServer);
      break;
    }
    else
      AfxMessageBox("Host name or IP address too long");
  }

  // initialize the datagram socket object

  m_pDatagram = new CDatagramSocket(this, WM_USER_DATAGRAM);
  if (m_pDatagram->CreateSocket() == CWINSOCK_NOERROR)
    plb->InsertString(0, "Datagram created");
  else
  {
    plb->InsertString(0, "Datagram creation failed");
    delete m_pDatagram;
    m_pDatagram = NULL;
  }
}

BEGIN_MESSAGE_MAP(CMainView, CFormView)
  //{{AFX_MSG_MAP(CMainView)
  ON_MESSAGE(WM_USER_DATAGRAM, OnDatagram)
  ON_WM_TIMER()
  //}}AFX_MSG_MAP
END_MESSAGE_MAP()

/////////////////////////////////////////////////////////////////////////////
// CMainView message handlers

/////////////////////////////////////////////////////////////////////////////
// CMainView::OnDatagram()
//
// Receives messages from the datagram object.
//
LONG CMainView::OnDatagram(WPARAM wParam, LPARAM lParam)
{
  LPVOID pDataWritten;  // pointer to data that is completely written
  LPVOID pDataRead;     // pointer to data just read
  int nLen;             // length
  SOCKADDR_IN sin;      // Internet address of data's sender
  IN_ADDR in;           // IP address of data's sender
  char pszMessage[1000];// informational message

  // get pointer to list box used for status messages
  CListBox *plb = (CListBox *)GetDlgItem(IDC_LIST_STATUS);

  switch (wParam)
  {
    case CWINSOCK_DONE_WRITING:
      // lParam = pointer to data that was sent
```

```
      pDataWritten = (LPVOID)lParam;
      wsprintf(pszMessage, "Data sent (%s)", pDataWritten);
      plb->InsertString(0, pszMessage);
      (*m_pszBuf) = '\0';   // same as (*pDataWritten) = '\0';
      break;

    case CWINSOCK_ERROR_WRITING:
      // lParam = pointer to data that generated error sending
      pDataWritten = (LPVOID)lParam;
      wsprintf(pszMessage, "Error sending data (%s)", pDataWritten);
      plb->InsertString(0, pszMessage);
      (*m_pszBuf) = '\0';   // same as (*pDataWritten) = '\0';
      break;

    case CWINSOCK_DONE_READING:
      // lParam = # data chunks in queue
      pDataRead = m_pDatagram->Read(&nLen, &sin);
      // display informational message (data must be NULL terminated)
      memcpy(&in, &sin.sin_addr.s_addr, 4);
      wsprintf(pszMessage, "Data received (%s) from %s, %d",
       pDataRead, inet_ntoa(in), ntohs(sin.sin_port));
      plb->InsertString(0, pszMessage);
      free(pDataRead);
      break;

    case CWINSOCK_ERROR_READING:
      break;

    default:
      break;
  }

  return 0L;
}

void CMainView::OnTimer(UINT nIDEvent)
{
  static int nSendCount = 1;  // used to generate unique message
  char pszMessage[1000];      // informational message

  // make sure we are not sending out of a bad datagram socket
  if (m_pDatagram == NULL)
    return;

  // get pointer to list box used for status messages
  CListBox *plb = (CListBox *)GetDlgItem(IDC_LIST_STATUS);

  // send the buffer unless the previous send hasn't completed yet
  if ((*m_pszBuf) == '\0')
  {
    wsprintf(m_pszBuf, "Hello %d", nSendCount);
    ++nSendCount;
    // be sure to send terminating NULL character
    if (m_pDatagram->Write(lstrlen(m_pszBuf) + 1, m_pszBuf,
     m_pszServer, 2000) != CWINSOCK_NOERROR)
    {
      (*m_pszBuf) = '\0';
```

continues

Listing 14.4. continued

```
      wsprintf(pszMessage, "Error sending data (%s)", m_pszBuf);
      plb->InsertString(0, pszMessage);
    }
  }

  CFormView::OnTimer(nIDEvent);
}
```

Running the Datagram Echo Server and Client

Following is a sample sequence of events that occur when the datagram echo client and server are run:

1. Run CDESRV.
2. Run CDECLNT on the same or a different computer. It prompts for the host name or IP address of CDESRV.
3. In five seconds the timer will trigger in CDECLNT, causing `CMainView::OnTimer()` to get called. The outgoing buffer is not in use, so the outgoing buffer is filled and written using `m_pDatagram's Write()` member function.
4. `CMainView::OnDatagram()` is called in CDECLNT with a `CWINSOCK_DONE_WRITING` notice. The outgoing buffer is then marked as unused so that it may be used with the next triggering of `CMainView::OnTimer()`.
5. `CMainView::OnDatagram()` is called in CDESRV with a `CWINSOCK_DONE_READING` notice. The data is read and immediately echoed back to the client.
6. `CMainView::OnDatagram()` is called in CDESRV with a CWINSOCK_DONE_WRITING notice. The data is then freed.
7. `CMainView::OnDatagram()` is called in CDECLNT with a CWINSOCK_DONE_READING notice. The echoed data is read and then freed.
8. Another timer goes off in CDECLNT and the process repeats.

Stream Echo Client and Server

These programs, CSESRV and CSECLNT, demonstrate the use of the `CStreamSocket` object. The CSESRV server application receives data and sends it back to the client. The CSECLNT client application sends data to the server and receives the echoed reply.

Stream Echo Server CSESRV

As in the SESERV program described in Chapter 8, this sample uses a CFormView-derived object named CMainView as its primary user interface. The CMainView header file is shown in Listing 14.5. The m_pWinSock member variable controls the starting and stopping of the WinSock subsystem for this program. The m_pStreamSrv member variable is a pointer to the stream socket object that waits for connections from clients. The m_pStream member variable is the stream socket that actually receives data from and sends data to the client. The OnStreamSrv() member function receives status information for the server stream socket object. It's triggered by the WM_USER_STREAMSRV user-defined message whenever a client requests a connection to the server. The OnStream() member function receives status information for the stream socket object that actually communicates with the client. It's triggered by the WM_USER_STREAM user-defined message whenever a client connection is made or lost and when data is available to be read or is finished being written.

Listing 14.5. MAINVIEW.H for CSESRV.

```
// mainview.h : header file
//

/////////////////////////////////////////////////////////////////////////////
// CMainView form view

#ifndef __AFXEXT_H__
#include <afxext.h>
#endif

#include "cwinsock.h"    // Windows Sockets classes

class CMainView : public CFormView
{
  DECLARE_DYNCREATE(CMainView)

private:
  CWinSock * m_pWinSock;          // WinSock sub-system startup/.shutdown
  CStreamSocket * m_pStreamSrv;   // Stream socket to wait for connections on
  CStreamSocket * m_pStream;      // Stream socket to receive from

protected:
  CMainView();       // protected constructor used by dynamic creation

// Form Data
public:
  //{{AFX_DATA(CMainView)
  enum { IDD = IDD_DIALOG_MAIN };
    // NOTE: the ClassWizard will add data members here
  //}}AFX_DATA

// Attributes
```

continues

Listing 14.5. continued

```
public:

// Operations
public:

// Implementation
protected:
  virtual ~CMainView();
  virtual void DoDataExchange(CDataExchange* pDX);  // DDX/DDV support
  virtual void OnInitialUpdate();
  // Generated message map functions
  //{{AFX_MSG(CMainView)
  afx_msg LONG OnStreamSrv(WPARAM wParam, LPARAM lParam);
  afx_msg LONG OnStream(WPARAM wParam, LPARAM lParam);
  //}}AFX_MSG
  DECLARE_MESSAGE_MAP()
};

/////////////////////////////////////////////////////////////////////////////

#define WM_USER_STREAMSRV (WM_USER + 1)
#define WM_USER_STREAM    (WM_USER + 2)
```

The implementation of the `CMainView` object is shown in Listing 14.6. This object performs most of the work for the CSESRV application. `OnInitialUpdate()` is called soon after the object is created. This function is responsible for starting the WinSock subsystem and creating a server stream socket that waits for connection requests to arrive on port 2000. When a client requests a connection, the `OnStreamSrv()` member function is triggered with `wParam` set to `CWINSOCK_READY_TO_ACCEPT_CONNECTION`. The `m_pStream` object is then used to accept the client connection request. When the connection is made, `OnStream()` is called with `wParam` set to `CWINSOCK_YOU_ARE_CONNECTED`. When data arrives from the client, `OnStream()` is called with `wParam` set to `CWINSOCK_DONE_READING`. Data is read and a write attempt is made to echo the data back to the client. When the write finishes, `OnStream()` is called with `wParam` set to `CWINSOCK_DONE_WRITING`. At this point, the data pointer is freed. When the server application is closed, `CMainView`'s destructor is called, destroying the two stream socket objects and shutting down the WinSock subsystem.

Listing 14.6. MAINVIEW.CPP for CSESRV.

```
// mainview.cpp : implementation file
//

#include "stdafx.h"
#include "csesrv.h"
#include "mainview.h"
```

```
#ifdef _DEBUG
#undef THIS_FILE
static char BASED_CODE THIS_FILE[] = __FILE__;
#endif

/////////////////////////////////////////////////////////////////////////////
// CMainView

IMPLEMENT_DYNCREATE(CMainView, CFormView)

CMainView::CMainView()
  : CFormView(CMainView::IDD)
{
  //{{AFX_DATA_INIT(CMainView)
    // NOTE: the ClassWizard will add member initialization here
  //}}AFX_DATA_INIT

  // initialize class variables

  m_pWinSock = NULL;
  m_pStreamSrv = NULL;
  m_pStream = NULL;
}

CMainView::~CMainView()
{
  // free the stream and WinSock objects

  if (m_pStreamSrv)
  {
    m_pStreamSrv->DestroySocket();
    delete m_pStreamSrv;
    m_pStreamSrv = NULL;
  }

  if (m_pStream)
  {
    m_pStream->DestroySocket();
    delete m_pStream;
    m_pStream = NULL;
  }

  if (m_pWinSock)
  {
    m_pWinSock->Shutdown();
    delete m_pWinSock;
    m_pWinSock = NULL;
  }
}

void CMainView::DoDataExchange(CDataExchange* pDX)
{
  CFormView::DoDataExchange(pDX);
  //{{AFX_DATA_MAP(CMainView)
    // NOTE: the ClassWizard will add DDX and DDV calls here
  //}}AFX_DATA_MAP
```

continues

Listing 14.6. continued

```
}

void CMainView::OnInitialUpdate()
{
  // get pointer to list box used for status messages

  CListBox *plb = (CListBox *)GetDlgItem(IDC_LIST_STATUS);

  // initialize the WinSock object

  m_pWinSock = new CWinSock;
  if (m_pWinSock->Startup() == CWINSOCK_NOERROR)
    plb->InsertString(0, "WinSock initialized");
  else
  {
    plb->InsertString(0, "WinSock initialization failed");
    delete m_pWinSock;
    m_pWinSock = NULL;
    return;
  }

  // initialize the stream socket object

  m_pStreamSrv = new CStreamSocket(this, WM_USER_STREAMSRV);
  if (m_pStreamSrv->CreateSocket(2000) == CWINSOCK_NOERROR)
    plb->InsertString(0, "Stream server created (port 2000)");
  else
  {
    plb->InsertString(0, "Stream server creation failed");
    delete m_pStreamSrv;
    m_pStreamSrv = NULL;
  }
}

BEGIN_MESSAGE_MAP(CMainView, CFormView)
  //{{AFX_MSG_MAP(CMainView)
  ON_MESSAGE(WM_USER_STREAMSRV, OnStreamSrv)
  ON_MESSAGE(WM_USER_STREAM, OnStream)
  //}}AFX_MSG_MAP
END_MESSAGE_MAP()

/////////////////////////////////////////////////////////////////////////////
// CMainView message handlers

/////////////////////////////////////////////////////////////////////////////
// CMainView::OnStreamSrv()
//
// Receives messages from the stream server object.
//
LONG CMainView::OnStreamSrv(WPARAM wParam, LPARAM lParam)
{
  // get pointer to list box used for status messages
  CListBox *plb = (CListBox *)GetDlgItem(IDC_LIST_STATUS);

  switch (wParam)
  {
```

```
    case CWINSOCK_READY_TO_ACCEPT_CONNECTION:
      // make sure the server is not already servicing a client
      if (m_pStream != NULL)
      {
        plb->InsertString(0, "Already servicing a client");
        break;
      }

      // accept the client connection
      int nStatus;
      m_pStream = new CStreamSocket(this, WM_USER_STREAM);
      nStatus = m_pStreamSrv->Accept(m_pStream);
      if (nStatus != CWINSOCK_NOERROR)
      {
        delete m_pStream;
        m_pStream = NULL;
        plb->InsertString(0, "Error accepting client connection");
        break;
      }
      else
        plb->InsertString(0, "Accepted client connection");

      break;

    default:
      break;
  }

  return 0L;
}

/////////////////////////////////////////////////////////////////////////////
// CMainView::OnStream()
//
// Receives messages from the connected stream object.
//
LONG CMainView::OnStream(WPARAM wParam, LPARAM lParam)
{
  LPVOID pDataWritten;  // pointer to data that is completely written
  LPVOID pDataRead;     // pointer to data just read
  int nLen;             // length
  char pszMessage[1000];// informational message
  SOCKADDR_IN sin;      // Internet address of client
  IN_ADDR in;           // IP address of client
  int nStatus;          // error status

  // get pointer to list box used for status messages
  CListBox *plb = (CListBox *)GetDlgItem(IDC_LIST_STATUS);

  switch (wParam)
  {
    case CWINSOCK_DONE_WRITING:
      // lParam = pointer to data that was sent
      pDataWritten = (LPVOID)lParam;
      wsprintf(pszMessage, "Data sent (%s)", pDataWritten);
      plb->InsertString(0, pszMessage);
      free(pDataWritten);
      break;
```

continues

Listing 14.6. continued

```
    case CWINSOCK_ERROR_WRITING:
      // lParam = pointer to data that generated error sending
      pDataWritten = (LPVOID)lParam;
      wsprintf(pszMessage, "Error sending data (%s)", pDataWritten);
      plb->InsertString(0, pszMessage);
      free(pDataWritten);
      break;

    case CWINSOCK_DONE_READING:
      // lParam = # data chunks in queue
      pDataRead = m_pStream->Read(&nLen);
      wsprintf(pszMessage, "Data received (%s)", pDataRead);
      plb->InsertString(0, pszMessage);

      // echo the data back to the sender
      if (m_pStream->Write(nLen, pDataRead) != CWINSOCK_NOERROR)
      {
        wsprintf(pszMessage, "Error sending data (%s)", pDataRead);
        plb->InsertString(0, pszMessage);
        free(pDataRead);
      }

      break;

    case CWINSOCK_ERROR_READING:
      break;

    case CWINSOCK_YOU_ARE_CONNECTED:
      // print out client information
      nStatus = m_pStream->GetPeerName(&sin);
      if (nStatus == CWINSOCK_NOERROR)
      {
        memcpy(&in, &sin.sin_addr.s_addr, 4);
        wsprintf(pszMessage, "Connected to client %s, %d",
         inet_ntoa(in), ntohs(sin.sin_port));
        plb->InsertString(0, pszMessage);
      }
      else
        plb->InsertString(0, "Error getting client name");
      break;

    case CWINSOCK_LOST_CONNECTION:
      // client closed the connection
      m_pStream->DestroySocket();
      delete m_pStream;
      m_pStream = NULL;
      plb->InsertString(0, "Client closed connection");
      break;

    default:
      break;
  }

  return 0L;
}
```

Stream Echo Client CSECLNT

The stream echo client, CSECLNT, is a reimplementation of the SECLIENT program described in Chapter 8. It uses a CFormView-derived object as its main interface. The header file for the CMainView object is shown in Listing 14.7. Its implementation is shown in Listing 14.8. This object performs most of the work for the CSECLNT application. OnInitialUpdate() is called soon after the object is created. This function is responsible for starting the WinSock subsystem, creating a client stream socket, prompting for the host name or IP address of the CSESRV stream echo server, and setting a five-second interval timer used for data writes. When the server accepts the client's connection request on port 2000, OnStream() is called with wParam set to CWINSOCK_YOU_ARE_CONNECTED. When the five-second timer goes off, OnTimer() is called. If there is no data waiting to be sent—denoted by the first byte of the outgoing buffer m_pszBuf containing a NULL—an outgoing data stream is formatted and the stream socket object's Write() member function is called to send data to the designated server. When the write completes, OnStream() is called with wParam set to CWINSOCK_DONE_WRITING. The first byte of m_pszBuf is set to NULL to indicate that the buffer is available. The CMainView object is continually waiting for its previously sent data to be echoed back. When data arrives on the stream socket, OnStream() is triggered with wParam set to CWINSOCK_DONE_READING. The data is read and the read buffer is then freed. When the client application is closed, CMainView's destructor is called, destroying the stream socket object and shutting down the WinSock subsystem.

Listing 14.7. MAINVIEW.H for CSECLNT.

```
// mainview.h : header file
//

/////////////////////////////////////////////////////////////////////////////
// CMainView form view

#ifndef __AFXEXT_H__
#include <afxext.h>
#endif

#include "cwinsock.h"    // Windows Sockets classes

class CMainView : public CFormView
{
  DECLARE_DYNCREATE(CMainView)

private:
  CWinSock * m_pWinSock;           // WinSock sub-system startup/.shutdown
  CStreamSocket * m_pStream;       // Stream socket to receive from
  char m_pszBuf[100];              // buffer to send
  char m_pszServer[100];           // host name or IP address of stream server
```

continues

Listing 14.7. continued

```
protected:
  CMainView();      // protected constructor used by dynamic creation

// Form Data
public:
  //{{AFX_DATA(CMainView)
  enum { IDD = IDD_DIALOG_MAIN };
    // NOTE: the ClassWizard will add data members here
  //}}AFX_DATA

// Attributes
public:

// Operations
public:

// Implementation
protected:
  virtual ~CMainView();
  virtual void DoDataExchange(CDataExchange* pDX);  // DDX/DDV support
  virtual void OnInitialUpdate();
  // Generated message map functions
  //{{AFX_MSG(CMainView)
  afx_msg LONG OnStream(WPARAM wParam, LPARAM lParam);
  afx_msg void OnTimer(UINT nIDEvent);
  //}}AFX_MSG
  DECLARE_MESSAGE_MAP()
};

/////////////////////////////////////////////////////////////////////////////

#define WM_USER_STREAM (WM_USER + 1)
```

Listing 14.8. MAINVIEW.CPP for CSECLNT.

```
// mainview.cpp : implementation file
//

#include "stdafx.h"
#include "cseclnt.h"
#include "mainview.h"
#include "servdlg.h"

#ifdef _DEBUG
#undef THIS_FILE
static char BASED_CODE THIS_FILE[] = __FILE__;
#endif

/////////////////////////////////////////////////////////////////////////////
// CMainView

IMPLEMENT_DYNCREATE(CMainView, CFormView)
```

```
CMainView::CMainView()
  : CFormView(CMainView::IDD)
{
  //{{AFX_DATA_INIT(CMainView)
    // NOTE: the ClassWizard will add member initialization here
  //}}AFX_DATA_INIT

  // initialize class variables

  m_pWinSock = NULL;
  m_pStream = NULL;
  (*m_pszBuf) = '\0';
}

CMainView::~CMainView()
{
  // free the stream and WinSock objects

  if (m_pStream)
  {
    m_pStream->DestroySocket();
    delete m_pStream;
    m_pStream = NULL;
  }

  if (m_pWinSock)
  {
    m_pWinSock->Shutdown();
    delete m_pWinSock;
    m_pWinSock = NULL;
  }
}

void CMainView::DoDataExchange(CDataExchange* pDX)
{
  CFormView::DoDataExchange(pDX);
  //{{AFX_DATA_MAP(CMainView)
    // NOTE: the ClassWizard will add DDX and DDV calls here
  //}}AFX_DATA_MAP
}

void CMainView::OnInitialUpdate()
{
  // start the timer used to trigger the socket writes

  SetTimer(1, 5000, NULL);    // 5 second timer

  // get pointer to list box used for status messages

  CListBox *plb = (CListBox *)GetDlgItem(IDC_LIST_STATUS);

  // initialize the WinSock object

  m_pWinSock = new CWinSock;
  if (m_pWinSock->Startup() == CWINSOCK_NOERROR)
    plb->InsertString(0, "WinSock initialized");
  else
  {
```

continues

Listing 14.8. continued

```
    plb->InsertString(0, "WinSock initialization failed");
    delete m_pWinSock;
    m_pWinSock = NULL;
    return;
  }

  // prompt for server information
  // (host name or IP address of stream server)

  while (1)
  {
    CServerDlg dlg;
    dlg.DoModal();
    if (dlg.m_stringServer.GetLength() < sizeof(m_pszServer))
    {
      lstrcpy(m_pszServer, dlg.m_stringServer);
      break;
    }
    else
      AfxMessageBox("Host name or IP address too long");
  }

  // initialize the stream socket object

  m_pStream = new CStreamSocket(this, WM_USER_STREAM);
  if (m_pStream->CreateSocket() == CWINSOCK_NOERROR)
    plb->InsertString(0, "Stream created");
  else
  {
    plb->InsertString(0, "Stream creation failed");
    delete m_pStream;
    m_pStream = NULL;
  }

  // connect the client to the server
  if (m_pStream->Connect(m_pszServer, 2000) == CWINSOCK_NOERROR)
    plb->InsertString(0, "Stream connect attempt made");
  else
  {
    plb->InsertString(0, "Stream connect attempt failed");
    delete m_pStream;
    m_pStream = NULL;
  }
}

BEGIN_MESSAGE_MAP(CMainView, CFormView)
  //{{AFX_MSG_MAP(CMainView)
  ON_MESSAGE(WM_USER_STREAM, OnStream)
  ON_WM_TIMER()
  //}}AFX_MSG_MAP
END_MESSAGE_MAP()

/////////////////////////////////////////////////////////////////////////////
// CMainView message handlers

/////////////////////////////////////////////////////////////////////////////
```

```
// CMainView::OnStream()
//
// Receives messages from the stream object.
//
LONG CMainView::OnStream(WPARAM wParam, LPARAM lParam)
{
  LPVOID pDataWritten;  // pointer to data that is completely written
  LPVOID pDataRead;     // pointer to data just read
  int nLen;             // length
  char pszMessage[1000];// informational message

  // get pointer to list box used for status messages
  CListBox *plb = (CListBox *)GetDlgItem(IDC_LIST_STATUS);

  switch (wParam)
  {
    case CWINSOCK_DONE_WRITING:
      // lParam = pointer to data that was sent
      pDataWritten = (LPVOID)lParam;
      wsprintf(pszMessage, "Data sent (%s)", pDataWritten);
      plb->InsertString(0, pszMessage);
      (*m_pszBuf) = '\0';    // same as (*pDataWritten) = '\0';
      break;

    case CWINSOCK_ERROR_WRITING:
      // lParam = pointer to data that generated error sending
      pDataWritten = (LPVOID)lParam;
      wsprintf(pszMessage, "Error sending data (%s)", pDataWritten);
      plb->InsertString(0, pszMessage);
      (*m_pszBuf) = '\0';    // same as (*pDataWritten) = '\0';
      break;

    case CWINSOCK_DONE_READING:
      // lParam = # data chunks in queue
      pDataRead = m_pStream->Read(&nLen);
      wsprintf(pszMessage, "Data received (%s)", pDataRead);
      plb->InsertString(0, pszMessage);
      free(pDataRead);
      break;

    case CWINSOCK_ERROR_READING:
      break;

    case CWINSOCK_YOU_ARE_CONNECTED:
      plb->InsertString(0, "Connected to server");
      break;

    case CWINSOCK_LOST_CONNECTION:
      // server closed the connection
      m_pStream->DestroySocket();
      delete m_pStream;
      m_pStream = NULL;
      plb->InsertString(0, "Server closed connection");
      break;

    default:
      break;
  }
```

continues

Listing 14.8. continued

```
  return 0L;
}

void CMainView::OnTimer(UINT nIDEvent)
{
  static int nSendCount = 1;  // used to generate unique message
  char pszMessage[1000];      // informational message

  // make sure we are not sending out of a bad stream socket
  if (m_pStream == NULL)
    return;

  // get pointer to list box used for status messages
  CListBox *plb = (CListBox *)GetDlgItem(IDC_LIST_STATUS);

  // send the buffer unless the previous send hasn't completed yet
  if ((*m_pszBuf) == '\0')
  {
    wsprintf(m_pszBuf, "Hello %d", nSendCount);
    ++nSendCount;
    // be sure to send terminating NULL character
    if (m_pStream->Write(lstrlen(m_pszBuf) + 1, m_pszBuf) != CWINSOCK_NOERROR)
    {
      (*m_pszBuf) = '\0';
      wsprintf(pszMessage, "Error sending data (%s)", m_pszBuf);
      plb->InsertString(0, pszMessage);
    }
  }

  CFormView::OnTimer(nIDEvent);
}
```

Running the Stream Echo Server and Client

Following is a sample sequence of events that occur when the stream echo client and server are run:

1. Run CSESRV.
2. Run CSECLNT on the same or a different computer. It prompts for the host name or IP address CSESRV is using. A connection to the server is attempted.
3. CSESRV's `CMainView::OnStreamSrv()` is called with the `CWINSOCK_READY_TO_ACCEPT_CONNECTION` event and, if the `m_pStream` socket is not yet connected to a client, a connection attempt is made.
4. When the server's connection accept succeeds, `OnStream()` is called with `wParam` set to `CWINSOCK_YOU_ARE_CONNECTED`.
5. CDECLNT's `CMainView::OnStream()` is also called with the `CWINSOCK_YOU_ARE_CONNECTED` event.

6. In five seconds, the timer will trigger in CSECLNT, causing `CMainView::OnTimer()` to get called. No bytes are waiting to be sent yet, so the outgoing buffer is filled and written to the connected server.
7. `CMainView::OnStream()` is called in CSECLNT with a `CWINSOCK_DONE_WRITING` notice. The outgoing buffer is then marked as unused so that it may be used with the next triggering of `CMainView::OnTimer()`.
8. `CMainView::OnStream()` is called in CSESRV with a `CWINSOCK_DONE_READING` notice. The data is read and immediately echoed back to the client.
9. `CMainView::OnStream()` is called in CSESRV with a `CWINSOCK_DONE_WRITING` notice. The data is then freed.
10. `CMainView::OnStream()` is called in CSECLNT with a `CWINSOCK_DONE_READING` notice. The echoed data is read and then freed.
11. Another timer goes off in CSECLNT and the process repeats.

If CSECLNT is closed first, `CMainView::OnStream()` is called in CSESRV with a `CWINSOCK_LOST_CONNECTION` notice. If CSESRV is closed first, `CMainView::OnStream()` is called in CSECLNT with a `CWINSOCK_LOST_CONNECTION` notice.

Summary

This chapter demonstrates the use of the `CWinSock`, `CDatagramSocket`, and `CStreamSocket` objects. These objects are designed to make socket programming easier for you.

It is hoped that the comparison of these sample programs with those of Chapter 8 proves that the design goals of the WinSock class library, described in Chapter 9, are met. A comparison also reveals one of the limitations of the `CDatagramSocket` and `CStreamSocket` objects. These objects don't have the capability of letting the WinSock subsystem assign an unused port to a server socket. Instead, the port must be specified in terms of its port number or service name, in this case to port number 2000.

The next chapter uses the WinSock class library objects in a sample client-server database environment.

15

Practical Client/Server Database Application

This chapter presents a practical client/server database application set that uses the WinSock class library described in the preceding chapters. The application set consists of a client application and a server application. The client sends database requests to the server and the server responds with a positive or negative acknowledgment.

The client (INICLNT) and server (INISRV) use the `CDatagramSocket` and `CStreamSocket` objects. In previous chapters, the server examples could handle only one client connection at a time. This server is more realistic in that it can service several clients simultaneously. The server is implemented as a Multiple Document Interface application in which each window represents a client connection. The client is a simple Single Document Interface application. A stream socket connection is used to transmit database commands and responses between the client and server. A datagram socket is used to send a *heartbeat* message from the server to the client. The heartbeat is a block of data that is sent between the client and server to let each know that the other side is still active and able to communicate. This heartbeat allows the client program to show a visual indication of the client/server link status.

The "database" in this example uses Windows' built-in INI file facility. An INI file is used to maintain configuration information for an application. An example INI file is shown below:

```
[boot]
386grabber=ajvga.3gr
oemfonts.fon=vgaoem.fon

[keyboard]
subtype=
type=4
```

`[boot]` is called the *section.* `386grabber` is an example of an *entry* or *key.* `ajvga.3gr` is its *value.* The `GetPrivateProfileString()` and `WritePrivateProfileString()` SDK functions are used to read and write an INI file string value, respectively.

Client INICLNT

The client application, INICLNT, uses a `CFormView`-derived object as its main interface. The header file for the `CMainView` object is shown in Listing 15.1, which appears later in this section. Its implementation is shown in Listing 15.2, which also appears later in this section. This object performs most of the work for the INICLNT application. `OnInitialUpdate()` is called soon after the object is created. This function is responsible for starting the WinSock subsystem, creating a client stream socket, creating a server datagram socket for the heartbeat, prompting for the host name or IP address of the INISRV server, and setting a timer interval used for the heartbeats. When the

server accepts the client's connection request, `OnStream()` is called with `wParam` set to `CWINSOCK_YOU_ARE_CONNECTED`.

Command Identifier

The user enters the read or write parameters into the appropriate fields and then selects either the Read or Write button, triggering `OnClickedButtonRead()` or `OnClickedButtonWrite()`, respectively. These functions format the database command and call `FillAndSendDBCmd()`, which assigns a unique identifier to the database command and sends it to the server. The database command has the following structure:

```
typedef struct tagDBCOMMAND
{
  int nID;                      // database command identifier
  int nCommand;                 // database command
  char szFile[DBBUFSIZE];       // INI file
  char szSection[DBBUFSIZE];    // section of INI file
  char szEntry[DBBUFSIZE];      // entry within section of INI file
  char szValue[DBBUFSIZE];      // value of entry within section of INI file
} DBCOMMAND, FAR * LPDBCOMMAND;
```

ClassWizard is used to limit the number of bytes that may be entered into the data entry fields of `CMainView`. This limit is set to 40 to match the `DBBUFSIZE` value used in the preceding `DBCOMMAND` definition.

Possible commands for the client are `DB_READ` and `DB_WRITE`. A unique identifier is assigned because there could be multiple outstanding database requests; the client and server operate totally asynchronously. The identifier may be used to correlate the command and its asynchronous response. Once the command is successfully sent, `OnStream()` is called with `wParam` set to `CWINSOCK_DONE_WRITING`. When the server is done processing the database command, it sends a response to the client, triggering `OnStream()` with `wParam` set to `CWINSOCK_DONE_READING`. The `HandleRead()` function processes the database response sent by the server.

Heartbeat Link Status Indicator

This application has a timer that's used to keep track of missing heartbeat messages. The `OnDatagram()` function handles reception of the heartbeats sent from the connected server. If one heartbeat message is missed, the traffic light status indicator changes to a yellow light. Missing two or more heartbeats causes the light to turn red. If the heartbeats are received without fail, the light remains green. This provides for a visual cue as to the state of the server.

When `CMainView`'s destructor is called, the stream and datagram sockets are destroyed and the WinSock subsystem is shut down.

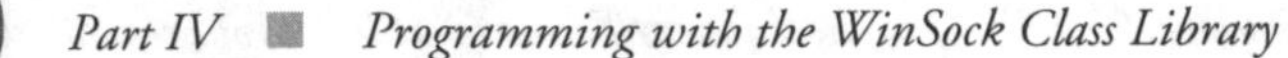

Listing 15.1. MAINVIEW.H for INICLNT.

```
// mainview.h : header file
//

/////////////////////////////////////////////////////////////////////////////
// CMainView form view

#ifndef __AFXEXT_H__
#include <afxext.h>
#endif

#include "cwinsock.h"   // Windows Sockets classes
#include "db.h"

class CMainView : public CFormView
{
  DECLARE_DYNCREATE(CMainView)

private:
  CWinSock * m_pWinSock;          // WinSock sub-system startup/.shutdown
  CStreamSocket * m_pStream;      // Stream socket to receive from
  CDatagramSocket * m_pDatagram; // Datagram socket to receive heartbeat
  char m_pszServer[100];          // host name or IP address of stream server
  int m_nHeartbeat;               // heartbeat count
  HICON m_hRed, m_hYellow, m_hGreen;   // link status icons

  void HandleRead();
  void FillAndSendDBCmd(LPDBCOMMAND pdb, LPCSTR szFile,
   LPCSTR szSection, LPCSTR szEntry, LPCSTR szValue = NULL);

protected:
  CMainView();      // protected constructor used by dynamic creation

// Form Data
public:
  //{{AFX_DATA(CMainView)
  enum { IDD = IDD_DIALOG_MAIN };
  CString m_stringFile;
  CString m_stringSection;
  CString m_stringValue;
  CString m_stringEntry;
  //}}AFX_DATA

// Attributes
public:

// Operations
public:

// Implementation
protected:
  virtual ~CMainView();
  virtual void DoDataExchange(CDataExchange* pDX);  // DDX/DDV support
  virtual void OnInitialUpdate();
  // Generated message map functions
  //{{AFX_MSG(CMainView)
  afx_msg LONG OnStream(WPARAM wParam, LPARAM lParam);
```

```
  afx_msg LONG OnDatagram(WPARAM wParam, LPARAM lParam);
  afx_msg void OnTimer(UINT nIDEvent);
  afx_msg void OnClickedButtonRead();
  afx_msg void OnClickedButtonWrite();
  //}}AFX_MSG
  DECLARE_MESSAGE_MAP()
};

/////////////////////////////////////////////////////////////////////////////

#define WM_USER_STREAM    (WM_USER + 1)
#define WM_USER_DATAGRAM (WM_USER + 2)
```

Listing 15.2. MAINVIEW.CPP for INICLNT.

```
// mainview.cpp : implementation file
//

#include "stdafx.h"
#include "iniclnt.h"
#include "mainview.h"
#include "servdlg.h"
#include "db.h"
#include "common.h"

#ifdef _DEBUG
#undef THIS_FILE
static char BASED_CODE THIS_FILE[] = __FILE__;
#endif

/////////////////////////////////////////////////////////////////////////////
// CMainView

IMPLEMENT_DYNCREATE(CMainView, CFormView)

CMainView::CMainView()
  : CFormView(CMainView::IDD)
{
  //{{AFX_DATA_INIT(CMainView)
  m_stringFile = "";
  m_stringSection = "";
  m_stringValue = "";
  m_stringEntry = "";
  //}}AFX_DATA_INIT

  // initialize class variables

  m_pWinSock = NULL;
  m_pStream = NULL;
  m_pDatagram = NULL;
  m_nHeartbeat = 0;

  // load link status icons
  m_hRed = AfxGetApp()->LoadIcon(IDI_ICON_RED);
```

continues

Listing 15.2. continued

```
  m_hYellow = AfxGetApp()->LoadIcon(IDI_ICON_YELLOW);
  m_hGreen = AfxGetApp()->LoadIcon(IDI_ICON_GREEN);
}

CMainView::~CMainView()
{
  // free the stream and WinSock objects

  if (m_pStream)
  {
    m_pStream->DestroySocket();
    delete m_pStream;
    m_pStream = NULL;
  }

  if (m_pDatagram)
  {
    m_pDatagram->DestroySocket();
    delete m_pDatagram;
    m_pDatagram = NULL;
  }

  if (m_pWinSock)
  {
    m_pWinSock->Shutdown();
    delete m_pWinSock;
    m_pWinSock = NULL;
  }
}

void CMainView::DoDataExchange(CDataExchange* pDX)
{
  CFormView::DoDataExchange(pDX);
  //{{AFX_DATA_MAP(CMainView)
  DDX_Text(pDX, IDC_EDIT_FILE, m_stringFile);
  DDV_MaxChars(pDX, m_stringFile, 40);
  DDX_Text(pDX, IDC_EDIT_SECTION, m_stringSection);
  DDV_MaxChars(pDX, m_stringSection, 40);
  DDX_Text(pDX, IDC_EDIT_VALUE, m_stringValue);
  DDV_MaxChars(pDX, m_stringValue, 40);
  DDX_Text(pDX, IDC_EDIT_ENTRY, m_stringEntry);
  DDV_MaxChars(pDX, m_stringEntry, 40);
  //}}AFX_DATA_MAP
}

void CMainView::OnInitialUpdate()
{
  // start the timer used to keep track of heartbeats

  SetTimer(1, HEARTBEAT_DELAY, NULL);

  // get pointer to list box used for status messages

  CListBox *plb = (CListBox *)GetDlgItem(IDC_LIST_STATUS);

  // initialize the WinSock object
```

```
m_pWinSock = new CWinSock;
if (m_pWinSock->Startup() == CWINSOCK_NOERROR)
  plb->InsertString(0, "WinSock initialized");
else
{
  plb->InsertString(0, "WinSock initialization failed");
  delete m_pWinSock;
  m_pWinSock = NULL;
  return;
}

// prompt for server information
// (host name or IP address of stream server)

while (1)
{
  CServerDlg dlg;
  dlg.DoModal();
  if (dlg.m_stringServer.GetLength() < sizeof(m_pszServer))
  {
    lstrcpy(m_pszServer, dlg.m_stringServer);
    break;
  }
  else
    AfxMessageBox("Host name or IP address too long");
}

// initialize the stream socket object

m_pStream = new CStreamSocket(this, WM_USER_STREAM);
if (m_pStream->CreateSocket() == CWINSOCK_NOERROR)
  plb->InsertString(0, "Stream created");
else
{
  plb->InsertString(0, "Stream creation failed");
  delete m_pStream;
  m_pStream = NULL;
  return;
}

// initialize the datagram socket object for the heartbeat

m_pDatagram = new CDatagramSocket(this, WM_USER_DATAGRAM);
if (m_pDatagram->CreateSocket(DATAGRAM_PORT) == CWINSOCK_NOERROR)
  plb->InsertString(0, "Heartbeat datagram created");
else
{
  plb->InsertString(0, "Error creating heartbeat datagram");
  delete m_pDatagram;
  m_pDatagram = NULL;

  m_pStream->DestroySocket();
  delete m_pStream;
  m_pStream = NULL;

  return;
}
```

continues

Listing 15.2. continued

```
  // connect the client to the server
  if (m_pStream->Connect(m_pszServer, STREAM_PORT) == CWINSOCK_NOERROR)
    plb->InsertString(0, "Stream connect attempt made");
  else
  {
    plb->InsertString(0, "Stream connect attempt failed");
    m_pStream->DestroySocket();
    delete m_pStream;
    m_pStream = NULL;

    m_pDatagram->DestroySocket();
    delete m_pDatagram;
    m_pDatagram = NULL;
  }
}

BEGIN_MESSAGE_MAP(CMainView, CFormView)
  //{{AFX_MSG_MAP(CMainView)
  ON_MESSAGE(WM_USER_STREAM, OnStream)
  ON_MESSAGE(WM_USER_DATAGRAM, OnDatagram)
  ON_WM_TIMER()
  ON_BN_CLICKED(IDC_BUTTON_READ, OnClickedButtonRead)
  ON_BN_CLICKED(IDC_BUTTON_WRITE, OnClickedButtonWrite)
  //}}AFX_MSG_MAP
END_MESSAGE_MAP()

/////////////////////////////////////////////////////////////////////////////
// CMainView message handlers

/////////////////////////////////////////////////////////////////////////////
// CMainView::OnStream()
//
// Receives messages from the stream object.
//
LONG CMainView::OnStream(WPARAM wParam, LPARAM lParam)
{
  LPVOID pDataWritten;  // pointer to data that is completely written
  char pszMessage[1000];// informational message

  // get pointer to list box used for status messages
  CListBox *plb = (CListBox *)GetDlgItem(IDC_LIST_STATUS);

  switch (wParam)
  {
    case CWINSOCK_DONE_WRITING:
      // lParam = pointer to data that was sent
      pDataWritten = (LPVOID)lParam;
      wsprintf(pszMessage, "Data sent (ID %d)",
       ((LPDBCOMMAND)pDataWritten)->nID);
      plb->InsertString(0, pszMessage);
      free(pDataWritten);
      break;

    case CWINSOCK_ERROR_WRITING:
      // lParam = pointer to data that generated error sending
```

```
      pDataWritten = (LPVOID)lParam;
      wsprintf(pszMessage, "Error sending data (ID %d)",
       ((LPDBCOMMAND)pDataWritten)->nID);
      plb->InsertString(0, pszMessage);
      free(pDataWritten);
      break;

    case CWINSOCK_DONE_READING:
      // lParam = # data chunks in queue
      HandleRead();
      break;

    case CWINSOCK_ERROR_READING:
      break;

    case CWINSOCK_YOU_ARE_CONNECTED:
      plb->InsertString(0, "Connected to server");
      break;

    case CWINSOCK_LOST_CONNECTION:
      // server closed the connection
      m_pStream->DestroySocket();
      delete m_pStream;
      m_pStream = NULL;
      m_pDatagram->DestroySocket();
      delete m_pDatagram;
      m_pDatagram = NULL;
      plb->InsertString(0, "Server closed connection");
      break;

    default:
      break;
  }

  return 0L;
}

/////////////////////////////////////////////////////////////////////////////
// CMainView::HandleRead()
//
// Receives data from the connected stream object.
//
void CMainView::HandleRead()
{
  char pszMessage[1000];// informational message
  LPVOID pDataRead;     // pointer to data read
  int nLen;             // length
  DBCOMMAND dbcmd;      // database command structure

  // get pointer to list box used for status messages
  CListBox *plb = (CListBox *)GetDlgItem(IDC_LIST_STATUS);

  // read the data
  pDataRead = m_pStream->Read(&nLen);
  plb->InsertString(0, "Received response from server");

  // verify that the data represented an entire
  // database command structure
```

continues

Listing 15.2. continued

```
  if (nLen != sizeof(dbcmd))
  {
    plb->InsertString(0, "This client cannot handle partial blocks");
    free(pDataRead);
    return;
  }

  // copy the data to a database command structure
  memcpy(&dbcmd, pDataRead, sizeof(dbcmd));
  free(pDataRead);

  // display database command results
  if (dbcmd.nCommand == DB_OK)
    wsprintf(pszMessage, "OK (ID %d, \"%s\")", dbcmd.nID, dbcmd.szValue);
  else if (dbcmd.nCommand == DB_ERROR)
    wsprintf(pszMessage, "Error (ID %d, \"%s\")", dbcmd.nID, dbcmd.szValue);
  else
    lstrcpy(pszMessage, "Invalid database response");
  plb->InsertString(0, pszMessage);
}

/////////////////////////////////////////////////////////////////////////////
// CMainView::OnClickedButtonRead()
//
void CMainView::OnClickedButtonRead()
{
  // get pointer to list box used for status messages
  CListBox *plb = (CListBox *)GetDlgItem(IDC_LIST_STATUS);

  // allocate memory for database command structure
  LPDBCOMMAND pdb = (LPDBCOMMAND)malloc(sizeof(DBCOMMAND));
  if (pdb == NULL)
    plb->InsertString(0, "Cannot allocate memory for command");
  else
  {
    memset(pdb, 0, sizeof(DBCOMMAND));
    UpdateData(TRUE);
    FillAndSendDBCmd(pdb, m_stringFile, m_stringSection, m_stringEntry);
  }
}

/////////////////////////////////////////////////////////////////////////////
// CMainView::OnClickedButtonWrite()
//
void CMainView::OnClickedButtonWrite()
{
  // get pointer to list box used for status messages
  CListBox *plb = (CListBox *)GetDlgItem(IDC_LIST_STATUS);

  // allocate memory for database command structure
  LPDBCOMMAND pdb = (LPDBCOMMAND)malloc(sizeof(DBCOMMAND));
  if (pdb == NULL)
    plb->InsertString(0, "Cannot allocate memory for command");
  else
  {
    memset(pdb, 0, sizeof(DBCOMMAND));
```

```
    UpdateData(TRUE);
    FillAndSendDBCmd(pdb, m_stringFile, m_stringSection, m_stringEntry,
     m_stringValue);
  }
}

///////////////////////////////////////////////////////////////////////////////
// CMainView::FillAndSendDBCmd()
//
void CMainView::FillAndSendDBCmd(LPDBCOMMAND pdb, LPCSTR szFile,
 LPCSTR szSection, LPCSTR szEntry, LPCSTR szValue/*= NULL*/)
{
  char pszMessage[1000];    // informational message
  static int nID = 1;       // database command identifier

  // get pointer to list box used for status messages
  CListBox *plb = (CListBox *)GetDlgItem(IDC_LIST_STATUS);

  // fill out command parameters
  pdb->nID = nID;

  lstrcpy(pdb->szFile, szFile);
  lstrcpy(pdb->szSection, szSection);
  lstrcpy(pdb->szEntry, szEntry);

  if (szValue == NULL)
    pdb->nCommand = DB_READ;
  else
  {
    pdb->nCommand = DB_WRITE;
    lstrcpy(pdb->szValue, szValue);
  }

  // send the command to the server
  if (m_pStream->Write(sizeof(DBCOMMAND), pdb) != CWINSOCK_NOERROR)
  {
    wsprintf(pszMessage, "Error sending data (ID %d)", pdb->nID);
    plb->InsertString(0, pszMessage);
    free(pdb);
  }
  else
    ++nID;
}

///////////////////////////////////////////////////////////////////////////////
// CMainView::OnDatagram()
//
// Receives messages from the heartbeat datagram object.
//
LONG CMainView::OnDatagram(WPARAM wParam, LPARAM lParam)
{
  LPVOID pDataWritten;  // pointer to data that is completely written
  LPVOID pDataRead;     // pointer to data just read
  int nLen;             // length
  char pszMessage[1000];// informational message

  // get pointer to list box used for status messages
  CListBox *plb = (CListBox *)GetDlgItem(IDC_LIST_STATUS);
```

continues

Listing 15.2. continued

```
  switch (wParam)
  {
    case CWINSOCK_DONE_WRITING:
      // lParam = pointer to data that was sent
      // should never happen but make sure the memory is freed just in case
      pDataWritten = (LPVOID)lParam;
      free(pDataWritten);
      break;

    case CWINSOCK_ERROR_WRITING:
      // lParam = pointer to data that generated error sending
      // should never happen but make sure the memory is freed just in case
      pDataWritten = (LPVOID)lParam;
      free(pDataWritten);
      break;

    case CWINSOCK_DONE_READING:
      // lParam = # data chunks in queue
      pDataRead = m_pDatagram->Read(&nLen);
      lstrcpy(pszMessage, "Heartbeat received");
      plb->InsertString(0, pszMessage);
      free(pDataRead);
      m_nHeartbeat = 0;
      ((CStatic *)GetDlgItem(IDC_ICON_STATUS))->SetIcon(m_hGreen);
      break;

    case CWINSOCK_ERROR_READING:
      break;

    default:
      break;
  }

  return 0L;
}

/////////////////////////////////////////////////////////////////////////////
// CMainView::OnTimer()
//
// Receives timer messages
//
void CMainView::OnTimer(UINT nIDEvent)
{
  ++m_nHeartbeat;

  if (m_nHeartbeat > 1)
    ((CStatic *)GetDlgItem(IDC_ICON_STATUS))->SetIcon(m_hYellow);

  if (m_nHeartbeat > 2)
    ((CStatic *)GetDlgItem(IDC_ICON_STATUS))->SetIcon(m_hRed);

  CFormView::OnTimer(nIDEvent);
}
```

Server INISRV

The INISRV program uses the Multiple Document Interface. The program has two views that are derived from the CFormView object. CMainView, shown in Listings 15.3 and 15.4, shows status information for the server socket that waits for connection requests from clients. CServerView, shown in Listings 15.5 and 15.6, shows status information for the connected socket that processes database commands sent by clients.

CMainView's m_pWinSock member variable controls the starting and stopping of the WinSock subsystem for this program. g_pStreamSrv is a global variable that points to the server stream socket object that waits for connections from clients.

The CMainView OnStreamSrv() member function receives status information for the server stream socket object. It's triggered by the WM_USER_STREAMSRV user-defined message whenever a client requests a connection to the server.

The implementation of the CMainView object is shown in Listing 15.4. This object performs the initialization work for the INISRV application. CMainView's OnInitialUpdate() is called soon after the object is created. This function is responsible for starting the WinSock subsystem and creating a server stream socket that waits for connection requests to arrive from clients.

Multiple Views

When a client requests a connection, the OnStreamSrv() member function is triggered with wParam set to CWINSOCK_READY_TO_ACCEPT_CONNECTION. A new view, of type CServerView, is then launched to accept the client connection. This new view is supported by having two document templates, as shown in Listing 15.3 and 15.4. One template uses CMainView and the other uses CServerView.

Listing 15.3. MAINVIEW.H for INISRV.

```
// mainview.h : header file
//

/////////////////////////////////////////////////////////////////////////////
// CMainView form view

#ifndef __AFXEXT_H__
#include <afxext.h>
#endif

#include "cwinsock.h"    // Windows Sockets classes

class CMainView : public CFormView
{
```

continues

Listing 15.3. continued

```
  DECLARE_DYNCREATE(CMainView)

private:
  CWinSock * m_pWinSock;          // WinSock sub-system startup/.shutdown

protected:
  CMainView();      // protected constructor used by dynamic creation

// Form Data
public:
  //{{AFX_DATA(CMainView)
  enum { IDD = IDD_DIALOG_MAIN };
    // NOTE: the ClassWizard will add data members here
  //}}AFX_DATA

// Attributes
public:

// Operations
public:

// Implementation
protected:
  virtual ~CMainView();
  virtual void DoDataExchange(CDataExchange* pDX);  // DDX/DDV support
  virtual void OnInitialUpdate();
  // Generated message map functions
  //{{AFX_MSG(CMainView)
  afx_msg LONG OnStreamSrv(WPARAM wParam, LPARAM lParam);
  //}}AFX_MSG
  DECLARE_MESSAGE_MAP()
};

/////////////////////////////////////////////////////////////////////////////

#define WM_USER_STREAMSRV (WM_USER + 1)
```

Listing 15.4. MAINVIEW.CPP for INISRV.

```
// mainview.cpp : implementation file
//

#include "stdafx.h"
#include "inisrv.h"
#include "mainfrm.h"
#include "mainview.h"
#include "global.h"
#include "common.h"

#ifdef _DEBUG
#undef THIS_FILE
static char BASED_CODE THIS_FILE[] = __FILE__;
#endif
```

```
///////////////////////////////////////////////////////////////////////////
// CMainView

IMPLEMENT_DYNCREATE(CMainView, CFormView)

CMainView::CMainView()
  : CFormView(CMainView::IDD)
{
  //{{AFX_DATA_INIT(CMainView)
    // NOTE: the ClassWizard will add member initialization here
  //}}AFX_DATA_INIT

  // initialize class variables

  m_pWinSock = NULL;
  g_pStreamSrv = NULL;
}

CMainView::~CMainView()
{
  // free the stream and WinSock objects

  if (g_pStreamSrv)
  {
    g_pStreamSrv->DestroySocket();
    delete g_pStreamSrv;
    g_pStreamSrv = NULL;
  }

  if (m_pWinSock)
  {
    m_pWinSock->Shutdown();
    delete m_pWinSock;
    m_pWinSock = NULL;
  }
}

void CMainView::DoDataExchange(CDataExchange* pDX)
{
  CFormView::DoDataExchange(pDX);
  //{{AFX_DATA_MAP(CMainView)
    // NOTE: the ClassWizard will add DDX and DDV calls here
  //}}AFX_DATA_MAP
}

void CMainView::OnInitialUpdate()
{
  // get pointer to list box used for status messages

  CListBox *plb = (CListBox *)GetDlgItem(IDC_LIST_STATUS);

  // initialize the WinSock object

  m_pWinSock = new CWinSock;
  if (m_pWinSock->Startup() == CWINSOCK_NOERROR)
    plb->InsertString(0, "WinSock initialized");
  else
  {
```

continues

Listing 15.4. continued

```
    plb->InsertString(0, "WinSock initialization failed");
    delete m_pWinSock;
    m_pWinSock = NULL;
    return;
  }

  // initialize the stream socket object

  g_pStreamSrv = new CStreamSocket(this, WM_USER_STREAMSRV);
  if (g_pStreamSrv->CreateSocket(STREAM_PORT) == CWINSOCK_NOERROR)
    plb->InsertString(0, "Stream server created");
  else
  {
    plb->InsertString(0, "Stream server creation failed");
    delete g_pStreamSrv;
    g_pStreamSrv = NULL;
  }
}

BEGIN_MESSAGE_MAP(CMainView, CFormView)
  //{{AFX_MSG_MAP(CMainView)
  ON_MESSAGE(WM_USER_STREAMSRV, OnStreamSrv)
  //}}AFX_MSG_MAP
END_MESSAGE_MAP()

/////////////////////////////////////////////////////////////////////////////
// CMainView message handlers

/////////////////////////////////////////////////////////////////////////////
// CMainView::OnStreamSrv()
//
// Receives messages from the stream server object.
//
LONG CMainView::OnStreamSrv(WPARAM wParam, LPARAM lParam)
{
// temporary code
CMDIChildWnd *pActiveChild;


  // get pointer to list box used for status messages
  CListBox *plb = (CListBox *)GetDlgItem(IDC_LIST_STATUS);

  switch (wParam)
  {
    case CWINSOCK_READY_TO_ACCEPT_CONNECTION:
      plb->InsertString(0, "Client requesting connection");

      // accept the client connection by creating
      // a CServerView window
      pActiveChild =
       ((CMainFrame *)(AfxGetApp()->m_pMainWnd))->MDIGetActive();
      CDocument *pDocument;
      if (pActiveChild != NULL)
      {
        if ((pDocument = pActiveChild->GetActiveDocument()) != NULL)
```

```
        {
          CDocTemplate *pTemplate =
           ((CInisrvApp *)AfxGetApp())->m_pServerTemplate;
          ASSERT_VALID(pTemplate);
          CFrameWnd *pFrame =
           pTemplate->CreateNewFrame(pDocument, pActiveChild);
          if (pFrame == NULL)
          {
            plb->InsertString(0, "Failed to create window to handle client");
          }
          else
          {
            pTemplate->InitialUpdateFrame(pFrame, pDocument);
          }
        }
      }

      break;

    default:
      break;
  }

  return 0L;
}
```

The CServerView object handles the actual communication with the client. Its m_pStream member variable is the stream socket that actually receives data from and sends data to the client.

CServerView's OnStream() member function receives status information for the stream socket object that does the actual communication with the client. It's triggered by the WM_USER_STREAM user-defined message whenever a client connection is made or lost, and when data is available to be read or finished being written.

The m_pStream object is then used to accept the client connection request. When the connection is made, OnStream() is called with wParam set to CWINSOCK_YOU_ARE_CONNECTED. When data arrives from the client, OnStream() is called with wParam set to CWINSOCK_DONE_READING. The database command is read and carried out. A response is formulated and sent back to the client. When the write finishes, OnStream() is called with wParam set to CWINSOCK_DONE_WRITING letting the server know the data send has completed.

CServerView also has a datagram socket that, in combination with the timer handled by OnTimer(), handles the periodic sending of a heartbeat message to the client. Notice the HEARTBEAT_TEST ifdef in the CServerView's OnTimer() function. By defining this variable, the client's traffic light feature is easily tested. After the client is connected to the server for 10 and then 20 seconds, the client's status should go from green to yellow to red, and back to green.

Listing 15.5. SRVVIEW.H for INISRV.

```
// srvview.h : header file
//

/////////////////////////////////////////////////////////////////////////////
// CServerView form view

#ifndef __AFXEXT_H__
#include <afxext.h>
#endif

#include "cwinsock.h"   // Windows Sockets classes

class CServerView : public CFormView
{
  DECLARE_DYNCREATE(CServerView)

private:
  CStreamSocket * m_pStream;      // Stream socket which communicates with client
  CDatagramSocket * m_pDatagram; // Datagram socket which sends heatbeats to client
  SOCKADDR_IN m_sinClient;        // Client's address
  char m_pszHeartbeat[20];        // Heartbeat message sent to client
  void HandleRead();

protected:
  CServerView();      // protected constructor used by dynamic creation

// Form Data
public:
  //{{AFX_DATA(CServerView)
  enum { IDD = IDD_DIALOG_SERVER };
    // NOTE: the ClassWizard will add data members here
  //}}AFX_DATA

// Attributes
public:

// Operations
public:

// Implementation
protected:
  virtual ~CServerView();
  virtual void DoDataExchange(CDataExchange* pDX);  // DDX/DDV support
  virtual void OnInitialUpdate();
  // Generated message map functions
  //{{AFX_MSG(CServerView)
  afx_msg LONG OnStream(WPARAM wParam, LPARAM lParam);
  afx_msg LONG OnDatagram(WPARAM wParam, LPARAM lParam);
  afx_msg void OnTimer(UINT nIDEvent);
  //}}AFX_MSG
  DECLARE_MESSAGE_MAP()
};

/////////////////////////////////////////////////////////////////////////////
```

```
#define WM_USER_STREAM     (WM_USER + 1)
#define WM_USER_DATAGRAM   (WM_USER + 2)
```

Listing 15.6. SRVVIEW.CPP for INISRV.

```
// srvview.cpp : implementation file
//

#include "stdafx.h"
#include <string.h>
#include "inisrv.h"
#include "srvview.h"
#include "global.h"
#include "db.h"
#include "common.h"

#ifdef _DEBUG
#undef THIS_FILE
static char BASED_CODE THIS_FILE[] = __FILE__;
#endif

/////////////////////////////////////////////////////////////////////////////
// CServerView

IMPLEMENT_DYNCREATE(CServerView, CFormView)

CServerView::CServerView()
  : CFormView(CServerView::IDD)
{
  //{{AFX_DATA_INIT(CServerView)
    // NOTE: the ClassWizard will add member initialization here
  //}}AFX_DATA_INIT

  m_pStream = NULL;
  m_pDatagram = NULL;
  (*m_pszHeartbeat) = '\0';
}

CServerView::~CServerView()
{
  // free the stream and WinSock objects

  if (m_pStream)
  {
    m_pStream->DestroySocket();
    delete m_pStream;
    m_pStream = NULL;
  }

  if (m_pDatagram)
  {
    m_pDatagram->DestroySocket();
    delete m_pDatagram;
    m_pDatagram = NULL;
```

continues

Listing 15.6. continued

```
  }
}

void CServerView::DoDataExchange(CDataExchange* pDX)
{
  CFormView::DoDataExchange(pDX);
  //{{AFX_DATA_MAP(CServerView)
    // NOTE: the ClassWizard will add DDX and DDV calls here
  //}}AFX_DATA_MAP
}

void CServerView::OnInitialUpdate()
{
  // start the timer used to trigger the heartbeat writes

  SetTimer(1, HEARTBEAT_DELAY, NULL);

  // get pointer to list box used for status messages

  CListBox *plb = (CListBox *)GetDlgItem(IDC_LIST_STATUS);

  // accept the client connection
  int nStatus;
  m_pStream = new CStreamSocket(this, WM_USER_STREAM);
  nStatus = g_pStreamSrv->Accept(m_pStream);
  if (nStatus != CWINSOCK_NOERROR)
  {
    plb->InsertString(0, "Error accepting client connection");
    delete m_pStream;
    m_pStream = NULL;
    return;
  }

  plb->InsertString(0, "Accepted client connection");

  // get address of client and convert it to be used for sending heartbeat
  if (m_pStream->GetPeerName(&m_sinClient) != CWINSOCK_NOERROR)
  {
    plb->InsertString(0, "Cannot get name of client");
    m_pStream->DestroySocket();
    delete m_pStream;
    m_pStream = NULL;
    return;
  }
  m_sinClient.sin_port = htons(DATAGRAM_PORT);

  // create the heartbeat datagram
  m_pDatagram = new CDatagramSocket(this, WM_USER_DATAGRAM);
  nStatus = m_pDatagram->CreateSocket();
  if (nStatus != CWINSOCK_NOERROR)
  {
    delete m_pDatagram;
    m_pDatagram = NULL;
    plb->InsertString(0, "Error creating heartbeat datagram");
```

```
    m_pStream->DestroySocket();
    delete m_pStream;
    m_pStream = NULL;

    return;
  }
  plb->InsertString(0, "Heartbeat datagram created");
}

BEGIN_MESSAGE_MAP(CServerView, CFormView)
  //{{AFX_MSG_MAP(CServerView)
  ON_MESSAGE(WM_USER_STREAM, OnStream)
  ON_MESSAGE(WM_USER_DATAGRAM, OnDatagram)
  ON_WM_TIMER()
  //}}AFX_MSG_MAP
END_MESSAGE_MAP()

/////////////////////////////////////////////////////////////////////////////
// CServerView message handlers

/////////////////////////////////////////////////////////////////////////////
// CServerView::OnStream()
//
// Receives messages from the connected stream object.
//
LONG CServerView::OnStream(WPARAM wParam, LPARAM lParam)
{
  LPVOID pDataWritten;  // pointer to data that is completely written
  char pszMessage[1000];// informational message
  SOCKADDR_IN sin;      // Internet address of client
  IN_ADDR in;           // IP address of client
  int nStatus;          // error status

  // get pointer to list box used for status messages
  CListBox *plb = (CListBox *)GetDlgItem(IDC_LIST_STATUS);

  switch (wParam)
  {
    case CWINSOCK_DONE_WRITING:
      // lParam = pointer to data that was sent
      pDataWritten = (LPVOID)lParam;
      wsprintf(pszMessage, "Data sent (ID %d)",
       ((LPDBCOMMAND)pDataWritten)->nID);
      plb->InsertString(0, pszMessage);
      free(pDataWritten);
      break;

    case CWINSOCK_ERROR_WRITING:
      // lParam = pointer to data that generated error sending
      pDataWritten = (LPVOID)lParam;
      wsprintf(pszMessage, "Error sending data (ID %d)",
       ((LPDBCOMMAND)pDataWritten)->nID);
      plb->InsertString(0, pszMessage);
      free(pDataWritten);
      break;

    case CWINSOCK_DONE_READING:
      // lParam = # data chunks in queue
```

continues

Listing 15.6. continued

```
      HandleRead();
      break;

    case CWINSOCK_ERROR_READING:
      break;

    case CWINSOCK_YOU_ARE_CONNECTED:
      // print out client information
      nStatus = m_pStream->GetPeerName(&sin);
      if (nStatus == CWINSOCK_NOERROR)
      {
        memcpy(&in, &sin.sin_addr.s_addr, 4);
        wsprintf(pszMessage, "Connected to client %s, %d",
          inet_ntoa(in), ntohs(sin.sin_port));
        plb->InsertString(0, pszMessage);
      }
      else
        plb->InsertString(0, "Error getting client name");
      break;

    case CWINSOCK_LOST_CONNECTION:
      // client closed the connection
      m_pStream->DestroySocket();
      delete m_pStream;
      m_pStream = NULL;
      m_pDatagram->DestroySocket();
      delete m_pDatagram;Listing 15.6. continued.
      m_pDatagram = NULL;
      plb->InsertString(0, "Client closed connection");
      break;

    default:
      break;
  }

  return 0L;
}

/////////////////////////////////////////////////////////////////////////////
// CServerView::HandleRead()
//
// Receives data from the connected stream object.
//
void CServerView::HandleRead()
{
  char pszMessage[1000];// informational message
  LPVOID pDataRead;      // pointer to data read
  int nLen;              // length
  DBCOMMAND dbcmd;       // database command structure

  // get pointer to list box used for status messages
  CListBox *plb = (CListBox *)GetDlgItem(IDC_LIST_STATUS);

  // read the data
  pDataRead = m_pStream->Read(&nLen);
  plb->InsertString(0, "Received command from client");
```

```
    // verify that the data represented an entire
    // database command structure
    if (nLen != sizeof(DBCOMMAND))
    {
      plb->InsertString(0, "This server cannot handle partial blocks");
      free(pDataRead);
      return;
    }

    // copy the data to a database command structure
    memcpy(&dbcmd, pDataRead, sizeof(DBCOMMAND));
    free(pDataRead);

    // verify database command
    if ((dbcmd.nCommand != DB_READ) && (dbcmd.nCommand != DB_WRITE))
    {
      plb->InsertString(0, "Invalid database command");
      return;
    }

    // perform the database request and format a response
    LPDBCOMMAND pdbcmd = (LPDBCOMMAND)malloc(sizeof(DBCOMMAND));
    if (pdbcmd == NULL)
    {
      plb->InsertString(0, "Cannot allocate memory for response");
      return;
    }
    memcpy(pdbcmd, &dbcmd, sizeof(DBCOMMAND));
    pdbcmd->nCommand = DB_OK;
    if (dbcmd.nCommand == DB_READ)
      ::GetPrivateProfileString(dbcmd.szSection, dbcmd.szEntry, "NOT FOUND",
       pdbcmd->szValue, DBBUFSIZE, dbcmd.szFile);
    else
      ::WritePrivateProfileString(dbcmd.szSection, dbcmd.szEntry,
       dbcmd.szValue, dbcmd.szFile);

    // send the response to the client
    if (m_pStream->Write(sizeof(DBCOMMAND), pdbcmd) != CWINSOCK_NOERROR)
    {
      wsprintf(pszMessage, "Error sending data (ID %d)", pdbcmd->nID);
      plb->InsertString(0, pszMessage);
      free(pdbcmd);
    }
}

/////////////////////////////////////////////////////////////////////////////
// CServerView::OnDatagram()
//
// Receives messages from the datagram object.
//
LONG CServerView::OnDatagram(WPARAM wParam, LPARAM lParam)
{
  LPVOID pDataWritten;  // pointer to data that is completely written
  LPVOID pDataRead;     // pointer to data just read
  int nLen;             // length
  char pszMessage[1000];// informational message
```

continues

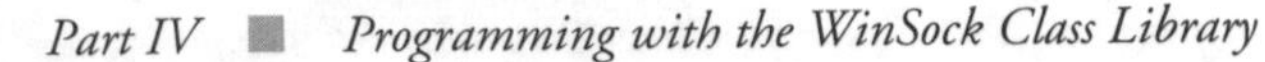

Listing 15.6. continued

```
  // get pointer to list box used for status messages
  CListBox *plb = (CListBox *)GetDlgItem(IDC_LIST_STATUS);

  switch (wParam)
  {
    case CWINSOCK_DONE_WRITING:
      // lParam = pointer to data that was sent
      pDataWritten = (LPVOID)lParam;
      wsprintf(pszMessage, "Heartbeat sent");
      plb->InsertString(0, pszMessage);
      (*m_pszHeartbeat) = '\0';   // same as (*pDataWritten) = '\0';
      break;

    case CWINSOCK_ERROR_WRITING:
      // lParam = pointer to data that generated error sending
      pDataWritten = (LPVOID)lParam;
      wsprintf(pszMessage, "Error sending heartbeat");
      plb->InsertString(0, pszMessage);
      (*m_pszHeartbeat) = '\0';   // same as (*pDataWritten) = '\0';
      break;

    case CWINSOCK_DONE_READING:
      // lParam = # data chunks in queue
      // should never happen but make sure the memory is freed just in case
      pDataRead = m_pDatagram->Read(&nLen);
      free(pDataRead);
      break;

    case CWINSOCK_ERROR_READING:
      break;

    default:
      break;
  }

  return 0L;
}

/////////////////////////////////////////////////////////////////////////////
// CServerView::OnTimer()
//
// Sends periodic heartbeats to the connected client through the datagram.
//

void CServerView::OnTimer(UINT nIDEvent)
{
  char pszMessage[1000];      // informational message

#ifdef HEARTBEAT_TEST
  static int nHeartbeatTest = 0;
  ++nHeartbeatTest;
  if ((nHeartbeatTest == 10) || (nHeartbeatTest == 11) ||
    (nHeartbeatTest == 20) || (nHeartbeatTest == 21))
    return;
#endif
```

```
  // make sure we are not sending out of a bad datagram socket
  if (m_pDatagram == NULL)
    return;

  // get pointer to list box used for status messages
  CListBox *plb = (CListBox *)GetDlgItem(IDC_LIST_STATUS);

  // send the buffer unless the previous send hasn't completed yet
  if ((*m_pszHeartbeat) == '\0')
  {
    lstrcpy(m_pszHeartbeat, HEARTBEAT_STRING);
    // be sure to send terminating NULL character
    if (m_pDatagram->Write(lstrlen(m_pszHeartbeat) + 1, m_pszHeartbeat,
     &m_sinClient) != CWINSOCK_NOERROR)
    {
      (*m_pszHeartbeat) = '\0';
      wsprintf(pszMessage, "Error sending heartbeat");
      plb->InsertString(0, pszMessage);
    }
  }

  CFormView::OnTimer(nIDEvent);
}
```

Figures 15.1 and 15.2 show the client and server in action.

FIGURE 15.1.
The client INICLNT.

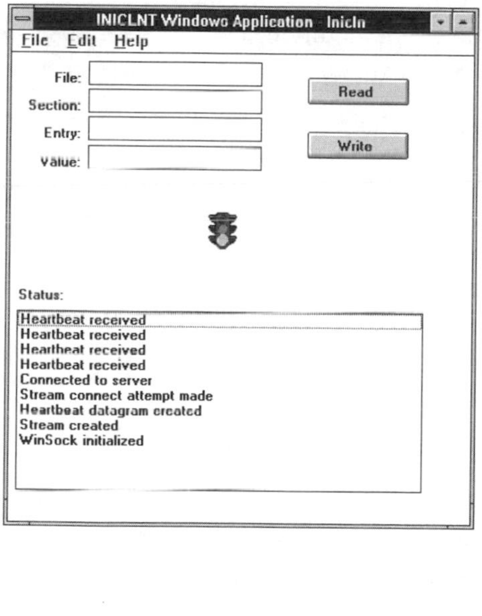

Summary

This chapter demonstrates the use of the `CWinSock`, `CDatagramSocket`, and `CStreamSocket` objects. It also shows how a server, which handles several clients simultaneously, is easily produced with the help of the WinSock class library.

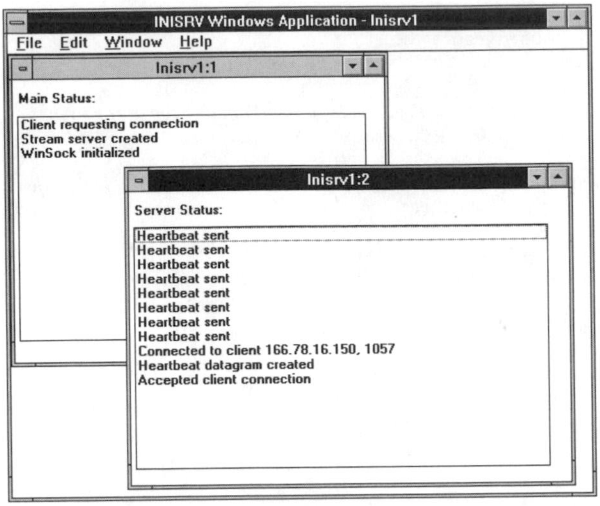

FIGURE 15.2.
The server INISRV.

There is much room for improvement in the client and server programs, though. One important enhancement might be the ability to handle database commands and responses that do not arrive in one contiguous block. Presently, the client and server can't handle such a circumstance. Luckily, however, the blocks of data being transferred are relatively small and hence have little fragmentation on a lightly loaded network. This enhancement would entail modifying the `CWINSOCK_DONE_READING` handlers for the stream socket objects to buffer the incoming bytes until an entire `DBCOMMAND` structure arrives.

The next chapter uses the WinSock class library object in a finger application for a heterogeneous UNIX environment.

16

Finger Application in a Heterogeneous UNIX Environment

This chapter shows how easy it is to interface a program written with the WinSock API to a program running on a UNIX computer. As discussed in the introductory chapters, WinSock has its roots in Berkeley sockets as implemented in that university's UNIX offering. Using the WinSock class library developed in Part III of this text makes writing such a program even easier.

This chapter presents a functional, if somewhat simplified, Finger client. A Finger client uses the Finger protocol to retrieve user information from a host running the Finger server, or the Finger daemon as it is called in the UNIX realm.

Finger Protocol

The Finger protocol is described in the Internet RFC 1288 authored by David Zimmerman. The groundwork for Finger was introduced in Ken Harrenstien's RFC 742 and by earlier work performed by Les Earnest, Earl Killian, and Brian Harvey. To understand the complete working of the Finger protocol and to gain the knowledge necessary to implement a Finger server, refer to RFC 1288. The simplified client presented in this chapter obeys the following flow:

Create a socket and connect it to port 79 on the host running the Finger server.

Wait for the Finger server to accept the connection.

Send the Finger request to the Finger server.

Receive the response to the Finger request from the Finger server.

Wait for the Finger server to close its end of the socket connection.

Close the socket.

The Finger request has one of two formats:

<CR><LF> requests basic information about all users currently logged into the specified host.

Username<CR><LF> requests detailed information about the specified user.

When the Finger server receives the Finger request, it responds with one or more lines of text delineated by a carriage return. When the server has sent all data, it closes the socket.

The Finger client presented here uses the `CStreamSocket` object. The client is a simple Single Document Interface application. A stream socket connection is used to transmit the Finger request and responses between the client and server.

Finger Client Design

The Finger client application, FINGER, uses the venerable `CFormView`-derived object as its main interface. The header file for the `CMainView` object is shown in Listing 16.1. Its implementation is shown in Listing 16.2 (both of these listings appear later in this section). This object performs most of the work for the FINGER application. `OnInitialUpdate()` is called soon after the object is created. The first thing this function does is to force the list box used for output to use a fixed-pitch font. This ensures that any data formatted for an ASCII terminal looks appropriate. The function starts the WinSock subsystem next and then initializes the data entry field used to accept a username.

When the operator of the Finger client selects the button labeled Finger, `OnClickedButtonFinger()` is called. First, the host and username fields are checked to ensure that they contain valid data. If the username is valid, a Finger request string is formatted. If the wildcard asterisk character (*) is entered for the username, the request string consists of just a carriage return followed by a linefeed. Otherwise, the request string is the username followed by carriage return and linefeed. Next, a stream socket is created and the asynchronous connect is made to port 79 on the selected host. Last, the Finger button is disabled to give the user visual feedback that the program is busy.

When the connect succeeds, `OnStream()` is called with `wParam` set to `CWINSOCK_YOU_ARE_CONNECTED`. In response to this event, the Finger request, formatted in the `OnClickedButtonFinger()` function, is sent. When the Finger request is sent, `OnStream()` is called with `wParam` set to `CWINSOCK_DONE_WRITING`. In response to this event, the list box used for output is cleared, readying itself for the response to the Finger request.

As data arrives, `OnStream()` is called with `wParam` set to `CWINSOCK_DONE_READING`. The `CWINSOCK_DONE_READING` handler calls `DisplayData()` to buffer a complete line of text, denoted by a carriage return, before adding the line to the output list box. The buffering is necessary because it is possible for the data to be received in several pieces with some lines only partially received.

When the Finger server is done sending its response to the Finger request, it closes its side of the stream connection, causing `OnStream()` to be called with `wParam` set to `CWINSOCK_LOST_CONNECTION`. This causes the client to destroy the stream socket. The Finger button is enabled, signaling that it may be used again, with the same or a different host/username combination.

Listing 16.1. MAINVIEW.H for FINGER.

```
// mainview.h : header file
//
```

continues

Listing 16.1. continued

```
/////////////////////////////////////////////////////////////////////////////
// CMainView form view

#ifndef __AFXEXT_H__
#include <afxext.h>
#endif

#include "cwinsock.h"   // Windows Sockets classes

class CMainView : public CFormView
{
  DECLARE_DYNCREATE(CMainView)

private:
  void DisplayData(LPCSTR pDataRead, int nLen);
  CWinSock * m_pWinSock;       // WinSock sub-system startup/shutdown
  CStreamSocket * m_pStream;  // Stream socket
#define MAXUSERLEN (100)
  char m_szUser[MAXUSERLEN];  // user name to query finger with
#define MAXBUFLEN (200)
  char m_szBuf[MAXBUFLEN+1];  // one line of finger output

protected:
  CMainView();        // protected constructor used by dynamic creation

// Form Data
public:
  //{{AFX_DATA(CMainView)
  enum { IDD = IDD_DIALOG_MAIN };
  CString m_stringHost;
  CString m_stringUser;
  //}}AFX_DATA

// Attributes
public:

// Operations
public:

// Implementation
protected:
  virtual ~CMainView();
  virtual void DoDataExchange(CDataExchange* pDX);  // DDX/DDV support
  virtual void OnInitialUpdate();
  // Generated message map functions
  //{{AFX_MSG(CMainView)
  afx_msg LONG OnStream(WPARAM wParam, LPARAM lParam);
  afx_msg void OnClickedButtonFinger();
  //}}AFX_MSG
  DECLARE_MESSAGE_MAP()
};

/////////////////////////////////////////////////////////////////////////////

#define WM_USER_STREAM (WM_USER + 1)
```

Listing 16.2. MAINVIEW.CPP for FINGER.

```
// mainview.cpp : implementation file
//

#include "stdafx.h"
#include "finger.h"
#include "mainview.h"

#ifdef _DEBUG
#undef THIS_FILE
static char BASED_CODE THIS_FILE[] = __FILE__;
#endif

/////////////////////////////////////////////////////////////////////////////
// CMainView

IMPLEMENT_DYNCREATE(CMainView, CFormView)

CMainView::CMainView()
  : CFormView(CMainView::IDD)
{
  //{{AFX_DATA INIT(CMainView)
  m_stringHost = "";
  m_stringUser = "";
  //}}AFX_DATA_INIT

  // initialize class variables

  m_pWinSock = NULL;
  m_pStream = NULL;
  m_szBuf[0] = '\0';
}

CMainView::~CMainView()
{
  // free the stream and WinSock objects

  if (m_pStream)
  {
    m_pStream->DestroySocket();
    delete m_pStream;
    m_pStream = NULL;
  }

  if (m_pWinSock)
  {
    m_pWinSock->Shutdown();
    delete m_pWinSock;
    m_pWinSock = NULL;
  }
}

void CMainView::DoDataExchange(CDataExchange* pDX)
{
  CFormView::DoDataExchange(pDX);
  //{{AFX_DATA_MAP(CMainView)
  DDX_Text(pDX, IDC_EDIT_HOST, m_stringHost);
```

continues

Listing 16.2. continued

```
  DDX_Text(pDX, IDC_EDIT_USER, m_stringUser);
  //}}AFX_DATA_MAP
}

void CMainView::OnInitialUpdate()
{
  // get pointer to list box used for status messages

  CListBox *plb = (CListBox *)GetDlgItem(IDC_LIST_OUTPUT);

  // change the font of the listbox so it is fixed pitch

  HFONT hFont = (HFONT)::GetStockObject(SYSTEM_FIXED_FONT);
  CFont *pFixedFont = CFont::FromHandle(hFont);
  plb->SetFont(pFixedFont);

  // set the tab stops because some finger
  // servers format their data with tabs

  LONG lDialogBaseUnits = GetDialogBaseUnits();
  WORD wDialogUnitX = LOWORD(lDialogBaseUnits) / 4;
  int nTabIndex, anTabStops[10];
  for (nTabIndex=0; nTabIndex < 10; nTabIndex++)
    anTabStops[nTabIndex] = wDialogUnitX * (2 * nTabIndex);
  plb->SetTabStops(10, anTabStops);

  // initialize the WinSock object

  m_pWinSock = new CWinSock;
  if (m_pWinSock->Startup() != CWINSOCK_NOERROR)
  {
    AfxMessageBox("WinSock initialization failed");
    delete m_pWinSock;
    m_pWinSock = NULL;
    return;
  }

  m_stringUser = "*";
  UpdateData(FALSE);
}

BEGIN_MESSAGE_MAP(CMainView, CFormView)
  //{{AFX_MSG_MAP(CMainView)
  ON_MESSAGE(WM_USER_STREAM, OnStream)
  ON_BN_CLICKED(IDC_BUTTON_FINGER, OnClickedButtonFinger)
  //}}AFX_MSG_MAP
END_MESSAGE_MAP()

/////////////////////////////////////////////////////////////////////////////
// CMainView message handlers

/////////////////////////////////////////////////////////////////////////////
// CMainView::OnStream()
//
// Receives messages from the stream object.
//
```

```
LONG CMainView::OnStream(WPARAM wParam, LPARAM lParam)
{
  LPCSTR pDataRead;      // pointer to data just read
  LPCSTR pOrigDataRead;  // pointer to data just read
  int nLen;              // length

  // get pointer to list box used for status messages

  CListBox *plb = (CListBox *)GetDlgItem(IDC_LIST_OUTPUT);

  // check for invalid stream socket object
  if (m_pStream == NULL)
  {
    plb->AddString("Invalid stream socket object");
    return 0L;
  }

  switch (wParam)
  {
    case CWINSOCK_DONE_WRITING:
      // lParam = pointer to data that was sent

      // lParam points to the static variable m_szUser
      // so it should not be freed

      // clear the list box
      while (plb->GetCount() > 0)
        plb->DeleteString(0);
      break;

    case CWINSOCK_ERROR_WRITING:
      // lParam = pointer to data that generated error sending

      // lParam points to the static variable m_szUser
      // so it should not be freed

      AfxMessageBox("Error sending finger request");
      break;

    case CWINSOCK_DONE_READING:
      // lParam = # data chunks in queue
      pDataRead = pOrigDataRead = (LPCSTR)m_pStream->Read(&nLen);
      if (pDataRead != NULL)
      {
        DisplayData(pDataRead, nLen);
        free((LPVOID)pOrigDataRead);
      }
      break;

    case CWINSOCK_ERROR_READING:
      break;

    case CWINSOCK_YOU_ARE_CONNECTED:
      if (m_pStream->Write(lstrlen(m_szUser), m_szUser) !=
       CWINSOCK_NOERROR)
      {
        AfxMessageBox("Error sending finger request");
        m_pStream->DestroySocket();
```

continues

Listing 16.2. continued

```
        delete m_pStream;
        m_pStream = NULL;
        GetDlgItem(IDC_BUTTON_FINGER)->EnableWindow(TRUE);
      }
      break;

    case CWINSOCK_LOST_CONNECTION:
      // server closed the connection
      m_pStream->DestroySocket();
      delete m_pStream;
      m_pStream = NULL;
      GetDlgItem(IDC_BUTTON_FINGER)->EnableWindow(TRUE);
      break;

    default:
      break;
  }

  return 0L;
}

/////////////////////////////////////////////////////////////////////////////
// CMainView::OnClickedButtonFinger()
//
// Called when the Finger button is pressed.
// Creates a socket, connects to a finger server, and send the request.
//
void CMainView::OnClickedButtonFinger()
{
  // inititalize the buffer used to display the results
  m_szBuf[0] = '\0';

  // make sure the user entered something for the host

  UpdateData(TRUE);

  if (m_stringHost.GetLength() == 0)
  {
    AfxMessageBox("You must enter a host name or IP address");
    return;
  }

#define MAXHOSTLEN (100)
  char szHost[MAXHOSTLEN];
  if (m_stringHost.GetLength() >= MAXHOSTLEN)
  {
    AfxMessageBox("Host name or IP address is too long");
    return;
  }
  lstrcpy(szHost, m_stringHost);

  // make sure the user entered something for the user

  if (m_stringUser.GetLength() == 0)
  {
    AfxMessageBox("You must enter a user name or *");
```

```
      return;
    }

    if (m_stringUser.GetLength() >= MAXUSERLEN)
    {
      AfxMessageBox("User name is too long");
      return;
    }

    // format the finger request

    if (m_stringUser.Compare("*") == 0)
      lstrcpy(m_szUser, "\n\r");
    else
    {
      lstrcpy(m_szUser, m_stringUser);
      lstrcat(m_szUser, "\n\r");
    }

    // initialize the stream socket object

    m_pStream = new CStreamSocket(this, WM_USER_STREAM);
    if (m_pStream->CreateSocket() != CWINSOCK_NOERROR)
    {
      AfxMessageBox("Stream creation failed");
      delete m_pStream;
      m_pStream = NULL;
      return;
    }

    // connect the client to the finger server on port 79
    // (the finger server usually listens on TCP port 79 but we
    // could replace the hard-coded 79 with the "finger" string
    // to do a service lookup)

    if (m_pStream->Connect(szHost, 79) != CWINSOCK_NOERROR)
    {
      AfxMessageBox("Stream connect attempt failed");
      delete m_pStream;
      m_pStream = NULL;
      return;
    }

  GetDlgItem(IDC_BUTTON_FINGER)->EnableWindow(FALSE);
}

/////////////////////////////////////////////////////////////////////////////
// CMainView::DisplayData()
//
void CMainView::DisplayData(LPCSTR pDataRead, int nLen)
{
  char szBuf[2];           // buffer for a one byte string

  // get pointer to list box used for status messages
  CListBox *plb = (CListBox *)GetDlgItem(IDC_LIST_OUTPUT);

  while (nLen > 0)
  {
```

continues

Listing 16.2. continued

```
    // ignore linefeed
    if (*pDataRead != '\r')
    {
      // don't add carriage return to string
      if (*pDataRead != '\n')
      {
        szBuf[0] = *pDataRead;
        szBuf[1] = '\0';
        lstrcat(m_szBuf, szBuf);
      }
      if ((lstrlen(m_szBuf) >= MAXBUFLEN) || (*pDataRead == '\n'))
      {
        // check to see if the buffer has data in it
        if (m_szBuf[0] != '\0')
        {
          plb->AddString(m_szBuf);
          m_szBuf[0] = '\0';
        }
        // check to see if we should insert a blank line
        else if (*pDataRead == '\n')
          plb->AddString(" ");
      }
    }
    --nLen;
    ++pDataRead;
  }
}
```

Running the Finger Client

Figure 16.1 shows the Finger client in action. A user needs only to enter the host name or IP address of a computer running a Finger server, or daemon. If the user desires information about all users on the host computer, the user field is left as an asterisk (*); otherwise, a specific user's name is entered. Simply pressing the Finger button begins the request.

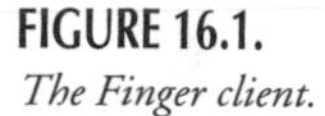

FIGURE 16.1.
The Finger client.

Summary

This chapter presents the last example of using the WinSock class library developed in Part III. It shows how easy it is to interface a Windows program with a computer running the same or a different operating system. With the help of industry-accepted protocols, some programs become quite trivial.

V

Appendixes

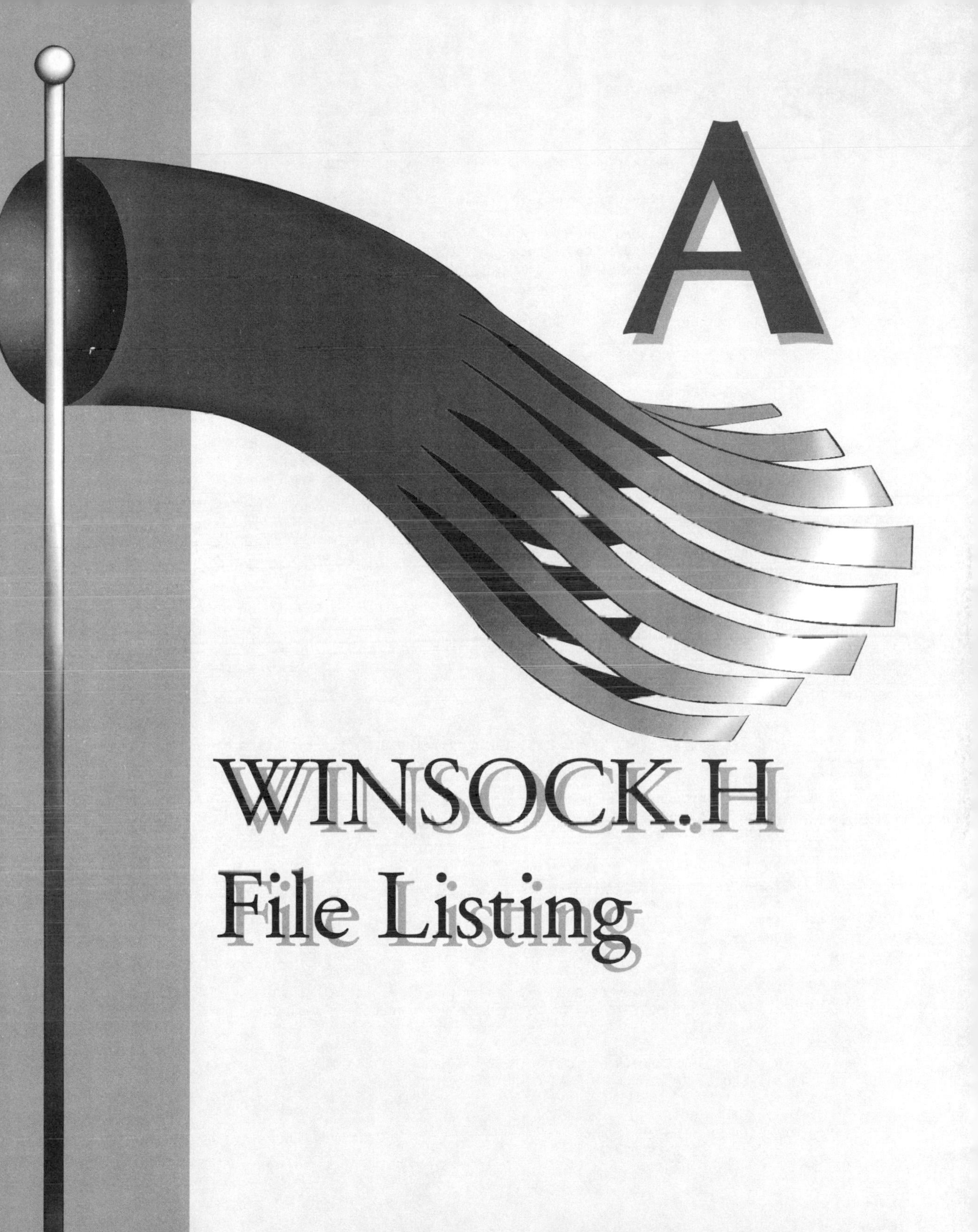

A

WINSOCK.H File Listing

```
/* WINSOCK.H—definitions to be used with the WINSOCK.DLL
 *
 * This header file corresponds to version 1.1 of the Windows Sockets specification.
 *
 * This file includes parts which are Copyright (c) 1982-1986 Regents
 * of the University of California.  All rights reserved.  The
 * Berkeley Software License Agreement specifies the terms and
 * conditions for redistribution.
 *
 * Change log:
 *
 * Fri Apr 23 16:31:01 1993  Mark Towfiq  (towfiq@Microdyne.COM)
 *  New version from David Treadwell which adds extern "C" around
 *  __WSAFDIsSet() and removes "const" from buf param of
 *  WSAAsyncGetHostByAddr().  Added change log.
 *
 * Sat May 15 10:55:00 1993 David Treadwell (davidtr@microsoft.com)
 *  Fix the IN_CLASSC macro to account for class-D multicasts.
 *  Add AF_IPX == AF_NS.
 *
 */

#ifndef _WINSOCKAPI_
#define _WINSOCKAPI_

/*
 * Pull in WINDOWS.H if necessary
 */
#ifndef _INC_WINDOWS
#include <windows.h>
#endif /* _INC_WINDOWS */

/*
 * Basic system type definitions, taken from the BSD file sys/types.h.
 */
typedef unsigned char   u_char;
typedef unsigned short  u_short;
typedef unsigned int    u_int;
typedef unsigned long   u_long;

/*
 * The new type to be used in all
 * instances which refer to sockets.
 */
typedef u_int           SOCKET;

/*
 * Select uses arrays of SOCKETs.  These macros manipulate such
 * arrays.  FD_SETSIZE may be defined by the user before including
 * this file, but the default here should be >= 64.
 *
 * CAVEAT IMPLEMENTOR and USER: THESE MACROS AND TYPES MUST BE
 * INCLUDED IN WINSOCK.H EXACTLY AS SHOWN HERE.
 */
#ifndef FD_SETSIZE
#define FD_SETSIZE      64
#endif /* FD_SETSIZE */
```

```
typedef struct fd_set {
        u_int   fd_count;               /* how many are SET? */
        SOCKET  fd_array[FD_SETSIZE];   /* an array of SOCKETs */
} fd_set;

#ifdef __cplusplus
extern "C" {
#endif

extern int PASCAL FAR __WSAFDIsSet(SOCKET, fd_set FAR *);

#ifdef __cplusplus
}
#endif


#define FD_CLR(fd, set) do { \
    u_int __i; \
    for (__i = 0; __i < ((fd_set FAR *)(set))->fd_count ; __i++) { \
        if (((fd_set FAR *)(set))->fd_array[__i] == fd) { \
            while (__i < ((fd_set FAR *)(set))->fd_count-1) { \
                ((fd_set FAR *)(set))->fd_array[__i] = \
                    ((fd_set FAR *)(set))->fd_array[__i+1]; \
                __i++; \
            } \
            ((fd_set FAR *)(set))->fd_count--; \
            break; \
        } \
    } \
} while(0)

#define FD_SET(fd, set) do { \
    if (((fd_set FAR *)(set))->fd_count < FD_SETSIZE) \
        ((fd_set FAR *)(set))->fd_array[((fd_set FAR *)(set))->fd_count++]=fd;\
} while(0)

#define FD_ZERO(set) (((fd_set FAR *)(set))->fd_count=0)

#define FD_ISSET(fd, set) __WSAFDIsSet((SOCKET)fd, (fd_set FAR *)set)

/*
 * Structure used in select() call, taken from the BSD file sys/time.h.
 */
struct timeval {
        long    tv_sec;         /* seconds */
        long    tv_usec;        /* and microseconds */
};

/*
 * Operations on timevals.
 *
 * NB: timercmp does not work for >= or <=.
 */
#define timerisset(tvp)         ((tvp)->tv_sec || (tvp)->tv_usec)
#define timercmp(tvp, uvp, cmp) \
        ((tvp)->tv_sec cmp (uvp)->tv_sec || \
         (tvp)->tv_sec == (uvp)->tv_sec && (tvp)->tv_usec cmp (uvp)->tv_usec)
```

```
#define timerclear(tvp)         (tvp)->tv_sec = (tvp)->tv_usec = 0

/*
 * Commands for ioctlsocket(),  taken from the BSD file fcntl.h.
 *
 *
 * Ioctl's have the command encoded in the lower word,
 * and the size of any in or out parameters in the upper
 * word.  The high 2 bits of the upper word are used
 * to encode the in/out status of the parameter; for now
 * we restrict parameters to at most 128 bytes.
 */
#define IOCPARM_MASK    0x7f            /* parameters must be < 128 bytes */
#define IOC_VOID        0x20000000      /* no parameters */
#define IOC_OUT         0x40000000      /* copy out parameters */
#define IOC_IN          0x80000000      /* copy in parameters */
#define IOC_INOUT       (IOC_IN¦IOC_OUT)
                                        /* 0x20000000 distinguishes new &
                                           old ioctl's */
#define _IO(x,y)        (IOC_VOID¦(x<<8)¦y)

#define _IOR(x,y,t)     (IOC_OUT¦(((long)sizeof(t)&IOCPARM_MASK)<<16)¦(x<<8)¦y)

#define _IOW(x,y,t)     (IOC_IN¦(((long)sizeof(t)&IOCPARM_MASK)<<16)¦(x<<8)¦y)

#define FIONREAD    _IOR('f', 127, u_long) /* get # bytes to read */
#define FIONBIO     _IOW('f', 126, u_long) /* set/clear non-blocking i/o */
#define FIOASYNC    _IOW('f', 125, u_long) /* set/clear async i/o */

/* Socket I/O Controls */
#define SIOCSHIWAT  _IOW('s',  0, u_long)  /* set high watermark */
#define SIOCGHIWAT  _IOR('s',  1, u_long)  /* get high watermark */
#define SIOCSLOWAT  _IOW('s',  2, u_long)  /* set low watermark */
#define SIOCGLOWAT  _IOR('s',  3, u_long)  /* get low watermark */
#define SIOCATMARK  _IOR('s',  7, u_long)  /* at oob mark? */

/*
 * Structures returned by network data base library, taken from the
 * BSD file netdb.h.  All addresses are supplied in host order, and
 * returned in network order (suitable for use in system calls).
 */

struct  hostent {
        char    FAR * h_name;           /* official name of host */
        char    FAR * FAR * h_aliases;  /* alias list */
        short   h_addrtype;             /* host address type */
        short   h_length;               /* length of address */
        char    FAR * FAR * h_addr_list; /* list of addresses */
#define h_addr  h_addr_list[0]          /* address, for backward compat */
};

/*
 * It is assumed here that a network number
 * fits in 32 bits.
 */
struct  netent {
        char    FAR * n_name;           /* official name of net */
        char    FAR * FAR * n_aliases;  /* alias list */
```

```
        short   n_addrtype;             /* net address type */
        u_long  n_net;                  /* network # */
};

struct  servent {
        char    FAR * s_name;           /* official service name */
        char    FAR * FAR * s_aliases;  /* alias list */
        short   s_port;                 /* port # */
        char    FAR * s_proto;          /* protocol to use */
};

struct  protoent {
        char    FAR * p_name;           /* official protocol name */
        char    FAR * FAR * p_aliases;  /* alias list */
        short   p_proto;                /* protocol # */
};

/*
 * Constants and structures defined by the internet system,
 * Per RFC 790, September 1981, taken from the BSD file netinet/in.h.
 */

/*
 * Protocols
 */
#define IPPROTO_IP              0               /* dummy for IP */
#define IPPROTO_ICMP            1               /* control message protocol */
#define IPPROTO_GGP             2               /* gateway^2 (deprecated) */
#define IPPROTO_TCP             6               /* tcp */
#define IPPROTO_PUP             12              /* pup */
#define IPPROTO_UDP             17              /* user datagram protocol */
#define IPPROTO_IDP             22              /* xns idp */
#define IPPROTO_ND              77              /* UNOFFICIAL net disk proto */

#define IPPROTO_RAW             255             /* raw IP packet */
#define IPPROTO_MAX             256

/*
 * Port/socket numbers: network standard functions
 */
#define IPPORT_ECHO             7
#define IPPORT_DISCARD          9
#define IPPORT_SYSTAT           11
#define IPPORT_DAYTIME          13
#define IPPORT_NETSTAT          15
#define IPPORT_FTP              21
#define IPPORT_TELNET           23
#define IPPORT_SMTP             25
#define IPPORT_TIMESERVER       37
#define IPPORT_NAMESERVER       42
#define IPPORT_WHOIS            43
#define IPPORT_MTP              57

/*
 * Port/socket numbers: host specific functions
 */
#define IPPORT_TFTP             69
#define IPPORT_RJE              77
```

```
#define IPPORT_FINGER           79
#define IPPORT_TTYLINK          87
#define IPPORT_SUPDUP           95

/*
 * UNIX TCP sockets
 */
#define IPPORT_EXECSERVER       512
#define IPPORT_LOGINSERVER      513
#define IPPORT_CMDSERVER        514
#define IPPORT_EFSSERVER        520

/*
 * UNIX UDP sockets
 */
#define IPPORT_BIFFUDP          512
#define IPPORT_WHOSERVER        513
#define IPPORT_ROUTESERVER      520
                                        /* 520+1 also used */

/*
 * Ports < IPPORT_RESERVED are reserved for
 * privileged processes (e.g. root).
 */
#define IPPORT_RESERVED         1024

/*
 * Link numbers
 */
#define IMPLINK_IP              155
#define IMPLINK_LOWEXPER        156
#define IMPLINK_HIGHEXPER       158

/*
 * Internet address (old style... should be updated)
 */
struct in_addr {
        union {
                struct { u_char s_b1,s_b2,s_b3,s_b4; } S_un_b;
                struct { u_short s_w1,s_w2; } S_un_w;
                u_long S_addr;
        } S_un;
#define s_addr  S_un.S_addr
                                /* can be used for most tcp & ip code */
#define s_host  S_un.S_un_b.s_b2
                                /* host on imp */
#define s_net   S_un.S_un_b.s_b1
                                /* network */
#define s_imp   S_un.S_un_w.s_w2
                                /* imp */
#define s_impno S_un.S_un_b.s_b4
                                /* imp # */
#define s_lh    S_un.S_un_b.s_b3
                                /* logical host */
};

/*
```

```
 * Definitions of bits in internet address integers.
 * On subnets, the decomposition of addresses to host and net parts
 * is done according to subnet mask, not the masks here.
 */
#define IN_CLASSA(i)            (((long)(i) & 0x80000000) == 0)
#define IN_CLASSA_NET           0xff000000
#define IN_CLASSA_NSHIFT        24
#define IN_CLASSA_HOST          0x00ffffff
#define IN_CLASSA_MAX           128

#define IN_CLASSB(i)            (((long)(i) & 0xc0000000) == 0x80000000)
#define IN_CLASSB_NET           0xffff0000
#define IN_CLASSB_NSHIFT        16
#define IN_CLASSB_HOST          0x0000ffff
#define IN_CLASSB_MAX           65536

#define IN_CLASSC(i)            (((long)(i) & 0xe0000000) == 0xc0000000)
#define IN_CLASSC_NET           0xffffff00
#define IN_CLASSC_NSHIFT        8
#define IN_CLASSC_HOST          0x000000ff

#define INADDR_ANY              (u_long)0x00000000
#define INADDR_LOOPBACK         0x7f000001
#define INADDR_BROADCAST        (u_long)0xffffffff
#define INADDR_NONE             0xffffffff

/*
 * Socket address, internet style.
 */
struct sockaddr_in {
        short   sin_family;
        u_short sin_port;
        struct  in_addr sin_addr;
        char    sin_zero[8];
};

#define WSADESCRIPTION_LEN      256
#define WSASYS_STATUS_LEN       128

typedef struct WSAData {
        WORD                    wVersion;
        WORD                    wHighVersion;
        char                    szDescription[WSADESCRIPTION_LEN+1];
        char                    szSystemStatus[WSASYS_STATUS_LEN+1];
        unsigned short          iMaxSockets;
        unsigned short          iMaxUdpDg;
        char FAR *              lpVendorInfo;
} WSADATA;

typedef WSADATA FAR *LPWSADATA;

/*
 * Options for use with [gs]etsockopt at the IP level.
 */
#define IP_OPTIONS      1               /* set/get IP per-packet options */

/*
```

```
 * Definitions related to sockets: types, address families, options,
 * taken from the BSD file sys/socket.h.
 */

/*
 * This is used instead of -1, since the
 * SOCKET type is unsigned.
 */
#define INVALID_SOCKET  (SOCKET)(~0)
#define SOCKET_ERROR            (-1)

/*
 * Types
 */
#define SOCK_STREAM     1               /* stream socket */
#define SOCK_DGRAM      2               /* datagram socket */
#define SOCK_RAW        3               /* raw-protocol interface */
#define SOCK_RDM        4               /* reliably delivered message */
#define SOCK_SEQPACKET  5               /* sequenced packet stream */

/*
 * Option flags per-socket.
 */
#define SO_DEBUG        0x0001          /* turn on debugging info recording */
#define SO_ACCEPTCONN   0x0002          /* socket has had listen() */
#define SO_REUSEADDR    0x0004          /* allow local address reuse */
#define SO_KEEPALIVE    0x0008          /* keep connections alive */
#define SO_DONTROUTE    0x0010          /* just use interface addresses */
#define SO_BROADCAST    0x0020          /* permit sending of broadcast msgs */
#define SO_USELOOPBACK  0x0040          /* bypass hardware when possible */
#define SO_LINGER       0x0080          /* linger on close if data present */
#define SO_OOBINLINE    0x0100          /* leave received OOB data in line */

#define SO_DONTLINGER   (u_int)(~SO_LINGER)

/*
 * Additional options.
 */
#define SO_SNDBUF       0x1001          /* send buffer size */
#define SO_RCVBUF       0x1002          /* receive buffer size */
#define SO_SNDLOWAT     0x1003          /* send low-water mark */
#define SO_RCVLOWAT     0x1004          /* receive low-water mark */
#define SO_SNDTIMEO     0x1005          /* send timeout */
#define SO_RCVTIMEO     0x1006          /* receive timeout */
#define SO_ERROR        0x1007          /* get error status and clear */
#define SO_TYPE         0x1008          /* get socket type */

/*
 * Options for connect and disconnect data and options.  Used only by
 * non-TCP/IP transports such as DECNet, OSI TP4, etc.
 */
#define SO_CONNDATA     0x7000
#define SO_CONNOPT      0x7001
#define SO_DISCDATA     0x7002
#define SO_DISCOPT      0x7003
#define SO_CONNDATALEN  0x7004
#define SO_CONNOPTLEN   0x7005
#define SO_DISCDATALEN  0x7006
```

```
#define SO_DISCOPTLEN   0x7007

/*
 * TCP options.
 */
#define TCP_NODELAY     0x0001

/*
 * Address families.
 */
#define AF_UNSPEC       0               /* unspecified */
#define AF_UNIX         1               /* local to host (pipes, portals) */
#define AF_INET         2               /* internetwork: UDP, TCP, etc. */
#define AF_IMPLINK      3               /* arpanet imp addresses */
#define AF_PUP          4               /* pup protocols: e.g. BSP */
#define AF_CHAOS        5               /* mit CHAOS protocols */
#define AF_IPX          6               /* IPX and SPX */
#define AF_NS           6               /* XEROX NS protocols */
#define AF_ISO          7               /* ISO protocols */
#define AF_OSI          AF_ISO          /* OSI is ISO */
#define AF_ECMA         8               /* European computer manufacturers */
#define AF_DATAKIT      9               /* datakit protocols */
#define AF_CCITT        10              /* CCITT protocols, X.25 etc */
#define AF_SNA          11              /* IBM SNA */
#define AF_DECnet       12              /* DECnet */
#define AF_DLI          13              /* Direct data link interface */
#define AF_LAT          14              /* LAT */
#define AF_HYLINK       15              /* NSC Hyperchannel */
#define AF_APPLETALK    16              /* AppleTalk */
#define AF_NETBIOS      17              /* NetBios-style addresses */

#define AF_MAX          18

/*
 * Structure used by kernel to store most
 * addresses.
 */
struct sockaddr {
        u_short sa_family;              /* address family */
        char    sa_data[14];            /* up to 14 bytes of direct address */
};

/*
 * Structure used by kernel to pass protocol
 * information in raw sockets.
 */
struct sockproto {
        u_short sp_family;              /* address family */
        u_short sp_protocol;            /* protocol */
};

/*
 * Protocol families, same as address families for now.
 */
#define PF_UNSPEC       AF_UNSPEC
#define PF_UNIX         AF_UNIX
#define PF_INET         AF_INET
#define PF_IMPLINK      AF_IMPLINK
```

```
#define PF_PUP          AF_PUP
#define PF_CHAOS        AF_CHAOS
#define PF_NS           AF_NS
#define PF_IPX          AF_IPX
#define PF_ISO          AF_ISO
#define PF_OSI          AF_OSI
#define PF_ECMA         AF_ECMA
#define PF_DATAKIT      AF_DATAKIT
#define PF_CCITT        AF_CCITT
#define PF_SNA          AF_SNA
#define PF_DECnet       AF_DECnet
#define PF_DLI          AF_DLI
#define PF_LAT          AF_LAT
#define PF_HYLINK       AF_HYLINK
#define PF_APPLETALK    AF_APPLETALK

#define PF_MAX          AF_MAX

/*
 * Structure used for manipulating linger option.
 */
struct  linger {
        u_short l_onoff;                /* option on/off */
        u_short l_linger;               /* linger time */
};

/*
 * Level number for (get/set)sockopt() to apply to socket itself.
 */
#define SOL_SOCKET      0xffff          /* options for socket level */

/*
 * Maximum queue length specifiable by listen.
 */
#define SOMAXCONN       5

#define MSG_OOB         0x1             /* process out-of-band data */
#define MSG_PEEK        0x2             /* peek at incoming message */
#define MSG_DONTROUTE   0x4             /* send without using routing tables */

#define MSG_MAXIOVLEN   16

#define MSG_PARTIAL     0x8000          /* partial send or recv for message xport */

/*
 * Define constant based on rfc883, used by gethostbyxxxx() calls.
 */
#define MAXGETHOSTSTRUCT        1024

/*
 * Define flags to be used with the WSAAsyncSelect() call.
 */
#define FD_READ         0x01
#define FD_WRITE        0x02
#define FD_OOB          0x04
#define FD_ACCEPT       0x08
#define FD_CONNECT      0x10
```

```
#define FD_CLOSE        0x20

/*
 * All Windows Sockets error constants are biased by WSABASEERR from
 * the "normal"
 */
#define WSABASEERR              10000
/*
 * Windows Sockets definitions of regular Microsoft C error constants
 */
#define WSAEINTR                (WSABASEERR+4)
#define WSAEBADF                (WSABASEERR+9)
#define WSAEACCES               (WSABASEERR+13)
#define WSAEFAULT               (WSABASEERR+14)
#define WSAEINVAL               (WSABASEERR+22)
#define WSAEMFILE               (WSABASEERR+24)

/*
 * Windows Sockets definitions of regular Berkeley error constants
 */
#define WSAEWOULDBLOCK          (WSABASEERR+35)
#define WSAEINPROGRESS          (WSABASEERR+36)
#define WSAEALREADY             (WSABASEERR+37)
#define WSAENOTSOCK             (WSABASEERR+38)
#define WSAEDESTADDRREQ         (WSABASEERR+39)
#define WSAEMSGSIZE             (WSABASEERR+40)
#define WSAEPROTOTYPE           (WSABASEERR+41)
#define WSAENOPROTOOPT          (WSABASEERR+42)
#define WSAEPROTONOSUPPORT      (WSABASEERR+43)
#define WSAESOCKTNOSUPPORT      (WSABASEERR+44)
#define WSAEOPNOTSUPP           (WSABASEERR+45)
#define WSAEPFNOSUPPORT         (WSABASEERR+46)
#define WSAEAFNOSUPPORT         (WSABASEERR+47)
#define WSAEADDRINUSE           (WSABASEERR+48)
#define WSAEADDRNOTAVAIL        (WSABASEERR+49)
#define WSAENETDOWN             (WSABASEERR+50)
#define WSAENETUNREACH          (WSABASEERR+51)
#define WSAENETRESET            (WSABASEERR+52)
#define WSAECONNABORTED         (WSABASEERR+53)
#define WSAECONNRESET           (WSABASEERR+54)
#define WSAENOBUFS              (WSABASEERR+55)
#define WSAEISCONN              (WSABASEERR+56)
#define WSAENOTCONN             (WSABASEERR+57)
#define WSAESHUTDOWN            (WSABASEERR+58)
#define WSAETOOMANYREFS         (WSABASEERR+59)
#define WSAETIMEDOUT            (WSABASEERR+60)
#define WSAECONNREFUSED         (WSABASEERR+61)
#define WSAELOOP                (WSABASEERR+62)
#define WSAENAMETOOLONG         (WSABASEERR+63)
#define WSAEHOSTDOWN            (WSABASEERR+64)
#define WSAEHOSTUNREACH         (WSABASEERR+65)
#define WSAENOTEMPTY            (WSABASEERR+66)
#define WSAEPROCLIM             (WSABASEERR+67)
#define WSAEUSERS               (WSABASEERR+68)
#define WSAEDQUOT               (WSABASEERR+69)
#define WSAESTALE               (WSABASEERR+70)
#define WSAEREMOTE              (WSABASEERR+71)
```

```
#define WSAEDISCON              (WSABASEERR+101)

/*
 * Extended Windows Sockets error constant definitions
 */
#define WSASYSNOTREADY          (WSABASEERR+91)
#define WSAVERNOTSUPPORTED      (WSABASEERR+92)
#define WSANOTINITIALISED       (WSABASEERR+93)

/*
 * Error return codes from gethostbyname() and gethostbyaddr()
 * (when using the resolver). Note that these errors are
 * retrieved via WSAGetLastError() and must therefore follow
 * the rules for avoiding clashes with error numbers from
 * specific implementations or language run-time systems.
 * For this reason the codes are based at WSABASEERR+1001.
 * Note also that [WSA]NO_ADDRESS is defined only for
 * compatibility purposes.
 */

#define h_errno         WSAGetLastError()

/* Authoritative Answer: Host not found */
#define WSAHOST_NOT_FOUND       (WSABASEERR+1001)
#define HOST_NOT_FOUND          WSAHOST_NOT_FOUND

/* Non-Authoritative: Host not found, or SERVERFAIL */
#define WSATRY_AGAIN            (WSABASEERR+1002)
#define TRY_AGAIN               WSATRY_AGAIN

/* Non recoverable errors, FORMERR, REFUSED, NOTIMP */
#define WSANO_RECOVERY          (WSABASEERR+1003)
#define NO_RECOVERY             WSANO_RECOVERY

/* Valid name, no data record of requested type */
#define WSANO_DATA              (WSABASEERR+1004)
#define NO_DATA                 WSANO_DATA

/* no address, look for MX record */
#define WSANO_ADDRESS           WSANO_DATA
#define NO_ADDRESS              WSANO_ADDRESS

/*
 * Windows Sockets errors redefined as regular Berkeley error constants.
 * These are commented out in Windows NT to avoid conflicts with errno.h.
 * Use the WSA constants instead.
 */
#if 0
#define EWOULDBLOCK             WSAEWOULDBLOCK
#define EINPROGRESS             WSAEINPROGRESS
#define EALREADY                WSAEALREADY
#define ENOTSOCK                WSAENOTSOCK
#define EDESTADDRREQ            WSAEDESTADDRREQ
#define EMSGSIZE                WSAEMSGSIZE
#define EPROTOTYPE              WSAEPROTOTYPE
#define ENOPROTOOPT             WSAENOPROTOOPT
#define EPROTONOSUPPORT         WSAEPROTONOSUPPORT
#define ESOCKTNOSUPPORT         WSAESOCKTNOSUPPORT
```

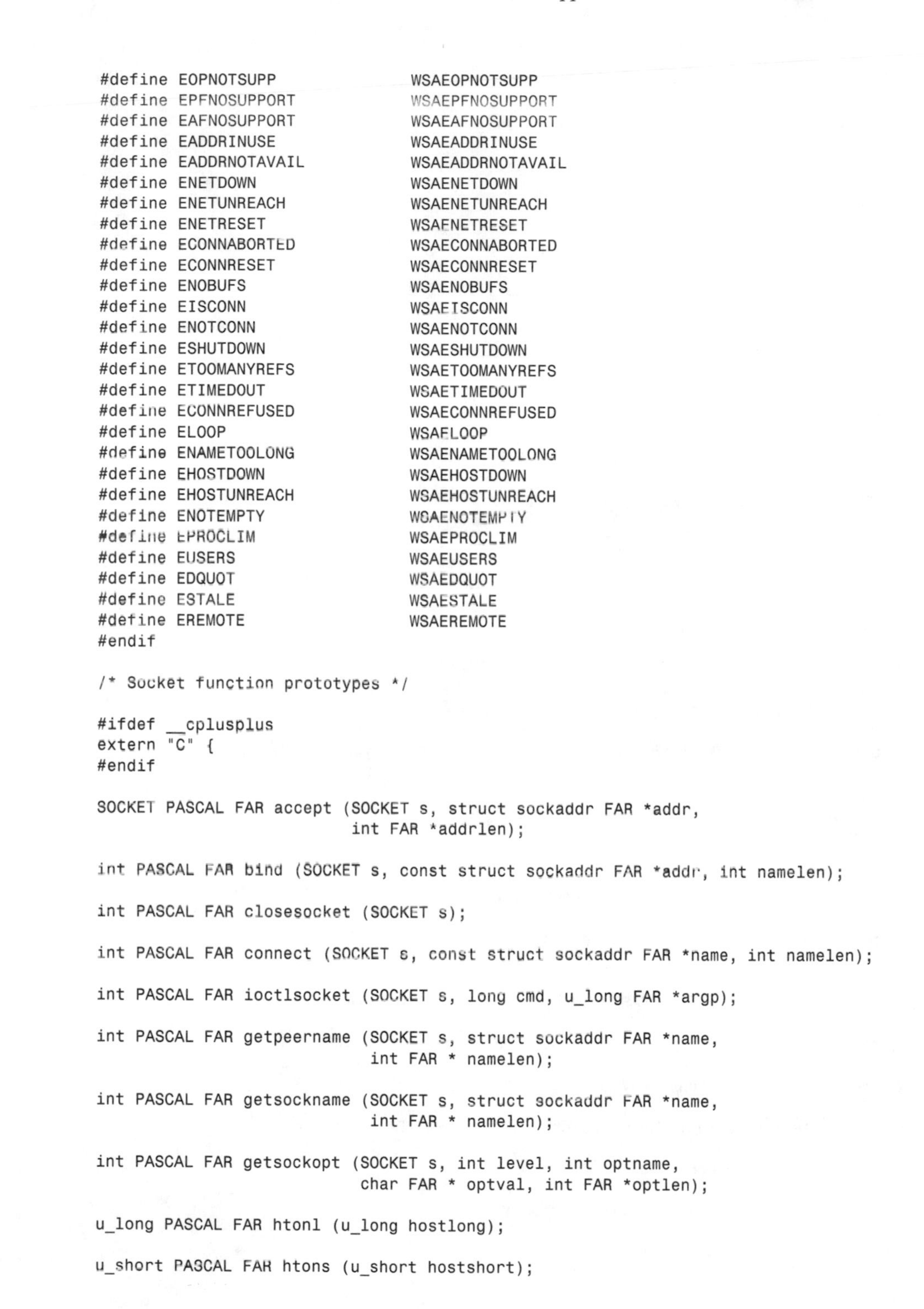

```
#define EOPNOTSUPP              WSAEOPNOTSUPP
#define EPFNOSUPPORT            WSAEPFNOSUPPORT
#define EAFNOSUPPORT            WSAEAFNOSUPPORT
#define EADDRINUSE              WSAEADDRINUSE
#define EADDRNOTAVAIL           WSAEADDRNOTAVAIL
#define ENETDOWN                WSAENETDOWN
#define ENETUNREACH             WSAENETUNREACH
#define ENETRESET               WSAENETRESET
#define ECONNABORTED            WSAECONNABORTED
#define ECONNRESET              WSAECONNRESET
#define ENOBUFS                 WSAENOBUFS
#define EISCONN                 WSAEISCONN
#define ENOTCONN                WSAENOTCONN
#define ESHUTDOWN               WSAESHUTDOWN
#define ETOOMANYREFS            WSAETOOMANYREFS
#define ETIMEDOUT               WSAETIMEDOUT
#define ECONNREFUSED            WSAECONNREFUSED
#define ELOOP                   WSAELOOP
#define ENAMETOOLONG            WSAENAMETOOLONG
#define EHOSTDOWN               WSAEHOSTDOWN
#define EHOSTUNREACH            WSAEHOSTUNREACH
#define ENOTEMPTY               WSAENOTEMPTY
#define EPROCLIM                WSAEPROCLIM
#define EUSERS                  WSAEUSERS
#define EDQUOT                  WSAEDQUOT
#define ESTALE                  WSAESTALE
#define EREMOTE                 WSAEREMOTE
#endif

/* Socket function prototypes */

#ifdef __cplusplus
extern "C" {
#endif

SOCKET PASCAL FAR accept (SOCKET s, struct sockaddr FAR *addr,
                          int FAR *addrlen);

int PASCAL FAR bind (SOCKET s, const struct sockaddr FAR *addr, int namelen);

int PASCAL FAR closesocket (SOCKET s);

int PASCAL FAR connect (SOCKET s, const struct sockaddr FAR *name, int namelen);

int PASCAL FAR ioctlsocket (SOCKET s, long cmd, u_long FAR *argp);

int PASCAL FAR getpeername (SOCKET s, struct sockaddr FAR *name,
                            int FAR * namelen);

int PASCAL FAR getsockname (SOCKET s, struct sockaddr FAR *name,
                            int FAR * namelen);

int PASCAL FAR getsockopt (SOCKET s, int level, int optname,
                           char FAR * optval, int FAR *optlen);

u_long PASCAL FAR htonl (u_long hostlong);

u_short PASCAL FAR htons (u_short hostshort);
```

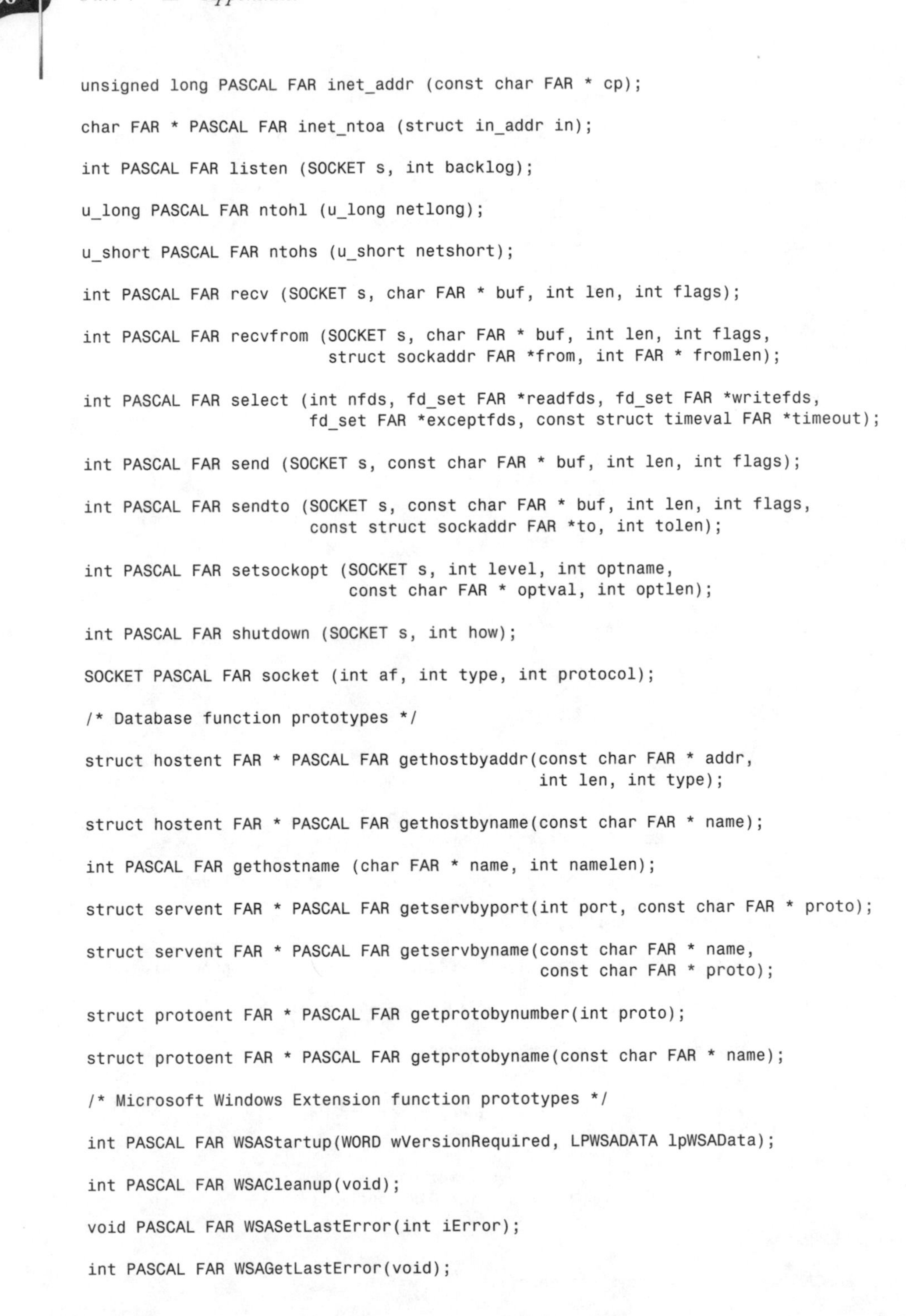

```
unsigned long PASCAL FAR inet_addr (const char FAR * cp);

char FAR * PASCAL FAR inet_ntoa (struct in_addr in);

int PASCAL FAR listen (SOCKET s, int backlog);

u_long PASCAL FAR ntohl (u_long netlong);

u_short PASCAL FAR ntohs (u_short netshort);

int PASCAL FAR recv (SOCKET s, char FAR * buf, int len, int flags);

int PASCAL FAR recvfrom (SOCKET s, char FAR * buf, int len, int flags,
                         struct sockaddr FAR *from, int FAR * fromlen);

int PASCAL FAR select (int nfds, fd_set FAR *readfds, fd_set FAR *writefds,
                       fd_set FAR *exceptfds, const struct timeval FAR *timeout);

int PASCAL FAR send (SOCKET s, const char FAR * buf, int len, int flags);

int PASCAL FAR sendto (SOCKET s, const char FAR * buf, int len, int flags,
                       const struct sockaddr FAR *to, int tolen);

int PASCAL FAR setsockopt (SOCKET s, int level, int optname,
                           const char FAR * optval, int optlen);

int PASCAL FAR shutdown (SOCKET s, int how);

SOCKET PASCAL FAR socket (int af, int type, int protocol);

/* Database function prototypes */

struct hostent FAR * PASCAL FAR gethostbyaddr(const char FAR * addr,
                                              int len, int type);

struct hostent FAR * PASCAL FAR gethostbyname(const char FAR * name);

int PASCAL FAR gethostname (char FAR * name, int namelen);

struct servent FAR * PASCAL FAR getservbyport(int port, const char FAR * proto);

struct servent FAR * PASCAL FAR getservbyname(const char FAR * name,
                                              const char FAR * proto);

struct protoent FAR * PASCAL FAR getprotobynumber(int proto);

struct protoent FAR * PASCAL FAR getprotobyname(const char FAR * name);

/* Microsoft Windows Extension function prototypes */

int PASCAL FAR WSAStartup(WORD wVersionRequired, LPWSADATA lpWSAData);

int PASCAL FAR WSACleanup(void);

void PASCAL FAR WSASetLastError(int iError);

int PASCAL FAR WSAGetLastError(void);
```

```
BOOL PASCAL FAR WSAIsBlocking(void);

int PASCAL FAR WSAUnhookBlockingHook(void);

FARPROC PASCAL FAR WSASetBlockingHook(FARPROC lpBlockFunc);

int PASCAL FAR WSACancelBlockingCall(void);

HANDLE PASCAL FAR WSAAsyncGetServByName(HWND hWnd, u_int wMsg,
                                        const char FAR * name,
                                        const char FAR * proto,
                                        char FAR * buf, int buflen);

HANDLE PASCAL FAR WSAAsyncGetServByPort(HWND hWnd, u_int wMsg, int port,
                                        const char FAR * proto, char FAR * buf,
                                        int buflen);

HANDLE PASCAL FAR WSAAsyncGetProtoByName(HWND hWnd, u_int wMsg,
                                         const char FAR * name, char FAR * buf,
                                         int buflen);

HANDLE PASCAL FAR WSAAsyncGetProtoByNumber(HWND hWnd, u_int wMsg,
                                           int number, char FAR * buf,
                                           int buflen);

HANDLE PASCAL FAR WSAAsyncGetHostByName(HWND hWnd, u_int wMsg,
                                        const char FAR * name, char FAR * buf,
                                        int buflen);

HANDLE PASCAL FAR WSAAsyncGetHostByAddr(HWND hWnd, u_int wMsg,
                                        const char FAR * addr, int len, int type,
                                        char FAR * buf, int buflen);

int PASCAL FAR WSACancelAsyncRequest(HANDLE hAsyncTaskHandle);

int PASCAL FAR WSAAsyncSelect(SOCKET s, HWND hWnd, u_int wMsg,
                              long lEvent);

int PASCAL FAR WSARecvEx (SOCKET s, char FAR * buf, int len, int *flags);

#ifdef __cplusplus
}
#endif

/* Microsoft Windows Extended data types */
typedef struct sockaddr SOCKADDR;
typedef struct sockaddr *PSOCKADDR;
typedef struct sockaddr FAR *LPSOCKADDR;

typedef struct sockaddr_in SOCKADDR_IN;
typedef struct sockaddr_in *PSOCKADDR_IN;
typedef struct sockaddr_in FAR *LPSOCKADDR_IN;

typedef struct linger LINGER;
typedef struct linger *PLINGER;
typedef struct linger FAR *LPLINGER;
```

```
typedef struct in_addr IN_ADDR;
typedef struct in_addr *PIN_ADDR;
typedef struct in_addr FAR *LPIN_ADDR;

typedef struct fd_set FD_SET;
typedef struct fd_set *PFD_SET;
typedef struct fd_set FAR *LPFD_SET;

typedef struct hostent HOSTENT;
typedef struct hostent *PHOSTENT;
typedef struct hostent FAR *LPHOSTENT;

typedef struct servent SERVENT;
typedef struct servent *PSERVENT;
typedef struct servent FAR *LPSERVENT;

typedef struct protoent PROTOENT;
typedef struct protoent *PPROTOENT;
typedef struct protoent FAR *LPPROTOENT;

typedef struct timeval TIMEVAL;
typedef struct timeval *PTIMEVAL;
typedef struct timeval FAR *LPTIMEVAL;

/*
 * Windows message parameter composition and decomposition
 * macros.
 *
 * WSAMAKEASYNCREPLY is intended for use by the Windows Sockets implementation
 * when constructing the response to a WSAAsyncGetXByY() routine.
 */
#define WSAMAKEASYNCREPLY(buflen,error)     MAKELONG(buflen,error)
/*
 * WSAMAKESELECTREPLY is intended for use by the Windows Sockets implementation
 * when constructing the response to WSAAsyncSelect().
 */
#define WSAMAKESELECTREPLY(event,error)     MAKELONG(event,error)
/*
 * WSAGETASYNCBUFLEN is intended for use by the Windows Sockets application
 * to extract the buffer length from the lParam in the response
 * to a WSAGetXByY().
 */
#define WSAGETASYNCBUFLEN(lParam)           LOWORD(lParam)
/*
 * WSAGETASYNCERROR is intended for use by the Windows Sockets application
 * to extract the error code from the lParam in the response
 * to a WSAGetXByY().
 */
#define WSAGETASYNCERROR(lParam)            HIWORD(lParam)
/*
 * WSAGETSELECTEVENT is intended for use by the Windows Sockets application
 * to extract the event code from the lParam in the response
 * to a WSAAsyncSelect().
 */
#define WSAGETSELECTEVENT(lParam)           LOWORD(lParam)
/*
```

```
 * WSAGETSELECTERROR is intended for use by the Windows Sockets application
 * to extract the error code from the lParam in the response
 * to a WSAAsyncSelect().
 */
#define WSAGETSELECTERROR(lParam)            HIWORD(lParam)

#endif  /* _WINSOCKAPI_ */
```

WinSock Error Codes

B.1. WinSock error codes, values, and meaning.

ror	Value	Meaning
WSAEINTR	10004	Interrupted system call
WSAEBADF	10009	Bad file number
WSAEACCES	10013	Permission denied
WSAEFAULT	10014	Bad address
WSAEINVAL	10022	Invalid argument
WSAEMFILE	10024	Too many open files
WSAEWOULDBLOCK	10035	Operation would block
WSAEINPROGRESS	10036	Operation now in progress
WSAEALREADY	10037	Operation already in progress
WSAENOTSOCK	10038	Socket operation on nonsocket
WSAEDESTADDRREQ	10039	Destination address required
WSAEMSGSIZE	10040	Message too long
WSAEPROTOTYPE	10041	Protocol wrong type for socket
WSAENOPROTOOPT	10042	Protocol not available
WSAEPROTONOSUPPORT	10043	Protocol not supported
WSAESOCKTNOSUPPORT	10044	Socket type not supported
WSAEOPNOTSUPP	10045	Operation not supported on socket
WSAEPFNOSUPPORT	10046	Protocol family not supported
WSAEAFNOSUPPORT	10047	Address family not supported by protocol family
WSAEADDRINUSE	10048	Address already in use
WSAEADDRNOTAVAIL	10049	Can't assign requested address
WSAENETDOWN	10050	Network is down
WSAENETUNREACH	10051	Network is unreachable
WSAENETRESET	10052	Network dropped connection on reset
WSAECONNABORTED	10053	Software caused connection abort
WSAECONNRESET	10054	Connection reset by peer
WSAENOBUFS	10055	No buffer space available

Error	*Value*	*Meaning*
WSAEISCONN	10056	Socket is already connected
WSAENOTCONN	10057	Socket is not connected
WSAESHUTDOWN	10058	Can't send after socket shutdown
WSAETOOMANYREFS	10059	Too many references: can't splice
WSAETIMEDOUT	10060	Connection timed out
WSAECONNREFUSED	10061	Connection refused
WSAELOOP	10062	Too many levels of symbolic links
WSAENAMETOOLONG	10063	File name too long
WSAEHOSTDOWN	10064	Host is down
WSAEHOSTUNREACH	10065	No route to host
WSAENOTEMPTY	10066	Directory not empty
WSAEPROCLIM	10067	Too many processes
WSAEUSERS	10068	Too many users
WSAEDQUOT	10069	Disk quota exceeded
WSAESTALE	10070	Stale NFS file handle
WSAEREMOTE	10071	Too many levels of remote in path
WSASYSNOTREADY	10091	Network subsystem is unusable
WSAVERNOTSUPPORTED	10092	WinSock DLL cannot support this application
WSANOTINITIALISED	10093	WinSock not initialized
WSAEDISCON	10101	Disconnect
WSAHOST_NOT_FOUND	11001	Host not found
WSATRY_AGAIN	11002	Nonauthoritative host not found
WSANO_RECOVERY	11003	Nonrecoverable error
WSANO_DATA	11004	Valid name, no data record of requested type

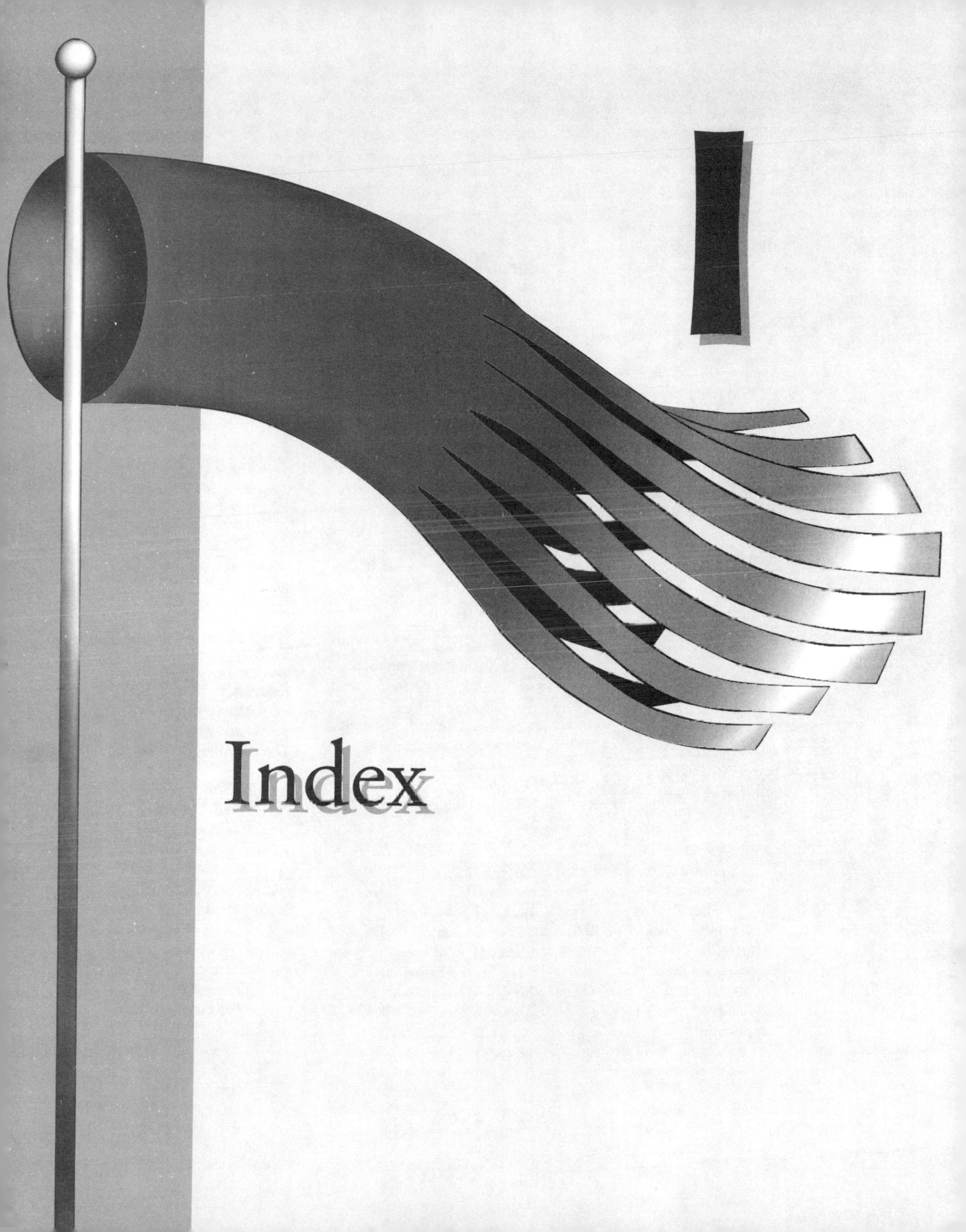

Index

SYMBOLS

A

B

C

D

E

F

J-K-L

N

S

T

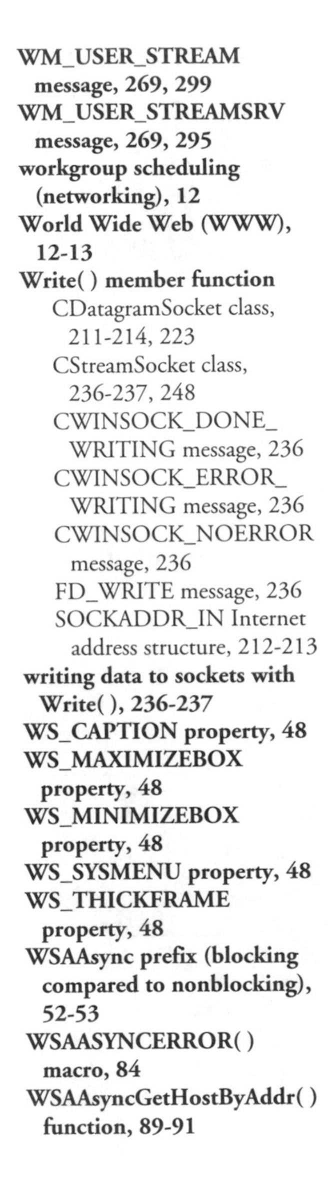

X-Y-Z

Book ISBN 0-672-30594-1

Disk Install

Installing the Disk

The software on the disk is stored in a compressed form and must be installed to your hard drive using the installation program, which runs from within Windows.

1. From File Manager or Program Manager, choose **R**un from the **F**ile menu.
2. Type *<drive>*\INSTALL and press Enter, where *<drive>* is the letter of the drive that contains the installation disk. For example, if the disk is in drive B:, type B:\INSTALL and press Enter.

Follow the on-screen instructions in the installation program. The files will be installed in the \PWINSOCK directory, unless you chose a different directory during installation. Be sure to read the file displayed at the end of the installation process; it contains information about the files and programs that were installed.

WINDOWS NT USERS NOTE:

To install the companion disk files, run the INSTPROG.BAT file. For more information, see the README.TXT file.